VICARIOUS DREAMING

—

With Jack Idriess on Madman's Island

ERNEST HUNTER

ETT IMPRINT
Exile Bay

This edition published by ETT Imprint, Exile Bay 2019

Reprinted May 2019

This book is copyright. Apart from any fair dealing for the purposes of private study, research, criticism or review, as permitted under the Copyright Act, no part may be reproduced by any process without written permission. Inquiries should be addressed to the publishers:

ETT IMPRINT
PO Box R1906
Royal Exchange NSW 1225 Australia

Copyright © Ernest Hunter, 2019

ISBN 978-1-925706-63-5 (paper)
ISBN 978-1-925706-64-2 (ebook)

Design by Hanna Gotlieb
Maps by Cameron Emerson-Elliott
Original line drawings for *Madman's Island* by Percy Lindsay
Cover photograph by Geoff Miller

Ernest Hunter trained as a psychiatrist and public health physician and has worked as a clinician and academic for more than three decades in remote northern Australia. He has published several hundred articles and monographs in the academic and popular press and is author of *Aboriginal health and history: Power and prejudice in remote Australia* (Cambridge University Press). Ernest and his wife, Trish Fagan, live in Kewarra Beach, north of Cairns – on the shores of the Coral Sea.

All men dream: but not equally. Those who dream by night in the dusty recesses of their minds wake in the day to find that it was vanity: but the dreamers of the day are dangerous men, for they may act their dream with open eyes, to make it possible.

T.E. Lawrence
Seven pillars of wisdom[1]

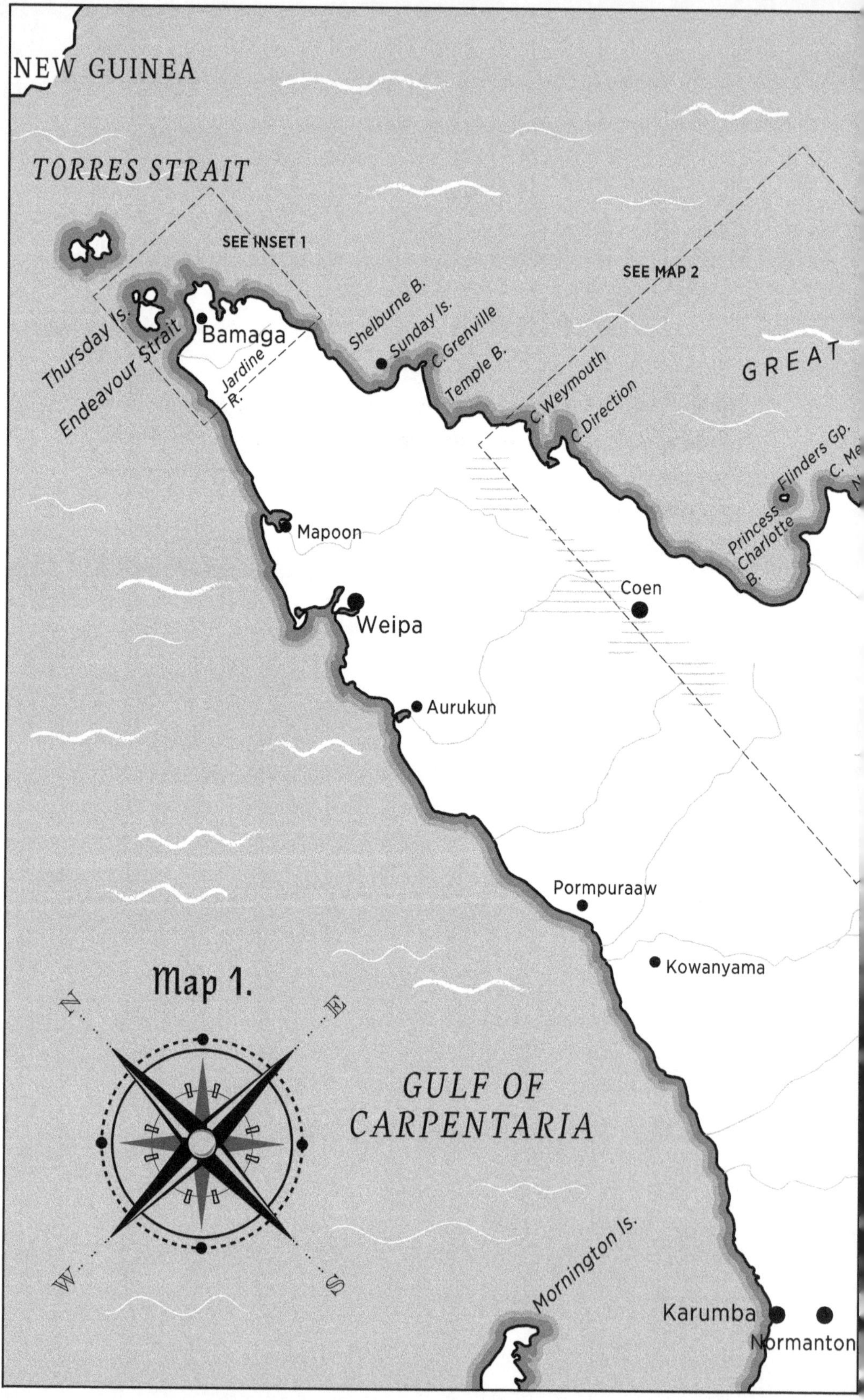

NEW GUINEA
TORRES STRAIT
SEE INSET 1
SEE MAP 2
Thursday Is.
Endeavour Strait
Bamaga
Jardine R.
Shelburne B.
Sunday Is.
C.Grenville
Temple B.
C.Weymouth
C.Direction
GREAT
Flinders Gp.
Princess Charlotte B.
Mapoon
Weipa
Coen
Aurukun
Pormpuraaw
Kowanyama
Map 1.
N
E
W
S
GULF OF CARPENTARIA
Mornington Is.
Karumba
Normanton

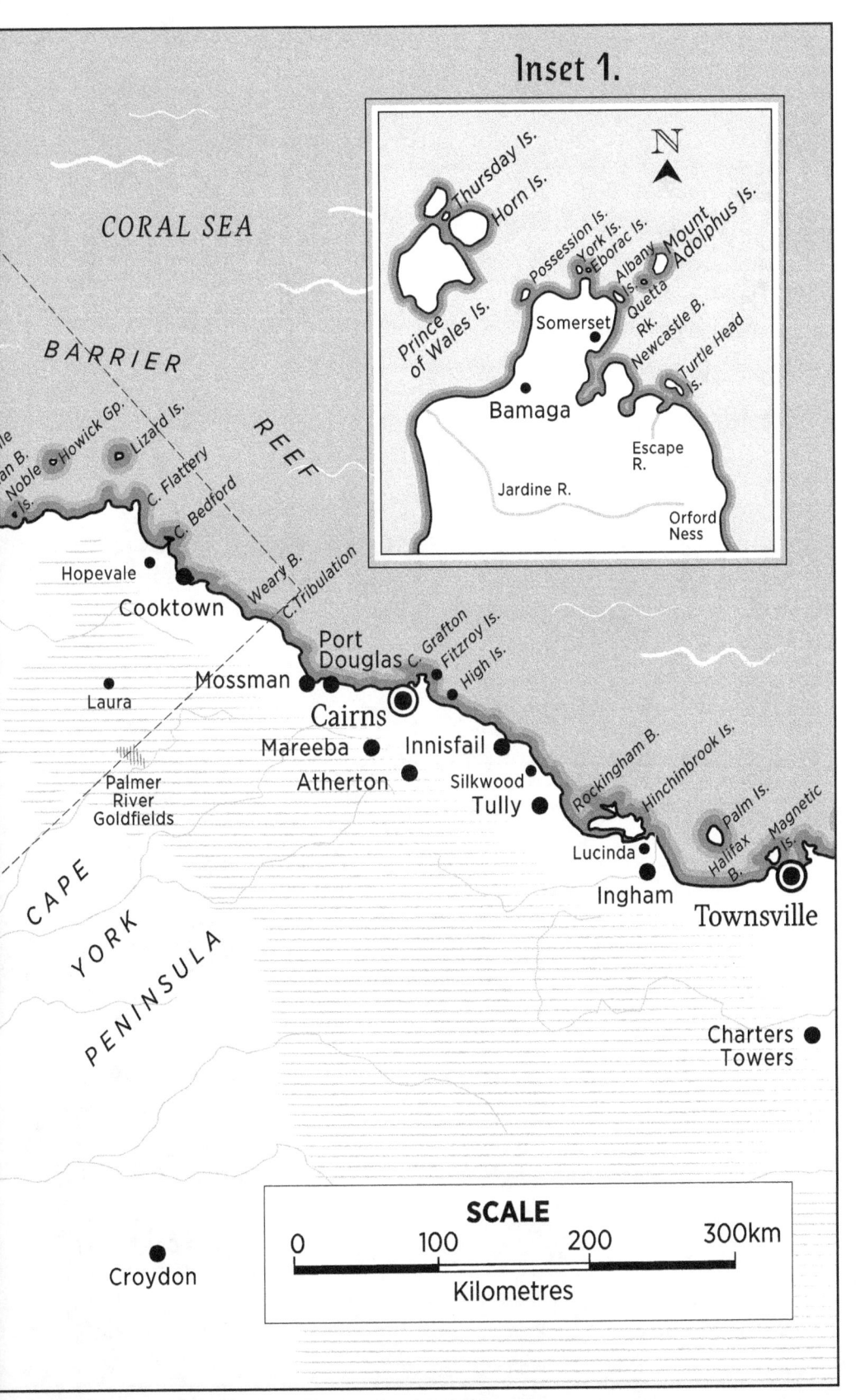

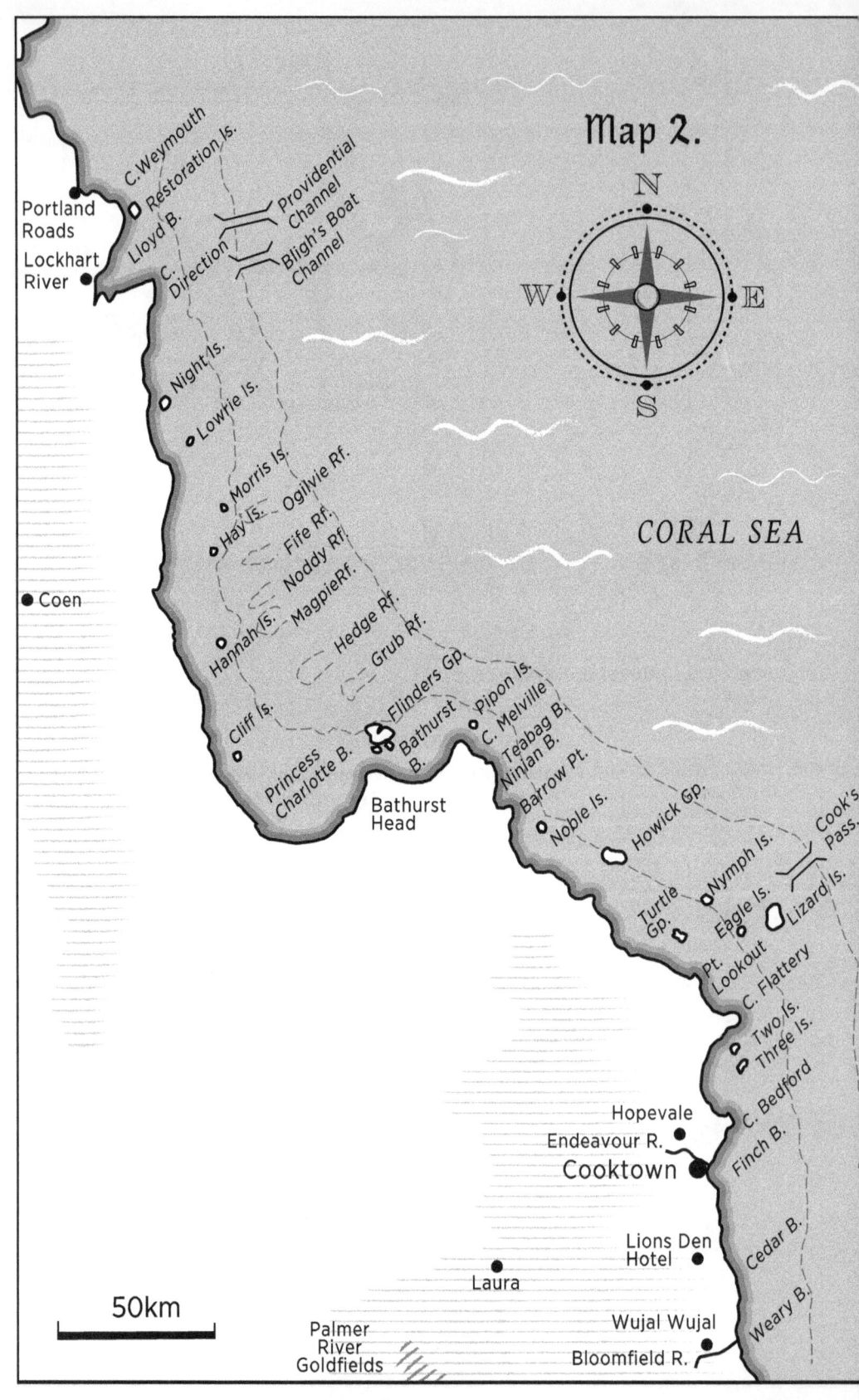

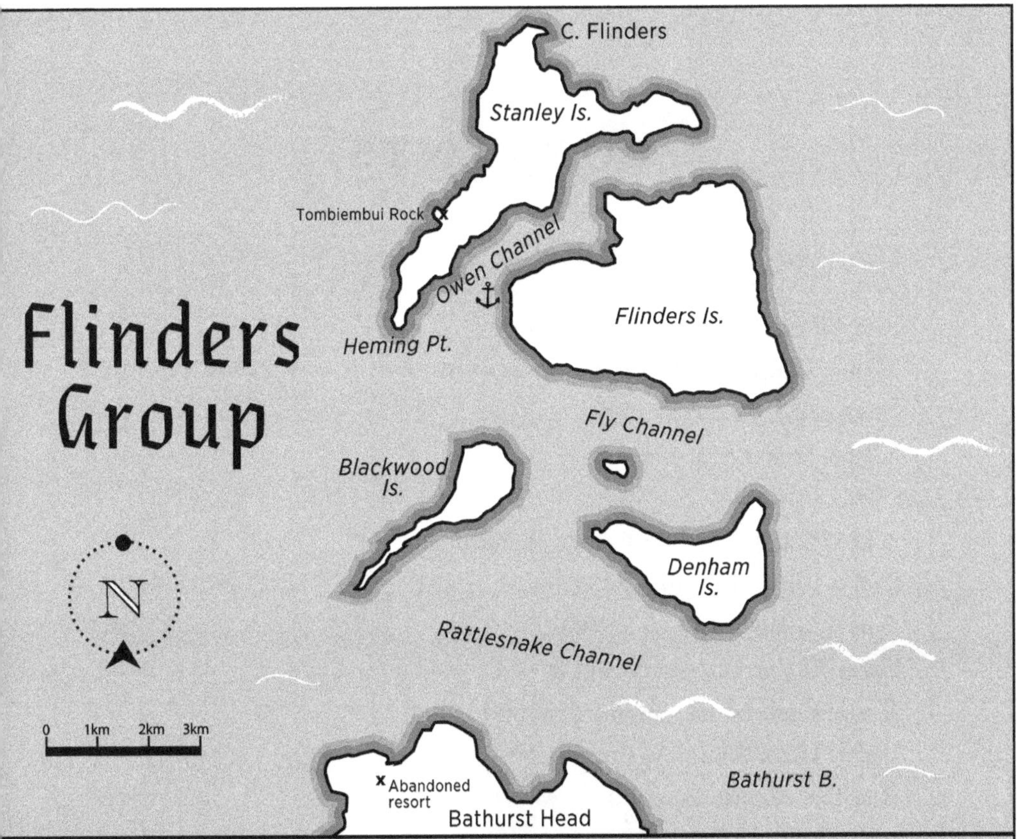
Flinders Group
C. Flinders
Stanley Is.
Tombiembui Rock
Owen Channel
Heming Pt.
Flinders Is.
Fly Channel
Blackwood Is.
Denham Is.
N
Rattlesnake Channel
0 1km 2km 3km
Abandoned resort
Bathurst Head
Bathurst B.

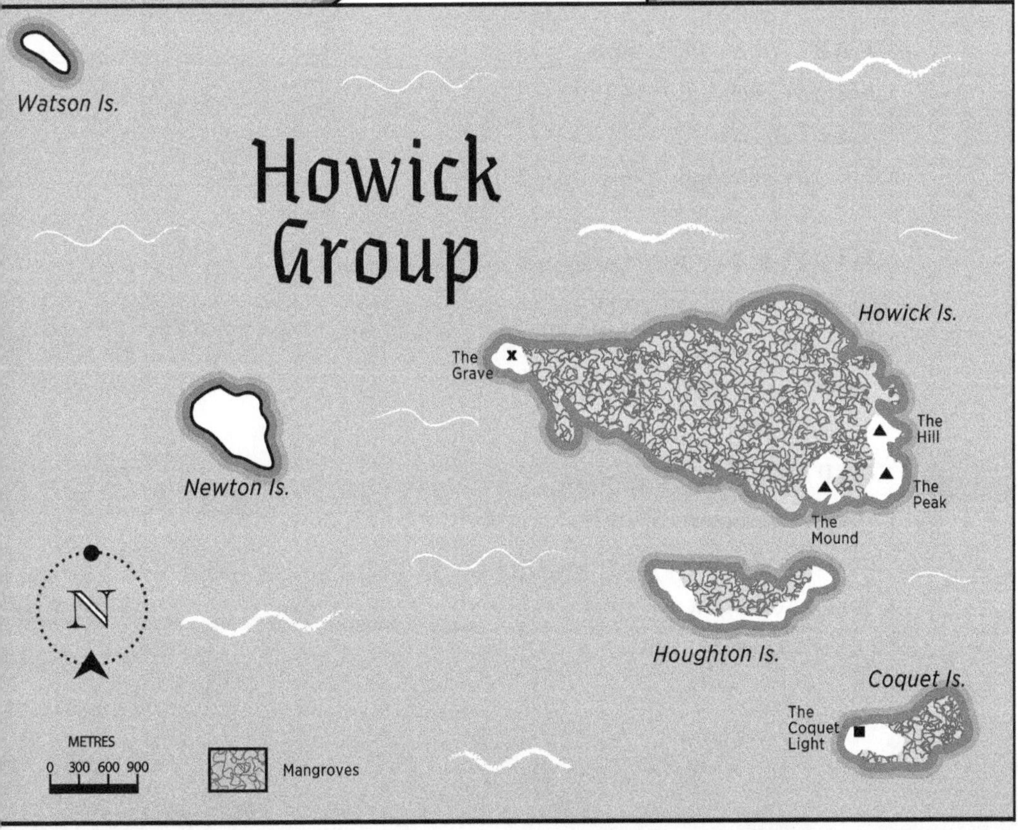
Watson Is.
Howick Group
Howick Is.
The Grave
The Hill
The Peak
The Mound
Newton Is.
N
Houghton Is.
Coquet Is.
The Coquet Light
METRES
0 300 600 900
Mangroves

CONTENTS

CHAPTER 1 - 1987-1993: *alpha* — 9
Glebe, December 12, 1987 — 11
Cooktown, August 18, 1992 — 12
Glebe, January 16, 1993 — 15

CHAPTER 2 - 2000: *Cairns to Bamaga* — 19
Noble Island, July 16, 2000 — 20
Sunday Island, August 7, 2000 — 26
Escape River, August 12, 2000 — 28
Turtle Head Island, August 12, 2000 — 33
Turtle Head Island, August 13, 2000 — 36
The Tip, August 14, 2000 — 41

CHAPTER 3 - 1993: *beta* — 47
Cooktown, February 10, 1993 — 47
Cairns, February 27, 1993 — 52
University of Sydney, November 25, 1993 — 54

CHAPTER 4 - 2003: *Cooktown to Lizard Island* — 61
Two Isles, August 21, 2003 — 62
Lizard Island, August 26, 2003 — 66
Lizard Island, August 28, 2003 — 75

CHAPTER 5 - 1994: *gamma* — 78
Cooktown, August 16, 1994 — 79
Cooktown, August 17, 1994 — 80
Cooktown, August 18, 1994 — 87
Cairns, August 21, 1994 — 93

CHAPTER 6 - 2003: *Lizard Island to Cape Weymouth*   96
Eagle Island, August 29, 2003   97
Noble Island, August 31, 2003   101
Bathurst Head, September 6, 2003   103
Flinders Island, September 7, 2003   108
Endeavour Bay, September 8, 2003   110
Hay Island, September 9, 2003   113
Cape Weymouth, September 14, 2003   114

CHAPTER 7 - 1995-1996: *delta*   117
Lion's Den Hotel, February 9, 1995   118
Silkwood, April 29, 1996   124
Cooktown, December 18, 1996   137

CHAPTER 8 - 2008: *Cooktown to Cape Weymouth*   145
The Turtle Group, July 8, 2008   146
Coquet Island, July 9, 2008   151
Teabag Bay, July 11, 2008   161
Lowrie Island, July 17, 2008   169

CHAPTER 9 - 2000-2001: *epsilon*   178
Finch Bay, July 9, 2000   179
Cooktown, September 27, 2000   181
Cairns, November 27, 2000   193
Tresta, April 18, 2001   197
Tresta, April 19, 2001   200
Cooktown, September 12, 2001   204

CHAPTER 10 - 2011: *Elim to Cape Weymouth*   219
Lookout Point, August 15, 2011   220
Night Island, August 25, 2011   238
Restoration Island, August 27, 2011   248

CHAPTER 11 - 2013-2015: *zeta* — 256
Le Mole sul Farfa, Mompeo, September 2, 2013 — 257
Cairns, July 23, 2014 — 257
Silkwood, August 6, 2014 — 261
Cairns, August 7, 2014 — 266
Cairns Base Hospital, September 16, 2014 — 272
James Cook University, October 3, 2014 — 276
Kowanyama, November 11, 2014 — 278
High Island, September 23, 2015 — 282

CHAPTER 12 - 2016: *psi* — 293
Cairns German Club, February 26, 2016 — 293
Melbourne, March 6, 2016 — 296
Cairns, July 16, 2016 — 299
Cooktown, September 13, 2016 — 301

CHAPTER 13 - 2016: *Cooktown to Howick – omega* — 309
Cooktown, September 23, 2016 — 310
Lizard Island, September 26, 2016 — 313
Madman's Island, September 30, 2016 — 317

Notes — 324
Acknowledgements — 342

CHAPTER 1

1987-1993: alpha

One of the gladdest moments in human life, methinks, is the departure upon a distant journey into unknown lands. Shaking off with one mighty effort the fetters of Habit, the leaden weight of Routine, the cloak of many Cares and the slavery of Home, one feels once more happy. The blood flows with the fast circulation of childhood... A journey, in fact, appeals to Imagination, to Memory, to Hope, – the three sister Graces of our moral being.
Richard Francis Burton[2]

The three sister Graces of our moral being – imagination, memory and hope; present, past and future. An imagined pause of time's arrow, the present is just a wave on the ocean – there and gone. Except in dreams. Dream-time arrows are timeless. I suppose it's the same with journeys, with adventures – it's all now. And like a dream there are more beginnings to a journey than we can know and we never reach the end. Maybe because we don't want to.

Arthur Ransome would have recognized what Richard Francis Burton meant by the blood flowing *with the fast circulation of childhood*. When

Burton died in 1890 after a lifetime of adventures, journeys and dreams, Arthur was a child of six, his own destiny being shaped along the shores and in the shallows of Coniston Water in the Lake District. And although he had more than a few adventures of his own as an adult, his inspiration as an author was the lake – and childhood. He knew that the end was something children didn't understand and he had the character, Titty Walker, a little girl and able seaman on the *Swallow*, say as much as she sat on the shore of *Wild Cat Island* in the years between Wars, dreaming of Robinson Crusoe: *There never ought to be an end*[3]– that's what she said to herself and to us. In *Swallows and Amazons* Titty was in the adventure, in the moment, in the never-ending journey. And for some people journeys and dreams blur. *Live the dream* – that was László's advice, and if anyone should know it would be an oneironaut.

I thought you might be a fellow oneironaut – that's what he said to me in Cooktown. I didn't know what he meant then and I'm still figuring it out now, eighteen years later on a remote island hill-top, one-hundred-and-fifty kilometres further north. And although I'm alone I think I catch glimpses of László, and maybe of Jack Idriess too, as the night is punctured by the Coquet light that fissures the darkness to silhouette a floating world every five seconds. Twenty metres high, the light on Coquet Island is only a few kilometres south of this hilltop on Howick Island with the coast of Cape York beyond lost in the night. Just after the First World War Jack Idriess sat in this place on Howick looking across at the *white pillar above the mangroves*[4] on Coquet. Not Ion Idriess, just Jack then; Ion would come later, after Howick, after *Madman's Island*.

Jack's journey to Howick began at the West Coast Hotel in Cooktown. But it also started much earlier. For László there was no beginning – he was always here and never arrived. And me… Well, in the sixteen years since the millennium this is the fifth time I've set course for Howick but the first time I've arrived, and those journeys and this one have multiple starting points – places and times. But one of them I know, it was a bookstore on Glebe Point Road and it was 1987. I'd just begun a stint as a researcher in the Kimberley and was back in Sydney for a meeting. It was a Saturday morning and I was walking to or from the Glebe Markets, the footpath channelling weathered locals from council row houses back from the street, and better-heeled new arrivals enticed by renovators' dreams a few blocks away, mixing them all into the stream. White, Aboriginal, from somewhere else or nowhere at all, ebbing and flowing around vibrant islands of discarded clothes, rescued implements and devices, questionable crafts and faux oriental objects. At various places pedestrians were funnelled between building and road as businesses spilt their wares onto the path. One of those was the bookshop, now long closed and soulless, its façade intact but frozen in heritage-listed limbo. Thirty years ago that shop – *specialist in antiquarian, rare and out-of-print Australian books* – had a soul.

Glebe, December 12, 1987

There's a bottleneck outside Cornstalk Bookshop. Hunched figures lean across two elevated trays, occasionally reaching forward to inspect or move an item. Whether on the outer because they failed the antiquarian test or to momentarily slow the stream and bring passers-by to a halt, the medley of paperbacks and beyond-redemption hardcovers casts a spell. Once stalled, the primed pedestrian is drawn to the two-metre-high shopfront window, through the reflections of people and traffic and into a dim chamber lined with what might be treasures.

Inside it's floor to ceiling books. Not the compact precision of recently shelved new merchandise, but worn-edged items in saw-tooth array with a subtle, sober scent lingering throughout, not the alerting sharpness of fresh print. And not the order and ranking of new releases – but order nonetheless, recognizable immediately to the collector. Like a chess master intuiting meaning through an unconscious sifting of familiar scenarios, the collector's gaze triggers comparisons across known and possible sets, individual items fixing attention as part of a calculus of exchange to some third or fourth level ordering of assets and absences.

But while the collector is on a mission, browsers like myself are drawn by ambience, including the background chaos that continues from room to room. There are piles of books threatening collapse, others open and being scrutinized for valuation or repair, Paul and his wife Gabrielle unobtrusively indistinguishable from absorbed customers. Even the uninitiated soon realize that this is more than a used-book store. The stacks are crammed with simple titles on faded cloth and embossed leather bindings rather than rows of color-cracked, spine-worn, serialized paperbacks. There are folio, quarto and octavo volumes, and antiquarian sheet music in protective binders labeled with content and provenance – almost all, somehow, connected to Australia. And for those without the collector's eye the shelves' contents still form categories – early botanicals, journals of the first fleets, first editions of Patrick White and so on. It's a short step from curiosity to collecting, from browsing to obsession.

Cooktown, August 18, 1992

Walking to the hospital from the Seaview Motel there's only one way to go, along Charlotte Street, past memorials to triumphs and tragedies. The sandstone column celebrating James Cook stands between Charlotte Street and the Endeavour River, rising to the height of nearby coconut palms. Even without the statue of the Great Navigator that in the original design topped the column, everyone was happy when it was officially dedicated in 1888. And just a few metres away a plaque on a pyramid of Cooktown granite that rises to a modest six feet, records the outcome of another journey of exploration:

EDMUND BESLEY COURT KENNEDY J.P.
Landed At Rockingham Bay 24 May 1848
On His Memorable Exploring Expedition
Of Cape York Peninsula.
Of The 13 Members, The Leader Was
Fatally Speared In December At Escape River
Within Sight Of His Goal.
Nine Perished En Route And Two Europeans And
The Aborigine Jackey-Jackey Were Rescued.
Unveiled 25 September 1948
W.C.H. Hodges, Chairman, Shire Council.

But the oldest memorial is further along Charlotte Street. Two years before the monument to Cook was dedicated the *Queensland Times, Ipswich Herald and General Advertiser* of 27 February 1886 recorded that, two days earlier:

The official unveiling of the memorial to Mrs Watson, in the shape of a drinking fountain took place this afternoon, before a large concourse of people. The battery of artillery, with the fire brigade band, and a large number of school children were present. The Mayor (Mr. John Davis), in a very appropriate speech, gave a short résumé of the circumstances connected with the death of the heroine and Miss Alice Newman, who was the first female born in Cooktown then untied the flags, the band meanwhile playing "God Save the Queen".

And it still stands, a book in stone inscribed folio:

In Memoriam
MRS WATSON
The Heroine of Lizard Island, Cooktown North Queensland, A.D. 1881
Erected 1886
Edward D'Arcy,
Mayor 1885

And verso:

Five Fearful Days Beneath
The Scorching Glare
Her Babe She Nursed
God Knows The Pangs That
Woman Had To Bear,
Whose Last Sad Entry Showed
A Mother's Care
Then – "Near Dead With Thirst."
John Davis, Mayor 1886

A drinking fountain for a woman and babe *Dead with Thirst*.[5] Mary and child – biblical resonances leaving no room for Ah Leung, killed on the island, or the injured Ah Sam who shared Mary's journey and fate. And just across Charlotte Street and up the hill is the West Coast Hotel, built in the 1870s when Cooktown was a scattering of buildings at the beginning of the trail to the goldfields. Before the memorials came the pubs and there were plenty of them. The first survey of the town in 1874 listed twenty-five and there were fifty by the end of the decade. Almost all are gone but, like the memorials, stories remain – of then and now. After I arrive at the hospital doctor Mick tells me one as he lurches towards the nurses' station in King Gee work-wear, Blundell lace-ups and a stethoscope swinging across his barrel chest. It was a few years ago but Mick was around when one of the West Coast regulars, Sledge Murphy, set up his drinking mate Slack, also a regular at the pub and with just enough common sense left not to drive his troopie home after the evening sessions. His blackouts were predictable and he never remembered what had happened the evening before, but wherever he was when he woke up he knew that the keys would be behind the bar so he always headed back to the West Coast before meandering into the day. One night after Slack had staggered off, Sledge moved the troopie into the middle of the road. It was more dents than duco and he left it with the driver's door open and an equine crime scene profile painted on the road. On cue, Slack arrived in the morning and even through the residual fog of intoxication, slowly giving way to the irritability and haze of hangover, the evidence spoke for itself. He might have told the story dozens of times but Mick still savors the scene: *Total panic, Slack couldn't get to the bar fast enough. Sledge was shitting himself.*

His eyes sparkling but somewhere else, with a snorting chuckle he detaches and slopes off towards the ward. Abrasive and much loved, a fixture on the Cape for a decade, doctor Mick thrives on frontier stories, tales of people escaping lovers, families, debts, police – themselves. Washing up in Cooktown as they have since the goldrush on the Palmer

River. From the beginning bringing recycled dreams and disappointments, as they did from New Zealand's west coast rush in the 1860s – thus the West Coast Hotel. About as east as you can get.

Glebe, January 16, 1993

A familiar space now, as much reading room as bookshop, and although the street still intrudes, crossing the Cornstalk threshold is calming. Someone enters and a wave of sound fills the front rooms and then dissipates, muffled by the closing door – and books. The volumes on the shelf in front of me are cloth covered, the spines worn, with titles in desert-coloured capitals across the top and at the base ANGUS & ROBERTSON. There's lightness to old hardcovers, as if some indiscernible substance has been lost with the relinquishing of words to past readers. Unlike the glued binding of new paperbacks these are stitch bound and open easily and flat. This one at *CHAPTER XX – THE OPIUM*, the title below a line drawing of two men in shorts, lying behind a coastal mound and peering through tussocks of grass, intently focused on a sailing vessel, maybe a lugger, in the middle distance. I start reading at mid-page:

The tide came lapping over the reef with hardly a ripple. And on it something came floating gently in. I had not noticed it, being wretchedly occupied in being miserable. That floating thing looked like a piece of seaweed, some floating weed had caught upon it. Suddenly I remembered last night and hurried down to the water's edge. The flotsam came nearer. It bore the tiniest of mastheads upon which was furled a wee flag. If there had been the faintest breeze that flag would have been bravely fluttering. It was the opium tin, brought back by the returning tide.[6]

Then further below:
Sitting on the reef I admired the thing, delaying to break it open. No doubt as to what was inside, for it was known in Cooktown and farther south in Cairns that opium was constantly thrown overboard that way, from China boats steaming down the coast.

I turn over thick yellowed pages to the inside cover – a profile map of Cape York Peninsula with Cooktown at its centre and a clutch of islands north to Cape Melville along a dotted line identified as *The Great Barrier Reef*. In the top right corner is an inset box with the outline of Australia and an arrow as the sole marker – MADMAN'S ISLAND. Three pages in is the book's only photograph, of a faded and stained document beneath which the title reads:

FASCIMILE OF PAGES FROM THE LOG OF THE WRECKED CUTTER SEA FOAM

Found by the author on the Reef at Howick (Madman's Island), and on the vacant pages of which he wrote the book.

Close by I see a similarly impressive section of Xavier Herbert works set next to a small group of Randolph Stow first editions – Geraldton boys. Stow was drawn to the Kimberley, like me I suppose, but for different reasons and by darker stories. I slide out a familiar volume, Stow's classic, reading at the first page:

A child dragged a stick along the corrugated iron wall of a hut, and Heriot woke and found the morning standing at his bed like a valet, holding out his daylight self to put on again, his name, his age, his vague and wearying occupation.[7]

To the islands – a book about violence and secrets. Reverend Ernest Gribble's secrets, that's who Heriot was based on. Stow was a young man when he sat under a tree listening to an old Aboriginal man tell stories about the killings that had occurred across the back country thirty years before. He was at Forrest River Mission, Oombulgurri later, the name of the massacre and a place of secrets then and now. Ernest Gribble – Protector of Aborigines – weighed down by rage and guilt for enabling what he'd tried to prevent. He'd been at the mission for more than a decade when special constables rode out of Wyndham in June 1926 with .44 Winchesters, side arms and a thousand rounds of ammunition. Leonard Overheu was with them, partner of Frederick Hay, whose spearing triggered the killings. They were soldier-settlers on Nulla Nulla station – Aboriginal land south of the mission. With them was their station boy, Tommy Doort, who made the mistake of talking about the shootings and

- specialist in antiquarian, rare and out-of-print Australian books -

And verso:

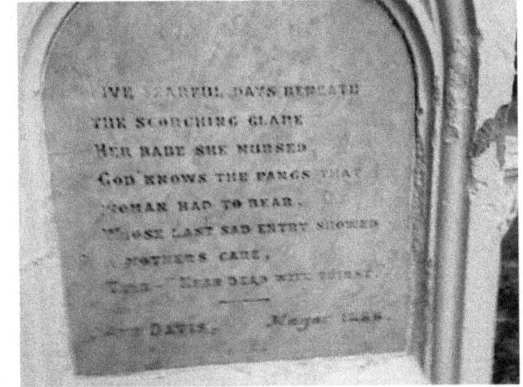

...two men in shorts, lying behind a coastal mound...
Madmans Island, 1938

that story got to Gribble. Tommy – station boy and witness. Overheu lured him out of hiding and that was that. Two riding out and one returning – no witnesses that time, black or white, other than Overheu and he didn't talk for decades.

Ernest Gribble railed against the pastoralists and police, against the Royal Commission – against fate. Muscular Christian and reluctant missionary, he'd tried to build on the legacy of his father, John, at Yarrabah near Cairns around the turn of century. Ernest was feared and admired at Yarrabah but eventually temptations of the flesh got the upper hand. A cyclone hit in 1906 and the following year his wife and children left for Brisbane. So did his sister Ethel who married her Aboriginal lover there. Tough and lonely times for Ernest and to cover the relationship that developed with Janie Brown, a woman who'd been removed to Yarrabah as a child because of her mixed descent, he organized her marriage to a local man, Willie Clark, but still fathered a child, Nora, born in 1908. It was an open secret that sealed his fate – he had to go.[8]

His father, John, had left Western Australia in controversy in the 1880s, but that's where Ernest headed in 1910. Nearly two decades later, after the Royal Commission into the Oombulgurri massacre he imploded and was banished – again – just like his dad. On Palm Island, over a quarter century, he rebuilt his reputation only to be taken as a failing old man, against his wishes, back to Yarrabah – full circle.[9] I slide the book back into its station.

The Kimberley and Cape York – a continent apart but bound by shared stories and by the silence of the human shadow-world beneath sun-drenched tropical landscapes. Heavy with research facts and fictions I left the Kimberley three years ago, and it's tales of Cape York that I'm searching out now. I walk back past the wall of Xavier Herbert and extract three early editions of Ion Idriess – *The opium smugglers*, *Coral Sea calling* and *Gold-dust and ashes*. Paul is almost hidden by a desk-top barricade of books but silhouetted on approach against the shop-front window and the flow on Glebe Point Road beyond. A computer monitor is the only sign that this is where business is transacted, where these tales become mine.

CHAPTER 2

2000: Cairns to Bamaga

Every five seconds the night cracks, the Coquet light slow-strobing glimpses of another world. Flashes of reassurance or signals of danger somewhere in the night. The difference is a map, the unseen world condensed to lines, symbols and names, the imaginings of long past voyagers in cartographic amber. Half-a-century and half-a-dozen mariners – the whole coast is a time capsule. Of illusions, dangers and disappointments – False Cape, Cape Tribulation and Cape Flattery. Also coincidence, correlation and ceremony – Providential Channel, Low Wooded Island and Possession Island. And people – thousands of people – honourable and humble, famous still and forgotten.

Most of the major features of this eastern shore were on the charts sent ahead by James Cook from Batavia along with descriptions of the transit of Venus. By the time the *Endeavour* ran up the English Channel in July 1771 and Cook began work on the fine copies, the names were set.[10] But not here, not this place. He was out to sea, beyond the reef when he passed these islands. Other explorers would fill the emptiness with line and letter on this stretch of the coast as they headed north – always north. But those threading through the rest of the labyrinth would have Cook's record and were – are still – comforted by his intuitions and imaginings.

So, maps take us back to other travellers and transits. From their experiences a chart warns the passage-maker of future dangers by correspondences to features of the seen world and with devices that signify the unseen. Like the black teardrop in a forest of nautical symbols that marks the light on Coquet Island. Though the rest of the world is unseen in the night, with the map and light in sight I'm oriented and I can imagine continuing the journey – heading north. Moving on but going back – journeys always involve return, even when it's all new, even when there's no going back. Familiarity, coincidence – connections to the unseen, the unremembered, floating or fixed beneath the surface. Going forward, going on – it's always going back.

Noble Island, July 16, 2000

Coles Islands consist of four bushy islets from a quarter to half a mile in extent; they are from four to six miles North-East from Point Murdoch. This group appeared to be merely the several dry parts of the shoal that extends from Point Lookout to Noble Island; between them and the latter island; are two patches of dry sandy keys, but it is probable that they may be covered by the tide.

Phillip Parker King (1827)[11]

Two weeks out of Cairns heading to The Tip. A short break in Cooktown to visit Finch Bay and say goodbye to doctor Mick, then on again, paddling with the wind. Three days later and to the east the Howicks are on the horizon. *Madman's Island* is there and that was the destination yesterday leaving the Turtle Group – midway between Lookout Point and Howick on the shorter, inner route north, bypassing Lizard Island. But things went wrong – self-deception. At the end of a long day in a kayak it's easy to give in to willing the destination closer, even when that contradicts experience and the map. Overestimating speed, underestimating wind and current effects – it's too tempting when you're tired. But by mid-afternoon it was clear Howick wasn't going to happen despite repeated appeals to the map. At 1:300,000 it seemed doable, just three centimetres, but that's nearly ten kilometres and around two hours into the wind.

Murdoch Island was the default destination, sitting on a four to five kilometre reef and separated from the mainland by a narrow channel. It looked good on the map but turned out to be an open, weather shore surrounded by mudflats. An hour more of dragging and portaging to a squall-scoured depression with just enough protection to stop the tent being blown away. Then a miserable night, alone with the wind and insects – and ghosts. In October 1881, reports of fires on Lizard Island and native canoes on the shore reached Cooktown and a police party was dispatched. That was three weeks after Mary Watson, Ferrier and Ah Sam had taken to sea. The settlement was found destroyed, property scattered and evidence of violence. A search was mounted with police and native troopers on the *Conflict* and the *Spitfire* and items from the household were located in Aboriginal camps from Cape Flattery to Murdoch Point. And there was talk of cannibalism. There weren't any bodies but there was plenty of outrage, quickly followed by calls for *action*. Recovery soon gave way to reprisal and native troopers from Bowen and Port Douglas under Inspector Hervey Fitzgerald returned on the *Spitfire* to do the job. A Canadian by birth, Fitzgerald came with experience – he'd been suspended five years earlier for whipping an Aboriginal woman but was back within three[12] – and he got confessions: *for the murder of Mrs Watson, her child and the two Chinese workers at Lizard Island ... Her body was then thrown into deep water.*[13] At least that's what Fitzgerald told reporters in November 1881 – nearly two months before three bodies were found on Howick No. 5 Island, thereafter Watson Island.

And one-hundred-and-twenty years later, with easterly headwinds continuing to build, it was going to be a long, hard paddle to get to the Howicks. July 16 on *Madman's Island* – an eclipse of the full moon – it would have been perfect. But it wasn't to be, and after launching from Murdoch Island this morning it's the shard-like profile of Noble Island to the north that I'm willing closer. Jack Idriess knew Noble too, and so did Charles Jeffreys – he named it, and the Howicks as well. In fact he did a lot of naming in these parts from the *Kangaroo* in 1815, filling in a gap in charts of the coast. Phillip Parker King followed in the *Mermaid* four years later and gave Jeffreys a backhanded compliment:

> *This officer drew a chart, with a track of his voyage up the coast; which considering the shortness of his time, and the other circumstances that prevented his obtaining the necessary data to lay down with accuracy so intricate and dangerous a passage, does him very great credit; he filled up the space between Endeavour River and Cape Direction which Captain Cook did not see; the only part that had previously been left blank upon the chart of New South Wales.*[14]

Lieutenant King was part of a fledgling aristocracy. Born on Norfolk Island just two years after the First Fleet, his father was Governor of New South Wales just before Bligh, who did his share of naming between Restoration Island and the Torres Strait.[15] After Bligh, and last Governor in the service of mad King George, was Lachlan Macquarie. Phillip Parker King got on well with Lachlan – Jeffreys didn't.

In fact, at least to the authorities in New South Wales – Governor Macquarie in Sydney and Lieutenant-Governor Sorell in Hobart – Charles Jeffreys was disobedient, devious, insubordinate and insolent. He smuggled hard spirits and lost souls, and was accused of *buccaneering* and *mutiny*. Against Macquarie's explicit orders to transport troops from Port Jackson to Ceylon without delay, Jeffreys slowly guided the *Kangaroo* through the reef's entire inner route – the first vessel to do so. Totally self-assured, he tried to publish an account of the voyage in the *Sydney Gazette* in February 1816 – which was suppressed, probably by Macquarie. Undeterred, and knowing the Governor had recommended that he be court-martialled on return to England, while discharging convicts in Hobart in April he had an account produced which appeared to have been in the *Hobart Town Gazette and Southern Reporter* of May 11, 1816 – a month before its first issue. He made sure that sole copy returned with him to England the following year and *Audentia* was the attribution of the anonymous covering letter introducing the supposed *Hobart Town Gazette* article in the *Statesman* and the Sunday *Constitution* in March 1818 in London, noting of Macquarie's suppression of it in Sydney that: *the right to do so was questioned by many, the justice by all.*

In case implicit comparisons to Cook weren't sufficient to garner favour, Jeffreys named the first island group he discovered between where Cook escaped from the labyrinth through Cook's Passage and where he returned through Providential Channel four days later, after the second Earl Grey, Viscount Howick – who went on to become Prime Minister. Whether it was sycophancy or the substance of his achievements it did the trick and in his reply to Macquarie in July 1818 Lord Bathurst noted that there were: *legal impediments to bringing that officer to a court martial.* But Jeffreys self-promotion didn't stop there and having plagiarized an unpublished manuscript on the geography of Tasmania he arrived back to take up land there in the same year that Phillip Parker King was off the Queensland coast.[16]

Nearly two centuries later, approaching Noble from the south the shore is battered rock backing scrubland rising to a saddle between two hills, the smaller of which to the south is fronted by boulders at water's edge. The peaks have been in sight for hours and have seemed no closer until, almost without warning, the details of the foreshore appear. With a strong following wind and sea the kayak surges with the swell, rounding the lesser hill with fractured cliffs towering above as the fragile craft bounces through reflected waves. And then into the wind-shadow, the air still as I glide past a fringe of mangroves rooted through clear water into white sand that continues above the tide-line as a northward-reaching spit. In the distance the mainland coast disappears into a midday haze that obscures the line between sea and sky.

In the lee of the hills the breeze gives way to stillness and radiant heat. Other than mangroves the only tree not struggling against the wind and sun is a solitary wongai – *Manilkara kauki*. Shade – in the middle of the day it's critical and trumps the nuisance of green-ants swarming over rotting fruit. Others have made the same decision – fishermen, yachties, maybe kayakers – a mandala of rubbish radiating out from the trunk. Cans, broken camp chairs, the remains of an old television, sheets of warped plywood – and plastic everywhere. As always there's the camp routine; clearing ground, rummaging through discards to find something to cook on, to hold the tent down, to give a bit of shade – for yet to be determined purposes. The lower branches of the wongai are festooned with paddling gear – life vest, spray-deck, gloves, sunglasses, hat – and later with suspended dry-bags to protect provisions from ants and rats. Slowly the kayak is rolled and dragged from the beach and tethered. With a full moon only a novice would throw the dice with a high tide. Nightmare scenario – waking up in the morning and looking out of the tent to see the beach cleared by the tide, and no kayak. Like Jack Idriess, stranded – and in sight of *Madman's Island*.

Exploring, on every island it's part of the routine, of claiming the space. The summit-climb is up a crumbling, dry rock-face, fired and glazed by constant northern exposure. Edging into shade in the solitary gully near the ridge, then vertical, cresting into fresh southern winds with Lizard in the distance – leaning into it, breathing it deeply, hearing nothing but the sounds of the unseen racing by. The Howicks are low on the horizon to the east, the mainland to the west now visible northward past Barrow Point and all the way to Cape Melville, with the languid drift of smoke from fires in the back-country.

Climbing down towards the saddle there's a cave that faces to the north – silence, shade and soft ground – an eyrie. Far below is a triangle of flat land behind the rock and boulder weather shore that was hidden from view as I was approaching Noble from the south. No trees, just struggling, windswept bushes, the only outstanding feature is abandoned machinery blending with the rust-colours of the surrounding rocks and scrub close to the base of the other, smaller hill and what could be a tunnel – or a mine.

Jack Idriess knew about mining on Noble, although he called it Nobel when he wrote about it years later, after he'd reverted to his birth-name – Ion. He was told by Formasini while they were working along the Bloomfield, or at least Formasini was probably the one working. Jack had a reputation for being averse to labouring for wages – he was called *Cyclone* by the *Murris*; a nice touch, a lot of wind but not much outcome. Anyway, in

The tin scratchers Formasini tells Jack he's just come back from digging for wolfram on the island with a mate. No water on Noble now or then and they relied on soaks behind the beach on the mainland, rowing about ten kilometres to get there:

> *then one would stand by the precious boat with rifle ready, while the other hurried across the beach to the swamp to fill the kerosene-tin bucket. The man guarding the boat had to cover his mate as he hurried through the tall grass to the swamp for the water, and he had to keep glancing back at their islet rock. For the opportunist natives raced their canoes across and tried to cut them off, each such attempt ending in a race back to the rock only won by rifle fire.*[17]

Wurrguulnyjin – that's what the *Guugu Yimithirr* called the island in those days, a place of stories about the tiger snake, protected by a spirit – *Yiirmbal* – a place to avoid. Formasini wouldn't have known that and probably knew very little about the mainland *Murris* who were already being scattered by missionaries, miners and mariners well before the first pastoral leases were taken up around Barrow Point just after the First World War. Jack would have understood the actions of the two men stranded on this remote island. At least with the advantage of firearms the situation was manageable – that is, until his mate sickened and Formasini was forced to row to the mainland for water alone under cover of darkness. To support the illusion that they were both still fighting fit he rigged up a dummy and crawled about out of sight showing his mate's hat. Although he was in hospital in Egypt at the time of the evacuation, Jack had been at Gallipoli and understood strategic deception. But eventually Formasini's mate died, the boat was stolen, and Formasini holed up in the mine with his rifle: *like a wombat in a walled-in burrow*. After a week without water he was raving when the lugger finally came to pick him up. That was before the War and it wasn't until Jack was back from Palestine that he stepped onto the island: *and walked into Formasini's lonely tunnel, vividly reconstructing his terrible ordeal*. The abandoned machinery – probably from a different time, different stories. And the mine, maybe Formasini's, maybe not. But Jack was here.

Sunday Island, August 7, 2000

Round Cape Grenville is Margaret Bay, fronted by Sunday Island, elevated and rocky, but not so high as Haggerston's Island with good anchorage under its lee.

Phillip Parker King (1827)

Sunday Island is at the south end of Shelburne Bay and that's where Paul's motor cruiser, *Thirsty Dog*, is moored after I pass Cape Grenville. I met Paul and Marlene a few days ago at Restoration Island. Bligh stopped at both as he struggled north in the longboat after the mutiny and almost had another to deal with on Sunday Island.[18] Paul is ex-military. Living the dream – an island-hopping, maritime retirement with his wife – or so it seems. And lots of stories, harvested over decades from the sea between Townsville and the Torres. Enough tales that it's never forced and he doesn't repeat. Marlene busies herself in the background, smiling as the events are brought to life again, tidying up the narrative without challenging it.

Their vessel is their home and somewhere below-decks is a trove of found objects from years of beachcombing and bartering, easily accessible props to complement almost every tale. I'm shown a small collection of natural pearls from Marlene's oyster-picking, souvenirs salvaged from dozens of the vessels wrecked by fate or design, and coins – a flat metal disc with almost no discernible markings rests in his palm: *This one is Spanish, or Portuguese – they were all along the coast. Some old people in the Straits told me about caves they know where there's lots of this stuff – and armor and weapons. Maybe from a galleon that hit the reef, who knows...*

Stories I've heard before; I remember eavesdropping on something similar at the Federal Hotel on Thursday Island nearly a decade ago. It might have been a group of consultants overnighting to or from the outer islands, maybe Native Title lawyers or trainers delivering one more course to bemused Islanders enticed by the lure of a free meal, *experts* with enough fleeting visits to count as experience and studiously referencing the *old people* and *elders*. Whether it was the gravitas of presumed authority or just the grog, the tale-teller was riffing on local knowledge he'd been privileged with. And although he and his audience probably hadn't heard of Ion Idriess, what he was repeating was the cultural and historical backstory that Idriess described in detail and within which his stories came alive. Idriess spent time in the Torres in the 1920s, he'd moved on from just plain Jack, he was a serious writer by then. And he did his research; he read the Cambridge Expedition[19] reports from-turn-of-century and visited outer islands on the *Herald* with the missionary ethnographer W. H. McFarlane. And he talked to locals wherever he went – watching and listening, weaving it all together. On Yam and Mer the line between fiction and ethnography was blurred and plot became history in the retelling. Across the table at the Federal and over another drink on *Thirsty Dog* I hear echoes of the *Drums of Mer*,[20] or maybe *The wild white man of Badu*[21] or *Coral Sea calling*.[22] Tales of warriors, custom and the collision of cultures across the few short decades that transformed the Torres Strait.

Paul jettisons an empty wine cask into a corner of the deck where a pile from the last few days stacks against the transom alongside ropes and fishing gear. Marlene is ahead of the action and has already retrieved another from below as Paul's commentary continues: *The Chinese were here too – Admiral Zhou Man. There's a perfectly round stone on the north of Badu. Only women go there – some of the old people told Marlene that it's got spiritual power. But I think it's a stone cannon ball from Zhou Man's fleet. I was thinking of going and getting it. Marlene reckons it's better to leave it where it is. But there were junks in these waters, lots of them.*[23]

Jack McLaren saw one just around The Tip from where Cook hoisted the colours on Possession Island. McLaren was a wanderer who became a writer. He'd left the throb and thrust of Melbourne to head north just a decade after Federation. And like Idriess his writings were about the places and people of the journey. His *crowded solitude* at Utingu-Simpson Bay, where he developed the region's first coconut plantation, lasted from 1911 through the War when his namesake was at Gallipoli and in Palestine – Jack Idriess, trooper 358 with the 5th Light Horse.[24] It was maybe a few years before that, while Idriess was fossicking around the Bloomfield, that Jack McLaren had unexpected visitors in a Chinese junk that had left Hong Kong bound for San Francisco, but which had been blown wildly off course by unrelenting winds until it: *miraculously escaped the dangers of the Barrier Reef, and finally came to anchor off my house.*[25]

Aboard the junk were five people: *a white man, his Chinese wife and three adult Eurasian sons.* What they found when they got ashore was a home assembled from native materials, found objects and exotic decorations from trade across the Straits. Jack McLaren had contrived a refuge from civilization and the wilderness – a domesticated space for his *crowded solitude.* At the whim of the wind and blown to that doorstep, it must have seemed paradise to his storm-swept visitors and was their last stop before both junk and journey were abandoned on Thursday Island. And soon after that Jack relinquished his *one man dwelling* and the life he'd built at Utingu; in 1919 the *wanderlust welled up,* and he moved on. *Wanderlust –* floating, unattached, unconnected. But Jack McLaren really was attached to the land and people. *Wanderlust –* probably just a literary device, glossing over the bonds of blood. Through the birth of a pale, sandbeach babe – Nicholas Fitzherbert – Jack was rooted in sandbeach soil.[26]

It wasn't the solitude that got to Jack McLaren but the crowded bureaucracies of racial control that the new nation had spawned. Jack's idyll was shattered as the prejudices of frontier administration caught him in a net of regulations for the *protection* of native peoples – and the preservation of the colonial order: *He had committed the impardonable sin for a white man; he had 'gone native'.*[27] So, in 1919 Jack left Wandihnu and his son, Nicholas, who grew up in a world of institutional control. Nicholas Wymarra eventually became a citizen of the new country into which he was born, and died in 1975 across the Endeavour Channel from the sandbeach soil of his birth. By that time, like his father, the world had moved on.

Escape River, August 12, 2000

Orfordness is a sandy projection of the coast under Pudding-pan Hill (of Bligh) the shape of which, being flat-topped, is very remarkable: the hill is in latitude 11 degrees 18 minutes 30 seconds, and longitude 142 degrees 43 minutes 35 seconds. The country between Cape Grenville and Cape York is low and Sandy, with but few sinuosities in its coast line: it is exposed to the trade wind, which often blows with great strength, from South-East and South-East by East.

Phillip Parker King (1827)

Orfordness astern with seas building from the south-east. Orfordness – four kilometres north of Pudding Pan Hill. Named by Bligh, Edmund Kennedy stopped there in the penultimate stage of his final journey of exploration – an overland route to the top of York Peninsula along the east coast.[28] They sailed from Sydney in April 1848 on the *Tam O'Shanter*, escorted by the *Rattlesnake* under Captain Owen Stanley, and landed horses, provisions and men in Rockingham Bay near Cardwell the next month. It was a disaster from the start and they were so delayed they missed their supply ship the *Bramble* in Princess Charlotte Bay in August. And it only got worse – Kennedy left eight men behind at Weymouth Bay and continued with four others, one of whom was an Aboriginal teenager, Galmarra, known by those with him and ever after as Jackey Jackey. At Pudding Pan Hill a rifle accident forced Kennedy to leave the other three Europeans. Kennedy and Jackey Jackey struggled on into history.

And struggle is what it's about now along the same coast, glimpsed through rain showers as the bad weather that forced landfall at Orfordness last night continues to build. Lit with an ethereal glow, fragments of shore and hills suddenly appear as sunlight pours through twisting aquamarine aerial chasms in the darkening sky – there for a moment then swallowed by the leaden cloudbanks racing north. A big day to escape the wind and building seas. Focus ahead and don't look back, it's a basic rule, just keep the rhythm. And keep the coast in sight. When that fails and the continent disappears behind sea-mist and squalls trust the basics – compass and elapsed time. Wind direction can change suddenly, waves are reflected and refracted by islands and reefs, tides and currents weave mysteriously. And even with fine weather and line of sight the trickster takes advantage of weariness and inexperience. A kayaker's eyes are just two feet above the waterline, so the horizon isn't far. What look like islands an hour later are mainland hills and headlands, and the shoreline that is tantalizingly close is not; even when the beach is clearly visible it's another hour or more away. Not just fooling you into believing what you hope for, the trickster can send you in circles – the comfort of locating a navigation tower in the distance can dissolve after paddling in an arc before the bulk of the tanker beneath it is finally exposed in a distant shipping channel. Sea-kayaking is not for those in a hurry.

At least the map doesn't change. Contours and names stamp the unknown with familiarity that suggests the certainty of time and tradition. But almost all of which through the labyrinth were bestowed by only four men over five decades – Cook, Bligh, Jeffreys and King. And of those it's Cook's marks that are all over the charts. He wouldn't let this coast out of sight – he knew there was a westward passage and that he was near it. He came back into the labyrinth just south of here from the safety of open sea to find it. As he passed these shoals and coastal sand dunes he recorded:

> *The world will hardly admit of an excuse for a man leaving a Coast unexplored he has once discover'd, if dangers are his excuse he is then charged with Timorousness and want of Perseverance and at once pronounced the unfittest man in the world to be employ'd as a discoverer; if on the other hand he boldly encounters all the dangers and obstacles he meets and is unfortunate enough not to succeed he is then charged with Temerity and want of conduct.*[29]

Within days he'd found the passage, reached The Tip, which he named York Cape, claimed the eastern seaboard for the Crown and was heading west, leaving in his wake a corridor of coastal landmarks that echo the social networks and associations of an eighteenth century navigator. Interspersed with the mundane – Double Island, Two Isles, Three Isles, Low Wooded Island, Sharp Point and more.

Through the salt-encrusted map-case strapped across the decking directly in front of my cockpit it's difficult to read the writing on the laminated A4 photocopies of coastal maritime charts. Around twenty from Cairns to Bamaga and only a couple more north of Orfordness and around The Tip to the end of the journey. Reassurance when out of sight of land or when the weather closes in that while the continent is unseen it's still there. And during long days of clear skies, progressing one stroke at a time off an unchanging shore, a glance assures against the sense of inertia. Compressing this passing world to manageable dimensions these fading sheets work other magic. Not only by triggering fantasies of voyages of discovery but through an alchemy of associations that float the unremem-bered into awareness. With just the sounds of wind on water to break the hypnotic cadence of paddling over uninterrupted hours, the thoughts that breach into consciousness usually quickly dissipate, like the spray on the hull in full sun – there, gone, there again. Almost unnoticed, some return – a friend, a lover, parents, a school play, a song, a childhood book – usually subliminal but sometimes soaring and held momentarily aloft in the thermals of memory. The map is a companion – it speaks of things present, and whispers of the past.

But bad weather leaves no space for reflection, just attention – to balance, to the shifting centre of buoyancy as the kayak is overtaken by following swells, to remaining true to the compass bearing against the sea's pull to port, to glimpses of low coast through the rain, to the slowness of time – elapsed time; it's hours until the bauxite-reddened cliffs around Sharp Point appear between squalls. Again, checking the map, that its magic will quell the storm, that the sanctuary is real.

In the lee of Sharp Point the wind abruptly dies and the following sea falls away as it progresses through the channel between the sandbanks and mangroves of Escape River to the west and Turtle Head Island to the north and east, towards Newcastle Bay and the mouth of the Jackey Jackey. From memory and map I know there's a cultured pearl farm on the island, and there it is, a few buildings and a jetty. And in the channel, a solitary vessel – junk-rigged with a furled, red sail – slowly swaying with the vestigial swell.

The mouth of the Jackey Jackey; one hundred and fifty years ago Jackey Jackey was here twice, the fist time at the end of the doomed push with Kennedy through the mangroves and creeks around the Escape River to rendezvous with the *Ariel* just a few miles north. Kennedy didn't make it, speared in the back at a place Idriess knew:

> *Aborigines have pointed out to me the very spot where Kennedy fell. A dismal place to die alone, among the gaunt mangroves by that weird river mouth enclosed by those scrubby little hills, by those strange pitcher-plant swamps.*[30]

But Kennedy wasn't alone, Jackey Jackey was with him to the end, and he pushed on to the *Ariel,* and then directed Captain Dobson back to Weymouth Bay where the two survivors of the eight men who had been left were found – William Goddard and William Carron, a botanist. His journal is the record of the expedition to that point. He described the deaths of the storekeeper Niblet and naturalist Wall who had: *abandoned themselves to a calm and listless despair.*[31] Nothing was ever found of the three who remained at Pudding Pan Hill.

The following year Jackey Jackey returned on the *Freak* under Captain Thomas Beckford Simpson and the bodies at Weymouth Bay were recovered and transported north to Albany Island. On his last journey, to survey the Louisiade Archipelago in 1849, Captain Owen Stanley of the *Rattlesnake,* who had been with the expedition when it set out, marked the graves – *Here lies Thomas Wall and C. Niblet, late of the Kennedy Exploring Expedition.* Buried just across the Passage from where Kennedy was speared then carried on by Jackey Jackey, who stared straight ahead as he bore the dead weight of his companion, one step at a time, to journey's end in dense tea-tree scrub. But after leading the second expedition to the earlier stations in that slowly-evolving tragedy, Jackey Jackey couldn't find where he'd: *digged up the ground with a tomahawk, and covered him over with logs, then grass.* Because he was totally focused on moving forward when he carried Kennedy he hadn't been able to look back, to check his path as he always intuitively did in the bush – he'd lost his bearings. They tried to recreate the circumstances, getting him to walk into the scrub pretending to shift the body from one shoulder to the other and *not to look back,* but he couldn't do it and they returned without Kennedy but with stories that became legend.

Tommy Doort from Forrest River in the Kimberley and Jackey Jackey from near Muswellbrook in the upper Hunter both rode out with European expeditions. Tommy died because he knew too much and maybe Jackey Jackey did as well. He went home – or tried to. They said he had a *fondness for ardent spirits* and in 1854, in his early twenties, he fell into a campfire somewhere near Albury and died. But not before being fleetingly feted as an example to his race, the *Sydney Morning Herald* of Thursday 31 December 1850 reporting the official presentation of a silvered breast plate on which was inscribed:

PRESENTED

by

His Excellency Sir CHARLES AUGUSTUS FITZ ROY, K.H.,
Governor of New South Wales,

to

JACKEY JACKEY,

an Aboriginal Native of that Colony, in testimony of the fidelity with which he followed the late Assistant-Surveyor E. B. C. Kennedy throughout his exploration of York Peninsula, in the year 1848; the noble daring with which he supported that lamented Gentleman, when mortally wounded by the Natives of Escape River, the courage with which, after having affectionately tended the last moments of his Master, he made his way through hostile Tribes and an unknown Country, to Cape York; and finally, the unexampled sagacity with which he conducted the succour that there awaited the Expedition, to the rescue of the other survivors of it, who had been left at Shelbourne Bay

Turtle Head Island, August 12, 2000

Escape River, in 10 degrees 57½ minutes, is an opening in the land of one mile in breadth, trending in for two or three miles, when it turns to the north, and is concealed from view; the land on the north side of the entrance is probably an island, for an opening was observed in Newcastle Bay, trending to the south, which may communicate with the river. The entrance is defended by a bar, on which the Mermaid was nearly lost. The

deepest channel may probably be near the south head, which is rocky. The banks on the south side are wooded, and present an inviting aspect.
Phillip Parker King (1827)

Nobody at the cultured pearl farm but it doesn't seem to have been abandoned and the buildings aren't locked. After portaging gear and setting up camp, and as the sun is setting beyond the mangroves that are disappearing into the night on the other side of the channel, I paddle out to the vessel at anchor. Junk rigged with a ferro-cement hull, the *Si Hai* rides heavily on the water. The two figures moving about on deck that I saw earlier are now standing just in front of the mast, monitoring my approach. Echoes of McLaren's visitors, an Englishman and his Chinese wife – Terry and Anna Walker – and on a junk. They've been living in Sydney and now sailing back to Singapore; no rush, taking their time. I tether the kayak to the stern and follow them below into what has for years been their home. Railed shelves filled with books, map-canisters, radio equipment and more. Barometer, family photos and a print of a schooner in full sail on the bulkheads. The galley is efficient and orderly; within minutes the kettle is boiling and tea served with biscuits, Anna taking the lead: *You should try this jam I made from wongais we collected just inside Cape Melville.*

I know the place. And the wongai plum, *taste it and you'll come back* – that's what they say in the Torres Strait. I did and went back, and to the coast around Lockhart where I first learned about it from John Pritchard. But I didn't expect to find it on offshore islands and there it was, just back from a narrow beach in the Turtle Group north of Lookout Point. That was a month ago, mid-July, and fruiting trees carpeted the earth with a penumbra of teak-dark, ripe and rotting fruit, with more falling as I shook the outer branches. Big-pitted and like a dry date, but wonderful as found food.

Anna floats around the cabin, exotic delicacies materializing with a pleasantly offhand commentary: *We were on the flatlands in the lee of Cape Melville for about a week and set up a beach camp under one of the wongai trees. There was so much fruit I decided to make jam. Terry thinks I should start a business. So what makes someone paddle a thousand kilometres up Cape York…*

What makes someone paddle a thousand kilometres up Cape York … Too many reasons and all self-deceiving. And any summary statement too trite. Maybe the truth is somewhere in the contrails left as memories circulate through the stratosphere of consciousness as the paddling day passes – the song, the play, the childhood book: *Hard to answer. But over the last month coming north I've noticed that I keep thinking about things that haven't been in my mind for decades. For instance, after I've been paddling for a few hours I'll suddenly realize that for the last ten minutes or so I've been thinking about a book I read as a child,* Swallows and Amazons.[32]

– Arthur Ransome, I've got it here. Anna, it's next to the galley.

SWALLOWS-AND-AMAZONS-FOREVER! Below the crossed pennants bearing the profiles of a swallow in flight and skull-and-crossbones, the motto stands out from the surface of the worn cover above a faded drawing of the four children sitting on a lakeside rise. Not just surprised – I'm unprepared. Unprepared for a cascade of connections and memories.

Arthur Ransome surprised just about everyone. A would-be man-of-letters, he was one of a handful of people who, as the second decade of the twentieth century began, had read the unabridged text of Oscar Wilde's letter from Reading Jail – *De Profundis*. Its intended recipient and Wilde's ex-lover, Lord Alfred Douglas, kept Arthur in court for a year after Ransome's biography of Wilde was released.[33] With that and the pressures of an unhappy marriage he was off – to Russia; he was in St Petersburg as troops were mobilized on the eve of the War. By its end the world was changed and Russia was no more. Ransome reported on it from as close as it was possible for a foreign correspondent to get – Lenin warned him personally that he was suspected by the Americans of being a spy and he met his partner, Evgenia Petrovna Sherapina, when she was Trotsky's personal secretary. Journalist, British spy, Bolshevik agent, Soviet apologist – probably all of those but also a sailor; he and Evgenia had the *Racundra* built in Estonia and his account of their Baltic wanderings was a hit in the 1920s. Arrested on his return to England and monitored by MI5 for a decade, he had the skills and was one of few people with the experience to write a first-hand account of the revolution – that's what was expected.[34]

He didn't – he wrote children's books. But not trifling amusements; his stories of four children and two boats, resetting memories of childhood holidays on Coniston Water and Lake Windermere, and his Baltic adventures in the *Racundra*, were the highest selling children's books in the English language for two generations – *Swallows and Amazons* was the first. Nearly four decades after being given a copy I'm holding it again – Terry has no idea what he's handing over: *Take it for the night and bring it back in the morning. Anna, get a jar of wongai jam for Ernest to take with him. They say that if you taste it you'll come back.*

Turtle Head Island, August 13, 2000

Newcastle Bay is nine miles in extent by six deep; its shores are low, and apparently of a sandy character; at the bottom there is a considerable opening bearing West ¼ North eight miles and a half from Turtle Island. Off the south head of the bay is Turtle Island, a small rocky islet on the east side of an extensive reef, in latitude 10 degrees 54 minutes, and longitude 142 degrees 38 minutes 40 seconds.

Phillip Parker King (1827)

Swallows and Amazons – the map inside the front cover glows with familiarity, triggering a cascade of subtle associations and feelings – almost too much to be held within the fragile fabric of remembering. *Unexplored Arctic, Antarctic, Rio Bay, Cormorant Island, Shark Bay, Long Island, Houseboat Bay, Wild Cat Island* – through a rabbit hole into childhood. Weeks in a small boat, an A4 representation of the seen world strapped in front of me, my guide on this journey – no wonder Ransome's book kept nudging me to the rabbit hole. In the uncertain light of a headlamp on Turtle Head Island I'm reading about ageless children camping on *Wild Cat Island* – an adventure within an adventure, a moment to live with: *But who would wave a flag to be rescued if they had a desert island of their own? That was the thing that spoilt* Robinson Crusoe. *In the end he came home. There never ought to be an end.*[35]

Ransome sought inspiration in simpler days before a doomed marriage, court cases and the War. He went back to childhood and summer vacations in the Lake District with family friends, the Collingwoods and their four children, Dora, Barbara, Ursula and Robin, and to afternoons on the water in a sailing dinghy – the *Swallow*. In writing the fictional adventures of the Walker and Blackett children a quarter-century later he conjured adventure through the layering of their imaginations onto simple, holiday activities. While their parents are close by, they realize that the Windermere holiday will end, and know that certain things have to be done properly with small boats, at the same time they are somewhere else, casting off from *Darien* and making course to *Wild Cat Island,* sharing another world with pirates and savages. As it was for a young boy with a tin canoe forty years ago on the Swan River. The limestone cliffs of Freshwater Bay were the dominant features of a map drawn and redrawn on exercise-book paper. The heights, the boathouse, the cave, the passage, the bamboo forest, the rocks, a compass rose of sorts – it had all the devices of Ransome's map and some of the same names, and like his child creations I could be there and somewhere else too, alone with my imagination. As I am, in my sleeping bag in a tent on Turtle Head Island as dawn breaks in a new millennium. Not *Wild Cat Island* but close enough.

The burrow beneath the rabbit hole is a maze of interconnected tunnels and I step into another. In May 1944 the Liberty Ship *SS Samspeed* was launched and, surviving the war, was sold to Lyle's Shipping Company of Glasgow in 1947. The following year was its maiden voyage to Australia. Its captain had been one of the youngest in the merchant marine when the fighting began and spent the war in Mediterranean and Atlantic convoys. In 1948 he was on a one-way trip to a new life. Lyle's had renamed the ship after an earlier vessel lost to enemy action in the North Sea off Kinnaird Head in August 1940 – the *Samspeed* was the *Cape York* and my father, Harry Hunter, was its master.

Sixteen years later Harry was on another Lyle's freighter, the *Cape Sable*. Again, a one-way trip, but he was not master – of anything. Worn down by the unrelenting pressure of unarmed responsibility in war, an unhappy marriage and grief, he'd been marooned on foreign soil – it wasn't his country. The sea remained his solace and it was his bridge across space and generations to a distant land. And across time to his father, David, and six uncles, proud Shetland Islanders who were all sea captains like Harry and his brother, Ernie. And Harry's firstborn was also David, killed on his first day at school. An unremarkable tragedy, there's not much more can be said. Harry's sister, Beatrice, who came to Australia the year before David died and had cradled him and his younger brother, me, tried:

In memory of Darling little David….
Just when his life was brightest,
Just when his fears were least,
He was called from this world of sorrows,
To a home of eternal rest.
Perhaps when God's message grows plainer
And hearts and souls are at rest
We will find in our grief and sorrow
God's ways are always the best.

Harry was on the bridge of the *Cape Sable* with Captain Ian Hamilton, an old friend, Fremantle far behind. He had with him his father's sextant – passed down to the firstborn. Inside a polished wooden box it sat in felt-lined housing with each lens precisely nested. Its provenance was inscribed on the inner lid along with the name of its first owner – *David Hunter* – it should have gone to another. Harry recognized it and knew it, but he no longer understood it. Ian Hamilton sensed the struggle and was gentle in his diversion: *Harry, let the lad have a feel of it. He should learn y'know. Even with the new gear we've got now there'll always be a need for a good sextant and the skill to use it. First Mate, get Captain Hunter a mug of tea. Right Ernie, your father and I are going to teach you about it, what d'you say…*

Captain Hamilton's palm enclosed my hand around the dark, worn handle. I'd seen this beautiful device but never held it. It was bigger and heavier than it seemed in velvet repose: *You hold it like this, we'll be trying to see the horizon in this wee mirror here. In fact it's going to bounce off the index mirror up here. These coloured glasses are to protect your eyes from the sun, you can swing them out and back. We need to screw in a wee telescope, we'll take this one here. Harry, you'll remember how we were taught when we were lads. You sailed with your uncle Adam did you not, he was a hard man but a fine captain, knew his navigation...*

But Harry didn't remember, his brain was broken and his mind has been set adrift, floating in uncharted waters where everything was unfamiliar. *The child is father to the man* – twelve years old and taking him back; back to Glasgow, back to detached memories, to a city where the ship was king a long time ago – another time. With him, but both of us alone. Ian Hamilton's soft, kindly voice continued in the background as Harry grasped the mug: *Harry, you remember what a cup of tea was like in the convoys at night. Nothing like it. Ernie, I'm supposing your father told you about the War, he was in the Atlantic and on Malta convoys. Captain Hunter saw a lot...*

No, he never told me and they didn't tell me his mind had gone – I just knew. They didn't tell me I was taking him to die, but I knew that too. To fade from life among moors and mountains that looked like the colour photographs in the *Scottish Field* magazines he aimlessly scanned – again, and again, and again. But Glasgow in the 1960s wasn't like that, and he didn't die. There was a final one-way voyage, three years later, back to Fremantle. Back to a place filled with sadness and confusion, to a house that was no longer a home, to where he didn't belong, where he didn't fit in.

Perhaps he ended up in a place where he did fit in. Maybe he didn't belong there but he fitted in. One day after school I visited him in a locked ward of Claremont Hospital. Half-way between Perth and Fremantle – that was the logic when they chose the site for the Claremont Hospital of the Insane in 1901, with a name change and about 1700 long-stayers by the time Harry was there in the late 1960s, and closed a decade later in the heady days of deinstitutionalization. But Harry didn't leave, he wasn't going anywhere. That was clear the last time I saw him, though he didn't see me – or much else. Hospital-gown for ease of cleaning, bare-bum and unshaven, brought into a high-ceilinged hall from who-knows-where by a chain-smoking attendant with a bad attitude and stained uniform. Metallic, cavernous sounds, guttural wailing – no wonder it was hidden away. The last image of my father was a glimpse through a glass panel in the closing metal door, Harry surrendering a banana and cake – my last gift – to a hovering inmate as the attendant turned his back.

Sitting in a tent on Turtle Head Island reading a children's book. Thirty-five years and a degree in psychiatry to find this rabbit hole. And in it a book given by Harry a few years before he gave another, an illustrated edition of *The old man and the sea*. Twenty-two shillings and sixpence from Loftus Bookshop in Atwell Arcade, Fremantle, just a short walk from the turn-of-century bank building on the corner of High and Cliff Streets that became RG Lynn's – shipping agents. Across the road from the Mission to Seamen and right next door to the Roma. Not the Roma restaurant, just the Roma. Two piece cutlery on Formica tabletops, laminate chairs that would never be retro – somewhere between milk-bar and restaurant. Chicken and spaghetti, about as cultural as you could get in 1960. RG Lynn's; 7 High Street, just an office but with a bank's vaulted intimidation and with back-rooms where only men and war widows were welcome. Shipping agent; where else could a superannuated merchant mariner find work – they were a dime-a-dozen after that war. Harry was hired because of his wife's connections and when things started to go wrong and he became a liability they told Edna it was her problem. He would have been losing it when he walked to the Loftus Bookshop. *Swallows and Amazons, The old man and the sea* – it wasn't random, he may not have known it but across a generation he was downloading the sea. But maybe he did know it, perhaps he was racing against time and the closing of his mind.

The Tip, August 14, 2000

Cape York, the northernmost land of New South Wales, has a conical hill half a mile within its extremity, the situation of which is in 10 degrees 42 minutes 40 seconds South, and 142 degrees 28 minutes 5 seconds East of Greenwich. There is also an island close to the point with a conical hill upon it, which has perhaps been hitherto taken for the cape; from which it is separated by a shoal strait half a mile wide.

Phillip Parker King (1827)

One day on from Turtle Head Island but suddenly I'm approaching the journey's symbolic end – The Tip. After unchanging shorelines Newcastle Bay has surprises. Distant turbulence off Fly Point at the southern entry to the Albany Passage transforms into standing waves, the agitated intersection of currents and tides that bounce the kayak as it's driven by fifteen knot winds. In the Passage a following current of two to three knots speeds me between Albany Island to the east and the headlands of the mainland shore. Past Somerset Bay where, in January 1865, nearly two decades after Jackey Jackey buried Kennedy, Frank and Alexander Jardine with four former Aboriginal mounted police from the Wide Bay area, were escorted in by local *Yadhaigana* – the end of a seven month overland journey from Rockhampton with dead blackfellows all the way.[36] Unlike Kennedy, they chose a western route up the peninsula. Their father, John, was waiting for them:

> *disturbed by a loud shouting, and looking out saw a number of blacks running up to the place. Imagining that the Settlement was about to receive another attack, (for the little community had already had to repulse more than one,) he seized his gun, always in readiness for an "alerte" and rushed out. Instead, however, of the expected enemy, he had the pleasure of seeing his long-looked-for sons, surrounded and escorted by their sable guides.*[37]

As the Rockhampton police magistrate John Jardine was already known for bloody, vigilante justice against Aborigines before he arrived at Somerset.[38] And the apparent goodwill at the time of his reunion with his sons didn't last – within a couple of years Jardine's *sable guides* had shot and killed eight to ten *Yadhaigana*. Supposedly in retaliation for black-fellow treachery – but there are two sides to every story. Even after the Society for the Propagation of the Gospel arrived a year later attitudes didn't change – at least according to Reverend Jagg: *The Aborigines have been described as the most degraded, treacherous and bloodthirsty beings in existence by the present Police Magistrate and those whose only idea is to shoot them down whenever they were seen.*[39] Probably not a lot of sympathy from the Jardines – by that time Frank was the Police Magistrate.[40] And, of course, he knew nothing about it:

I had returned home some time before I heard anything about the killing part of the expedition, which was kept from my knowledge so well that I was the last person to hear of it ... but instead of speaking to me about it allowed a stranger to give the particulars and also to tell me that Mr. Jagg was going to "put a stop to that sort of thing". I then inquired into the matter and made out that ten Yardaigans had been killed but none of their heads taken. The skulls alluded to were those of two blacks speared at Cape York, the heads and the body of a child were bought by the servant of Dr. Horan the Medical Superintendent here.[41]

Bought to advance science and empire.

Albany Passage fast astern as the kayak is propelled on, the Carnegie Range to the west the last rump elevation of the Great Dividing Range before it reappears to the north as islands between the peninsula and Papua New Guinea. The Tip doesn't look remarkable – a rocky bluff separated by a short channel from the first small islands of the Torres Strait – but it is. The coast falls to the southwest with Peaked Hill obscuring Possession Island where, more than two centuries ago, the flag was raised with a volley of small arms answering from the deck of the *Endeavour*. At midday on the day before, Cook was still hours from passing The Tip and took sightings of Mount Adolphus Island to the east, Little Adolphus to the north, and Eborac Island to the west – an eroded slab of the Great

...*a solitary wongai*...

... the Si Hai *rides heavily on the water.*

- the Sam Speed *was the* Cape York...

Dividing Range surfacing less than a kilometre to the north as the kayak rounds the Tip into flat water and mangrove-fringed shores in its lee.

From the east, Eborac Island is indistinguishable from York Island, which is higher and immediately to the west.[42] It was to guide vessels coming from the east that a lighthouse was built on Eborac in the early 1920s. Cook's sightings locate the *Endeavour* in what is now the Adolphus shipping channel, which splits to avoid Mid Rock, the light on Eborac being the direction of safe passage to its south. The other channel to the north-west passes between Mid Rock and a submerged peak halfway between the mainland and Mt Adolphus Island. The *Endeavour* was within a few kilometres of that sea-veiled massif, and with a draught of around eleven feet may have been able to pass right over if its course had been different. One hundred and twenty years later the Royal Mail Ship *Quetta*, drawing nineteen feet at the bow and twenty-two at the stern, and travelling at around ten knots, was in almost the same position as Cook – but not quite.

Timing is all – looking south-east from The Tip, the headlands of Albany Island mark the northern entry to the Albany Passage. The Jardines had hoped that Somerset, in the middle of the Passage, would be a major stopping point for shipping through the Torres. Although currents, tides and poor anchorage ensured that Thursday Island prospered instead, it was still regularly visited in the 1890s when Joshua Slocum anchored next to the *Tarawa*, a Californian pearler. Singlehanded, Slocum was on his way around the world in the *Spray* out of Boston, and was interested in characters:

> They were Mr. Jardine, stockman, famous throughout the land, and his family. Mrs Jardine was the niece of King Malietoa, and cousin to the beautiful Faamu-Sami ("To make the sea burn"), who visited the Spray at Apia. Mr Jardine was himself a fine specimen of a Scotsman. With his little family about him, he was content to live in this remote place, accumulating the comforts of life.[43]

And a few years earlier, in 1890, a quarter century after he rode into Somerset with his brother, Frank Jardine was there as the *Quetta* approached Albany Island from the south on its twelfth round trip between Brisbane and London; it had stopped at Cooktown and was heading for Thursday Island. For Torres Strait Pilot, Captain Eldred Pottinger Keatinge, it was his thirteenth passage though the Straits. The sun had just set and rather than risking Albany Passage in the dark, Keatinge advised Captain Alfred Sanders to alter course for the safer, outer route through the Adolphus Channel, keeping between Mid Rock and Mount Adolphus Island. Just after 9:00pm on the 28th of February they hit the mass of granite rising to just fifteen feet below the surface and within minutes the *Quetta* was gone – taking nearly half of the 292 passengers and crew.

Sanders and Keatinge were both in the boat that made it to Somerset where Frank Jardine met them, and four days later they were on the *Albatross* back at the scene of the disaster. Reverend Albert Maclaren, later founder of the Quetta Memorial Church on Thursday Island, was also on board: *We passed over the scene of the terrible wreck, and, at the request of Captain Reid, I read the service of the Church of England, in the presence of the captain, Mr. Corser, Pilot Keating, Dr. Salter and the crew.*[44] It began: *I am the resurrection and the life. He who believes in Me, though he may die, he shall live. And whoever lives and believes in Me shall never die...* As Reverend Maclaren sought comfort in the Gospel according to John, his words just lifting above the whisperings of the wind, Pilot Keatinge might have had the other mariners' Book in mind – *Moby Dick* – and Ishmael's passing reference to *Rokavoko*, island home to Queequeg: *It is not down in any map; true places never are.*

True places never are – the following month David Reid sailed the Albatross back to the site. Keatinge and Sanders were again on board and the *Quetta* was found, but not the *true place* – Quetta Rock. That was later as the *Albatross* was returning from Cairncross Island after a final sweep for survivors – at sixteen feet corrected for the tide. Keatinge was absolved of blame by the inquiry into the tragedy and he returned to sea. But Jardine and Keatinge met again; eleven years later the exhausted pilot came ashore at Somerset with crewmembers of the grounded *Duke of Devonshire*. He'd fallen asleep before it passed Hannibal Island where the course had to change by thirty degrees. It didn't, and the next stop was Hunter Reef – timing is all. No third life in the Labyrinth for Eldred Pottinger Keatinge. Decades later Jack Idriess passed close by in the *Somerset*, a lugger skippered by Frank Jardine's grandson, Bootles.[45] The four-month journey from Brisbane nearly ended in disaster but Jack eventually made it to Thursday Island, staying at the Federal Hotel where the manager showed Idriess the register in which the survivors of the *Quetta* had signed their names thirty-seven years before.

CHAPTER XXV

THE SECOND SINGAPORE

The Jardines hoped that Somerset ... would be a major stopping point for shipping...
Coral sea calling, 1957

CHAPTER 3

1993: beta

Lost to the sea or consigned to it – becoming one, again, with the ocean, with its moods and movements. The Coral Sea; heard but not seen as the sounds of waves caressing Howick's shore drift up through the darkness to *The Peak*. Oceans warped by forces bent across time and space tightening their tidal embrace. Entwined with currents, driven by winds, checked and channeled by geography – its movements are different everywhere. And not – the sea comes in; it goes out. It's the same with memory, the flow determined by intersections, coincidences and the submerged terrain of shame and denial. And like returning to familiar islands, recollections are always different, memory never revisits in precisely the same way. But like tides they go back and forward, back and forward – and back again.

Cooktown, February 10, 1993

The mouth of the Endeavour with Indian Head in the distance – that's the view north from the Seaview Motel. Trawlers and ageing sailboats are scattered off the mangroves edging the river as it arcs to the west, with the jetty, boat ramp and Bicentennial Park in the foreground. On a rise behind the main wharf the motel's predecessor, the Sea View Hotel, was one of the first buildings Jack Idriess saw as he arrived in 1912 on the *Musgrave*:

> So this was Cooktown, port to the "Land of Gold". Dubiously I gazed down from the steamer rail at the weather beaten little wharf, now crowded with cheerful citizens. A shirt-sleeved lot, cool and unworried looking, the womenfolk in whites, animated faces turned upward to friends calling from the steamer.[46]

And *animated faces* at the Sea View once he was ashore, Mrs Wilson's daughters forming a *row of lively young girls gazing down from the balcony at the lone swaggie now adopted by an outcast blackfellow's dog*.[47] Six pounds in his pockets and dreams of making it in mining up the peninsula. Boat day for the town with a small crowd gathered to meet the steamer – white, black, Chinese, Malay, Japanese – all part of the polyglot community brought together by commerce. Charlie Patching was there, a solicitor who Jack was told was the *Father of Cooktown*, and George Love, mayor and proprietor of the Great Northern Hotel. And in the background was a giant of a man with a coal-black beard, Captain Dan Monaghan. Idriess would get to know him well and two years later it would be Captain Dan who let him know – far from Cooktown – that there was a war on in Europe.

Cooktown was past its prime but boat day was still a draw. Horses and loaded drays in the background with dogs roaming between bags of tin and stacks of sandalwood, sniffing at sacks of smoked sea slugs and other produce from the Coral Sea ready for on-loading. Jack had only one way to go – along what's now Weber Esplanade that becomes Charlotte Street but in Jack's day was known as the Western Road. By the railway wharf he might have seen the B13 steam locomotive, *Cooktown No. 2*, near the end of its life and running on a line that had ceased to be profitable almost as soon as it was operating two decades earlier. As he crossed Adelaide Street that curled down along the edge of the mangroves to run west parallel to Charlotte Street, he would have had his first glimpse of the Cooktown Railway Station, its stately verandas and vaulted sheds testifying to the hubris of the town's founding fathers. Maybe it was then that he first *listened to the old-timers of the early* bêche-de-mer *days yarning under the "Tree of Knowledge"*.⁴⁸ Then past the picket-fenced police barracks and, on the other side of the road, the post office and the monument to Cook opposite the Court House Hotel, still bearing the scars of the 1907 cyclone. Just beyond was the Little Wonder Store – *everything a prospector needed in one place* – that was the claim and the owner, James Dick, knew just about everything there was to know about mining in the region.⁴⁹

Next door to the Little Wonder Store was the Boatsman's Arms Hotel and as he kept walking he would have passed the Sovereign Hotel, and the New Guinea and Worth's Hotels. And more. Two decades later, after most had been long abandoned, someone who knew more than a little about pubs – Errol Flynn – was still impressed by Cooktown.⁵⁰ Flynn's first book, *Beam ends*, is a rollicking tale of frolicking, fighting and fucking from the Sydney Heads to the Gulf of Papua. It's the story of the last voyage of the *Sirocco*, a forty-four foot cutter built in 1881 that he bought while drunk in Sydney in 1930 with money he'd made from gold-mining in New Guinea. Broke and looking for adventure he decided to use it to get back to New Guinea with three mates. But they didn't make it – the *Sirocco* sank in a cyclone-season storm two days out of Port Moresby with one of his mates, Dook, lost at sea.

Charlotte Street was wide enough for teams of twelve horses pulling drays loaded with steel pipe for the Annan River tin-fields, or bringing sandalwood from beyond the Daintree. Walking on, Jack would have passed the Bank of North Queensland and the Bank of New South Wales and might have noticed on the road leading up to Grassy Hill, now covered in trees but barren then as it was when Cook named it, St Mary's convent, looming over bungalows backing the commercial heart of the town. Along the high side of the road there were double-storied buildings, some with elegant columns and filigree wrought-iron lacework. From their shaded verandas there were views across Charlotte Street and the row of planted trees that were by then mature and tall, to the single-storied houses that continued down to the railway and the distant mangroves around Chinaman's Creek.[51]

Alerted by the aroma outside Spearritt's Federal Bakery he may have lingered before passing the monument to Mary Watson, after thirty years with the patina and permanence of a foundation stone. Just beyond, on the slope down to Adelaide Street and the railway, were the crowded buildings of Chinatown – homes, shops, the joss house, fan-tan rooms and opium dens – all just across the road from the West Coast Hotel and a few steps further on the Commercial. Charlotte Street continued west but Jack stopped at the West Coast – it was a bob for dinner and the same for a bed: *And thus I met Paddy and kindly Mrs Devaney, and their lively crowd of growing daughters. Their happy-go-lucky hospitality was to lure many of us back to the West Coast in between wanderings.*[52]

Eighty years later, the walk from the Seaview to the West Coast takes five minutes; the Commercial that was next door is now the Cooktown Hotel. Charlotte Street is still wide and slowly coming alive with four-wheel-drives and trucks, but not many pedestrians. It was different last night with pubs and bottle shops relieving slack-week blues as fast as money and grog could be exchanged. Bonhomie followed by bedlam, intentional and collateral casualties, black and white – but mainly black.

Just where Chinatown used to be there's a café and, prowling outside, doctor Mick. Amiably bear-like a few days ago, he's no teddy now. Pacing and preoccupied, he twists his head and seems to gnash at the collar of his khaki shirt – always a khaki shirt. You wouldn't know it from his gaze but I'm in his sights and there's something on his mind: *Those bastards… fucking bastards…* Tight-jawed and with his eyes averted, as I come to a halt the phrase loops before Mick elaborates: *You spend years getting to know a community, trying to get proper services. We ran it all from Cooktown. It's been running well. Now that bunch of arseholes in Cairns think they know everything about this place. The Regional Health Authority – lots of authority and not much health – bastards…*

I'm still trying to get my head around who all the players in the local service are, and ask if he's referring to anyone in particular. The answer is immediate: *Everyone in particular. We had a hospital board that worked OK, now it's run from Cairns and nurses think they've hit the jackpot. Not good enough to be a matron, you have to be a manager. Someone with no experience with the* Murris *rocks up and because they've read a few books about Marxism they think we're all part of some oppressive political system. It's all bullshit.*

Bullshit – Mick projects the word as if it's something so foul that it's been spat out and, instinctively, I look down, as if I might see it lying as a stain on the pavement. He's flushed and breathing fast, his system in overdrive. I haven't been around long enough to have opinions, but I can listen: *You're the first shrink to come near this place, let alone the communities. You've been down to Wujal, imagine how hard it is to get specialists to leave their offices and come out to the bush. Some do, not many – and those that come do it because they've got relationships with community.*

Getting Mick onto specifics is difficult: *What about Wujal…* I'm trying to move through the vitriol to the substance. For a moment he stops and his eyes meet mine as he takes a deep breath and continues in a different register, as if talking to someone who should not need to be told: *I've been trying to get some services for the oldies. There's fuck all for them there. So I finally get the geriatric assessment team to agree to fly up. Wouldn't stay but willing to come for the day if we put on a plane. Anyway, better than nothing. Now this new DON gets it into her head that there's a cultural problem, that there hasn't been consultation. She thinks it's all about institutional racism. She's been there six months and says I'm paternalistic – she's the fucking gatekeeper and thinks she's got the moral right to decide what's in their best interest.*

Their best interest – a real concern and a convenient foil. Mick and I both fall back on it, all doctors do and are protected by legislation. Although it's still about power, it usually involves someone with whom there's a relationship – it's not anonymous and we have to explain it face to face and wear the consequences. But when it comes to Aboriginal populations and communities the phrase has form, more often than not rationalizing decisions driven by ideological agendas and bureaucratic expedience. I get it, I'm part of that too. After I ask what he wants the geriatric team to do Mick sighs, whether marking exhaustion, resignation or both isn't clear: *Just assess them, the one's who aren't being looked after. Sooner or later some of them will need more care and probably a place here in town. So what we do now is wait till it all fucks up and put them on a waiting list then – the waiting lists are years long. Anyway, they've sent it to Cairns to decide. Fuck them. Want a lift...*

Cairns, February 27, 1993

- *Cornstalk Bookshop, Gabrielle speaking, can I help you...*
- *Gabrielle, I bought some books a couple of months ago. I'm calling from Cairns about one in particular. When I was in Cornstalk I was looking at some Ion Idriess books...*
- *Cairns in summer – the Wet – it must be uncomfortable up there now. Let me get Paul. He's the Idriess expert – hang on.*

The Wet in north Queensland. Tropical Cyclone Nina, first of the season, hit the coast as a Category 2 near Weipa on Christmas day, passed across the peninsula and continued on to the Solomons. No wind to speak of in Cairns but plenty of rain. Rain – day after day after day. On the Cape the roads are still out. The rivers flowing east are up; there's no getting across the Pascoe or Wenlock to Lockhart River. Maybe not even past Laura. And in the west the floodplains draining to the Gulf are saturated. From the air the course of the overflowing, sediment-heavy Mitchell will be impossible to make out, just lazy dark lines of trees and mangroves marking dry-season creeks – brown to the horizon. In three months the rivers will have reappeared with everything between a radiant green. Idriess knew what it was like *putting in the Wet* in Derby.[53] That was the Kimberley but he knew the Wet in tropical Queensland much better, in the mining communities around the Palmer River and along the Bloomfield. He knew Cooktown well too, the country and the characters – always characters in Cooktown.

The sound of footsteps and fumbling from half-a-continent away brings me back to Glebe Point Road and a familiar voice: *Paul here, can I help you. Gabrielle tells me you have a question about Ion Idriess…* I explain who I am, that I moved to north Queensland from Sydney a few years ago. That's enough for Paul: *You bought several Idriess books while you were here, I remember. You used to live in the Kimberley. We also got in another book for you, a republication of John Gribble's* Dark deeds in a sunny land. *I remember it had some sheets stapled inside the front cover with photos and a family tree. From somewhere up your way.*

Paul's memory is precise. *Blacks and Whites in North-West Australia*[54] is the rest of the title. John Brown Gribble, Ernest's father, did outrage well. Outrage over the treatment of Aborigines, outrage over murder, outrage over cover-ups and European complacency. He started by taking on the Western Australian pastoralists and, in the end, all the other established interests; he even complained to the Secretary of State for Colonies about the Governor. He took on too much and left the West a humiliated and broken man, heading back east to Queensland – to Yarrabah. I have the book, and stapled inside the cover there's a photocopy sheet with a family tree and a photograph taken in the 1890s. It shows three men, with John sitting between his two sons. He appears relaxed, his hands, brightly contrasted against the dark background of his frock-coat, loosely held over crossed legs. His face is at a slight angle and he stares confidently at the camera. Deep, dark eyes, the poor copy revealing his clerical collar as a white slash below his full beard. On his right Ernest also engages the camera's eye but he's less at ease, arms firmly crossed over his chest and legs seeming to grip the chair. Arthur's gaze is somewhere else, maybe to show his profile to full effect, his hands on his lap. All carefully posed for effect with, behind them, the stilted props of a studio screen – columns and ferns. Certainly not Yarrabah.

Paul also remembers that I'm *a psychologist or something*. Close enough, I shift the conversation from the Kimberley back to north Queensland: *You're right about all of the books. The Gribbles, father and son; controversy followed both of them from the West to Queensland. Idriess went the other way and I have* The Nor'-Westers *and* One wet season. *Recently I bought three that were set in Queensland, the Torres Strait and New Guinea. I thought one was a book I'd been looking at by the shelves. About opium smuggling near Cooktown...*

That must be The opium smugglers *– difficult to get, but I thought you did buy it, we had only one copy.* Paul is on the money again, I did buy that, the title confused me and I ask if there's another that involves opium smuggling. Without missing a beat he has it: *You might be thinking of* Madman's Island. *I believe we have a copy, do you want me to check...* That's it, *Madman's Island,* I remember the title and the map inside the front cover with an arrow pointing to somewhere near Cooktown. In a borderland between fiction and autobiography – like all Idriess. Plenty of madmen in north Queensland – crazy for money, crazy for grog, crazy with hate, crazy with love. And just crazy, white and black. But it's the white ones that are truly lost, drawn into the deep north to where the roads end in rainforest shadows, sharing crowded solitude with hippies, druggies, deros and swampies. After a while it's hard to tell the difference when they're dragged into town by the police or end up emaciated and on a drip in hospital. Paul's back: *I've found it; it had been misplaced. It was in the Stow stack. Happens sometimes. But, anyway, I have it and it's in good condition. I can hold onto it if you're coming down or post it up ...*

University of Sydney, November 25, 1993

Down Glebe Point Road and past Cornstalk, through the schoolyard – empty now, the market stalls and stands gone on this Thursday morning. Crossing Parramatta Road into the university reminds me of driving into Beverley Hills at the end of a road trip in the summer of 1984, coming in from San Diego, through downtown LA and up Wilshire Boulevard for the hell of it, the hills just a background smudge. Once over Santa Monica Boulevard it all suddenly changed – as if some magic or device had sucked out all particulate matter – the air was clear, the views fabulous, the street-noise muted and the grass greener. Beverley Hills – even the cops were nice. It's like that crossing the chaos of Parramatta Road as it disappears into grim, inner-west greyness. Sandstone and grass replace cement and bitumen, and there's a horizon with the skyline of the city in the distance rather than looming vertically. The University of Sydney; the traffic sounds far away, the morning breeze is fresh – you can walk rather than run.

Past the Great Hall, nineteenth century sandstone allusion to medieval gravitas – to a time before Phillip, before Cook, before the Dutch touched Cape York. That stone is from the country of the *Gadigal* and *Wangal*, Bennelong's people. Through the open door, soaring solemnity supported by timber from along the Clarence River and the Queensland border, *Bundjalung* country, grounded in marble from *Gandangara* lands beyond the Nepean.

Through the quadrangle, across Science Road, and there's the Holme Building – Federation meets Gothic with hints of the Mediterranean, probably appropriate for the student union. And for the first national Aboriginal mental health conference. Next door to collections of artifacts from ancient civilizations, and from a world much closer and more ancient. In a mongrel, architectural homage to European heritage – and on *Gadigal* land, *Eora* land.

Somewhere between six and eight hundred in the audience with only a sprinkling of white faces, mainly towards the front where Gough Whitlam sits with Margaret in the first row. Just behind them are Bev Raphael and Pat Swan, authors of the first national report on Aboriginal mental health and the reason that I'm here – the token white psychiatrist in the first plenary session. Where trouble lurks of my own making. A young psychiatrist, cloaked by circumstances and coincidences with the mantle of expert, masking insecurity with polemic and looking for the angle. The angle – the hook – the controversial point of departure. And the local newspaper gave it last year. A week after classic *Cairns Post* hysteria about violence at Aurukun, front page headlines for March 1, 1992: *NURSES IN FEAR – Health workers assaulted, flee Cape communities*. The article started: *Cape York health workers fear for their lives after a series of assaults they blame on an Aboriginal backlash after years of neglect.*

The hook – Aboriginal violence to white nurses. And I have first hand experience. In the year or so I've been working across Cape York, nurses have been assaulted in every community I visit. Perhaps predictably the institutional responses were higher fences, more locks, security staff, reduced after-hours services and protocols for self-defense. No argument that nurses need protection but it's not clear from whom – as they've repeatedly told me they feel blamed by the system, compounding their sense of victimization.

But in three years working across the Kimberley before moving east, visiting every remote community, there was no comparison with the violence in Cape York. And it doesn't seem to happen to anywhere near the same degree to other Europeans on the Cape, like teachers or council staff. So – the hook leads to questions: why whites, why women, why nurses, why far north Queensland, and why now…

Provocative, but a lead into familiar and safer territory – history. Specifically, of Queensland's policies of separation, concentration, ghettoization – euphemistically, protection. Missions expedited government purposes in remote Queensland and missionaries were grateful for the opportunities they were given – Moravians, Seventh Day Adventists, Anglicans, Presbyterians, Plymouth Brethren, Lutherans and more. It didn't last; the Department eventually took over and whether missionary or administrator they were all functionaries, part of a process of total control – the Gribbles, Thiele, Schwarz, Hey, McKenzie and all the others. Until the 1980s and transparently sham institutions of local government and community autonomy funded through the sale of grog, which was rationalized as rights by Joh Bjelke-Petersen and his erstwhile co-conspirator, Russ Hinze. And now with the administrators gone, or at least in the background, it's nurses who unwittingly symbolize that history of emasculating paternalism. Grog is the accelerant and the spark can come from anywhere. That's the message. Maybe too smart, maybe way too smart. Especially from a pony-tailed, white psychiatrist.

Gough separates from Margaret, slowly mounts the stage and settles in behind the lectern. He's among friends, some may have been there when he sprinkled sand and stardust into the hands of Vincent Lingiari. He recalls that moment and explores it slowly – painfully slowly – there are other tales to tell too. The schedule for the morning is out the window but who could ring the bell on Gough Whitlam – maybe in 1975, but not now. Eventually he's finished – a standing ovation as the legend returns to Margaret's side. Tightness in the throat, pulse quickening, doubt – too smart by a long way. There are land rights colours across the auditorium on hat-bands and T-shirts, and appetites for revolution not reflection. The next speaker is Gary Foley and he gives it to them, starting slowly in the wake of Gough. He represents the old guard who were at the barricades and on the bus, and he knows the audience, understands its moods and shares their memories. And he knows me – or thinks he does from one meeting in Redfern. I carry all sorts of baggage – white, professional, researcher – so-called expert. And my partner, Trish, who's sitting next to me and aware of the hole I've dug for myself, was at that meeting too – she and Gary had been together for years. They'd broken up well before we reconnected and moved to Queensland – but a bloke thing is a bloke thing. If anybody understands how bad things could get – it's her. Gary looks at me then back to his audience for affirmation as he shifts effortlessly through the rhetorical gears. He peaks with the refrain of psychiatric imperialism – *they used to call us bad now they call us mad*. I've heard it before.

More applause and Foley, like Gough, soaks it up, a spring in his step as he leaves the stage and moves to take up his position for what will follow – the humiliation, and I've probably made that inevitable. Heart now bounding and needing to breathe deeply – try to control it – and the tremor of my hands, holding a prepared speech about black on white violence that I can feel shaking against my leg. It doesn't matter that the purpose is exploring a history of oppression; I'm already anticipating the faltering voice, forgetting the thread, losing the plot – fucking up.

It gets worse. There's a break after Foley as the last speakers before my downfall approach the stage. Four figures move slowly to the podium, one standing to the microphone. I know the walk – hobbled, with shoulders

...but in Jack's day was known as the Western Road.
The tin scratchers, 1959

It shows three men, with John sitting between his two sons...

...boat day was still a draw...
The tin scratchers, 1959

bent and faces drained of expression, eyes downcast, hands shaking. The Largactil shuffle – the side effects of high doses of antipsychotic drugs. The woman who speaks for the group stands straight, her face is covered by an intricate *moko* – Cook would have recognized it. She introduces the group – *Maori psychiatric survivors* – each member able to testify to having been scarred by an oppressive system of post-colonial social control. And they do. For thirty minutes their stories come alive – dispossession, cultural disrespect, abuse, violence, coercive treatments, institutions, prejudice, shame and fear, finishing with a *Maori* chant that echoes through the auditorium. A few people stand and within seconds the entire audience – including me – has joined them, the applause continuing as the psychiatric survivors shuffle back to their seats leaving an ominously vacant space on the stage. And silence – time is collapsing on itself as a voice filters through: *Our next speaker is doctor Ernest Hunter. Ernest has done extensive research in the Kimberley including for the Royal Commission into Aboriginal Deaths in Custody. He is now working as the Regional Psychiatrist with the Peninsula and Torres Strait Regional Health Authority in Cairns, covering Cape York and the Torres Strait. Please welcome Ernest Hunter.*

Probably thirty seconds between my third row seat and the microphone. Walking across the front of the auditorium, past Margaret and Gough – he seems to be somewhere else, maybe still with Vincent, in that moment. Turning to face the rows of faces I see Trish next to an empty seat and from her expression I know she knows I'm in trouble. So does Foley at the end of the row but it's sweet for Gary, it's how it was scripted. At the podium I arrange my notes, look into the eyes of those few I recognize and turn to the woman with the *moko* and her three fellow survivors. It's all on automatic: *Before I start I'd like to thank our* Maori *friends who have come across the sea to share their stories. As they did, and talked of surviving abusive systems, my mind went to another place, another time, which was called but did not give asylum, and to someone huddled in a hospital gown, unwashed and uncared for. That person did not survive. That was my father.*

Like the moment you enter Beverley Hills or cross Parramatta Road into the university – suddenly the atmosphere changes – as it does in the Holme Building auditorium. Spoken with a faltering voice it's the first time that story has been told and it means something, changes something – for me. It took more than training, therapy and analysis to get to that point – I've had plenty of those – it was self-preservation, survival.

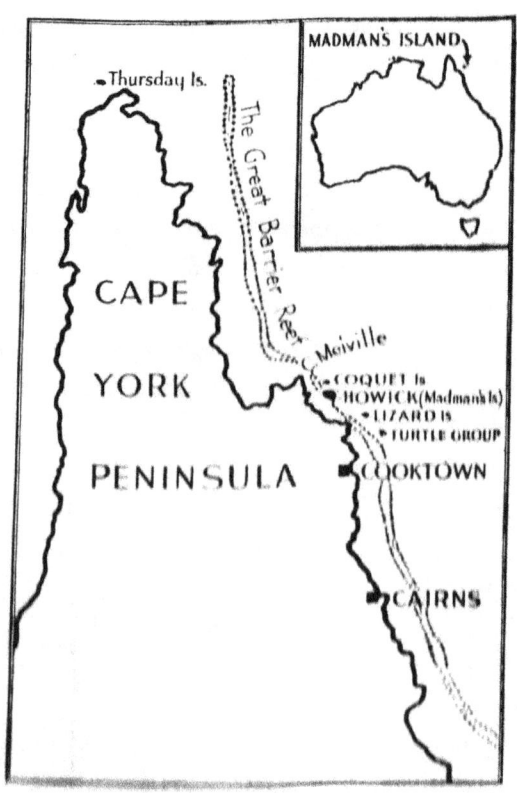

Madman's Island – the title and the map...
Madman's Island, 1938

CHAPTER 4

2003: Cooktown to Lizard Island

We're all alone at the end, as we step off the stage and into the night. Until that time there are companions; we're never entirely unaccompanied – even when we're on our own. Solo mariners know; when they're alone on the ocean, with senses starved, they're often visited – a voice, a presence, a fellow traveller – each understands it differently. And whether they realize it or not, familiar or frightening, it always connects – somehow – to what they've left behind. Imagination or hallucination – it's the past speaking.

A companion brings another set of eyes, a different sensibility – and their own baggage. The journey is changed, it's anchored in the present, in the shared experience. The personal past is muted as it's entwined with that of the other. Woven together as observations are shared and compared, as tales are told. On remote islands the amalgam is flame-fused as stories are drawn into the campfire before being carried up – into the night.

Two Isles, August 21, 2003

Two Isles are also low and wooded, and surrounded by a reef: the largest islet is in latitude 15 degrees 1 minute 20 seconds, and longitude 145 degrees 22 minutes 10 seconds.

Phillip Parker King (1827)

Heading north again by kayak but not alone this time, with Axel. Leaving Cooktown two days ago we were driven past Indian Head and Nob Point by following winds and waves. The layered dome of South Cape Bedford seemed to promise respite but delivered another hour of churned backwash from the cliffs and slippage along the fractured base of the dromedary ridge until we turned west around Cape Bedford into flat water and sudden stillness.

We spent last night behind mangroves on a rock-strewn sandspit then two hours pushing north-north-east with the wind on the beam before the first hint of a beach on Three Isles appeared. And another hour before the keel rested on sand on its leeward shore on which are a few coconut palms backed by scrub and bare earth. A helipad and navigation tower, the lock on its gated entry an invitation to climb around and up, past an eagles' nest to take in 360-degree sky with Two Isles directly east and Lizard's peak just above the horizon. To the west the coastline from Bedford and Flattery was obscured by heat haze and smoke from distant bushfires, with Low Wooded Island seeming to float in the middle-distance. Axel's gaze followed mine and he queried who was responsible for such an uninteresting name; that much I knew: *Cook, he passed just a few miles from us. Maybe there was an unstated agreement that if it didn't merit sycophancy then keep it simple. Or a quick whip around to see who on board hadn't had a turn. After a couple of years at sea even the lowliest midshipman, stranded in the Bermuda triangle of boredom, brutality and buggery might expect to get on the map – services rendered. There's a plane wreck on it from the War.*

Sixty years ago the Sydney Harbour Bridge was just a decade old as Captain Hayes Brown looked up at it from *Steak & Eggs*. Burnished metal, its fuselage flashed as it banked to Mascot. A Douglas A-20 Havoc of the 89th Bomb Squadron, in a past life it had been *Little Hellion*, flak damaged over Lae and left strip-side at 7-Mile out of Moresby after it bellied in on November 1, 1942. It was resurrected a few months later by Joe Long and Kip Hawkins with grafts and grease from another fallen war bird, *Yellow Fever*. Second life as *The Steak and Eggs Special*, weapons sacrificed for cargo, ferrying men and materiel from Australia to New Guinea. Then a third incarnation, with its war-paint stripped for speed and its name cut to the basics – *Steak & Eggs*. It was November 1943 that Hayes Brown took the dare and a boy warrior banished fear with adrenalin – under The Coathanger. Must have looked grand from the bridge.

June 11, 1944, in bad weather and low on fuel fifty miles north of Cooktown she bellied in again, this time on a beach half way between Capes Bedford and Flattery. Cook came this way and named them both, Flattery because he thought he'd beaten the reef.[55] He hadn't. And on Friday 10th August 1770 he saw and named a low wooded island to port, the same one Lt. Rude Vucelic brought his gasping plane down on. There was no fourth life for *Steak & Eggs*.[56]

The *Steak and Eggs Special* flew this coast regularly and there were other wartime American visitors. On May 17 1942, close to where we camped last night, trucks of the United States Army arrived to take *Guuugu Yimithirr* with English and German given names into exile. And also Georg Heinrich Schwarz, known to them by his breast plate beard as *Walaar,* or as *Muni*[57] because of its youthful blackness when he arrived at Cape Bedford Mission from Höchst as a twenty year old Lutheran missionary in 1887. *Muni* still but silver-backed over five decades later, he was marched off to Cooktown jail amid mutterings of German sympathies and Japanese luggers at Elim.

Battered and bewildered, the *Guuugu Yimithirr*, whose ancestors stood with Cook in the founding act of Aboriginal-European reconciliation[58] at *Gun-gaar* as the *Endeavour* was careened in June 1770, finally came to rest in open internment a thousand miles distant in Woorabinda Mission. *Muni* joined them around the time *Steak & Eggs* beached on Low Wooded Island. In 1949 they returned north but not to Cape Bedford, and *Muni's* journey ended in a Cooktown flat on Charlotte street – just up the road from the West Coast Hotel.

Leaving Three Isles and its tower-top vista there's another three hours in the kayaks with the afternoon wind beam-on then shifting to the east. Paddling into it with the beachline on the northern, leeward shore of Two Isles fixed in the distance – no closer, no closer – then suddenly there. Falling out of the cockpit with spray deck, life vest, hat, gloves – all the vestments of paddling still in place – and floating, suddenly weightless in cool, clear water. Coastal Sheoaks fringe the high tide mark with leaves like the plumage of the cassowary, *kasuari,* for which it was named, *Casuarina equisetifolia* – thriving on almost every island as its namesake struggles in ghettos of contracting, mainland, rainforest. Welcoming with shade and sound – a soft drone in dying breeze, hints of melody diminuendo with day's end stillness.

Axel has already selected his own tent site and is portaging camping gear from his kayak – always one step ahead. Soon his tent will be up and he'll be gone, off on an undisclosed mission to reappear unexpectedly, minutes or hours later, from shadows. As on our previous trip – Townsville to Cairns, that time with Jon – Axel's phantom presence is expected but disconcerting. The elements seem to fit – beard and braided ponytail, beads, rings and bracelets, multiple ear piercings, rose-tinted, wire-rimmed glasses, discrete tattoos of runic symbols, a just discernible accent, and his ability to materialize out of nowhere. Enigmatic, but in a premeditated way, like his stories – unfinished but suggestive, some critical ingredients strategically withheld.

Exploring on my own, following a beach smoothed by the retreating tide. The eastern border of the reef is now a dry coral causeway to another island, a mangrove cay – sand sharks, rays and turtles darting as I approach, and gaping, iridescent giant clams in isolated, crystal-clear pools. The veneer of windward mangroves gives way to dry coral with a chaotic mound of sticks and a few old feathers from long-departed eagles, then a carpet of succulent Waxflower, *Hoya australis,* with delicate branching flowers like *Chamaelaucium uncinatum* – the Geraldton wax of my childhood a continent away. Beyond that and into the tall leeward mangrove forest, its canopy dense with fruit bats, *Pteropus electo*, and through the stilled air a shrill cacophony as the colony prepares to depart for the mainland.

As I wade back across reef that's slipping beneath the advancing tide there's a sudden sense of incongruous familiarity – flashes of the Glebe markets – walking past stalls filled with throw-away stuff with only the occasional item inviting a second glance. It's like that along the western shore of the island with scattered and heaped debris hinting at something of interest. I'm in the browsing zone when Axel emerges from a thicket of island rainforest. He points to a barnacle-encrusted metal case, recently dug from sand and rocks just above the high tide mark. A military ammunition box with a stencil still legible across the top – *DUMN*. Surprisingly, the lid opens easily to reveal spent ammunition: *Probably 20mm. Left behind after an exercise.*

Axel is probably right about the caliber but I don't understand why there would be military training here when there's a huge exercise area at Shoalwater Bay and Axel's elaboration doesn't help: *They train everywhere – to be prepared, to be unnoticed.*

They – always a hint of conspiracy. Maybe understandable for someone who keeps his cash buried in the bush, who hides things and who has things to conceal. Not quite paranoia – not quite. Charisma and paranoia, both from the Greek and often fellow travellers. And maybe one from the other; to stand out risks unwanted attention and there are rumors. Not only of eccentricity but, as always, of money. Rumors that Axel allows to persist, that add to the mantle of mystery. Even tales of packages found washed up on beaches near here, consignments received or intercepted, or stumbled on by coincidence – by fate. Attention and mystery, a delicate balance, stories are passed on and draw more attention. Shaman, showman or shyster – an open verdict.

Axel selects three spent shells from the ammunition box and stops to pick up a section of bamboo, then pieces of vibrant blue twine that he disentangles from a knot woven through the roots of a casuarina struggling at water's edge. Iridescent, the strands glow with the colour of the electric starfish we floated over crossing the reef. Like the fleeting change that catches the paddler unaware crossing from cobalt depths to sand-bottomed azure, the blue of jetsam plastics persists and becomes more intense while other colours fade. Somehow it resists the vibrancy-sapping energies of sun, salt and wind that leave mounds of photo-degrading, milky polycarbonates – bottles, floats, canisters, jerry cans, thongs, insulation, rope, nets, more bottles, more thongs, on and on.

Walking past our own footprints he seems to be searching, looking for specific items and stoops to select feathers, maybe from an eagle, and coral, some pieces burgundy others the signal-red of my genoa sail, and next to one piece the mottled leg-armour of a lobster. That's taken too and back in camp Axel is totally focused in an artisanal moment until it comes together; the base of the bamboo jammed into a spent shell-case, feathers fixed into the tip with three inches of tight blue coils below ending in blow-away, frayed tips tied through the coral and carapace, all dancing with wind and movement, the colour of the twine catching the blue of his eyes: *There, that's all, it's a Mace.*

Lizard Island, August 26, 2003

Lizard Island, about three miles long, is remarkable for its peaked summit. The latitude of which is 14 degrees 40 minutes 20 seconds, and longitude 145 degrees 23minutes.

Phillip Parker King (1827)

Climbing to Cook's Look from the camp on Watson's Bay in the afternoon the kapok, *Cochlospermum gillivraei*, is in flower and, higher up, there are Golden orchids, *Durabaculum undulatum*, with a heather-like ground cover at the summit. The peak of Lizard Island; Cook would have looked back and retraced the *Endeavour's* course between Three Isles and Low Wooded Island, past Cape Flattery and then to Lookout Point. Hoping that he'd found the way west. But he hadn't, and after sending a yawl to check out the Turtle Group further north, he went in the pinnace to the highest island in sight. He was looking for open sea but wasn't giving up on the passage:

It was with great regret I was obliged to quit this coast unexplored to its Northern extremity which I think we were not far off, for I firmly believe that it doth not join to New Guinea, however this I hope yet to clear up being resolved to get in with land again as soon as I can do it with safety and the reasons I have before assigned will I presume be thought sufficient for my having left it at this time.[59]

He climbed this hill twice. The first time visibility wasn't good, but not so bad that he didn't realize from the breakers to the east that the outer reef was close. Joseph Banks was with him when they sighted what looked like several channels to the open sea:

Through one of these we determined to go which seemd most easy: to ascertain however the Practicability of it We resolved to stay upon the Island all night and at day break in the morn to send the boat to sound one of them, which was accordingly done. We slept under the shade of a Bush that grew on the Beach very comfortably.[60]

After the pinnace returned with encouraging news they headed back to Lookout Point but stopped off on: *a low island where we shot many birds; on it was an Eagles nest the young ones of which we killd, and another built on the ground by I know not what kind of bird, of a most enormous magnitude.*[61] Eagle Island - the *Endeavour* kept it to windward as it headed for the passage and open sea. From Cooks Look, Eagle Island is in clear sight with Nymph beyond in the distance. Our course to Lizard was more southerly – Three Isles, Two Isles, Rocky Island, keeping South Direction and North Direction to windward, and into Blue Lagoon between Lizard Head and South Island. Blue Lagoon – the water was so clear that it was like gliding over coral worlds with turtles undisturbed as the kayak followed the breeze curling around the Head.

Now on the summit, Cooks Look, Axel is here but not. Behind me a minute ago and gone again. But the aura is broken. He's been worried since we set out from Cooktown, building to a crescendo after he got to a public phone in the Yachties' Bar on Lizard. Now he's got one purpose – to get back to Cairns, to his money, to his lawyer – to try and avoid jail. Tales now of the cops bugging his telephone, following him, setting him up. He says it's *all bullshit* and they don't have anything on him, just some gunja they found in his car, and they didn't have a proper warrant, his lawyer can deal with it, there are other things to do, people to see, people to avoid – he's got to get back to Cairns.

But two days ago the veneer was still intact as Axel disappeared towards the horizon between Two Isles and Rocky Islet, about half way to Lizard with the Direction Islands to the south. It was a good kayaking day, my sail was up, the genoa bulging to port with a fifteen knot south-easterly. Paddling for a while, drifting, sailing, paddling again – lost in rhythm and thoughts of the day before. Thoughts of a whale and her calf that appeared in the late afternoon off Two Isles and their songs after dark, a vibration somewhere between Tuvan throat singing and the low registers of Marvin Gaye, Axel called it the *god sound*. Shining a torch out into the sea-misted darkness there was nothing, just light-eating night.

The sounds of ocean kayaking are constant and rhythmical – wind and water, and paddles. Alone at sea any other noises are startling – the cry of an unseen frigate bird, a flying fish, an unexpected wave breaking over the aft-deck… Between Two Isles and Rocky it was a loud, sphincteric exhalation to windward, and as I twisted in the cockpit to look over my right shoulder I glimpsed a smooth, dark, cetacean curve disappearing about fifty metres away. It was a moment of startled wonder as I fumbled to drop the genoa, the kayak silently drifting forward. And then there it was, less than twenty metres ahead – so close that the blowhole was visible, with a hint of its dorsal fin as it disappeared. Gone but fixed in memory, held fast as much by the apprehension of unseen mass below, a momentary expectation of turbulence – but there was nothing, just calm water and bubbles as I passed over. Seconds later a whale surfaced fifty metres to the left, maybe it was the same one, or a mother and calf, or a pod, but like us – heading north.

...*past an eagles' nest to take in 360-degree sky...*

... *it's a Mace.*

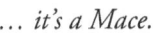

The black lugger had gone.

... *probably the same rakish black lugger that cruises around Howick...*
The opium smugglers, 1948

Approaching Rocky Islet an hour later Axel reappeared from behind exposed rocks beyond which dozens of coral heads darkly puckered the surface as swells rolled by, the reef continuing north-east toward South Direction Island. Threading through the shallows a beach appeared to the south-west backed by dense groves of succulent plants and tortuously tangled trees bursting from and growing around fissured rocks that seemed intentionally set one on another. It had the appearance of an ancient ruin, the walls of a long abandoned fortress breached by a landslide exposing rubble and bare earth. The ground was friable and loose, and clambering over it difficult, the powder soil giving way unpredictably. With every few steps the surface collapsed and we sometimes fell to mid-calf, as if the islet had a thin mantle, a crust, enough for us to call it the *Island of Hollow Earth*. Hollowed by burrows – everywhere – but with no hint of burrowing animals. No clues.

At least not until later. Sitting at the northernmost point looking towards the sunset a few birds appeared in the sky, returning from the mainland. Within twenty minutes there were thousands swirling in tight formations around boulders and trees. Streamlined and agile in the air, they waddled gormlessly on the ground, oblivious of us and our tents. The wedge-tailed Shearwater, *Puffinus pacificus*, dark chocolate brown above and below, tail long and flared – beautiful in the air, less so on the ground. They nest in tunnels and crevices and we'd arrived as they were preparing for the breeding season. And then the noise began – a droning, mournful dirge, hollow, like the earth – across the island and right outside the tent. All night.

Then to Lizard and after being made unwelcome at the Lizard Island Resort yesterday, now at Cooks Look. There's a brass compass rose at the summit with distances to major cities around the world – and fifty-seven kilometres to Howick Island. And an information plaque with a wooden box at its base inside which is a book recording visitors' mundane memorials. From here you can see most of the island. A valley below and a ridge in the mid-ground, beyond that the airstrip and resort. Dense melaleuca clusters at the base of the hill with a grove of pandanus around a freshwater soak in the valley. Parallel to the shore there's a line of mangroves marking a creek that connects at high tide at the eastern end of the bay. Beyond that a ridge of dunes and scrub, then a crystal crescent of beach between two headlands. And from there to the horizon, a palate of blues that darken into the distance, with around twenty vessels close by – a few catamarans up to the sand and, further out, mono-hulls riding at anchor.

For a moment Axel's back, writing in the visitors book, but when I turn away for a moment I'm alone, just a glint of blue out of the corner of my eye and he's gone – again. In the shadow-land of the late-afternoon's light-play, observation gives way to imagination, night's approach draining the island's colours and shifting contours. At the far end of the beach it's just possible to make out the remains of the house that Robert Watson brought his young bride to soon after their marriage in Cooktown in May 1880. She was a twenty-year-old Protestant girl from Cornwall and he an Irish Catholic in his forties, both recent arrivals in the colony. A stop on the tourist trail now, just the foundation square of the main building, but back then there were outhouses for preparing *bêche-de-mer* for shipment, and fenced gardens. Mary left the island only once, for the delivery of her baby, Ferrier, in Cooktown in June 1881, a year to the day after she'd stepped ashore on Lizard. Before she left Cooktown Ferrier was christened by Father Hacket in a Catholic ceremony and the divisions of the day were in place – Mary didn't attend.

Just a couple of months later Robert and his business partner left, and within two weeks she and the two Chinese servants, Ah Leung and Ah Sam, realized there were *negroes* on nearby islands. In her diary she recorded that on 29 September: *Ah Leung killed by the blacks over at the "farm". Ah Sam found his hat which was the only proof.*[62] From there things rapidly got worse and the next day Ah Sam was speared. A desperate situation for a twenty-one year old new mother; it was another two days before they dragged the *bêche-de-mer* curing tank, just over a metre square, down to the waterline and loaded supplies, including a small camphor chest which contained a pencil and the paper on which she recorded the last eight days of the tragedy. A vessel of desperation; unsteerable and with a large section missing from one side which would have given them only inches of freeboard – drifting precariously into history.

The Heroine of Lizard Island – no similar status for Ah Sam or Ah Leung, but maybe that wasn't just about race but also because Mary was a mother who fought to live for her baby and suffered his death. Ferrier – iron in the name and doomed to die in a metal tank. Mary – the eternal mother, crazed by thirst and mad with despair. And Mary wasn't the only mother crazed by loss on Lizard; Mrs Schultz went mad here fifty years later. When the *Sirocco* approached in 1930 Errol Flynn and his crew saw three men on the beach, two of whom ran into the bush as they approached. The third, Schultz, was almost incomprehensible. Eventually he explained that they'd gone to Lizard to make money from trochus shell and *bêche-de-mer*. There had been a fourth member of the original syndicate who'd taken their cutter to go to the mainland three months earlier to get supplies – and to arrange for the pregnant Mrs Schultz, who like Mary had gone with her husband to Lizard, to have her baby in Cooktown. Tragically, as it turned out, all of their fishing gear was on the cutter – which didn't return. Over the following months they nearly starved, and after the child was born the weakened mother couldn't produce milk. Although she struggled desperately to keep the baby alive it died two weeks later. The men restrained her with ropes as she struck out wildly trying to kill herself. Mad with grief – she was still bound when Flynn was taken to see her, a sight he said he never wanted to see again.[63] A flash of blue and a daydream interrupted. Axel is back, standing by the box. It looks like an infant's coffin.

Jack Idriess would have daydreamed too when he sat up here looking towards Howick. He was on Lizard for a month with his best mate Dick Welsh and he knew all about Mary Watson – as he said about the monument in Cooktown: *seldom did anyone pass without glancing at it.*[64] The *opium smugglers*, true story or fiction… Jack said it was true and Dick Welsh really was his best mate and had also been to the War – he was at the Somme while Jack was in Palestine. Dick was a north Queenslander by birth, born in Cooktown. That's why he was wise to what was happening

– he knew all the locals and he'd heard the stories. And while early on in the tale Cross-Eyed Joe, the captain of the *Nancy Bell*, had Jack and Dick believing they had gone to Lizard for trochus, he was actually scheming with two of the crew, Alor San and Ah Matt, to intercept a consignment of opium. It was dropped off by one of the China steamers to be picked up by the crew of a Japanese lugger – maybe the same *rakish black lugger* that cruises around Howick in *Madman's Island*. And in *The opium smugglers* Cross-Eyed Joe takes the *Nancy Bell* off to Howick with the black lugger following as part of the plot. In the end it all comes unstuck but Jack and Dick end up with a decent load of trochus and lots of stories.

Washed up drugs – it happens, even if Axel is keen to prove it doesn't any more. But it certainly did back then. Errol Flynn knew about it. While he and his mates were heading north on the *Sirocco* he stopped in Townsville and noticed a black-hulled pearling lugger with low, raking lines, down from the Straits with a Japanese captain and mixed Asian and Islander crew, and he was treated to a lesson in seamanship as it made sail.[65] Just a few weeks later he was in Cairns and in a fight at a *Fan-Tan frolic* or, more accurately, an all-in brawl between cane cutters and Chinese in a gambling den. The next day he was approached by a local Chinese businessman, Gabriel Aloysius Achun, who wanted Flynn to take him out in the *Sirocco* to pick up a delivery of opium being dropped from the steamer, the *Taiping*, the same steamer that Dick Welsh told Jack Idriess had been off Lizard Island to deliver a similar package. Short of money Flynn agreed, and the next night they waited off Green Island, hoisting a signal when the *Taiping* passed. They followed, and when the consignment was eventually sighted Flynn watched Achun secure the floating object and hoist aboard a metal box. It was sealed and marked as an Admiralty tide testing device to deter the curious – but not Gabriel Aloysius Achun.

When Jack was with Dick on Lizard they didn't get to see the opium, but Jack described the object he and Charlie found washed up on Howick:
A watertight kerosene tin it appeared to be at first sight. But it was actually larger, supporting a clever "topmast" of wire built just like those steel trellis-masts on some American battleships. This mast rose two feet above

the tin and right at the top was the neat little flash lamp... Above the mast projected a tiny wooden flagpole.[66]

True stories... Well, that's what Jack and Errol claimed. Jack was on Lizard and Howick in the early 1920s and the unsuccessful first version of *Madman's Island* was 1927, with the version he swore was fact not coming out until 1938, the same year that Errol Flynn published *Beam Ends*. Flynn's voyage in the *Sirocco* had been in 1930 and soon after he made his move to acting and, eventually, Hollywood. Maybe he'd read Idriess but, whether or not, in Flynn's account the *Taiping* approached from the north and they found the opium floating just past Fitzroy Island. Two years before the crew of the *Sirocco* and Gabriel Aloysius Achun were desperately scouring the horizon, the *Cairns Post* of Monday 20 February, 1928 reported:

Opium Found
A VALUABLE PARCEL
Yarrabah Boys' Honesty
WORTH A REWARD
A big opium discovery was made on Friday near Deception Point in the vicinity of Fitzroy Islands by Yarrabah Mission Boys.
A parcel was seen floating about in the sea and when opened it was found to contain 98 tins of opium which is valued at approximately £1500
The Mission boys brought the parcel to the Mission Station and it was subsequently conveyed to Cairns.
SPECULATION
The last steamer from the East was the Arafura which arrived here during the early part of last week and after a short stay left for the South.
It is surmised that the opium was thrown overboard from this vessel but possibly the persons for whom it was intended had failed to get it.[67]

Yarrabah – the drugs were found around the time Ernest Gribble was hounded back east after his time at the Forrest River Mission – later he'd be taken to Yarrabah to die. The Superintendent of the mission, Mr McCulloch, who took the opium to the police, would have known all about Ernest Gribble. Errol was anything but a missionary; he was in it for the money though he ended up being hoodwinked by Gabriel Aloysius Achun who disappeared from the tale.

Roll on eighty years and the same stories are going around, but this time of mysterious containers washed up north of Elim and somewhere south of Cape Flattery. And Axel is in the thick of it. Fact or fiction, Axel won't confirm or deny, but now he's more likely to opt for denial – a lot of it. Suddenly he's back with me on the summit and keen to get going: *I need to make a few calls.*

Lizard Island, August 28, 2003
Lizard Island ... on its south side is an extensive reef encompassing three islets, of which two are high and rocky: the best anchorage is on its western side under the summit.

Phillip Parker King (1827)

Axel is gone. Each time he returned from the public phone at the Yachties' Bar you could see the tension mounting, the cool dissipating – the real world reaching out and grabbing him. Within a day he had a ticket on the plane out and appointments with his lawyers in town. And business to settle, maybe a house to sell. When lawyers are involved you need ready cash and where it comes from the lawyers probably won't ask. Even Jack Idriess was silent on those matters. The opium that Cross-Eyed-Joe purloined at Howick was reclaimed by the Japanese on the black lugger back on Lizard. But the opium that Jack and Charlie found on Howick in *Madman's Island* is a different matter. There's no mention of what happened to it, at least not in the second version – the one he said was a true story. But in his first book, published a decade earlier, the version tizzed-up with a romance to sell as fiction and which flopped, the main character, but still Jack, took the opium with him and sold it. By the time Idriess re-wrote *Madman's Island* as fact he was no longer Jack, he was Ion Llewellyn Idriess again, a successful writer with a reputation to protect. Whether it was eliminating an unnecessary plot device or a tactful omission, only Idriess knew.

And only Axel knows the back-story to the charges he's facing and when he flew out he left his kayak, which is still tethered to mine on the beach in front of the National Parks campground. The only other campers are two young women, continental tourists who flew in soon after we paddled through the clutch of vessels in Watson's Bay two days ago. Some of the yachties wander by and Karl has come ashore each night to schmooze with the women, whose tents are next to mine. He's in electronics and from Salzburg via three decades in New Zealand. He looks younger than his fifty years and attributes it to vegetarianism, on which he's been expounding in polite but redundant detail with the women. Karl told me how difficult it is to retain female crew and I know why.

Riding at anchor in a fleet of production cruisers, his yacht is three decades old, a replica of the *Joshua* that Bernard Moitessier sailed in the first, solo around-the-world yacht race in 1968.[68] Named for Joshua Slocum who sailed out of Cooktown and to the west of Lizard in July 1897, heading north and to a meeting with the Jardines. Slocum had been in Cooktown three decades earlier on a steamship, the *Soushay* from Batavia, but was on the sick list and couldn't go ashore. Maybe that's why he chose his subject when he was asked by the citizens of Cooktown to give a lecture at the Presbyterian church about his solo journey: a story of the sea, and how the crew of the *Spray* fared when illness got aboard her.[69]

But as of this morning there are two of us again, Axel has been replaced by Jon – or Chris. Chris is his name in the world of work and family, but in the journey it's always Jon. It regularly causes confusion to the uninitiated – he's Jon, I'm Jon, it's a Bruce thing. The only other person I know with multiple names is Axel – but for other reasons. In Axel's case it's not a Bruce thing and now he's gone, leaving his kayak and provisions for another two weeks. A few phone calls and Jon was on his way to replace him for the rest of the journey north. He was flown in by Geoffrey Wordsworth, the pilot of the only seaplane that's ever been rooted by a crocodile. Or that was the story in Cooktown and it spread – it was reported on the ABC. The seaplane was moored next to a trawler three years ago at Princess Charlotte Bay. That night the crew and pilot:

> *were caused to awaken by the noise of crashing and splashing going on around the area of the seaplane. They turned the lights on and much to their horror they spotted a very large salt water crocodile trying to mount the flotation pontoon on the left-hand side of the aircraft.*[70]

Amorous tales – maybe appropriate that the next stop is Nymph Island.

...just the foundation square of the main building...

CHAPTER 5

1994: gamma

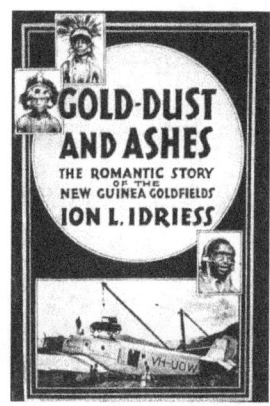

Intersecting journeys – sharing the same path for a while. But only ever for a while. Forever only happens in myth – blessed or cursed to be free of the passage of time, locked into the eternal present. And maybe in imagination and dreams too, and in stories – holding time fast in an unchanging now. Ion Idriess was obsessed with the past – outback history and the War. He was driven by a pioneer vision of the future – diverting rivers, clearing the bush, building mines, ports and railways, populating the outback – unleashing the potential and unlocking the treasures of the north. But his visions of the future were wrapped in a frontier past, the world of a young nation, its characters hardened in the furnace of the War and waiting for their fortunes to change, for: *luck to unearth a little nest of those earthy-yellow, though often rusty-black, little eggs*[71] – gold. Or tin, or wolfram – or sandalwood or pearl-shell.

That was the world Idriess re-created and which remains with us in print. And he's in it, but not as Ion: *I called myself Jack when I took to the*

Bush.[72] He'd had enough of being taunted as *Little Lord Fauntleroy* and it's as Jack that he's bound in a past-present with his best mate, Dick Welsh, at the West Coast Hotel and on Lizard Island. And with Charlie, here, on Howick, with the light on Coquet flashing in the distance. And though their stories are different and their paths diverged, Dick and Charlie are together forever in Cooktown cemetery. Maybe László is close by. In his dreams he was, they were all together, there and here. Forever.

Cooktown, August 16, 1994

Doctor Mick is standing on a pathway winding between unfamiliar plants that have seen better days. An elderly Aboriginal woman slowly passes by following a zimmer frame towards a rear entry to the hospital, stopping every few, hesitant, steps to look around. Outside the ambulance entry two ward nurses are sitting silently, smoking. Mick is in the shimmering shade of a sapling, directing a hose toward a bed of struggling shrubs: *We made this garden with some of the oldies who still remember bush medicines and bush tucker. Got a prize for it. Not just something to do, it was about pride – helping to pass on knowledge. It was a hit for a while, the long stayers still like to come out and water sometimes. But I suppose it's ended up being my responsibility – can't get any of the nurses interested.*

Aiming the hose towards the base of the tree Mick inspects the foliage – new growth against a cloudless sky: *This is sandpaper fig* – Ficus opposita. *It was used for skin infections – just rub it on the skin until it starts to get raw. A few years ago I was on Resto with John Pritchard. There was a yachtie who'd stopped over and John had him believing you could use it to sand down a gasket. He'd run out of sandpaper but there were plenty of these trees on the island. We just kept up the encouragement and a supply of leaves, telling him he was making a real go of it. Told him the* Murris *sometimes used it for gaskets.* Turning his head, Mick seems to gnash his teeth on his collar to suppress a snicker, revelling in the memory of being back on Restoration Island, enjoying a home-brew with John as the visitor struggled to sand a copper gasket with a leaf. Just another day on Resto: *By the way, there's an old fellow in the ward from Hopevale. I wouldn't bother you 'cos he's in here for R&R. Just slack, not his old self. I don't think he's depressed but I thought since you were in the hospital you could check him out.*

Another hour on the end of the day, another story to be heard. Mick smiles without looking up after I ask for a name: *You'll like this, your namesake – Ernie. Not many about up this way but we had another a few years ago, a whitefellow who decided he was going to walk to The Tip. He took seeds with him that he was going to plant along the way – Johnny Appleseed type. Mad bastard. Picked up by a trawler somewhere near Port Stewart. Said he knew there'd be a boat around the next headland and there it was. A lot thinner when he got back to Cooktown but otherwise just the same. Lots of mad bastards about here but mostly harmless. It's the ones that aren't mad that are the problem.*

Mick is right, Ernie doesn't need treatment. Other things, perhaps, but not treatment. And he has lots of stories; growing up at Cape Bedford Mission, *Muni*, the rounding up during the War and the journey south. *An old man with clouded eyes* – that's how he appeared when he spoke to Paul Theroux, who seemed to have liked Ernie Bowen. Maybe as a foil to lampoon redneck white Australians. Cooktown gave him plenty of scope and was his first stop on a trip that became the *Happy isles of Oceania*.[73] Kayaking was the device for the book but despite loading up with heavy weaponry for rogue crocodiles and feral pigs he didn't get far from Cooktown, which gave more scope for caustic commentary on outback social divides and boorish behaviour as he sat chatting with locals at the Sovereign Hotel.[74] The Sovereign – the Cooktown equivalent of five-star. Theroux sure as hell wasn't going to stay at the West Coast.

Cooktown, August 17, 1994

Another day and new names on the clinic list. There are four patients seated in what serves as a waiting room, an alcove hidden from the main entry and reception desk, and screened off from the business end of the hospital by a Coke machine. Just a few steps to the cross-roads – right to the ward, left to outpatients and ahead to the operating theatre, the kitchen and staff dining room, and just out the back, the morgue. Choose wisely, there's always danger at the crossroads. But although the name I've called out is unfamiliar the face of the man who stands and walks towards me is not.

The suspicious glances and furtive avoidance are gone, and he's scrubbed up compared to when we last met. It's the same man – but it's not Gordon. That was the name I was given when I first met him in Bamaga two years ago. I'd only been to Bamaga once, a journey of exploration up the peninsula stopping at clinics along the way. My first taste of Aboriginal communities on Cape York – chaos in paradise. Then across the Jardine River by ferry and onto Injinoo land – all the way to the Tip. That is, except for four excisions that with Injinoo itself make up the five communities of the Northern Peninsula Area that's now home to several thousand souls. Injinoo, or Cowal Creek as it used to be known and Small River before that, concentrated survivors of disease and brutality at the hands of the likes of Frank Jardine and his native troopers from Somerset. They're gone but you still have to cross the Jardine to get there.

At Red Island Point along the coast from Injinoo there's an Islander community. In 1947, after king tides inundated the gardens and fouled the fresh water supply on Saibai Island just a few kilometres from mainland New Guinea, families left on the luggers *Millard* and *Macoy* and set up camp near the site of a wartime radar station at Muttee Heads. Within a few years they moved to join other Saibai families at Red Island Point where fresh water was more reliable, the community renamed acronymically in the 1970s after the Sunai, Elu, Ibua, Sagaukaz, Isua and Aken founding families – Seisia.

Islanders also went on to develop the township of Bamaga six kilometres inland, the administrative centre for all five communities. Between Injinoo and Bamaga, Umagico was set up in the 1960s with families from Lockhart River after the Anglicans decamped. Somewhere in the Department a decision had been made to relocate the whole Lockhart community to a projected supercamp at Bamaga to expedite bureaucratic management – a remote Indigenous version of the panopticon. Most of the Lockhart *Murris* refused but were moved anyway from old site to the other side of Cape Direction, where access was easier for the swelling ranks of Department functionaries, who had very different agendas to their missionary predecessors – Lockhart River Aboriginal Community.[75]

Tjungundji people from the Batavia River Mission had no choice. The Presbyterian Board of Missions and the Queensland government decided that the thirty or so families at Mapoon, north of Weipa, would be relocated nearly two-hundred kilometres further north to Hidden Valley between Bamaga and Red Island Point. Their protests were ignored and maybe the deafness of those making the decisions in their interest was influenced by rich bauxite deposits. Whether or not, in 1963 the MV *Gelam* brought police and Islander workers from Thursday Island to demolish their homes and to take the remaining traditional owners away. Although some drifted south to Weipa most ended up at Hidden Valley. Eventually the perverse irony of the name was recognized and Hidden Valley was diplomatically re-christened – New Mapoon. Five communities within fifteen minutes of each other – the administrators loved it, a model of efficiency.

By the 1990s a semblance of local governance and economy was in place – struggling but way ahead of the ghettoized Aboriginal communities further south. The canteen is an outlet for grog and a financial windfall for the local council and there's a struggling motel – the Golden Orchid. The council offices, a few shops and a bakery are scattered along the main street and further back there's some light industry and support services. The high school, police station and hospital are in Bamaga with small shed-like aid-posts in each of the discrete communities. Injinoo manages the lands of traditional owners and the resort at The Tip – Pajinka. Seisia has basic tourist facilities and the ferry to Thursday Island – *Waiben*. The discovery of the golden lip oyster, *Pinctada maxima*, off Warrior reef a hundred years ago was the nail in the coffin for Somerset, concentrating administrators and bureaucrats on TI ever since. But although Bamaga across the Endeavour Strait was the junior partner, the 1990s brought lots of activity with changing governments each promising new investments and opportunities. Including a hospital that's going up not far from the primary care centre by the police station. And there's a new cadre of Islander health workers, all sensing that something of substance is happening to their communities and for their futures. Maybe.

One of them approached me on the first day of my second visit. Philomena had just been appointed as the mental health liaison worker, a position that might have been created to keep an eye on me. There had never been a psychiatric service and the only experience of that system was the reasonably rare evacuation of someone who was acutely psychotic – and that was usually left to the police. Luckily the station is next door and Trevor, the senior officer, understands the process; a minimum of fuss and questions. Straight to Cairns and the Base Hospital. A psychiatrist on the ground was a different matter – it wasn't clear to the nurses and health workers who could benefit from seeing a mental health specialist. But after I'd been politely told there were no *mental problems*, within a week there was an avalanche of referrals. Not just mad and sad blackfellows, but occasionally very mad whitefellows. Drawn by isolation and anonymity, or by the idea of power and redemption from somewhere over the horizon, like Cooktown, Bamaga is a place where they regularly wash up.

Gordon had come by land, and to the locals who are generally remarkably unphased by weird Europeans, he managed to raise eyebrows. Philomena was still trying to determine who, exactly, should see the *mental doctor*, and it wasn't clear to her if this man and the old woman he was travelling with were in the frame: *Some women at church bin give dempla kaikai. They don't cause trouble. Quiet mainly. But mipla no sabe dempla – we don' know them – some people worry for them.*

— *Them – who's them Philomena…*
— *Waitman at servo. He got old woman with him in that car, they been there nearly a week now. He bin tell Jason that he fixing up that car. But they got no kaikai – nothing to eat. And old woman don't talk much, just laugh sometime.*
— *Where are they going…*

— *No sabe, they don't talk straight. Hard figuring out what they doing or saying. But they don't do nobody harm. Just sidaun with their car and the dogs.*
— *Dogs…*
— *Wa, plenty dogs.*

My next stop was the police station and I arrived as Trevor was preparing his lunch in the kitchen. He was already on to it and keen to get me in on it too, summarising the intelligence he'd collected as the microwave hummed in the background: *Gordon Smith, thirty-year-old male from New South Wales, in a mid-70s Falcon station wagon. All the way up the telegraph track in a two-wheel drive. Seems to be mechanically savvy and would need to be. At the back of the servo for nearly a week, living out of the car.*

Trevor's summary was only momentarily interrupted as he extracted what looked like last night's leftovers steaming with new life. A place cleared at the cluttered kitchen table and he was back on task: *The old lady seems happy but not quite with it. Doris is her name and Gordon always refers to her as his wife though she's probably twice his age. He seems reserved, maybe even suspicious. They haven't caused problems but don't seem to have much money and locals are getting wound up. They'd like them gone and for us to do it. No records in Queensland and the New South Wales registration checks out. And then there are the five dogs. We figured this one was for you.*

Half-an-hour later I was at the servo and made the mistake of parking too close to the Falcon. As soon as I opened the door I was conscious of my breathing, of trying not to recoil from the stench – stagnant and miasmal in the humid air. There were fast-food wrappers scattered around, and bones that had been passed from dog to dog – some on the ground, others in the car. The back of the vehicle was open and inside were swags and milk crates filled with pots and pans, the surfaces of plastic dishes on the tray encrusted with ants and flies. An exhausted looking bitch lay on the back seat with two puppies playing outside, another pair of mature dogs lying, panting, in the shade of a nearby tree that also provided some shelter for a concrete picnic table next to a board with a map of the Northern Peninsula Area – Bamaga's version of the tourist information centre. At least there was a toilet at the back of the servo.

There were car parts scattered across the table and at one end the elderly woman I presumed was Doris sat in a camp chair that was just holding together. She was slouched forward with her back and shoulders forming a single curved surface, her head bowed so that her hair fell in tangled strands, an incongruous and functionless pink hairclip in a lock hanging at the side of her face. She was so low that the seat of the concrete table was her bench-top on which an old pannikin half-filled with tea queued flies along the rim. Doris seemed to be rocking slightly and was undistracted from wherever she was by my approach. A much younger man was seated a few feet away, clean-shaven but with a look that nothing else got quite the same treatment. He'd been manipulating one of the car parts strewn across the table but was totally still from the moment I stepped out of the Toyota. Only his eyes moved – following me.

Even before I spoke I knew that Gordon had been through this before and that their passage had regularly attracted unsolicited attention from functionaries and agencies – like Trevor. Starting a conversation in situations like that isn't easy and that day in 1992 with Gordon in Bamaga was no exception – it didn't start well and didn't get better. What I did manage to glean was that he and Doris were married. She was seventy-six. They liked to travel but he wouldn't say why they were in Bamaga, or where they started from – or where they were going. His 78 CX Falcon had a buggered-up radiator and Mario at the workshop in town was going to get a replacement from a wrecked Falcon at the dump. They had enough food, locals were helpful and Doris was on a pension. He wouldn't say anything about himself, demanded to know who I was and why I was talking to him, and became agitated as I tried to direct questions to Doris, whose vacant smile was framed by her matted hair. *Hello, hello, I'm all right, everything is all right* – the only words she uttered, like a mantra, without looking up.

I guessed that somewhere along the line Gordon's path had crossed mental health services and that he'd learned that the best course was movement and silence – don't stay too long, don't say too much. For a clinician without a back-story to go on it was a classic bind; they probably needed help of some kind but would almost certainly reject any health – let alone mental health – involvement. Of course it might have been possible to take some action through guardianship legislation without their consent, but that would have stretched legal provisions and would have been messy – getting the police involved, detaining one or both in Bamaga and transporting them to TI or directly to Cairns. Very messy, and there was no suggestion that Doris was being coerced. And while she didn't look like she was in good shape she didn't appear to be in distress. So I reported back to Trevor that it was not a good situation but also not a crisis. He seemed to have had his expectations of psychiatrists confirmed when I didn't come up with an immediate action plan. I clarified: *My inclination is to temporize. I head over to TI tomorrow, I'll be there three days and back on the morning ferry on Friday. They seem to get on with the local older women and I might ask the health workers, maybe Jenny or Philomena, to drop by and keep an eye on them in a low-key way.*

I didn't get to temporize long. The next afternoon as I was being dropped off at the Red Island Point jetty for the TI ferry a small crowd was gathered around the Falcon, parked near a large *Ficus*. Gordon had managed to get it going but it hadn't gotten far. He was pacing about outside the vehicle with the passenger-side door open and Doris lying awkwardly across the front seats. She was fitting, and the small crowd parted as I approached: *Are you doctor… she's sick doc… she take fit or something like that… she need help doc…* They were right. The ambulance came down the dirt road from Bamaga within a few minutes, preceded by Trevor and an Islander aide in the police Land Cruiser. For the ten minutes it took to review her, get an airway in and an oxygen mask on, an IV line in place, transfer her to a stretcher, and into the ambulance and away, Gordon maintained an agitated stream of comments, that were either irrelevant or denied the obvious: *The radiator's fixed… we can drive on… we'll be fine… she just needs some water… we've got to look after the dogs... it's just the sun... she's OK... she just needs to be left alone... we don't need any help, don't do anything to her...*

But they did – the chopper took her from Bamaga hospital over to TI and she was there soon after I arrived by ferry. Gordon had to stay in Bamaga and that gave me an opportunity for some sleuthing and dot-connecting. Eventually he made his way to TI but she'd already been flown to Cairns. Gordon returned to Bamaga and then he and the Falcon disappeared. A few weeks later I found out that Doris had had a massive stroke – she never left the Base hospital. And when they finally traced her records it turned out she wasn't Doris, she was Elizabeth – Elizabeth Grace, from Tenterfield.

But Gordon didn't disappear entirely and in 1993 the police brought him into the clinic in Lockhart River. He'd been living in the Falcon in a rainforest clearing near Wongai Point at the end of Chilli Beach north of Lockhart – two-hundred kilometres by unsealed road south of Bamaga. Even against the variegated backdrop of deros, swampies, hippies and the occasional junkies squatting along Chilli Beach, Gordon didn't fit in and the final demise of the Falcon stripped him of a critical means of dealing with an intrusive world – moving on. He was stuck, and raving by the time the police got out to Chilli Beach. He'd probably been on something but nobody would say anything about drugs – to anyone but especially the cops. Anyway, he was quickly evacuated from Lockhart to the mental health unit in Cairns and now, two years later, he's here in Cooktown. Same man, but different name. It's not Smith, it's Halassy. And he's not Gordon – he's László.

Cooktown, August 18, 1994

— *Needle-dependent psychopaths.*
— *Sorry...*
— *Needle-dependent psychopaths. All the rapists, the psychos, psycho-the-rapists, the functionaries of the system, needle-dependent psychopaths with constrained degrees of freedom...*

...Wongai Point at the end of Chilli Beach.

*Read a bit of Idriess and you know why —
he was all over this country.*
The tin scratchers, 1959

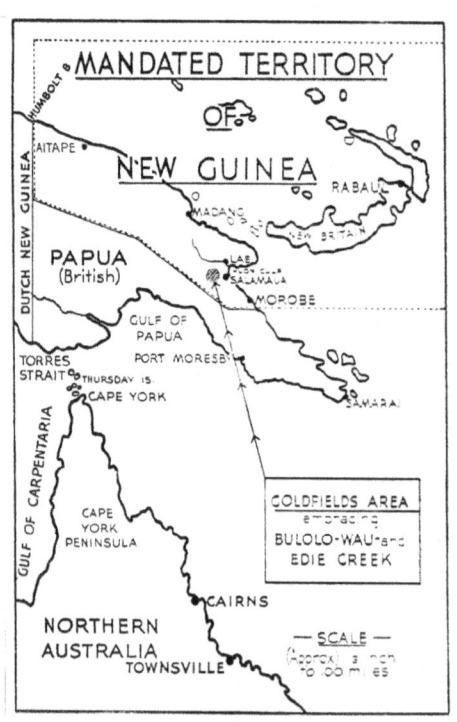

*... a long way from where gold
was found on the Wau...*
Gold-dust and ashes, 1947

Gordon or László – like yesterday, he's sitting in the waiting area. It's early morning and there are five people seated, the others probably there for fasting blood tests, but there's nobody sitting next to László, who stares ahead as he talks at me: *Needle-dependent psychopaths – hello doctor – are you part of the conspiracy doctor, are you dependent on needles, do you need needles doctor, are you driven by needling, a needling psychopath or needling psychopaths doctor, which is it… Shall I follow you doctor…*

— *That sounds like a great idea, let's see if we can find somewhere quiet…*

We can't – as usual the procedural medicos have all the consult rooms booked, even the dental suite. Just about everything has priority over mental health. The only option is the operating theatre. László seems entirely unphased and minutes later we're sitting on rotating stools next to the operating table, under a discoid theatre light jointed through arachnoid steel to the wall behind. Unphased but not unnoticing: *Do you have something you'd like to tell me doctor. You can trust me, we can trust everyone – trust everyone except the needle-dependent psychopaths…*

He's nailed it, it could be a 1960s B-grade thriller with G-men extracting a confession under arc-lights. And whatever we talk about we'll come back to needles – about coercive treatments and depot medications – about power. *You can trust me.* He's got it – it's asymmetrical, what better place to make the point, next to an operating table. Don't look, don't see the straps, the probes, the machinery of ECT and lobotomy – *we can trust everyone* – of course. But first things first – names: *You can call me László or call me Larry doctor, and I'll call you doctor, doctor. Doctor doctor, a very skilled needle-dependent psychopath doctor…*

— *László then, I like the ring of it.*

— *The ring of it doctor, if it rings your bell doctor…*

It goes on – and on. Psychotic rambling, but telling truths all the same. The theatre chair is on rollers and with his toes he drifts it across the floor, tracing the curve where the line of light might fall, forcing me to rotate to face him. He has me on the defensive, I'm the one under the arc-lights. And as much as I try to pin him down I'm swept along in his stream. Although the thought disorder is obvious and his discharge diagnosis is probably correct, it took a full hour in our first meeting and another today to grasp enough information from the torrent that a story coalesces and a person starts to emerge, a person that is not new to Cooktown. I learned that from Mick.

Yesterday, before I realized the Bamaga connection, Mick had told me what he knew about Larry, that's the name he knows him by. He helped me make sense of the hospital discharge summary I found in his file, a series of clinical statements with the ghost in the machine redacted. When Larry woke up in Cairns Base Hospital after being air-evacuated from Lockhart he looked, sounded and smelt crazy – all boxes ticked, schizophrenia. I can't argue with that but it's a clinical stick figure, the essence of a life magically disappeared.[76]

Mick is no magician but he described a person, not just a patient, and a story that goes back to when Mick arrived in Cooktown in 1988. Larry had been in town for a year or so, living in the Peninsula Caravan Park. He'd walk to Finch Bay every day and then in to town – quiet type. Maybe a bit of gunja but no trouble, he spent more time at the library than at the pub and that had to be a positive. Mick had him do some work for cash on the fruit trees he and Jan had planted on their block on the way out of town; Larry was diligent but not a conversationalist. With time he began to trust Mick and Jan, and over a year told them that his parents had both died, his mother, Doris, just a few years earlier. He didn't talk much about his father but they were all from Europe and he'd been raised in Sydney. The story reminded Mick of Michael Fomenko but Larry was no Tarzan. And lots of people in Cooktown avoided talking about their past lives – again, no surprise. As usual I had to keep bringing Mick back to the clinical matters: *Well, he was never what you'd call social, but nothing obviously mad. Not until a woman was involved. A local* Murri *woman, a girl. He was besotted and totally misread the signs, no fucking idea, it was all foreign territory. I doubt that there was any sex, but he was way out of his depth.*

— *Out of his depth…*
— *Yeah, she was underage and probably using him to jealous a local* Murri *guy she was with. It worked. Then the shit hit the fan. She*

told the boyfriend Larry had put the word on her. Not likely, but he told her grandmother who fronted Larry – that was probably the worst thing for him, that old lady going for him in public. So then the police were in on it – they knew it was a beat up but it was too much for Larry. Between the cops and her family leaning on him he totally lost it. I'd never seen him psychotic but he was then, terrified that the Murris *were using* purri purri*. Once the cops were on the game he was convinced he was being followed and monitored by secret police. Kept talking about the Ah-voe and started using foreign words. Turned out to be Hungarian and I eventually figured out he was talking about the* ÁVO *– Államvédelmi Osztály – the State Security Department just after the war. I looked it up. Nasty bastards.*

ÁVO – Államvédelmi Osztály – plenty of paranoid projections involve security organisations but the Hungarian secret police was new to me. Mick glanced to the door as a nurse placed a new chart in the box outside; that made three patients waiting to be seen. On the desk and scattered about the floor lay dozens of files, some closed and others open, with a precarious pile reaching almost to the window-sill in the corner. A virtual community constituted by the processes of recording and review, a unique constellation, some transiting with short-order entries, others held back in an eddy of tests and consultations, and a few that will never return, waiting for sign off to be laid to rest in the *deceased* stacks. Files, I bet the *ÁVO* had lots of them, maybe one on László's father. I pushed Mick about what happened when Larry lost the plot in Cooktown: *A week in Cooktown hospital and some haloperidol. He settled and told me that he had an aunt in Silkwood – Bea, I called her up. Not a lot of detail, she met him for the first time when he turned up on her doorstep. Unhappy childhood, turned out Doris was his stepmother. His parents were refugees, his father was from Hungary. I guessed that was where the ÁVO came from. Not much on his mother. And then around 1990 he disappeared. I checked at the caravan park and they said that he'd told them he was going home. He'd never talked about that, it seemed like an alien category. But leaving looked to me to be a wise move. He was fucked if he stayed here.*

Disappeared – a geographic solution. He moved on as he did two years later, from Bamaga to Chilli Beach. But probably with the same baggage: *The next I heard was a call from a registrar in the psych unit a couple of months ago. Larry put me down as next of kin. They didn't know I'd had him in hospital here. All they knew was that he was from New South Wales and lost it up near Lockhart. They thought his name was Gordon. Took me a while to figure out what was going on. Now he's back. Glowing in the dark with antipsychotics. And back at the Caravan Park. Like he never left. There and the library.*

With Mick's backstory in mind I'm trying to get a fix on László as he continues to roll the stool across the operating room floor, always facing me. He looks like he's been on antipsychotics for years, not just months – the flattened facial features and distant stare. There's a fine tremor in his hands and occasional movements of his legs – less obvious as he moves about: *You can take the fifth doctor, always take the fifth. Amend it or bend it and say nothing, anyone can do it. But not here in Australia doctor, we don't have a Bill of Rights doctor, just bills of wrongs doctor. But you can take the fifth doctor, choose to say nothing, don't incriminate yourself…*

— *Larry, sorry László, we talked earlier about the trip you made to Bamaga a few years ago, when I first met you, you used the name Gordon then and you were with an old woman, Doris. You said she was your wife. How long had you been together…*

— *A wifetime doctor, a wifetime of woes and a lifetime of lows, it's all the same, we were commoners, married in common, lawed in common. Love conquers all. We knew what we had to do, where we had to go.*

— *Where you had to go…*

— *To New Guinea doctor, we had to go to the highlands. That's where the money is doctor, you rob banks for the money, that's where it is, in the banks, in banks of rivers doctor, in the highlands.*

— *Money in the highlands, what money…*

— *Gold, doctor, gold. Shark-eye Park knows it all. But sorry, doctor, I have to take the fifth. And the fourth, and the third, and the second. I have to take the first too doctor. Or two first…*

And, as he predicted, we come to the needle in the end. Despite protestations he quietly follows me out of the operating suite and towards a nurse who will do the deed. *Quite an interrogation room doctor, who do you work for…* Again, on the money, The State. Five minutes later I'm called back to the reception desk, Larry wants to see me before he leaves – some advice: *Don't forget doctor, you can always take the fifth. Even needle-dependent psychopaths can take the fifth.*

Cairns, August 21, 1994

The coast road from Cooktown to Cairns through the Daintree passes the Lion's Den then through Rossville and Ayton, past the turnoffs to Home Rule, China Camp and Shipton's Flat, and over the Bloomfield with Roaring Meg in the distance. In the last few years I've driven it maybe half-a-dozen times, through a landscape in which each new name seemed familiar. Read a bit of Idriess and you know why – he was all over this country. Then, as I was waiting at the Daintree ferry, I thought about László. Maybe because the only other ferry on the Cape is across the Jardine near Bamaga. Two years ago, after our first meeting, I was waiting at the Jardine crossing to drive south to Cairns and was still thinking about the elderly woman who'd been living in a car with five dogs. Then I remembered the young man who seemed more driven by mission than destination – heading north. Just as that memory formed, László's words from our meeting in Cooktown filtered into consciousness: *Gold, doctor, gold. Shark-eye Park knows it all.* Idriess was on my mind all the way to Cairns.

Gold-dust and ashes – the book sits in a set of what has grown to six Idriess early editions in the office of our beachside home looking north to the Coral Sea. It was from Cornstalk, probably one of the first I bought. And there, on the first page:

Gold! Yellow gold – heavy gold! He stared at it with burning eyes, this man on the mountain tops. His are unusual eyes that, when startled, instantly cloud over in a wary waiting. Throughout New Guinea he is known as "Shark-eye Park," or "Shark-eye Bill." Rarely as William Park. He is a jungle-man, master too of the forest and the wild men who dwell in both.[77]

The rush started in New Guinea in 1926. Idriess was there soon after but mainly around the Fly River, a long way from where gold was found on the Wau, though that's what *Gold-dust and ashes* is about. Someone who was where the action was at that time was Errol Flynn – he wrote that he walked out to Salamua, what had been the German settlement of Samoahafen and is now Salamaua, probably down the Black Cat Track from the Wau in 1929 or 1930. He worked his way back to Sydney on a tramp ship and after he landed he headed to Ushers, a pub where the New Guinea hands gathered and where the barmaids knew all the gossip. The latest was that Lady Turray, the governor's wife, had publicly taken on Shark-eye Bill Park for keeping native wives, to which Shark-eye shot back that there was no doubt about his choice if all options were on the table – or on the couch.[78]

Shark-eye Park – my gut tells me it's not Errol Flynn but Ion Idriess that László read. Although they were both interested in gold, Idriess wrote books about how to mine the stuff – *Cyaniding for gold: A complete, simple and detailed account of the process written especially for the working miner and small syndicate*. And Idriess was a popular writer, not many people have heard of Errol Flynn the author. But whichever, it's there in László's psychosis. And if I'm right it was Idriess directing László – even when the craziness wasn't declared – across the Torres to Papua, to where Shark-eye Park was just after the Australians took over from the Germans nearly a century ago. And László was taking Doris with him – mother, step-mother, wife.

László – son of a Hungarian refugee whose paranoia about the *ÁVO*, the secret police, was probably well-founded. Drifting or driven – even before I met him in Bamaga he'd been heading north like lots of others, and had landed in Cooktown with a new name and old problems. Then a crisis, probably inevitable and brought on by the twisted cords of attachment. Maybe at that point he wasn't psychotic, just tensed to breaking point by an impossible relationship. Perhaps psychosis was a solution. Whichever, it came to a head with a public humiliation by a *Murri* matriarch, murmurings of black magic, and then the police – all knowing, all seeing. Allegations; if not in practice, then in possibility and in desire, he was guilty. No wonder he lost it, no wonder he fled. To Tenterfield. To Elizabeth, who became Doris – mother, step-mother, wife. All I know about Tenterfield is from Peter Allen and that's about death – *Time is a tale-teller, Tenterfield saddler* – wonderful song, grim message. And then together with wife or mother, on the road to New Guinea, to a meeting with Shark-eye Park somewhere in the jungle.

...where the gold was found on the Wau... Gold dust and ashes, 1947

CHAPTER 6

2003: Lizard Island to Cape Weymouth

Mates and fellow travellers – not necessarily the same but when they are it's special. As it was for Jack Idriess and Dick Welsh, special enough for a book – *My mate Dick*.[79] They had a lot in common; young men drawn to wild places and then the War, they returned to north Queensland with youth sucked dry. Both were wounded and probably never healed, alcohol their common balm. Jack was five years older but lived another four decades after Dick died in 1933, a broken man at thirty-nine years of age. By that time Jack had left the bush and was a successful writer – once again, Ion Idriess.

His stories of Dick continued for another three decades. Tales of fossicking on the frontier of a rapidly changing world that was long gone by the time it was published, *My mate Dick* was one of his last books. Past friendship is like that, anchored in the best of times, lit favorably in the hall of remembering that forgives what remains hidden in shadows. It is what it is, but it's not what it was. Fortunately, I suppose, elsewise that corridor would be all darkness.

But then there are people who seem not to need those connections to light their path through the world. Idriess wrote of some he called *jungle men,* who held nature close to their heart and for whom solitude illuminated a relationship to the world that was always in the moment, always in the present – not the past. He would have recognized Michael Fomenko – Tarzan – as a jungle man. But not László; he would have struggled with László and he wouldn't have understood this person who was born when Idriess was entering old age, around the time he wrote *My mate Dick,* and who claimed to be a fellow traveller. Friendship is usually reciprocal – but not always, and not for László.

Friendships – *lit favorably in the hall of remembering.* Staring directly towards Coquet, I try to condense an image from the afterglow of each flash of the navigation light. Moments and friendships freeze-framed for a second then fading. People and places – islands. And one of them, just over the south-east horizon now disappeared by night, is Eagle Island.

Eagle Island, August 29, 2003

Eagle Island is low and wooded, and situated at the north end of a considerable shoal; its latitude is 14 degrees 42 minutes 20 seconds, and longitude 145 degrees 18 minutes 30 seconds.

Phillip Parker King (1827)

Twenty-five knot winds on the beam from the east. Yesterday, on Jon's first day, we were heading from Lizard to Nymph but we only made it to Eagle Island. Lizard is still in sight across a large reef exposed by the falling tide. The rest of Eagle is flat with a sandy, coral-rock centre, some dense low scrub and a tidal causeway along the southern and eastern shores. Not much protection from the wind, as uncompromising as Chris – Jon: *You're a cunt Jon.*
— *How's that Jon…*
— *You might enjoy this but it's not my idea of a pleasant paddle.*
— *It's a headspace thing Jon.*
— *Fuck the headspace. And fuck the wind.*

Fuck the wind – howl at the wind, be lost and buried in the wind. Wind and whitecaps. In high winds and swells a kayak thirty metres away is out of sight, only the flash of wet blades appearing and disappearing behind moving mounds of water. Salt and spray; don't look back, look ahead and not at the water chasing you down. That was the problem yesterday, Jon looked back, always a trap for beginners. And the swells that distracted him made getting back in after he capsized difficult, and emptying his cockpit even harder. One swell breaking over the deck with the cockpit cover off can re-swamp a kayak – sometimes pumping is futile. Other than a foot-pump or electric bilge pump, which we don't have, the solution, if all that's available is a hand pump, is to have a sealable hole in the cockpit cover which allows the kayaker to pump with the cover in place. That still means letting the paddle go so that you can have both hands on the pump, and in a kayak that's full of water in big seas that's a major balancing act, even for an experienced paddler. And for someone out there alone it may be impossible.

Axel's cockpit cover doesn't have a port for the pump and Jon doesn't have experience in rough conditions. As we were pushed towards the reef surrounding Eagle Island, even after rafting up for stability and some directional control, it took thirty minutes to half-empty his cockpit. Three hours after leaving Lizard we drifted into the lee of the kilometre-long reef off Eagle, a line of white agitation separating wild and tame water. Waves gave way to chop then to calm and the beach, and the reassuring scrape of keel on sand. There was no way we were going to push on to Nymph, which left time for exploring.

Following the shore, at the eastern end of the island a piece of industrial steel impaled into the reef at the high tide mark with a coconut pithed at the top stood sentinel as an anonymous challenge to the wind. We continued around the windward shore then into the centre where about half-a-dozen gale-stunted trees rise above the tangled scrub. Jon was standing across a small clearing watching me. Or watching the tree next to me, and then I realized that immediately above me, blasted by the wind and taking up the entire exposed surface of the tree was an eagles' nest. No surprise

on Eagle Island, and visitors other than Cook and Banks, who named it, have commented on the raptors. HMS *Rattlesnake* under captain Owen Stanley passed by after landing the Kennedy Expedition at Rockingham Bay in April 1848. On board were scientists, including Thomas Huxley and John MacGillivray, and during the two weeks spent around Lizard Island, they visited Eagle and speculated about what Cook had sighted there: *a huge nest 26 feet in circumference and nearly 3 feet high, made of sticks. An American professor thought this must be the nest of some North Australian moa. Gould and McGillvray thought it was the nest of the big fishing eagle.*[80] No moas here, but eagles for sure, gulls hovering over the nest, bouncing in the wind – swooping down, landing, a few lunging pecks and gone. Two eagles up high, then near, and two humans circling at ground level. Shouting at the gulls – shouting at nature. Shouting into the wind – shouting at each other: *Jon, you're still a cunt.*
— *How so now Jon…*
— *You promised clear sky, dolphins, turtles and mermaids. You didn't say anything about survival in extreme conditions.*
— *Karma Jon. Don't fight it.*

And now, the morning, we're huddled in a bracken cave around a struggling camp-stove as the sun rises. In the only wind-challenging spot on the island – a minor flaw in the otherwise laminar flow across this desolate aerofoil. A tempest outside, a small gale within. There was no way we were going to start an open fire this morning after nearly incinerating the camp last night. Cold, hungry and frustrated, after half-an-hour blowing on rounds of beach tinder that produced smoke but refused to take, we took the easy option – Shellite. Within seconds a flicker became a swirling knot of fire lashing tails of embers through the nearby bracken and on into the night: *The whole fucking island could have gone up Jon. That would have been hard to explain.*

Particularly as the fire started under the National Parks sign – *No fishing, No camping, No fires, No firearms, No cats or dogs. By Order. To protect the island.* But for now we spin out the morning rituals before going back into the water and wind. It's a standard script; I supply the fillers and connectors to a string of anecdotes from Jon's past, each a vehicle for a joke – some new, most recycled. This morning it starts with a passing bird: *I was the bird-man at the Novotel a few years ago. All I knew was what a bush turkey nest looked like. The rest was bullshit. I read a few books to get some names. When someone would ask what a particular bird was I'd say it was a red-breasted booby or something like that. Then some smart bastard would say that's not a booby and give a lecture about speckled drongos or something.*

— *Spangled drongos; but how did you deal with it…*
— *I turned the bird walk into a masters' class. Told them that they had all the knowledge, flattered them, and said that my role was simply to harness their expertise, to help them tap their collective knowledge. So I'd point to a bird and ask who knew what it was. There was always some smart-ass dying to show off, then someone else would get into the act and I'd just sit back until I could say that, sadly, this terribly interesting discussion would have to end because we'd run out of time.*
— *What if nobody knew…*
— *I'd tell them it was a red-breasted booby.*

Good one Jon, even if I've heard it before. I don't have Jon's gift of puns and persiflage, but I have the advantage when it comes to sea-kayaking, and some answers for Jon: *Tides, I know it's related to the moon and currents, but why nothing here and huge tides somewhere else. And navigation, even if you can see something, how do you know how far away it is if you haven't got the gear…*

— *Geometry Jon, you can use a kamal. Arabic – you take a body ratio that relates to an angle that can be projected into the distance. Like holding four fingers at arm's length, which is about one tenth of the distance from eye to hand. If you know how far objects in the distance are from each other then you can figure out how far you are from them. So if we look at our map we can see that Lizard is about three k wide, if I hold my arm out I need about two hand-widths to cover it. So, our distance from Lizard can be figured out by multiplying the kamal ratio – that is, ten over however many hand-widths, in this*

case two – by the distance we know from the map, which is around three k – that comes to thirty over two or fifteen k.
— *The map says we are around seven or eight.*
— *Margin of error. When in doubt carry a GPS.*
— *Do we have one...*
— *No.*

Noble Island, August 31, 2003

Noble Island is a rock, having a sandy, or a coral beach at its north-west end; although small it is very conspicuous; and, when first seen from the southward, has the appearance of a rock with a double rounded top.
Phillip Parker King (1827)

Three years ago I approached Noble from the south. Now it's from the east – from Howick, although we didn't make it to where Jack stepped ashore. That was the destination yesterday but it didn't happen. With strong following winds we passed sand beaches on the most southerly of the Howicks – Coquet Island – and were blown directly on towards Howick itself, to what on the map seemed to be a break in the reef with an inlet between three low hills on the south-east. On the map perhaps, but not in reality. Off from a stretch of clear ground there was an exposed reef extending fifty to one-hundred metres from the shore and breaking waves along the drop – we weren't going to get ashore in kayaks. But that's where Jack landed at a high tide over eighty years ago.

Teardrop-shaped, Howick is about three kilometres long with the areas of high ground on a rim at its windward base. Along its leeward shore mangroves extended as far as we could see to the north. It was too difficult to head back into the wind to Coquet, to what seemed an ideal landing, so the only alternative in sight was a small beach two kilometres south-west on the north of Houghton Island. Beam on to the wind, half-an-hour later the shoreline resolved into rocks and exposed reef with not a lot to recommend the high ground behind. But from Houghton we could see the full leeward coast of Howick, two small islands at the extremities of a reef separated by a colonizing mangrove forest in limbo between sea and soil. All we could make out of the northernmost islet was that it wasn't mangroves, but that's where we headed, from Houghton back to Howick with the sun low on the horizon, dragging the kayaks by their bowlines to the only feasible landing through a narrow trench in the reef which was already disappearing with the outgoing tide. Once on – no off.

On the same island but separated by two or three kilometres of mangrove forest from the campsite Jack Idriess and Charlie set up. While there was no way for us to land there, Mary Watson and Ah Sam made it in an iron tank – maybe the tide was just right as it drifted in. They knew they had to find water but didn't know about the well between the hills that the *Murris* knew: *Ah Sam went ashore to try and get water, as ours was done. There were natives camped there so we were afraid to go far away.*[81] That's what Mary recorded before they set out on the last stage in their journey – to Howick No. 5, Watson Island. Jack and Charlie had heard about the well at the West Coast before they left Cooktown and located it soon after they landed. Even so they nearly died of thirst when it was fouled by king tides. If that wasn't enough, Jack had to deal with being stranded on the island with a madman who had the only rifle. *Madman's Island* – I was near but not there.

So we had a night at the wrong end of Howick. And not alone, at least that's what we discovered next morning after tracking a scatter of sapphire blue plastic through the campsite to the destroyed mouthpiece of Jon's Camelback water pack. *Rattus rattus*, probably attracted by fragments of deck snacks transferred with saliva. Rats and ghosts; just back from the landing is a grave, the perimeter marked by grey rock-coral that's been decorated over time with shells and bottles, a weathered post at one end the remains of a marker. Maybe a crew-member on a lugger, or a victim of Cyclone Mahina. It faces north, to Watson Island. At the inquiry held on the *Spitfire* Captain Bremner of the *Kate Kearney* described the discovery of the remains of Ah Sam there in January 1882: *covered with a quilt up to the ribs. The skull rested on a small Chinese pillow. Between the skull and pillow was some human hair attached to which was tape forming a Chinese tail or queue.*[82] A little after that the tank was found among the mangroves on the south-west side of the island and the ship's mate, William Scott, informed the inquiry:

I saw in the tank what I took to be the body of a woman, nearly covered by fresh water, in the last stage of decomposition and clad. I perforated with an axe the bottom of the tank, also the sides by a snider bullet to allow the water to escape and then recognised the skeleton of a child on the woman's breast encompassed by her arm. A loaded revolver by her side, full-cocked, and a camphorwood box.[83]

[A] *child on the woman's breast encompassed by her arm* – the image that has come down to us of the *Heroine of Lizard Island*, and in the box was a pencil and Mary's record. Knowing she and her child were about to die she continued to write – and placed it carefully aside.

And now back on Noble, under the wongai with its familiar rubbish including the junked Korean TV. Exploring with Jon this time – to the summit, the cave and the mine – being with someone changes the experience, it all seems new. Three years ago I didn't get up close to the mine and now we find abandoned vehicles, old decayed pipes, and the remains of a shack against the cliff. Quartz seams and green staining on the rockface; it may have been where Formasini's tunnel was, but this is from a later time – there will be other tales from this mine. But whoever was here probably knew Jack's account and looked to the east, to where Formasini rowed for water and raced back to beat the mainland *Murris*. Wandering on, back to the camp beneath the wongai tree, passing along the eastern shore where there are two slides in the sand behind the fringing mangroves. Last night with ghosts and tonight with crocodiles – and tomorrow north, past Barrow Point and on to Cape Melville.

Bathurst Head, September 6, 2003

Cape Melville, sloping off into the sea to the north, terminates this remarkable promontory in latitude 14 degrees 9 minutes 30 seconds, and longitude 144 degrees 24 minutes 50 seconds: the coast trends round it to the

SouthSouthWest and SouthWest, and forms Bathurst Bay, which is nine miles and a half deep, and thirteen wide, the western side being formed by Flinders' Group.

Phillip Parker King (1827)

Five days ago, just before Cape Melville, a trick at Jon's expense: *See if you can read the rocks – find the fresh water spring.* In and out of his kayak at promising gaps between lichen stained rock before, finally, two metres high in white paint – WATER HERE – arrows pointing to sea level caves between the boulders. Inside it was cool, with pooling fresh water draining over firm, alabaster sand to the sea. Then it was just ten minutes to round the Cape with the Flinders Islands in the distance to the west. Three hours later we were approaching the headland separating Bathurst and Princess Charlotte Bays with the Flinders Islands to the north. Jeffreys named them, and Bathurst Bay, and called this headland Cape Gill but now it's Bathurst Head. I've been here before, a shit of a place to land at low tide, which it was.

Keels stuck fast in mud sixty metres short of firm ground. Two uniformed figures back from the shore watching from behind reflector sunglasses – *what next…* What next was wading in through sole-sucking sludge, the only alternative to sitting in the sun for six hours as the tide drifted us in. Mud-caked from thigh down, we met Mick and Anita, AQIS[84] workers camped at the abandoned resort on a ridge overlooking the bay. Along the beach was a deserted tent city that Anita explained belonged to an all-male party of fishermen from Warren, near Cobar in New South Wales. Each year they drive three-thousand kilometres to the same spot to set themselves up with all the conveniences of home, including generators running twenty-four hours a day – even when they're off fishing. At night, videos and beer – boy stuff. Like us I suppose, same but different.

We followed Mick and Anita to what was left of the resort, built by a Joh Bielke-Petersen-era developer who believed in the sanctity of a nod and a wink but who didn't count on regime change. Finished, fitted out and ready to receive high-value anglers by helicopter from Cairns and

Cooktown, it was denied an operating permit and that was that. The AQIS team had taken over the veranda – three mosquito domes with million dollar views. The Supervising Inspector, Phil, was reclining at ease, binoculars and VHF at the ready, keeping watch for Australia with jam and scones within arms reach. They'd colonised the best spot – a shaded deck on a headland in a north-facing valley about half-a-kilometre wide, with granite ridges on either side protecting it from the easterly winds but with enough elevation to get some breeze. The view to the north is towards the Flinders Group with Princess Charlotte Bay to the west.

The structures are in much worse condition than when I stopped here in 2000 just after the caretaker decamped. In the three years between it's been picked over and vandalised, with trail-bike tire marks through the main building. Everywhere, graffiti: *Swagbaggers 2003; Fucken Fish; Bitch.com; Drifter and Crafty 8/5/00; Bazacca; Candice 03; Dickheads; what a waste; Maggie 1/7/01; I wish my missis was this dirty* – and more. Three years ago there was a bar in this main activity area, books still on shelves, and the rooms were intact. Not now, just a shell with the remains of campfires and mounds of garbage.

But there's still shade and after a hard paddle, struggling through mud in broiling heat and with hours to wait before we can float the kayaks ashore, the best position is horizontal. Phil is on watch, his view the horizon, ours the roof – always a problem with an ex-carpenter: *Jon, they haven't harassed the edge of the rafters and battens. From a carpenter's perspective. Harassed, with an h, you don't sound it. And they've used Oregon pine – white ants love it. Cheap and nasty. And definitely not cyclone-rated.*

And this is exactly where the big one hit – on Saturday evening, 4 March, 1899. Mahina was a Category 5 cyclone and came in from just west of north, right across Bathurst Head. Constable Kenny was on high ground at Barrow Point south of where we camped the day after Noble and he recorded that at 5am on the morning after Mahina hit, the wind:

Shifted to the north east and, if possible, blew harder than ever, with torrents of rain. Shortly after ... an immense tidal wave swept in ashore, and reached waist deep on the ridge with the camp on it, completing the misery of myself and troopers. Here the wave stretched between two and three miles inland.[85]

Just north of Barrow Point is Pipon Island, home to the carpet snake hero – there were stories that the carpet snake could drown seafarers. Harry Cape Melville, who was also known as King Harry said: *He's not a little one like an ordinary carpet snake – he's big, he float like bloody big rock, he drown you when you go close up.*[86] And some said that the carpet snake was responsible for sinking the *Channel Rock* lightship at her moorings by Pipon during the cyclone. The wrong place at the wrong time, the Thursday Island fleet had gathered in what was usually the sheltered safety of Princess Charlotte and Bathurst Bays, protected to the north by the Flinders Islands. Aboriginal people had watched this for years from the heights of Stanley Island where among the rock-face images of turtle and dugong are luggers and four-masted sailing vessels.

Mahina tossed those schooners – *Meg Merrilles, Wai Weer, Olive, Sagitta, Silvery Wave, Crest of Wave, Admiral, Aladin,* and *Tarawa,* tore them from their moorings, wrecked some – and sank dozens of luggers. It was nearly a week before the *White Star* arrived from Thursday Island, passing islands stripped bare and shorelines smashed by tsunami-like, fifteen-metre-high storm surges. More than three hundred mariners dead, nobody knows how many among the coastal *Lama Lama, Guugu Yimithirr, Umpila* and tribes further away. Certainly hundreds, and some died trying to help seamen, swept out to sea as the wind and waves shifted capriciously.[87] And if there were any Aboriginal survivors on the islands from where the fleets had been watched and on which they were recorded on stone, an island world known by different names to them – *Wurrima, Yindayin, Ngurromo* – they didn't stay. Those not taken by the sea were caught by a different tempest and their descendants are far away.

Mahina's devastation wasn't confined to the coast. North of Coen and well inland, eighty kilometres from the cyclone's path, miners took refuge wherever they could from the wind and torrential rain that turned creeks into torrents. Some died and the survivors told stories of the tempest for decades. One was Charlie, who talked about the *Cape Melville cyclone* to Jack Idriess just after they'd arrived on Howick twenty years later.[88]

... a rock with a double rounded top...

...read the rocks...

... trussed up like a working bullock...

No cyclone this time of year but, courtesy of AQIS, the off-shore forecast is for thirty knot winds. Only two options: either fifty kilometres across Princess Charlotte Bay to Cliff Islets or, as suggested by Phil, check out the Australian Customs Vessel – ACV *Botany Bay* – anchored off Flinders Island, maybe even sleep on the *Indo deck* which, we're told, is where boat people are detained. It's probably a lot more comfortable than the floor of the resort and if it's good for boat people it's OK for us. Maybe even hitch a ride north on the trawler supply ferry, the *Endeavour Bay*, due in a couple of nights and Phil knows the captain, Brian. Courtesy AQIS, again, we make a sat-phone call forewarned that Brian is a man of few words. None, in fact; in the early evening we're put through to a crew member unwilling to make any commitment or to disturb the skipper during his nap. But it's worth a try.

Flinders Island, September 7, 2003

Flinders Group forms the west head of Bathurst Bay; they are high and rocky, and consist of four islands, two of which are three miles long. The peak of the largest island, in latitude 14 degrees 11 minutes 5 seconds, and longitude 144 degrees 12 minutes 5 seconds, is visible from a distance of twelve or thirteen leagues; and the higher parts of the islands may be seen generally at seven or eight leagues. On the eastern side of the northernmost island there is a bay fronted by a coral reef, but it is too exposed to the prevailing winds to be safe. It is here that the Frederick (merchant ship) was wrecked in 1818.

Phillip Parker King (1827)

Paddling into the wind through Rattlesnake Channel, between Denham and Blackwood Islands then across Fly Channel and into the protected water behind Flinders Island in the Owen Channel, looking north to Stanley. On the other side of Stanley are Stokes Bay and Cape Flinders. The names capture a high point of Australian maritime exploration – Flinders of course, who sailed as midshipman with Bligh, who had been on the *Resolution* during Cook's last Pacific voyage. And Owen

Stanley on the *Rattlesnake* in 1848 supporting the Kennedy expedition. Owen Stanley had been midshipman on the *Beagle* under Wickam when Darwin was on board with Stokes second in command, and was with Blackwood on the *Fly* in 1842. Before Wickham, Phillip Parker King had been in command of the *Beagle* as it surveyed the high-latitude coasts of South America between 1826 and 1836. Paddling through the waves and currents of history.

Between Flinders and Stanley Islands trawlers are getting ready for the arrival of the *Endeavour Bay*. Booms up with metal shoes and nets hanging to the waterline, they rotate in formation with the tide. Above the background diesel hum there's the whine of outboards, tenders accelerating from one to the other or to the beach for a break from close quarters. It's a motley fleet thrown together by chance and necessity and in stark, burnished contrast, is the ACV *Botany Bay*, anchored in deeper water and with no crew visible. It's sleek, menacing, and hermetically sealed. Paddling around it with calls and whistles, a figure with long blond hair wearing a bikini finally appears on the bridge deck, takes a quick look and disappears to re-emerge minutes later in uniform overalls with an invitation to come on board.

Ushered into the mess, we're seated beneath a full-colour, detailed poster mounted on the bulkhead, a cutaway of a Glock pistol. Introduced to the crew including the bull-like captain, Paul, who indulges us while we eat a meal that seems to materialise from nowhere with an account of the most recent Customs excitement, the pursuit of a Uruguayan fishing boat in the Antarctic for infringing restrictions on taking Patagonian toothfish. A different ambience to AQIS – a sense of being the *serious* arm of non-military interdiction.

We're given a formal tour – thirty-eight metre Bay Class vessel built in Fremantle but being superseded by bigger and better fifty metre vessels. We pass the radio room with Paul huddled over a screen as our escort's commentary continues: *Communication is in clear and encrypted.*

— *Can we go in...*
— *I'm afraid if you step beyond the door we're obliged to kill you.*
— *What...*
— *He's kidding Jon.*

Hopes of a place to sleep dashed, Paul re-emerges with a gift before we depart – packets of *Potato-n-gravy Snack Stop* – *they're a meal in themselves.* Casting off as the doors close, ACV *Botany Bay* is hermetically sealed again. Nobody visible, but we now know that behind the tinted windows on the bridge are two crew surrounded by instrument banks – on watch for Australia. And if there's trouble they've got a Glock or two. Now, nothing to do but wait on the beach for the *Endeavour Bay*.

Flinders Island; on shore the sand-spit beach gives way to a rocky causeway behind mangroves. There are large stone circles, long abandoned wells that had been used to water passing vessels, with the mangroves cleared to manhandle barrels to the shoreline. Nearby, cut into a rock along the low, backing cliffs – *HMS Dart 1899*. And on almost every other surface more recent graffiti – names of people and boats, and in giant letters – *Darryl Braithwaite*.

Endeavour Bay, September 8, 2003

Princess Charlotte's Bay is an extensive bight in the coast, twentytwo miles deep, and thirtyone broad; its shores are low, and at the bottom in latitude 14 degrees 29 minutes there is a mangrove opening.

Phillip Parker King (1827)

Last night, on the dot at 8:00pm, the lights of the *Endeavour Bay* appeared in Owen Channel. In the darkness we passed between fishing boats manoeuvring into position around the stern of the mother ship, their engine-chorus floating across the water. Floodlights on the aft-deck high with containers, movement everywhere, there was none of the quiet professionalism of the Customs crew. But it was purposeful chaos and as we paddled into the fall of light, trawlers impatient behind us, there was no time for the niceties of considered boarding options. Dry bags and water-bottles were thrown to waiting arms, slings descended, the kayaks hoisted aboard and unceremoniously shoved aside.

Standing awkwardly in dripping paddling gear we were directed off the aft deck and out of the way of the real business, into the mess-area where bulkheads were festooned with posters dense with boobs and bums. Shown to a cabin with six berths, a crew member appeared and fast-forwarded through instructions: *Don't eat when the crew are eating, don't interfere with the crew's activities, don't use the showers when crew are changing, don't go on the fore or bridge decks, don't talk to the captain and never go beyond the black bollards on the maindeck – got it…*

— *Jon, I wonder what happens if you go past the black bollards…*
— *Just like the radio room – they may be obliged to kill you Jon. Don't give them the excuse.*

Somewhere around mid-morning there was a leisurely exodus of crew wearing life-vests. Jan, the only woman on board, informed us that it was the emergency drill and pointed to a cupboard with a collection of what appeared to be floatation devices. Suitably buoyant we assembled on the foredeck with everyone except the captain and were immediately dismissed. Jan has worked on trawlers for years. She fell off one in big seas a few years ago, missed the dead-man's rope but was seen by the skipper who was able to circle back to get her – then: *I just got back to work*. Lots of stories of mad or mongrel skippers, and a crew that she'd heard about who deserted in a life-raft to a nearby island, only to have the skipper sailing offshore taking pot-shots with a rifle.

Through the afternoon the crew work at a leisurely pace compared to last night. Jim, the chief engineer and Jamie, second engineer, are sitting at the mess-room table smoking and intent on fixing a switch. It goes on for about half an hour. Constant banter and jokes where opportunity presents; Jim starts, Jamie picks it up: *Jamie, in a different life you could have been a surgeon.*

— *Yeah. Did you hear about the mechanic that wanted to be a surgeon…*
— *Not that one Jamie.*
— *I haven't heard it. Have you Jon…*

— *No Jon.*
— *Well, no, actually it was a mechanic that wanted to be a gynaecologist.*
— *OK...*
— *Anyway he passes his exams and stuff and has to do a practical. Take apart all the bits and put it back together again and he finished before any of the others. The instructor gives him 95%. He says he can't give him 100% because... Anyway, when the final marks come out he's got 110%. He's stoked. He asks the instructor how come. The instructor says... Wait, no...*
— *Jamie's fucked it up again. Every time.*
— *But the build up is great, isn't it Jon...*
— *Great buildup Jon, but needs attention to detail.*
— *That's why he'll never be chief engineer.*

The conversation turns to the captain who hasn't made an appearance in almost a day on board: *You don't see the skipper much...*
— *He's upstairs. Been driving all day. Maybe a couple of hours in the afternoon Phil takes over while the skipper takes a nap.*
— *You never see him down here...*
— *No. Good like that.*

But we do see him – we're invited to the bridge. Inside there's a cot, pretty basic instrumentation by comparison to the *Botany Bay* and more bulkhead blondes. The vessel is forty-nine metres, an ex-rig tender, the *Pacific Endeavour*, built in the States in 1967, renamed the *Endeavour Bay* and now near the end of its working life given fuel inefficiencies. A crew of eight, they head north from Cairns dropping off supplies to trawlers, sometimes picking up product as far as Yorke Island in the Torres. A one-day turn around then south loading more product. Arrive in Cairns on a Friday and leave again Monday – and so it goes.

Captain Brian turns out to be very chatty and keen to provide correctives on just about everything. Geoffrey Wordsworth – a real disappointment, Brian was in the area when the seaplane went down after it tipped over on a piece of coral when the tide went out, no crocs involved. Spanish treasures – he said he saw Spanish inscriptions on rocks in the Sir Edward

Pellew group; also, he was on Boot Reef in the Torres when a Jardine lugger was caught in the lagoon and they had to hack their way through the coral to free it, in the course of which they found silver coins, and; Brian was on Badu when a local diver came up with gold coins but refused Brian a closer look. Chinese explorers – on a beach on the western side of Badu he saw a precisely rounded stone that nobody seems to know the origin of. Echoes of Paul on *Thirsty Dog* and Brian reckons it's a Chinese cannon ball too. True or not, it's the stories that count. Also, he's not impressed by our comments about Customs hospitality. A year ago they boarded the *Endeavour Bay* all glocked-up after he told them to *piss off* when they demanded to do an inspection. One constant throughout, to every question about islands along the way where we might get off: *There's crocs there too.*

Hay Island, September 9, 2003

Islet 6, in latitude 13 degrees 29 minutes, longitude 143 degrees 38 minutes 26 seconds, is a very small, low, woody islet, with a reef extending for threequarters of a mile off its north and south ends.

Phillip Parker King (1827)

An hour of frenetic activity, three trawlers at a time pulling to stern and sides, 12kg cartons of frozen shrimp flying along a roller conveyor – up to 1000 cartons from a fully loaded trawler. Fuel, beer and water going one way, product the other. Jon and I trying not to get in the way and staying well behind the black bollards. Then, suddenly, the transfers are complete and two kayaks are being hoisted over the stern. Trying to force dry bags and camping gear through fore- and rear-deck hatches as the boats bounce against the ship's metal hull – messy. Finally floating free as Brian appears on the bridge deck, shouting a warning into the wind as the engines power up: *Watch out for that old croc boys, he's four-feet-wide* – his words floating on the wind, we know all about crocs, they're everywhere, been there done that – *and the pythons.*

— *Pythons. What pythons…*

My plea lost in the wind. Just a smile and a wave in return. The *Endeavour Bay* is off and soon we've landed on Hay Island, a quadrant-shaped mangrove forest sitting on drying reef with a solitary beach to the northwest backed by a garden-sized area of higher ground. Within five minutes we've located a python, curled through driftwood piled above the high tide mark: *Tread carefully and keep an eye out for that four-feet-wide croc.*

And watch out for the surf – surf inside the reef. Hay Island sits in the middle of an inner-reef navigation channel that splits around the island. Piled driftwood and debris across the elevated ground shows the reach of shipping wash at high tide, presumably amplified when two ships travelling in opposite directions pass nearby at the same time. Fortunately unlikely, but prudence demands colonizing the highest point on the island for the night.

Cape Weymouth, September 14, 2003

Cape Weymouth is an elevated point, sloping off from a high summit; its extreme is in latitude 12 degrees 37 minutes 15 seconds, and longitude 143 degrees 20 minutes 35 seconds... The coast then extends towards Bolt Head, and forms several sinuosities, one of which is Weymouth Bay.

Phillip Parker King (1827)

Dismiss the vigil. I said I was going to start a little documentary. Action... John Pritchard is masked by a camera, recording our arrival as we struggle up towards an hexagonal pole house, open to the north and east, with a chaos of machinery, building materials, spare parts and projects-in-development beneath. Alerted to the strangers, Wilma and Pluto bound down the slope – all sound and saliva. Toughened to survive, with Lockhart's classic Great Dane frame – every camp has its signature dogs.

In full kayak gear – *trussed up like a working bullock* – John's words, it's all recorded. There forever – or parts thereof. *The second mate is on his way up* – the commentary continues as Jon appears on the stone track below, same gear and wearing my reading glasses. His are on the seabed somewhere off Eagle Island. He's carrying the Mace, made on Two Isles by Axel – whose journey has taken him elsewhere. And now Jon and a real John as well.

Cape Weymouth, north of Chilli Beach with Restoration Island just offshore. *Kuuku Ya'u* land – Hobson country – *Wuthathi* to the north and *Uutaalnganu* to the south, *Umpila* beyond that and *Kaanju* country inland. Thirty kilometres south, Lockhart River is as home as it gets now. But it wasn't always so. Camping on Night Island two days ago we looked across to where the mission was until the 1960s – Old Site. Like Cape Bedford Mission, the War came there too, and just after American soldiers arrived to take the *Guuugu Yimidhirr* away from Cape Bedford, airmen of the 90th Bomb Group began flying B-24D Liberators out of Claudie and Gordon fields at Iron Range. But the Lockhart mob weren't taken away, just left to fend for themselves until the War was over. Anglicans – no threat. Then it was all about administration, expedience, efficiency – convenience. Department days – new ways and a new home – Lockhart River Aboriginal Community.

Cape Weymouth – a few Aboriginal shacks facing south along Chilli Beach and half a dozen freehold blocks on the northern slopes with houses hidden from sight – around here people prefer it that way. Views north across the mangroves towards Portland Roads. Stories everywhere. Of survivors, like Bligh, landing on Restoration Island then heading north along the coast, and others, like the men left behind at the mouth of the Olive by Kennedy. The plaque at Portland Roads tells that story:

> EDMUND BESLEY COURT KENNEDY J.P. ON 13
> NOVEMBER 1848 WHILE EXPLORING IN CAPE
> YORK PENINSULA LEFT CARRON, WALL, DOUGLAS,
> NIBLET, TAYLOR, CARPENTER, GODDARD AND
> MITCHELL NEAR THE MOUTH OF PASCOE RIVER
> AND SOUGHT SUCCOUR AT CAPE YORK. EN ROUTE
> HE WAS FATALLY SPEARED AND 3 MEN DIED.
> ABORIGINE JACKEY-JACKEY SOLE SURVIVOR
> OF ADVANCE PARTY REACHED WAITING
> SHIP "ARIEL" WHICH RESCUED SURVIVORS
> CARRON AND GODDARD AT WEYMOUTH BAY
> ON 30 DECEMBER. UNVEILED 13 NOVEMBER 1948.

An hour after arrival and John is still filming, the camera shifting and selecting. Two young Aboriginal women playing pool in the background – questioning eyes, avoiding direct contact but watching, listening and taking it in, their electrifying smiles digitally captured with a sweeping, slow shot of the pool table. Close up of black hands on cue, the sharp crack of balls colliding and their dulled rebound from felt edges. Laughter, questions, fleeting glances - observing. We're watching the replay an hour later as it cuts to me – kayak gear gone, coloured-zinc-flecked full beard, the view shifting for effect, playing to the camera, John's voice in the background: *Ernest, tell us about arriving at Lizard Island with Axel.*

— *Club Rude – we got there dreaming of freshening up and having a good time. So Axel and I got out of the boats; I was covered in yellow zinc, he had red zinc, and we had all of our gear – life-vests, and hats and stuff – looking like some weird Nordic invasion. We went up to the boatshed and there were these young guys who seemed to have been picked out of Pump magazine. And they deferred to the management and wouldn't make a decision except to say it's nine-hundred-and-ninety dollars per person, twin share, clearly anticipating that we couldn't pay – which was correct. But we said we'd go up to reception anyway, and when we got to the office they slid us a pam-phlet that just had a big picture of Lizard Island on it so I said, look, I know we're on Lizard Island. And then they told us that the resort was expensive but you got access to all the amenities – which seemed to be the beach. But then they said we could go to the National Park where there's a toilet and fresh water – and considerable savings. So I asked how much it would cost, and they said two fifty. I said two hundred and fifty and they said no, two dollars fifty. I figured we'd save nine hundred and eighty-seven dollars fifty each. So we headed off and as we went out the door a woman with a bee-hive hairdo and an attitude to match rushed out after us. She'd been watching us in the reception area and I imagine she was in there with the Wettex and Brillo, scouring it after we left.*

Lizard Island Resort – not for the bootless and unhorsed, and certainly not for kayakers.

CHAPTER 7

1995-1996: delta

Horns of light somewhere in the darkness, a waning crescent moon that will crest the unseen ocean horizon in the early hours of the morning and begin its journey to landfall, a phantom fading in the lightening sky as the sun follows in its wake. But for now just stars and the Coquet light. And the void – wrap-around night so close you can feel it.

Cities of light mask nature's rhythms. Camping on remote islands those cycles are irresistible – it doesn't take long to fall into step. In the minutes or hours between twilight and sleep, before the night claims another soul, the fissures in the darkness are insistent – but in very different ways. Campfires comfort and illuminate a space for sharing and disclosure – for stories. The focus is inwards, looking down, away from the shadows and the unknowable. It's not the same looking out into a clear, moonless, star-crowded sky; even when you're with someone you're on your own.

But most of us don't look up, we avoid engaging with our solitude. The beyond threatens the fragile illusion of connectedness. *Stargazer* – not a compliment, as if what's above is less important than whatever happens to be in front of you. Perhaps because rejecting connection threatens the status quo. And the stargazers who are lost in their private beyond and who don't return the social gaze – they really threaten the order of things. Even though they're on their own – or because of it.

Lions Den Hotel, February 9, 1995

Jack Idriess knew the Lion's Den – it was more than two decades old when he stayed here just before the War and he probably spent time with Dick Welsh at the bar swapping stories. And maybe with Formasini as well – tin scratchers. They'd all come down from the hills for one of Mrs Watkins' feeds, and sometimes for her doctoring, using remedies she'd coaxed from native women, or organising a passing pack team for a ride to Cooktown hospital. The Lion's Den – a sanctuary for them all, as it seemed the first time Jack came by:

I really tried to plod past the long veranda shadowed by branches. There was another side veranda covered with creepers, a veranda running back among banana palms, pawpaw-trees and mangoes dimly loaded with luscious fruit. As I walked past they were lighting the lamps inside. The lions were warming up the den for a comfy night.[89]

It's still off the beaten track but in a tourist-kind-of-way. And still surrounded by fruit trees; close by are trellises of passionfruit in the wedge of land sloping down between Mungumby Creek and the Little Annan River and a for-sale sign on the fence – dream the dream each time I drive the coast road between Cairns and Cooktown. Jack was dreaming when he was here – and writing. About everything and everyone.

Thursday evening and I'm on my way back to Cooktown from a clinic at Wujal Wujal – an Aboriginal community nestled on a bend of the Bloomfield just back from Weary Bay. Cook again – deservedly weary after the path through the labyrinth was blocked by yet another reef, and exhausted by the exertions of freeing and fothering the *Endeavour* just south of Cape Tribulation. Saved by a coral head that stuck in the hull. Weary Bay – there's a photo of Michael Fomenko running along the beach that stretches north from the mouth of the Bloomfield. He was there on and off from the 1960s when he befriended Cedar Bay Bill, by then already an old timer at the Bay. He was there when the hippies came to Cedar Bay in the 1970s, to where the tin scratchers camped in Jack's time a half-century earlier. The biggest over-reaction in a state known for over-reactions, that was the view years after the combined Police, Customs and Narcotics Bureau raid that saw the hippies' shacks burnt and the squatters driven off in the mid-1970s. The whole pseudo-legal charade was eventually undone, featuring Terry O'Gorman who went on to a career unmasking corruption and over-reactions in Queensland – he was never going to run out of work.

Like the hippies, Tarzan moved on – to the weather slopes of Grassy Hill at Cooktown where he set up a camp near the abandoned Wireless Telegraph Station with a drift of wild pigs as companions. *Pig man*, that's what the kids called him when he wandered into town carrying a rough-hewn walking staff and his sack, clad only with an old beach towel worn like a kilt. But they saw more than weirdness and respected his connection to the wild: *we're just coming by, we don't mean any harm…* they'd call out if they were approaching his camp or the track down to Cherry Tree Bay – he was fearfully protective of his pigs, his family. As the 1970s ended he was a familiar figure in Cooktown where he might stop for a pannikin of tea at the ice works with Suzanne Bayliss and her boys. Wild but gentle, that was their take, a man on a solitary journey. She might have been thinking of him when, years later, she wrote:

His road is stony
Along the way
However, truth he tells,
Be what may.[90]

Decades earlier, before the hippies were embracing nature at Cedar Bay, Michael Fomenko was living off the land from Deeral to Cooktown and building dugout canoes. Hollowed by adze and fire, he built more than six along the banks of the Russell River. He rigged primitive sails and outriggers, and over eighteen months in the late 1950s he made it from Cooktown to Merauke, a Dutch outpost on the Maro river, a hundred kilometres to the west of what was then the Australian protectorate of Papua New Guinea. The authorities didn't know how to deal with someone like Michael. *Tarzan* – that's what they called him in the press and it stuck, maybe because of his superb physique and lack of clothes, but probably because he chose the jungle.

Michael Fomenko wasn't the first jungle man in these parts – Jack Idriess knew many, including one who took him on a journey of discovery through the tableland forests and bush back of Cairns. Like Michael Fomenko, Jack's jungle man: *loved loneliness, loved all the lonely places and the beauty that so often broods there*. Idriess understood that the jungle man lived and knew something he didn't, that he had: *secrets of the wild bush that he had learnt in loneliness.*[91] Idriess was still writing when Michael Fomenko arrived at the Bloomfield and Cedar Bay, fifty years after Jack was in that same place before the first War, wondering how some men had come close *to the heart of the Wild*:

> *Some few men merge right into the heart itself. They are perhaps "queer" and are very few and far between. I have met one or two in the Far North, men who have slipped right back until they have become literally Children of Nature. They can do that phenomenally hard thing, exist in the bush on what their cunning, endurance, and sharpened "animal" intelligence secure them.*[92]

But Michael Fomenko's origins were far from the jungle. He was born in Russia, his father a Ukrainian academic and mother an aristocratic Georgian – that's part of the legend. They fled the Soviets with Michael and his older sister through Manchuria to Japan where they managed to get Italian passports. From there his polyglot father, Daniel, went on to Australia, arriving in Sydney in 1937, two years before his wife and children. Daniel taught at an elite boys school where Michael was educated – a competent student and outstanding all-round athlete.

But by the mid-1950s Michael had left Sydney and his family, and had made his way north to the sugarcane country south of Cairns. Unlike the other Europeans who had drifted to the fringes and whose lives were frugal by necessity. Michael was a master of subsistence, willingly doing without society's encumbrances – making do with whatever was at hand. Michael wasn't escaping – he knew what he wanted, and what to do and where to go to get it. In 1958, while he was on Horne Island before crossing the Torres Strait to New Guinea, he met John and Mary Caldwell who were sailing around the world on their yacht, *Outward Bound*. Years later Mary recalled that he told her:

> *I am not running away from anything… I like company. But life is never wholly what you want. You have to accept the balance of things. So, in finding solitude, I also found loneliness. Sometimes in my canoe I felt terribly lonely. But then again, on balance, I like to be on my own.*[93]

Michael's life has been embellished by rumour and retelling. The essence of it, the truth of his life, is in his denial of the world of things and events, his rejection of conventions and comforts. He lived in and by isolation. But even in remote Australia there are no unclaimed spaces and his solitude wasn't complete; he wasn't alone and didn't go unnoticed. Fleeting as they were, his interactions with pastoralists and their families in the back-country pushed buttons – a decision was made by someone, somewhere, that something had to be done. Eventually they caught him outside Laura in the 1960s and took him in police custody to Brisbane, to an asylum. He was in hospital more than once and given ECT – fitting for not fitting in. And he didn't – Tarzan rejected the system, which its functionaries couldn't accept, so he had to be caught and classified – as mad. But he wasn't, he was a jungle man. When he was finally released he headed north again, back to his jungle.

Mick met Tarzan in the 1980s and he knows others who had *slipped right back*, who went on personal odysseys north along the coral coast by foot and by boat. Some of those were mad but others were not, including Michael Fomenko. And even in old age, living in riverside camps, Michael still continues to build dugout canoes, emerging only to tramp between Innisfail and Cairns, barefoot and bare-chested with his hessian sack over his shoulder. Along the Bruce Highway as the semi-trailers and motorhomes speed by – his new patch of jungle.

Doctor Mick understands jungle people – there are many communities of protest in the Daintree and back of the Bloomfield. Feisty rainforest *Murris – Kuku Yalanji –* who refused to be Lutheranised and continue to resist the pallid pressures of enlightened bureaucrats. And there are the newcomers – from before Jack and Formasini and since, drawn by dreams of difference and marooned on islands of filtered rainforest light.

There are always a few of them at the bar of the Lion's Den, either studiously ignoring or obsequiously grooming tourists in awe of any hint of bush authenticity. Mick knows there's no such thing – just survival in a shadow-world of feigned self-sufficiency that masks welfare dependence and, more often than not, petty crime – delinquency, drugs, duffing. He has intelligence on them all, and they know him – doctor Mick. He slowly rotates his beer can in the circle of its own condensation on the bar. Turning it slowly, deliberately, as if the cycles are linked to the story he's telling – of a service in transition: *they've got no idea what they're destroying. Not just neglect, wilful destruction. And not just here. But this is where I know about, and Cooktown is meaningful to me – it's my home. For them it's just another statistic, a set of personnel and resource management problems. There'll be an algorithm for sorting it somewhere. There are no people in that formula and no fucking patients.*

When I arrived fifteen minutes ago Mick was sitting in front of the same can of beer on which his gaze seems to be blindly locked. Our conversation has a liturgical flow, as I echo the terminal phrase – *no patients* – the response is triggered: *No patients. Patients aren't just bed numbers. They've got complex needs that don't end when they wander out of the hospital. I see them in the pub, in the supermarket – and out here. Sometimes as a doctor you need to make judgments, not just rely on a flow chart. Now the services are run by nurses who've got management degrees not experience. As far as they're concerned they don't need to know the history or context. Memory isn't valued.*

Memory isn't valued... I know exactly what he means, but the recitation is more like communion than communication and I push for an example: *Well, like we tried doing such and such to make sure the* Murri *kids* get their bicillin injections for rheumatic heart disease, but it didn't work and then we do so and so, which may mean talking hard or bribery – who cares as long as they get it. But for the new masters, that doesn't respect rights. Like the right to a slow death from heart failure. And they don't respect the knowledge or needs of the nurses who do know the community, like Jade.*

I know Jade, a rough diamond but always reliable if I have to make sure someone stays in the ward overnight, she intuitively knows how to relate no matter where they come from. Mick adds some background I wasn't aware of: *Jade's been here for decades living with a guy who's a violent prick more interested in the pub and his dope patch. They have three kids who are a bit wild but doing OK considering. She holds it all together and it would be better if she told that mongrel to piss off. But that's complicated and she probably couldn't work then. So every now and again she cracks but settles with a bit of valium. And probably some of the mongrel's gunja. I know about it – she tells me. Doesn't feel good about it but tells me. And gets on with work. I get it and I'm watching, she's probably the most competent nurse we've got.*

The can comes to a halt as Mick breaks his concentration to glance at new arrivals from a rental four-wheel-drive that pulled up outside, taking in the scene from the door before moving tentatively to the bar. But his gaze quickly shifts to the few regulars checking them out and weighing up their options as the strangers order two beers. Germans – high mark targets, well-heeled and suckers for the exotic, whether it's secret-sacred blackfellow business or Idriess-esque tales of the bush. And too polite or uncertain to tell the locals to *fuck off.* It'll all start after the first beer. Mick's focus returns to the can that has started again, around and around – he knows the players and the script. I bring him back to his story, to the nurse, Jade: *Jade… The problem is that she believed the bullshit about a sharing and caring workplace. She asked for leave when things got tough, broke down and made the fatal mistake – she shared. Told them what was happening at home. About the mongrel, about his drinking and dope, about it all. The shit hit the fan. Police and child welfare involved and the mongrel loses the plot. Jade's in hospital with a broken jaw, the mongrel arrested, kids likely to go who knows where, patients without a competent nurse who cares*

about them — because she's lived it too and they trust her. And I'm the villain in the piece.
— You're the villain...
— *They didn't talk to me about it, just did it. And I'm to blame because if I'd taken appropriate action none of this would have happened. It doesn't matter that I've managed it for years. So they expect me to roll over for some pimply-faced wanker from Human Resource Management and get fucked.*
— What do you mean...
— *They'll supervise my practice, tell me how to relate to my patients and neighbours to make sure everyone's safe — from me. They know I won't accept that — they just want me to leave.*

Movement at the bar, it looks like the Crocodile Dundee play, the dinky-di outback experience. Usually works well with continentals. Mick doesn't even look up, he seems lost in the can that is now still: *for our new breed of fucking managers it's about the system, in the end about their jobs. It'll happen to you if you stick around long enough. Don't start to care. For fuck's sake don't care about them — particularly the* Murris *— they don't give a shit about them unless there's a complaint. Scared shitless about a ministerial. So, if I can't work in a way I think is in the best interest of patients and fits with who I am then it's time to move.*

In the background the play is evolving: *I bet this beer's got nothing on German beer... Have you ever been to the Oktoberfest... I wouldn't mind a Captain Cook — sorry mate, that's one of our Aussie sayings...* He's moving it towards the homely bushie show — slow burn. Mick sits back, the can on the bar motionless, as if it's reached the end of its journey: *Mick, where would you go...*
— Collinsville.
— Where the fuck is that, I've never even heard of it...
— Probably a good thing. A long way away.

Silkwood, April 29, 1996

Driving south and passing Edmonton he appears in the distance heading north, his hessian sack draped across sun-darkened shoulders, face set to some unfathomable mission. He seems to be willing himself forward, leaning into his journey, undistracted by the highway-scape he's passing through. Later today he'll be returning south and will look just the same – hessian sack, shorts and old runners. That's his concession to old age, a pair of Dunlop Volleys, probably from a dumpster.

Hundreds-of-thousands have seen him as they speed by and tens-of-thousands will recognize him as the man they call Tarzan. Far fewer realize he's Michael Fomenko, and only a dozen or so will have noticed the fine definition of his ageing muscles, or his blue eyes beneath tangle-weed brows. Or thought that this man has remarkably good skin and a fine head of hair for someone who had tramped tracks and trails unclad for over six decades. Unwilling to concede ground to age or social conventions, an old man still on an unshared mission. He's somewhere behind me now, step-by-step towards Cairns.

Ten kilometres south of Innisfail the Bruce Highway crosses the junction of the Silkwood-Japoon Road to the west and Murdering Point Road to the east. Turn left and you head to Kurrimine Beach. Kurrimine, supposedly a *Djirbalngan* word for rising sun – sounds nicer than Murdering Point, which is what it was called before the 1930s. That name went back to 1878 when the Sub-collector of Customs at Cardwell telegraphed the Colonial Treasurer:

> *Mr. Sub-inspector Johnstone reports finding the bodies of two men in a native oven on the mainland opposite King's Reef. The skulls were smashed in, and the bodies partly roasted, parts of the flesh being absent. The features were not recognizable. One is supposed to be 6ft. high, with dark hair mixed with gray. The other man of medium size, with light brown hair and sandy whiskers. From papers found in the native camp in proximity to the bodies, there can be little doubt that these are the remains of the crew of the Riser cutter, the wreckage of which was found a few days since on King's Reef. An enquiry is being held today.*[94]

At the beach a historical marker with an image depicting the scene of the massacre that followed informs passing tourists:

An aboriginal tracker led the troopers to a thick mangrove swamp through which a saltwater creek ran. They crossed this at low tide and found the tribes' camp, which they surrounded and invaded at dusk. The murdered crewmen's clothes, axes, and other odds and ends were found within the camp. The troopers never reported on the exact events nor the outcome of the dusk raid.

The *exact events*, the *outcome*. Almost certainly no *Djirbalngan* left to report on the exact events – that was the outcome. And the name change – well, who would celebrate two massacres… Except maybe the Murdering Point Winery, half way between the Bruce Highway and the beach. Open for tastings and cellar door sales, their label emblazoned with a cutter in full sail. And at $35 including GST you can get a bottle of The Riser – *a smooth, yet rich coffee liqueur of attractive deep brown colour, enticing scents and bittersweet coffee bean and roasted chestnut.* Bittersweet – bad luck and bad liquor if you turn left.

Turn to the right, away from the coast, and a belt of sugarcane becomes Silkwood – a town without a centre, a place to pass through without arriving. Nothing but a straggling line of unpretentious brick and fibro cottages, each surrounded by a clear-zone of close cut lawn – midtown north Queensland. Except for a crenelated and domed concrete apparition looming from behind the rural streetscape. Silkwood Castle seems to be channelling Watts Towers – another never-to-be-finished New World Italianate folly. But it isn't – 1990 from the inscription across the gate and no Italian connections. Except for Silkwood itself and there's no giveaway in the name although it's a town that's as Italian as can be as far as you can get from the mother country. There are flags out and a festive arch nearly completed across what passes for a main street. Getting ready for the Feast of the Three Saints – Alfio, Filadelfo and Cerino. They came up with the goods and answered a migrant Italian worker's prayers to intercede when complications of childbirth threatened his wife's life. Rosario was so grateful he commissioned a statue of the trio in Italy. Silkwood has been home to the statue and the festival since 1950, the biggest event on the north Queensland Italian calendar.

Suddenly I'm through Silkwood without realizing it and five minutes and a few turns later there's a gate marked by a life-sized structure built of discarded machinery welded into android form – *you'll know when you get there. Look for Benno by the drive, he's yellow and holding a post box, you won't miss him.* And I don't, parking a few minutes later next to a work-worn pickup at the end of a gravel drive that loops lazily around an almost empty concrete pond with a central structure that at one time might have passed for a *lipicai* stallion. Paving stones lead to a weatherboard Queenslander that's survived serial renovations, set between barn-sized sheds spilling the stuff of tropical farming. The stringers of the steps grind as I climb to a small landing and try to knock on the rim of a screen-door. It's a lame sound – the rocking of the door in its frame – but enough.

A middle-aged woman appears across the darkened veranda from a more substantial entrance flanked by vertical panes of green and red stained-glass. From Mick's description two years ago of speaking with Biata when he had the man he knew as Larry in Cooktown Hospital in 1989, and from my own conversation with her a few months ago when László finally agreed that I could call her, I'd conjured an image of a blue-rinsed matron who might be heard chatting in heavily accented tones in the snug of one of Double Bay's central European coffee shops. The woman who invites me in looks around the age I expected but is obviously more familiar with the banter of worksheds and fields than hairdressers and café society. There's no rinse in her greyed hair, which is fastened into a neat bun that is probably for convenience rather than appearance. She has on a floral dress that's been recently pressed, and against a tanned and lined face her emerald eyes shine – she looks her age but seems younger.

Just inside the front door I'm introduced to two men who are on their way out: *I was christened Biata. I took Beatrice when I came to Australia in 1950, but everyone calls me Bea. This is my husband, Gino, and Dom – Dom is our second. We always have lunch with the boys here.* In an accented voice Gino acknowledges my presence without engaging. I'm struck by his hands, which seem too large for the ageing body, like wooden pulley-blocks worn by time and toil. Behind Gino is a powerfully built younger man with a friendly smile. But like his father few words, just *hello doctor* and *you're here to talk to mum about uncle Larry* – then they're gone, the screen door and creaking staircase tracking their progress, followed by the static of wheels on gravel as the pickup returns them to the world of farm work. Leaving me with Biata in the living room. Larry, László, Gordon – it's not clear who I'm talking to her about.

The walls and surfaces of the living room I'm led into track family history and connections – photos and grandchildren's drawings, trophies and ribbons marking local milestones, postcards with glimpses of the world beyond – somewhere else. Biata motions me to an armchair that seems positioned for the head of the family that has been covered with colourful drapes – perhaps for the visitor. Biata sits opposite on one half of a settee, the rest covered by photograph albums and an open folder with clippings from magazines and newspapers. On top is a faded and frayed sheet of aged newspaper, the banner just readable: *The Stars and Stripes, 1949*. Lifting that sheet so delicately that it seems suspended in her gaze, held fast by memory, she points to a photograph of ten adults and a child looking at the camera, a moment and a message from forty-five years ago. Five men, five women and a girl – they appear relaxed and from the suits, dresses and overcoats, probably reasonably well-to-do. At the right of the group, standing in front of a woman in her thirties or forties who has one arm around her, is the girl. Biata sighs and seems lost in the image: *That's me, I was eight when that photo was taken, in Munich*. The title above the photograph reads *Hungarian Refugees Who Fled Terror in Their Homeland*, but Biata points to a column on the opposite page:

Magyar Refugees Seek Life Free of Red Fear

Munich, Jan. 7 (S&S) – The 20 refugees who fled Hungary by taking control of a national airliner and flying to Munich, all hope to settle in countries beyond the sphere of Russian domination.[95]

From Biata's eyes I know the picture evokes memories too dense to unpack for a stranger with no connection: *I had just had my eighth birth-*

day, my last birthday in Budapest. The city was still a wasteland but we went to a park by the Danube, across from the university – my mother, my uncle and I. That's my mother behind me, and my uncle Géza at the very end – he was tall and very handsome.

So he is, standing at an angle to the camera, looking over his shoulder with his right hand in his trouser pocket and the left bent in front of his chest, holding a cigarette. Of the five men he is the only one who doesn't seem to be with a woman: *We lived with uncle Géza in an apartment on Rákóczi Avenue after my father died at the end of the war. It was in the centre of the city and all the buildings were damaged, but we were lucky compared to others. Géza was very clever, we got by on what he made teaching and on the black market.*

As Biata replaces the half-century old page its edge catches on the pile of photos and clippings below. She carefully smooths the newspaper as if caressing a foundation document. Reaching over to an album she opens it to an envelope marking a photograph of herself with her uncle against the backdrop of a war-ravaged city: *Géza organized for my mother and I to go with him on a trip to Prague, but when we crossed the border into Czechoslovakia the men took over. They only told me later that they were worried the Soviets would shoot us down. We were treated like heroes when we got to Munich. Some of the group had relatives in Germany but we went to a camp for refugees. Just six months later we sailed from Genoa to Sydney – that's where most of the Magyars wanted to go.*

Biata fetches a tray from the kitchen, already set for afternoon tea with home-baked strudel: *We call it Rétes.* Humming softly, she pours tea and loads a plate as if for sons and grandsons working in the fields and sheds. The conversation wanders slowly from Hungarian delicacies via Italian families and back to her story: *My mother met Aldo, my stepfather, at a Catholic dance – in Strathfield. He was good looking and full of stories about relatives who were living in Silkwood. He told her they had mansions and servants. My mother wanted to believe him. She thought she was coming to a country estate. Silkwood – imagine, it sounded so romantic – selyem*

– soft, beautiful silk. She wouldn't listen to my uncle. I think he knew it was all stories.

Another album, relationships woven through networks of family and fate. A young woman in a floral skirt standing next to what looks like a Holden FC sedan – chrome dreams. Next to her a tanned young man in high-waisted, dark trousers and a white shirt leans back on the vehicle with an air of ownership – the car and the girl. In the background the main street of Silkwood is filled with people. Maybe the Feast of the Three Saints: *That's Gino there. He was so proud of that car. That was 1960, just before we married. But we arrived in Decembe*r *1955 – it was such a shock. There were lots of Italians but none living in mansions. Aldo's family were here and they had a farm – but it was no estate.* A moment of silence, maybe to reflect on decisions and destiny, then Biata continues, her speech slowed as if by the effort remembering: *And it was hot – so hot, I thought I must have died and gone to hell, I wanted to be back in Budapest, to be anywhere but here. But I've lived around Silkwood ever since. Gino's family came from Calabria and their farm was near my stepfather's – this is it. It's the only home I've known in thirty-five years.*

Another album – other lives. She opens at a page marked with a used envelope and points to one of two figures in a posed photograph: *That is László's father, Béla, before the war.* Young adults, probably about the same age as Biata at the Feast of the Three Saints, around eighteen or nineteen. It's not a good photograph and their features are indistinct but they're looking directly to the camera. Béla is the shorter but both have broad chests and muscular arms. Wearing white shorts and nothing else, they each hold a paddle that crosses the other's, framing their torsos. I imagine their hair neatly combed – the photo may have been taken in a studio and there seems to be the shell of a kayak or canoe forming the base of the image: *Béla would have been in the 1940 Olympics – if the war hadn't come. He took after his uncle János who played water polo and was on the team that went to Los Angeles in 1932. Hungary won the gold in 1932. And in 1956 too – everyone knows about that. But with the war everything changed – lives and dreams did not go on as usual. It all changed. That photo must have been around 1938.*

Bea – Beatrice – over the course of the afternoon it becomes clear that it's Biata that I'm speaking with, her voice changing, becoming more accented as she recites the names of places and people from decades ago, a world away. Lives intersecting and diverging as she explains convoluted bloodlines. Béla's mother was related by marriage after the First World War to a Serbian Jewish family that had Magyarised and done well. One distant relation, Mátyás Rákosi, had been a Russian prisoner from 1915 and had returned after the War and revolution in Russia to become a founder-member of the Hungarian Communist Party which briefly held power. That didn't last long and he ended up back in Russia after being imprisoned by the Miklós Horthy regime that ousted the Communists – wrong side of history but, as it turned out, the right side after 1944. A Russian puppet, Rákosi was First Secretary of the Party until 1956, one of the most reviled figures in post-war Hungary.[96] A distant relative to Béla but, as it turned out, life-saving. Even so. Biata doesn't hide her contempt or her anti-Semitism.

Biata is of Béla's paternal family – establishment Budapest academics and professionals originally from near Lake Balaton southwest of the capital. They had vineyards there until the war and it was on Lake Balaton that uncle János taught Béla to swim. He was proficient but wasn't going to be a champion and it was on the lake not in it that he excelled, and by the 1936 Olympics Béla was a junior kayak champion. A certain, they said, for the 1940 Games – then another war. He was studying electrical engineering at the Palatine Joseph University of Technology under Professor József Liksa. Biata smiles as the cityscape of her birthplace seems to float through her recollections: *I remember my mother talking about Professor Liksa after the war. And the university, it was on the river in Buda, very grand, like a palace with columns and arches. On my last birthday in Budapest we went for a walk along the river and looked across at the citadel on the cliffs – the university was right next to it. Even after all the fighting it was beautiful. But we lived on the other side of the river – we just looked.*

Electrical engineering – an essential industry in a country at war and Professor Liksa saved Béla from the military and the eastern front. Connections – valuable one day, tainted the next. In the early years of the war local fascists were active in the universities – *Nyilaskeresztes Párt*, the Arrow Cross. Biata is quick to point out that Béla wasn't a member and reading between the lines he was probably an opportunistic hanger-on – relationships of convenience. Less convenient as the war progressed and Miklós Horthy began negotiations with the Russians. The Germans weren't going to allow that and the Arrow Cross under Ferenc Szálasi took control in October 1944, resuming the transports to Auschwitz that Horthy had expeditiously ceased, shooting Jews and anyone else who crossed their paths and throwing the bodies into the river – they could be seen floating past the University of Technology.

Béla was not really involved – so Biata says – he was just caught up in events. Too caught up to escape notice after the guns fell silent and the citizens of what had once been a Habsburg imperial capital emerged into its ruins in February 1945 – into a new world order. Fast-forward past a brief window of democratic opportunity and Mátyás Rákosi was back in power. Connections – previously tainted and now life-saving. Béla was lucky not to be summarily shot, but his engineering career was over and he certainly wasn't going to represent Hungary in the 1948 London Olympics. Past his peak by the 1952 Helsinki Games, he'd been rehabilitated enough to be an assistant coach and by 1956, married and with a daughter, he was with the kayak team preparing for the trip to Melbourne.

Nine-teen-fifty-six – Biata says it slowly and then is quiet, as if the effort of summoning up its associations has exhausted her. The year after she arrived in Silkwood. Where the talk in the street was what was happening at the sugar mill. Not Hungary – or Suez or Melbourne: *I couldn't understand that nobody was interested. It was so important for us but people in Silkwood didn't seem to care. So we listened to the radio and my mother phoned relatives in Sydney. She had to go to Innisfail to make a call in those days, to the post office. She went nearly every day.*

A wagon load of "hydraulic" pipes stopped beside the mango-trees of the Lion's Den.

*Jack Idriess
knew the Lions Den…*
The tin scratchers, 1959

*Silkwood castle seems to be
channeling Watts Towers…*

THE STARS AND STRIPES
Hungarian Refugees Who Fled Terror in Their Homeland

Eleven of the 26 Hungarians who arrived in the U.S. Zone this week after seizing a Hungarian airplane. The refugees, who told a story of "Communist terror" in their homeland, all said they wanted to settle in countries beyond the sphere of Russian domination. (See story on Page 2.) — S&S Photo

*… a moment
and message from
forty-five years ago.*

Twelve days – that's how long the revolution lasted. Twelve days and thousands of lives. Biata talks rapidly about the uprising, shifting from album to album to find exhibits – newspaper clippings, photos of relatives killed or imprisoned – evidence for the prosecution. And the Olympic team was in the middle of it; several members died in the early days of the uprising and Dezső Gyarmati, already a national hero as the captain of the water polo team, rallied the Olympic athletes as they returned form the Red Star hotel in the Svábhegy foothills just outside the capital, and from the Tartar training grounds seventy kilometres further west. They gathered at the Grand Hotel on Margit Island, surrounded by parklands ablaze with autumn colours and separated from the fires of Budapest by the Danube, heavy with sediment and history. And more blood and bodies.

Gyarmati formed a revolutionary committee that adopted the Kossuth flag that replaced the communist heraldry on the Hungarian tricolour with the coat of arms of the short-lived Republic of 1919. As the team met the fighting had stopped – for the moment – and a decision was made that the team would still go to Melbourne, to represent what they thought was a new nation. They left the next day by bus for Prague without knowing if they'd be able to get flights out and it was another six days before 156 team members boarded chartered planes at Ruzyně airport for the journey to Melbourne. Just a day before, Russian tanks had surrounded Budapest, and by the time they were airborne it was split by armoured thrusts along the Danube; fighting went on for nearly a week. The day that the Hungarian Olympic team touched down in Darwin was also the first day of a brief silence in their homeland between revolution and reprisals. [97]

Biata doesn't know how involved Béla was, he was older than most of the athletes and he'd learned to keep his head down. He marched under the Kossuth flag at the opening ceremony in Melbourne and rallied the canoe and kayak team on the water at Lake Wendouree near Ballarat. He must have been a good coach; although they won only one gold, Hungary ended up with seven of twenty-four kayak and canoe medals, the same number as Russia. There was daylight to the rest. Béla's job was over by December 1, five days before the water polo semi-final between Hungary and Russia that saw Dezső Gyarmati's team triumph 4:0, the photo of team-mate Ervin Zádor's bloodied face, overnight, an iconic image of the Cold War. Two days later, just before the closing ceremony, a reduced Hungarian team flew out of Melbourne and gold medal-winner Dezső Gyarmati went with them: *He had a wife and daughter in Budapest.*

Biata repeats it slowly and precisely: *He had a wife and daughter in Budapest, a young daughter just two years old. He went back.* She knows this history in day-by-day detail, what the back-stories were and what happened afterwards – to all of them. Including the thirty-four who left Australia just before Christmas for the United States – *Operation Griffin.* Béla also had a wife and child in Budapest but he didn't go back. And he wasn't on the plane to the United States. Uncle János probably would have been shocked. With members of the soccer team that played on the last day of competition, he stayed in Australia.

He was no hero – Biata is blunt. And of his decision not to return to his wife and daughter: *I don't judge him for that.* But she does, despite her hatred of the communists she doesn't respect Béla – too often flying a flag of convenience, even when it was the Kossuth flag. And always seeming to land on his feet, even when he'd tramped on others'. Ballarat – the middle of nowhere, but not far from the Snowy Scheme. Unlike those who went to America and the *Freedom Tour*[98] or stayed in Australia to play soccer, his sporting career was over. But his training as an electrical engineer finally paid off. And maybe connections – again. Some members of the Arrow Cross who fled Hungary after the fall of the fascist government in 1945 made it to Australia and were as active as the Americans encouraging Hungarians to defect. Béla knew one of them: *He called himself Josef but that wasn't his name, Béla knew him from the last months of the war.*[99] Biata knew about him, he'd been living in Melbourne for years – an open secret in the Hungarian community. There were lots of *Nyilaskeresztes Párt* in Australia and they lived to hate Communists. Glossing over their fascist origins and sharing their anti-Soviet obsession, Biata focuses on the pragmatics of 1956: *He gave Béla a place to stay until he got a job. It didn't take long.* It didn't take long for a whole new life.

His marriage wasn't happy – Biata skims over the fascist connections and family abandonment, she seems to be clawing for some way to excuse Béla: *He wasn't Dezső Gyarmati, he wasn't a hero in Hungary.* And within a couple of years he'd met a Polish woman at Cooma – twenty years younger than him and also working on the Snowy Scheme. But it didn't last and in 1962 she left him for a local man her own age; left Béla and the child they had in 1960 – László. The story is about to move on but a child is more than baggage, and a mother leaving is a rupture not a departure. I repeat her statement: *She left László…* After a moment of hesitation Biata picks up the dropped thread: *Béla was a difficult man, angry, always thought he had been hard done by, that he was better and everyone else was wrong. And he had the law on his side. She left for another man – it was black and white in those days. But Béla tried to do the right thing, he moved to Sydney with László and he found another woman – Doris. A good woman I was told, she didn't have children. She was older than Béla, but the only woman that László ever knew as mother.*

The approach of a vehicle on the gravel driveway draws Biata back to the Silkwood present. The engine stops, the door slams, footsteps moving away from the house and moments later an engine starts in one of the nearby sheds. Over the sounds of cane farm life Biata continues the story: *Béla died young, around 1975, he must have been in his mid-fifties, stomach cancer – very quick. The stepmother was about sixty then, László was just fifteen. Then she died too. I only know this from my uncle Géza who was still in Sydney. He tried to look out for László but Géza died in 1980. They all died within five years. László was alone – and he disappeared.*

Disappeared… Although that seems to fit with the man I know from Bamaga and Cooktown, László was just twenty then, alone after a lifetime of losses and with nowhere obvious to go: *We heard nothing until he arrived in Silkwood five years later. It was the first time I had ever met him. He had found his real mother – but it didn't work out. He wouldn't talk about it but I think she was sick – mental. He didn't stay long, he wanted to go further north. He didn't say where to, just north. The next I heard was from a doctor in Cooktown years later. I don't remember his name but he told me*

László was staying in the hospital there, he'd had a breakdown of some sort. The doctor seemed very caring.

We talk of much else, but most of the rest I know from Mick.

Cooktown, December 18, 1996

There's no sense of history at the Tropic Breeze caravan park at the other end of town from the Seaview. The only reference to the past is a sad sculpture of a prospector panning for gold, maybe trying his luck on the way to the Palmer River by foot, or waiting to get a lift on the Cooktown to Laura railway that passed by just a stone throw away, although the rush was pretty much over by the time that was operational. Jack Idriess may have walked by, perhaps to the racecourse or to farewell a mate at the cemetery, someone who died young and close to town. A drunken brawl or a prank gone wrong. Someone like Charlie Goodall, the *Bad Boy of the Two Mile*, who liked to stir up the police:

A piercing yell drew startled eyes up the street to a clatter of galloping hooves. Necks craned to blood curdling screeches as a bareback rider in pants and with bare hairy chest raced past, his whiskers mixed with the horse's mane as he resoundingly spanked his mount's rump with a battered felt hat. Arms and legs going hammer and tongs he flew past yelling defiance at the police station and charged right on down the long street to the Sea View. I thought he would leap straight up on to the Musgrave and plunge over the side, but he wheeled on a threepenny bit and came galloping back to ear-splitting yells.[100]

As Charlie Goodall was heading back that day the police were waiting for him with a rope across the road and he was probably tempted to take it at full gallop. He might have died in the fall if he'd tried. But he didn't, and avoided the trip down Charlotte Street to the cemetery. Even so, probably lots of opportunities for Jack to be graveside in those days, then on to a wake at the West Coast or the Commercial that the old timers still remembered as the Whitehorse. Or Jack might have passed this way while visiting the grave of an old mate on his way back from the Torres and the Fly River in Papua in the late 1920s. By that time the gold rush in New

Guinea inland from Lae was in full swing. William Shark-eye Park had kept the finds secret long enough to make his pile and was long gone from the Wau. He'd taken the money and Annie Agnes Quinn to a new life in Canada.

From this end of town it's a short walk to the hospital, but I drive. Better to have options as the day progresses. New systems – people and processes – and new layers of language. Floating on top are the inflated phrases of vision and mission pasted from policy documents designed for elevator interviews – like the froth on a cappuccino, it's sweetened and insubstantial with a dark coating that sticks to the lips. Beneath that there's a tepid and tasteless stratum of policy and practice directions, and directives that conflate technical jargon with substance and meaning. And for those who persevere what's left is a grim sediment of gravel and grinds – the language of subalterns whose mimicry is devoid of understanding or interest. The new managerialism – one size fits all.

It didn't fit doctor Mick – he went to Collinsville. It would have meant a lot of personal disappointment to leave Cooktown, to take his whole family from what he talked about as a tropical paradise to an inland coal-mining community. And his work was more than the job; he valued his relationships with the community and loved the connection that it provided with society's outriders. Nobody was too mundane or marginal to escape his interest and no patient would be dismissed. Bluntly abused, maybe, but never dismissed.

Behind the hospital, builders and labourers are easing themselves into the day. The slab for a new primary care clinic is down on the other side of two demountables, one of which is the base for the mental health team. There's a clutch of chairs nearby in the shade of Mick's sandpaper tree, all that's left of the bush medicine garden. A nurse and two health workers smoking and drinking tea sit at one end, László at the other, his eyes fixed at some point in the middle distance. His posture is rigid, straight-backed and head immobile, elbows at right angles with forearms flat along the arms of the chair. He's wearing something that looks like a caftan and he's very early – I point out that his appointment isn't for another couple of hours: *That's exactly correct doctor, for ten o'clock. For ten o'clock, Wednesday December eighteen, 1996. That's today doctor, you're exactly right, the wonders of science, of technology, of technoscience, the atomic clock, time and tide doctor. No waiting for them but I'm waiting for you...*

László's monologue seems to be projected to join his gaze somewhere beyond me. I cut through to offer a cup of tea that he declines and accepts in the same breath and as I head to the pantry, just after I offer to meet early if there's a no-show, it resumes: *But it's ten o'clock on my card doctor, in blue and white, the order of things. You can't change the order of things doctor. Even psychiatrists can't alter reality, only if they use drugs that bend reality, bend time doctor, spacetime...*

Spacetime – bent out of shape. Minds distorted by illness, drugs, medicines – by life. But it's relative; from my own spacetime continuum László seems all over the place despite drugs, talking, challenging, supporting. I've tried imagining how I seem to him from the realities he experiences. Over the two years we've been meeting there have been moments when we may as well have been in different dimensions, but others when, for a moment and sometimes longer, we're in the same plane where our realities come close to harmonising. Whether it's the medications or something else I don't know. But I still seem to represent incompatible qualities of being. I'm *psycho-the-rapist*, a *drug dependent psychopath*, the *antichrist* – and *Ördög*. After spending an hour or so on the internet I figured out that *Ördög* is from Magyar mythology and represents the devil in some form, creator of just about everything bad for humanity. And then I'm doctor Hunter again and he thanks me for my time and effort. He doesn't act out, keeps appointments, and never refuses recommendations even when he assures me that he knows I'm driven by malice or ignorance. Whatever it means, he seems to trust me, maybe even to like me.

The only other person that applied to was doctor Mick. That was a special relationship, enough for László to identify Mick as next of kin when he surfaced from delirium and drugs in Cairns Base Hospital after being evacuated from Lockhart. And when he came out of hospital he returned to Cooktown and the same caravan park he'd lived in four years before, and eventually ended up working at Mick's place again. Mick, Jan and their kids were his social world but he'd learned to keep his other realities to himself. Now they've all gone. On the surface there's no indication that their departure affected him in any way. I can imagine László's parting remarks after Mick's tortured goodbye, probably something like: *Doctor McLoughlin, I'm sure your replacement will be a competent doctor. I've just managed to get another Idriess book in at the library, maybe you can get it in Collinsville, I've read it before and it's a good read…*

If you read between the lines. When it comes to Idriess, László is always reading between the lines – and writing between them. He's been banned from taking Idriess books from the library because they either don't come back or are filled with notations. Mostly indecipherable, I've seen them. After I commented on his reference to Shark-eye Park two years ago it forged a connection of sorts – a metalanguage I suppose. But it's almost impossible to separate his exposure to Idriess, his understandings of the books, and his beliefs about Jack – László always talks about Jack, never Ion.

Making sense of it hasn't been straightforward, the relevant elements need to be sifted out as they float by in the turbulent, unfiltered stream. Every now and again something suggestive appears and I grab it. Like the passing mention of Shark-eye Park, a piece of the jigsaw that gave nothing away about what the big picture was – except that it involved New Guinea and Idriess. Another piece was Doris, who was Elizabeth Grace from Tenterfield. From Mick and Biata I now know that Doris is not just an elderly dementing woman in Bamaga, but the stepmother who appeared in László's life after his mother walked out when he was a toddler. But there seemed to be no pieces connected to his father, Béla, who's always referred to as *uram* Halassy, a stilted, formal Magyar version of mister Halassy.

That is, until another piece appeared, fleetingly. It surfaced as the flow of ideas became more than usually tortured, as if by unseen boulders beneath the surface related somehow to childhood and family. I was trying to talk in displacement about his father, but I was probably clumsy and transparent, speculating about how difficult it would be for a foreigner to fit into a society with different values, manners and language. It set him off on a tangent about the *ÁVO* and *Ördög*, then: *It's all in the cards doctor, you should know that, in the flush of life doctor. Ace, King, Queen, Jack. All in spades doctor, in the dark doctor and not in clubs. It's the spades doctor, the Jack of spades. Prospectors doctor, digging for the truth, to understand…*

The Jack of spades, Jack the prospector – Jack Idriess again. But it was more, and as we continued to talk I realized he was telling me about Ion Idriess the teacher – Béla's mentor. With some informed guesswork I began to get a clearer fix on László's early life. When his father defected after the Olympics he had virtually no English but was a quick learner. And his tutor was the most popular Australian novelist of the 1950s, whose writing was simple and clear, and who told interesting stories about this country – Ion Idriess. Béla had dozens of Idriess books that taught him about his adopted land and language, its idioms and idiosyncrasies.

But that's just about László's exposure to Idriess, not about how Jack and the books became meaningful. Since visiting Biata in Silkwood I know that although he had an older paternal sister in Hungary, and may have younger maternal siblings in Australia, his experience was as an only child who was probably just dimly aware that something terrible had happened earlier in his short life, some unfathomable trauma of which nobody would speak and about which he could only fantasize. Whatever the relationship was like between his parents during the first year of his life, it wasn't happy, and his mother may have been depressed – maybe that's why she left. Whether or not, when he needed her to support him she was gone. After that it was *uram* Halassy, until Doris arrived a year or so later.

Older and childless, Doris couldn't have been blind to the gulf between Béla and his son and I presume she tried to fill it. And I know that at night it was Doris who sat next to László reading to him as he fell asleep, he was able to tell me that much. She read what was in the house – Idriess – each chapter a story in itself from what seemed like another world. Idriess, fantasy, mother, intimacy, dreams – all woven together. As he grew older she included the tales of head-hunters and cannibals, exciting and threatening in equal measure, like his father's stories about *ÁVO* and *Ördög*.

And László continued to read Ion Idriess as he went through high school. Soothing and exciting in its other-worldliness, perhaps it filled an emotional void. It was all adventure – and it was so real.

And then there was Bethlehem. I was trying to gather together the fragments fitting between his first stay in Cooktown and when I met him outside the service station in Bamaga a few years later. I knew he'd gone to Tenterfield, and then Bethlehem came up: *Bedlam doctor, I really went to Bedlam – Bedlam, Bethlam, Bethlehem. Into the Inn doctor or out of the out, out of Bethlehem. Out before* Ördög, *out before the beasts and onto the road. Out of Bethlehem, out of Tenterfield and north doctor – north...*

Bethlehem, the birthplace of Jesus, the virgin birth. Possibly a reference to his stepmother, she who'd never birthed a child but was his mother. Not quite immaculate conception but in the frame if the connections are loose. And maybe he could never imagine *uram* Halassy having sex. Back on the internet I found that the Tenterfield Tourism site has a page titled *Famous Sons & Daughters*, even though it recognized no famous daughters. But they claimed Major JF Thomas who defended Breaker Morant in South Africa, the last time an Australian soldier was tried by a British court martial. And Captain Thunderbolt, Sir Henry Parkes and Peter Allen. The same search brought up a familiar name, but not on the Tourism site, on a filmography site – Gary Foley. All interesting, none revealing. And then I entered Tenterfield and Idriess – bingo.

Born on 20 September 1889 at Waverley in Sydney, to Walter Owen Idriess and Juliette Windeyer, her second marriage – *Ion Llewellyn Idriess.* But his father had moved to Tenterfield three months earlier, and that's where Ion spent the first four years of his life, and where his earliest memories were cast. More than sixty years later he remembered, as a child, walking along the railroad that had arrived in town just a few years earlier:

Timber and shrubbery then came right up to the back yards of the little mountain township of Tenterfield. Now those humble homes, those dark, low-built stores have grown into a prosperous town, the forest vanished to the open, grassy paddocks of developed closer settlement.[101]

In 1893 the family moved to Lismore but the Tenterfield/Idriess connection was too obvious not to be relevant to László's thought-chains. Those were the only pieces that seemed to fit into a coherent image – until I talked to Biata. And it took six months to get his permission for me to go to Silkwood to meet her. But eventually he agreed – sort of: *I have no relatives in Silkwood doctor, not Bea – or C or D or any other person related to* uram *Halassy. Only psychopaths go there doctor, maybe they will let you go because of your needle-dependent psychopath status but it will avail you not, or knot you in travails. They will have your souls doctor, Magyars and Italians, feasting on saints doctor, that's what they do there. But go if you must.*

I did, I went to Silkwood, but from his reactions in our meetings over the eight months since, I know that even though he'd agreed, he was angry that I had – I'd gone outside his story, his reality. Any mention of Silkwood or his family still triggers a torrent of agitated connections and today is no different. After waiting for an hour to see me László is silent. But after about ten minutes I mention family and, as if he's been waiting for the pretext, he's off: *Opening doors doctor, you can't open doors in the madhouse doctor. Seclusion for protection – protection from the needle-dependent psychopaths, the rapists doctor, from the volts on the skull. Why do you do it doctor Hunter, why did you join them. Was it your complex doctor or a doctor complex. Hunter – where does it come from doctor, your hunter past. Take the fifth doctor, or go to the island…*

It goes on and on, twisting, dipping and plunging, like being in a kayak that's bouncing through rapids before emerging into a calm stretch as the stream deepens and widens. Even then, what's going on beneath the surface remains a mystery but there's time to try and make sense of what's passing by. As long as I don't give in to the temptation to dismiss all of the turbulence as psychotic rambling – as meaningless babble – a moment to consider what's bubbling up before the next cataracts begin, the next surprises. And surprises there are – what comes to the surface is not just about László, today it's about me.

Most psychiatrists are promiscuous in pursuit of understanding, using any sources available – adding to a collage that's constantly changing and expanding. If it's going well patterns coalesce into a cohesive picture. Of course it depends on the clinician; lazy ones rely on their predecessors' assessments, some are inflexible after they've made their minds up, and others mix in their own issues and projections so that the patient is always seen through a distorted lens – a glass darkly that reflects as much light as it transmits. As long as they're not passed from one practitioner to another, patients do the same. They take note of what's said to them and how – of psychiatrists' attitudes and prejudices. The opinions of other patients, comments of nurses and receptionists, a wedding ring, photographs on a desk, the number of framed degrees cluttering the walls, items of clothing, how often a session is allowed to be interrupted by phone calls or people at the door, the tone of responses and the words they use about other patients – nothing is irrelevant. How it's put together is another matter – but it all goes into the mix. And some patients are more skilled than their therapists at detecting hesitation, ambivalence, mistrust, vulnerability, indifference – and bullshit. Those with particular personality disorders are standouts – intelligent borderline patients can draw a therapist into a net of their own narcissism. And there's plenty of that, some psychiatrists as lost as the outsiders who fall into their web. Put them together and it's a recipe for chaos and blurred boundaries – again, plenty of that.

László doesn't have a personality disorder. His issues are very different – he has a carapace, a rigid shell of difference. There's no enmeshment; he's detached, isolated – but observant. Everything is being noted, even when he seems elsewhere, it's all being sorted and stored. Filed in idiosyncratic ways and retrieved through connections and in sequences encoded in his psychosis. Sometimes it's like listening to a foreign language with phrases and neologisms that are decipherable only if I can pick up on obscure associations. And then there are questions which seem somehow prescient, that feel like he's intuitively on the money about me, questions that are statements – *Why are you a psychiatrist... Why are you here... Who are you...* And then there are comments that seem to be background static but which I know aren't, even when I don't know why – *take the fifth doctor Hunter, or go to the island.*

CHAPTER 8

2008: Cooktown to Cape Weymouth

Take the fifth doctor Hunter, or go to the island. Maybe he was just rambling; I could have dismissed it but, as it turned out, I didn't – it stuck. Even though I didn't understand what he meant back then, two decades ago, I recognized that it wasn't a meaningless conjunction of words. In fact it was the conjunction itself – *or* – that signaled non-randomness and ensured that it would filter back into awareness over the years since, and on *The Island* now. Whether he intended it or not he pushed a button, and each time that phrase floated back into awareness it would take hold. I might not even be aware of it until I realized that I was ruminating, trying to figure out why it carried personal weight. Lots of ideas and associations but no answers. And whatever it means for me I have no idea what it meant to László.

Or – either *or* – one or the other. *Take the fifth*, choose not to incriminate myself – avoid being compromised. *Or* – go to *The Island*. And now I've done it, I'm on *The Island*. And thinking about László. Again, attempting to distill meaning and intent where, perhaps, there was never any in the first place. In a way it's like how it felt when he was my patient and I was trying to unravel his dream experiences – it did my head in then and still does now. I know it would be better to let it all go, but it won't go – or I don't want it to. Maybe because of the meanings I think I find, the interpretations I layer onto his words from my own life and experiences. That much is real, and it has to do with making choices, being authentic or compromised – getting involved or choosing to be a bystander.

Particular moments and places; that's what it takes to hold on to memories and thoughts, to think them through toward some sort of clarity. And this is one of those places. Jack Idriess knew this spot well and would have sat here looking in the same direction a century ago. Waiting to be remembered, waiting to be rescued. Eventually a lugger appeared and he was off to a new life, from tin scratcher to pen pusher. In the end Charlie left too. And he didn't – he was trapped by fate and by the ink on the page – he left Howick but he's still on *Madman's Island*. And over the months Jack and Charlie were together on Howick they probably climbed *The Peak* together on a moonless night – to this spot – and looked towards the Coquet light – the only sign of the rest of the world. But sometimes you have to look past the light – into the darkness beyond. And beyond the Coquet light, thirty-five kilometres from Howick, is the Turtle Group.

The Turtle Group, July 8, 2008

The Turtle Group is four miles to the north of Point Lookout; the islets are encircled by a horse-shoe shaped coral reef, and consist of six islands, all low and bushy.

Phillip Parker King (1827)

Heading north again, for me the third time threading the necklace. The Queen's necklace, the only living structure visible from space – living for the time being but maybe not for long. The last time I kayaked this part of the coast was 2003 and in the five years since I've paddled thousands of kilometres along the coast, but never alone and always heading northwards to Cairns from points further south. From as far away as

Clairview. *The only spot the Bruce Highway meets the sea between the Gold Coast and Bowen* – that's the claim. With Jon but also with Jethro then and now, three middle-aged men together each year, camping on and exploring dozens of islands – little worlds, lots of stories.

Clairview – as south as we've gone and about as low as we're willing to go. Low enough to interrupt our night-before-departure routine of organizing and reorganizing dry-bags and provisions ready for an early morning, high tide launch. It was mid-evening and we were just in the fall of light outside the bar area of the Clairview Beach Holiday Park where a few locals and barra-tragics, taking time out from the air-conditioned comfort of their $200k mobile homes, were performing. Lucky to be in the shadows – out of sight and out of the action. Everyone else was part of the act, from the loud, inebriated young man pretending to butt-fuck a mate too drunk to realize or care, to the circle of similarly pissed middle-aged men getting down a few more Bundys while slurring encouragement, to the women in the party, either too far gone to feign surprise or simply accepting that this is what blokes do. And the barmaid – unphased and, presumably, not surprised. Paul Theroux enjoyed the opportunities that Cooktown provided for caustic social commentary – he would have loved Clairview. But those were different journeys, still with the south-easterly behind but taking us to other islands – Keswick-St Bees, the Whitsundays, Gloucester Island, Cape Upstart, Cape Bowling Green, Cape Cleveland, Magnetic Island, the Palm Group, Hinchinbrook, the Brooks, the Family Islands, the Barnards, Fitzroy – always heading home.

Now we're back at sea north of Cairns in the Turtle Group, three days paddle out of Cooktown – I landed here in 2000 on my solo trip to the Tip. These islands were rich grounds for turtle and dugong hunting by *Guugu Yimithirr* and a calm to moderate weather anchorage for coastal shipping under sail in the nineteenth and early twentieth centuries. Not just maritime explorers, Ludwig Leichardt came ashore on his way back to Sydney after his 1845 expedition to Port Essington – like Somerset doomed to disappoint as a *Singapore of the north coast*. In early 1846 he was on the *Heroine* under Captain Martin McKenzie *en route* to Sydney. They over-nighted on Turtle and Leichardt went to the mainland to look for water. They weren't alone and McKenzie took no chances in setting up their camp:

> *The stores and all necessaries were landed, firearms and ammunition for the number of men, and two two-pound swivel guns, which could command all parts of the island, or rather sandbank, as the natives seemed to have a number of canoes, and were well armed with all the Australian weapons.*[102]

McKenzie was near the Turtle Group again a month later. He was heading back to Port Essington as commodore of a small fleet, with the *Enchantress* and the *Sapphire*, which had the *Ariel* in tow, two years before it would pick up Jackey Jackey on the shore of Newcastle Bay. But around midnight on 24 April the *Heroine* hit a reef. In the confusion the lifeboats on the weather side couldn't be launched and went down with the *Heroine* and seven passengers and crew including the captain's infant son. The rest were picked up by the *Ariel*, but not McKenzie who was in the water with his daughter:

> *For myself, having a young child three years old, in one arm, and being heavily clothed, I could not fetch the boat, the tide running along the edge of the reef carrying me away. After considerable time I got into a heavy tide ripple and eddy which turned me round and round several times, and took me under: in my drowning struggles I must have parted with the child. I fortunately rose in a smoother spot, and when a little recovered, took off my clothes and merely floated until daylight, the heavy seas often breaking over and completely swamping me. At daylight I saw the Sapphire some distance from me, and was picked up by her boat when I was in speaking distance of them.*[103]

McKenzie was transferred to the *Enchantress* which stopped at the Turtle Group as the journey continued to Port Essington. Don't look back.

Half-a-dozen cays and infant islands on a cluster of reefs that frustrate landing except at high tide, which it's not and so we wait, with the wind at twenty knots from the south-east. It's been unrelenting since leaving Cooktown and swept us north past Indian Head, to a first night camp at Cape Bedford, and on yesterday to Three Isles and the mandatory climb of the navigation tower, Jon and Jethro leaning at twenty degrees to the vertical into winds gusting at thirty to forty knots at the top. My third time on Three Isles, the first time for Jon and Jethro – new eyes. Familiarity and difference everywhere. In 2003 Axel and I climbed past an eagles' nest on the fourth level of the tower. That's gone, replaced by an even bigger nest at the top. The air was clearer than I recalled and in the afternoon light the shadow of the tower was so sharp that our profiles were silhouetted against the dense foliage in the centre of the island. In 2003 I was here six weeks later in the year and the island was bare, the air heavy with the heat, dust and smoke off the mainland at the end of the dry season. And the horizon indistinct – Lizard was just visible then but yesterday the conical form of Cooks Look stood sharp against the sky. As was the humped outline of the Direction Islands just to its south with Two Isles in the foreground. And to the west a long line of hills in the distance passing behind the mesa-shaped profile of North Cape Bedford to the south-west, ending behind the trapezoidal form of South Cape Bedford and Mound Stone. And all around, the nightshades of deep water flecked by wind-whipped whitecaps drew the gaze toward the source.

At around eighty feet above ground the platform hummed with the gusting south-easterly, vibrating in tune with winds driven across thousands of miles of unbroken ocean, funnelled along the edge of the continent and racing unchecked across, around and through that insignificant lattice. All that was left was the vibration and, for the three passengers on the bridge deck of the wind vessel, a moment of connection in being – a moment more powerful for being shared.

Then, in the afternoon with those winds beam-on, to Two Isles, the now familiar casuarina-backed beach, the reef walk to the windward island, the succulent garden and eagle nest, the mangrove forest and fruit-bat colony. Same and different – the ammunition box found by Axel long buried or swept away. In the centre of the island the trees are now draped in an impenetrable, iridescent filigree vine. Dodder laurel – *Cassytha filiformis* – so dense Jon was wrapped in and suspended by it, hammocked in a chrysalis that refused to surrender him back to us until we tore him free. In the evening the familiar lights of Cape Flattery were in the distance. Three figures around the fire, and in the faltering light three tents at the edge of darkness. And three kayaks tethered to the trees above the high tide line – never take the tide for granted.

And today to the Turtle Group and a tide-delayed landing across reef and intertidal beach-rock – nature's cement. Onto a shore that from a distance promised sand but delivered coral rubble. But a place for the night with Nymph Island a line on the horizon to the north and, just out of sight to the northwest, the Howicks – and *Madman's Island*. That's for tomorrow, but as the driftwood starts to flare up the campsite is transformed by the fire's glow, the empty distance now a foreshortened cocoon of warmth and light. But still, begging comparisons: *Not quite a dingly-dell Jon – where was it…*

> — *St Bees, Jon – Jethro wasn't on that trip but you and I paddled through the channel between St Bees and Keswick, just south of the Whitsundays. The coast along the channel didn't look good. Then just around the northern tip of St Bees there was an outrageous flat, fine sand beach on clear water, with the dingly-dell tucked into the northwest corner. Trees to the waterline, shaded flat campsite, a small creek in the background and nobody there. Except for an American couple rowing ashore with beer.*

Jethro wasn't there but wants to know: *What makes a dingly-dell…* Another headspace thing, part of journeying. Like Jon, Jon and Jethro – no longer Ernest, Chris and Geoff – signifying that the conventions of work and home are left behind. The journey brings a different reality that is moment-focused, and relationships that are intimate and transparent. It allows a safe return to a less complicated and youthful space. Not escape, just a privileged suspension, with its own unstated codes – like *what makes a dingly-dell*.

A dingly-dell is so by consensual agreement, a comfortable and intimate space in a setting that's spectacularly beautiful and where there's no possibility of others intruding. A deserted island is a good starting point and that beach on St Bees was it. An afternoon with Jon singing to accompaniment on pots and shaker, my contribution *Danny-boy* on the E-flat tin whistle. And a retired couple from San Diego living their dream – it was special for them too. That was the dingly-dell by which all are judged and found wanting and Jethro wants to know what's in store: *What about tomorrow, any chance of a dingly-dell there...*

— *Jon, tell Jethro about the island with the grave where we stopped last time, a shit of a place.*
— *Well, Jethro, he speaks the truth – it was on the northern end of Howick and it was a shit of a place. But hopefully we'll get to a different part, where we weren't able to stop last time. After that it's a pretty short paddle to Noble where there's a real dingly-dell under a wongai tree, and a lot more.*
— *Why not go straight to Noble...*

Why not go straight to Noble... Bypass the Howicks and forget about *Madman's Island*. Let Idriess rest – let Jack and Charlie rest. Maybe let László rest. Not likely.

Coquet Island, July 9, 2008

The passage between 2 [Houghton] and 3 [Coquet] is safe, and has seven and eight fathoms: the north-west side of 3 is of rocky approach; but the opposite side of the strait is bold to; the anchorage is tolerably good. The Mermaid drove, but it was not considered to be caused by the nature of the bottom, which is of soft sand, and free from rocks.

Phillip Parker King (1827)

It was a great start but not sustained. Leaving the Turtles the sails were up early to winds building under a clear sky, probably around fifteen to twenty knots consistently and gusting to thirty by midday, shifting from south to south-east. A kayak under sail is a lot less predictable than a yacht. To stay upright without a keel and with winds on the beam the paddler has to lean into the wind to counter the pressure on the sail, or use the paddle as an outrigger to leeward when the kayak is going fast enough that the blade levers off the surface. Either way, paddling or sailing a kayak in high winds is difficult and there's constant pressure on the hull to turn into the wind. Where there's a swell, particularly if the waves are big enough to be breaking, the situation is more complicated. The natural response of a kayak to waves cresting on the beam is to roll and capsize. Waves from the stern can accelerate a kayak down the face and, again, it's likely to turn side on to the wave – and to roll and capsize. And that can happen quickly when the swell lifts the stern out of the water, suspending the rudder in mid-air – no steering. Meanwhile, the course to a destination also requires compensating for windage drift by maintaining a heading to windward of where you want to go, increasing the kayak's tendency to turn. That was the situation – demanding but manageable. Maybe compounded by being a lot of fun – surfing waves at sea, out of sight of land, is exciting; add a sail and it's exhilarating.

A spirit sail is an inverted triangle, a small version in sailcloth of the woven mat sails that drove Polynesian and Micronesian sailing canoes across the Pacific – that's what Jon and Jethro have on rigid kayaks. Mine is a collapsible kayak made of high-tech fabric on an aluminium frame. It's a double configured for one paddler and is much bigger than theirs – they call it the *mother-ship* – and it supports a two-and-a-half metre collapsible mast fixed to the base keel-rods and mounted through the mid-deck, carrying either a genoa or a spinnaker. For a kayak, my sails are enormous – a plus or a minus depending on circumstances. That afternoon it was a plus, but maintaining course against slippage from winds moving to the east was difficult – and Jon and Jethro were off playing. Which was a problem. When the moment focuses one's attention, what's happening to others is lost. With a divergence of just fifteen degrees, after a few minutes two kayakers can be separated by hundreds of metres. At that distance, with swells of two to three metres, not only does the other kayak disappear, so do the blade flashes.

That morning there were three kayakers doing their own thing. Fortunately the skies were clear – add rain and visibility can collapse to a few paddle-lengths. But between the Turtles and the Howicks it was all play and no precaution – until the others were gone, the horizons clear and clouds gathering to the south. That was a problem; I was the one who knew where we were going, the only one with maps and who understood what the default options were which, given the wind, looked a certainty. To communicate and regroup in emergency, other than by VHF radio – which we don't have – the options are limited. The whistles tethered to our life-vests can be heard up to fifty metres – in good conditions without a lot of wind. Also in my life-vest is a packet of eight small aerial pencil-flares which are easy to get at and fire, giving a loud report and six to eight seconds burn at around one hundred feet, visible across kilometres even in daytime – as long as someone's looking. If needed, a carefully directed flare would probably deter a crocodile, but although we've seen lots of crocs we've never had to fire a flare in anger.

The mast on my kayak is the default signaling system. With the genoa down and my iridescent, sun-safe hat tethered to the halyard with a couple of metres play from the masthead, the wind lifts it to about three metres above deck height, and it's visible at greater distances when the kayak is on the crest of a wave. It worked, we regrouped by mid-afternoon and the options were laid out. We could have proceeded as planned to Howick, but with no chance of turning back into winds gusting to thirty knots if it wasn't possible to land. And from the 2003 trip it was pretty clear that where Jack Idriess went ashore is not a good landing option in high winds, and where Jon and I camped at the other end of the island was *a shit of a place*. Or we could take the safe option and head to Coquet, the first of the Howick group from the south, to the appealing beach that Jon and I paddled past five years ago and were unable to turn back to. Phillip Parker King also thought it was a reasonable high wind anchorage when he arrived on 12 July 1819 in the cutter *Mermaid* but, as it turned out, not without problems:

The island, No. 3, being low, protected us only from the swell, and as the wind blew fresh from the South-East during the night, with a cross tide, the cutter rode very uneasily. At four o'clock the next morning the cutter was found to have drifted at least half a mile to leeward, but whether during the first or middle part of the night, it was not easy to discover; had the island No. 2, been a quarter of a mile nearer, we should have had little chance of escaping shipwreck, for the night was very dark, and her distance did not exceed that when she was brought up by veering cable.[104]

As for the *Mermaid* so for us – the beach and anchorage are protected from the prevailing swell but not the wind. Coquet is a vegetated cay with a few coconut trees and sisal, *Agave sisalana*, in the scrub backing a fine-sand beach looking north and west, with a twenty metre high navigation tower at the western end, just behind the beach. To the north, Howick's granite mounds shadow purple against the horizon in the late afternoon light. Soon after Jack Idriess and Charlie arrived on Howick in September 1920, Jack stood on *The Peak* and looked directly at where we're camped:
Three miles away – it seemed only half a mile, looking down from the Peak, was a little sand-bank on top of a coral reef capped by the dense green of mangroves. This was Coquette Island, and visible like a white pillar above the mangroves was its automatic light.[105]

And in the evening, just metres from the modern Coquet light, after a dinner of couscous and tinned tuna, followed by dried fruit and nuts and finished with a hit of chocolate, and as the fire moved into a mature middle age, I mused on connections with Howick in *Madman's Island* and *The opium smugglers*. And also a chapter in *The yellow joss*, published in 1934, midway between the first and second versions of *Madman's Island*, a collection of stories Idriess had heard in his travels, written to *record happenings or incidents in men's lives* along the coast of north Queensland. He insisted most were *transcripts of fact or are largely based on fact, unusual though an occasional one may seem*. But Idriess added a rider; *based on fact* – but – *with two exceptions*, and it's not clear whether *Account rendered* is one of those – or not.

... as the driftwood begins to flare up the campsite is transformed...

... as Jethro was finalising his repacking...

Tombiembui – we called it Dali Rock...

Account rendered has two main characters, Harris and Reynolds, on a pearling cutter anchored at *Coquette Island*, probably where Phillip Parker King thought was a *favourable place*. Looking north from the cutter, just *three miles across the channel loomed the two conical peaks of Howick Island.*[106] And at midnight, from somewhere in the mangrove heart of Howick, they clearly heard twelve bells. The next night, after being rowed across by a terrified *blackboy crew* they were washed through channels in the mangrove forest by the incoming tide, eventually finding what seemed like an ocean steamer with an officer pacing its bridge deck on which was fixed a: *white-painted lifebelt, and the men in the dinghy below read in black letters "S.S. Tait"*[107] As they approached they were able to make out that the bridge was a *framework of driftwood and wreckage built from tree to tree across the creek, and fastened to it, a broad sheet of canvas formed the bridge.* Harris then understood that the figure on the contrived deck was Captain Tersh of the *S.S. Tait* who'd been drunk when he *piled her on a coral reef in the Strait just as twelve bells struck* four years before. They realized that Tersh *had gone clean mad* and tried to call out to him. The response that came back wasn't welcoming:

> "I thought you were they come from the sea," he screamed. "Curse you! Can't you leave me alone even here? Go off into the darkness and drown, you swine! As I saw them drown."[108]

At that moment the tide turns and they're swept back through the maze of channels and out to sea, unsure of what they've just experienced and inclined to put it down to the play of moonlight and imagination. That is, until two days later. Four years to the day after the sinking of Tersh's ship, on a falling king tide they see an object floating out from the mangroves: *"It" was a white-painted lifebelt carrying in bold black letters "S.S. Tait."* [109]

Jon and Jethro listen but they're not really interested in Jack, his life and writing, or penetrating the mists between fact and fiction. Polite or patient – there's a limit and Jon switches tracks when I press the Idriess marginalia related to Howick: *Jon, I know it's hard but I have to say it – Howick Island gets me as excited as, say, free tickets to the Tamworth country music festival, or returning to repping for cigarette companies.* More stories I've heard before, wild times on the backroads of north Queensland. Tales of different times when the economies of towns like Mareeba relied on tobacco and when girls still dreamed of being crowned the Tobacco Queen. Before the industry and its reps were cast among the social pariahs. But for Jethro it's new, Jon and Big Tobacco don't seem to fit, but it was a different time and Jon was on a different journey: *Jethro, it was the '80s. I was a carpenter but getting over it. I had a cousin who worked for them. Seemed like a good gig – travel, a vehicle, perks – so I joined, putting up display cabinets in shops and pubs. And then I went to rep school.*

Jon's gaze doesn't shift, buried somewhere in glowing driftwood embers. Jethro's does, the conjunction – *rep school* – has broken the fire's spell. He looks up and seems to be scrutinizing Jon's face as if suspecting it's a joke. But it's not and the tale moves to the tactics: *Product placement, talking owners into replacing other companies' stock with whatever we were flogging. I worked for WD & HO Wills, they had Craven A, Players and Benson & Hedges. We got a company car, loaded it up with smokes and inducements. We also had darts and roulette – and girls. We'd go to a pub, throw free smokes at the manager. The girls would wander around in bikinis, spot a bloke smoking a different brand – say, Winfields – tell him he was better than to be smoking that crap, and that they'd give him a carton of B&H for his packet of Winfields. Worked every time – brand switching. I even wrote for the company newsletter,* Smoke Signals. *Small but dedicated readership. Hard to squeeze good news out of something that's killing people.*

A forlorn wail penetrates the background static of wind and waves. Maybe an Eastern Curlew – *Numenius madagascariensis* – nearing the end of its intercontinental journey, like us dropping in to the Howicks for the night. Jethro turns on his headlamp, its beam drowned in the darkness. The birds' calls continue, fading into the wind. Jethro probes to understand why Jon eventually gave up on repping. Leaning towards the fire, his face framed *chiaroscuro* against the night, Jon's answer seems to come from the fire as the tale moves towards its end: *Well, I'd been transferred to Cairns but it was still the same gig – long days on the road, lonely nights in cheap motels listening to another rep rooting in the next room. It was time for a change so I went back to carpentry. That was the beginning of* Tropical Erections. *That was the name I traded under, I even put it in the personal columns. Just* Tropical Erections *and a number. Worked a treat.*

Three men's gazes fixed at some point deep in the belly of the flames. Bits of lives spoken into the circle, hanging for a moment in the light then gone in the darkness. Sometimes a conversation, other times isolated memories or reflections inviting no response. Although the night has a direction of its own my thoughts are still on Howick – and Idriess. In the 1970s, a half-century after he spent months just a few kilometres from where we're camped, the ABC journalist, Tim Bowden, interviewed him. It was two or three years before Idriess died but even after fifty books he thought there was more writing to be done and he was still up for challenges, or so it seemed when the conversation drifted to the first time he'd seen hang-gliders: *these two damned things flying all over the damned place right outside our bloody front lawn.* Bowden went along with the frail man in his mid-eighties and asked Idriess if he'd like to try:

Oh, I would and by crikey don't I wish I wasn't toothless, broken leg, one leg in the grave and the other halfway there. This arm had been broken five bloomin' times, it's quite okay again now, and that little lump is from Lone Pine only tiny pin heads of things but they swell up now and I can't bloody well use it.[110]

But the start of that interview was about *Madman's Island* and he told Bowden about the fateful meeting at the West Coast:

Oh, an old prospector from Cape York Peninsula and me were in the West Coast pub one day, from the tin fields, and a Malay came in and his schooner wrecked on a place called Howick Island, and he threw some black stones on the counter and said, "Here Jacky, are these any good?", and I picked them up and they were specimens of wolfram and tin and I said, "Yes, where did you get them?", and he explained he was wrecked off Howick Island, and when he was waiting there for someone to come and pick him up, he walked along the beach and he picked up these black stones, because he'd heard that tin was black and he put them in a sarong and here he was, see. So, me and this fossicker from one of the real savage rivers up the north, we hired a boat and went up there and we landed there and we found the little reef alright, but worked it out, we got a couple of tons of mixed wolfram and tin out of it before it cut right out... But then it turned out that my cobber had nine feet of his intestines taken out in London from German shells - a war wound, and they patched him up at Guy's Hospital and he had to report there every year - write how he was getting on, because he had instruments and things that went into a silver tube that burrowed down right inside, and he had to pour chemicals down this every day to flush out the gas. Well of course, he'd been so drunk in Cooktown he forgot all his gadgets and things.[111]

All his gadgets and things – it's hard to imagine Charlie's injury, or what the surgical treatment consisted of. In the charnel house of First World War military hospitals unorthodox operations were the norm and hundreds of thousands of survivors lived with the consequences.[112] Jack did, and so did Charlie. He was able to get by on Howick without his *gadgets and things* by jury-rigging a replacement from fencing wire, a jam tin and canvas. Instead of the *chemicals* he'd left in Cooktown he used seawater, and: *poured that down his insides and gradually he got rid of this gas. After about three or four hours, his belly went down and down and down.*[113]

Jack saw it all and in *Madman's Island* he described a *fearful scar* on the side of Charlie's body with a *gruesome looking hole, the flesh all bunched around it.*[114] That sounds like a stoma. Maybe it was the times – acceptable to write about horrific injuries but not about shit. If it was the stoma of a colostomy that's what you'd expect – a primitive bag and a messy procedure. But Jack only wrote about gas, and Charlie talked to him about his routines as a *treatment*, which he was supposed to do daily, although he added: *I don't treat myself every day as I should, but only when a headache warns me attention is overdue.*[115] And it doesn't sound like a discharging opening of the small bowel onto his abdomen – an ileostomy – because when Charlie had finished fashioning his instruments, Jack watched him start his first *treatment*:

Climbing up, he sat down and made a pillow of his shirt. Then, partly twisted to one side, he fumbled about, poking the 'scope down the hole in his side. Stretching out on one side he poked the funnel end into the 'scope and reaching over, filled the billy. He filled the funnel, and lay stretched out there, a black shadow on the big grey rock.[116]

Whatever it was, he was lucky to be alive and he told Jack that the doctors in London probably thought so too. Maybe they could have explained his episodes of irritability, irrationality – derangement. Idriess still remembered it when he spoke to Tim Bowden:

Well, he went west. He got nuts and swelled up with gas and he went crazy, and the only weapons we had was his, he had a .22 pea-rifle and he chased me with it - poor devil went nutty. And each time this happened I'd jump across and somehow get across a big open space there where the waves and tide used to come and in I'd get among a heap of rocks and at high tide it was quite safe, and then … he'd get rid of the gas sort of business and then he'd be quite alright - a real good mate.[117]

A real good mate – they were there for months and there were moments when Jack was in fear of his life. For much of that time they didn't share or cooperate, came to blows, sabotaged each other's gear – *and then he'd be quite alright - a real good mate*. But Charlie really was *alright* when it counted, when the Japanese lugger came looking for the opium that had been thrown overboard from a passing China steamer and washed ashore. They kept out of sight until the lugger left – maybe the same lugger that Jack and Dick Welsh ran into when they were collecting trochus on Lizard Island with Cross-Eyed Joe. But when another lugger came by in February 1921 Jack was quick to hitch a ride back to Cooktown and even signed over to Charlie his share of the tin and wolfram they'd collected – he wanted out. He never saw Charlie again.

And now Howick is in the darkness just a few kilometres away. Three elevations that from Coquet appear as two – *The Hill* and *The Peak* joined by a short, low ridge – and a separate collection of boulders to the east they called *The Mound*, where Jack hid out when Charlie *went west*. Those were the only parts of the island not flooded with the high tide and the three stations around which their story wound. Just names of convenience, they don't appear on any map. Just in Jack's book. But the whole coast is covered by names of convenience, each of which is meaningful in some way and part of a story. And there are other names for these features that represent sites of redemption far from Howick. From a distant time and in another place that takes its name from the Aramaic, the skull place – Golgotha. That was László's map.

Teabag Bay, July 11, 2008

Between Ninian Bay and Cape Melville the coast is high and rocky, but appeared to be fronted by a reef, which in some places extends for a mile and a half from the shore; in this interval there are two or three sandy beaches, but I doubt the practicability of landing upon them in a boat. The summit and sides of the hills that form the promontory, of which Cape Melville is the extreme, are of most remarkable appearance, being covered with heaps of rounded stones of very large size.

Phillip Parker King (1827)

Yesterday, from Noble's summit, we looked across to the Howicks, faces into the wind swirling up the bare rockface. Jon was leaning into it, defying gravity at the drop off – *Wind Boy*. Navigation tower, rock, hill, cliff-face – always a whispered invitation to climb into the blue and be wrapped in the wind. Tilting forward, eyes closed, I imagined floating off the edge, the wind becoming the rush of air racing past in free-fall to the shore – flying. You can't do it in cities or towns where you're grounded by vertical surfaces that cut through sightlines, and by surround-sounds that hold you in place. On the edge of an ocean-wrapped, remote windward cliff it's possible. I opened my eyes and I was alone, back on the peak of Noble, Jon and Jethro already heading to the cave and on down the lee slopes to the mine-site – exploring. Later, we waded and swam back to the campsite through a mangrove forest with roots and twisted limbs disappearing into white sand through clear water, with refracted and reflected, canopy-filtered sunlight dancing through the shallows. A night under the wongai again, third time for me, second for Jon but a first for Jethro – familiar rubbish and the TV still there. All the usual routines of camp and many of the same stories.

And the routines of the day's beginning – breakfast, breaking camp, loading kayaks. Predictably, for Jethro, an expanded routine of packing, unpacking, repacking … and unpacking again – it's a Jethro thing. But we all suffer from it to some extent; even with planning the dry-bag you need most is rammed into the nose or the stern and usually it's easier to pull everything out and start again. That can lead to surprises. On Coquet Jon gave in and emptied his forward storage compartment looking for something to replace the paddle-tie that had floated off with the tide. Bent over the deck with his head through the hatch, torch gripped in his mouth, the exclamation we heard was muffled and indecipherable, but a second later we were back in previous journeys: *Boys, look at this – Axel's Mace. I'd forgotten about it. It must have been stuck up there for years.*

Made by Axel on Two Isles in 2003 and carried on by Jon and I when Axel left Lizard in his doomed attempt to sort out his legal options. The Mace is on film, carried by Jon – *trussed up like a working bullock* – as he struggled up the pathway to John Pritchard's house when we arrived at Cape Weymouth three weeks later. Its travels didn't stop there; we took it on southern trips from Mackay and Clairview with Jethro, in memory of Axel. But it's been lost even to memory, hidden away in the most inaccessible recess of Jon's kayak for two years. Hidden away like Axel in Lotus Glen Correctional Facility. Jon and I have been up to see him there. Not much of the shaman without the amulets and adornments – prison fatigues are drably levelling. Clothes do not make the man in jail, but Axel is making clothes in the prison sewing room. He even tried to look smart, but that's a bad strategy in a place where there's safety in being inconspicuous. So he plays it quiet, keeps his head down – he's out next year. But for a moment he's with us again.

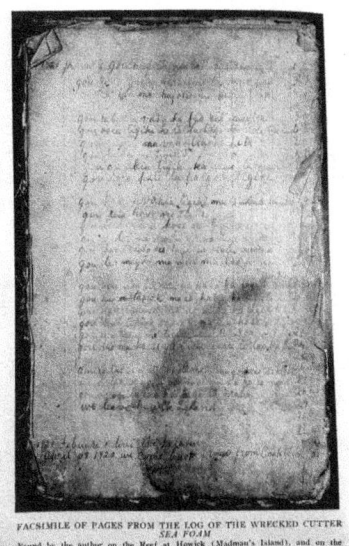

FACSIMILE OF PAGES FROM THE LOG OF THE WRECKED CUTTER
SEA FOAM
Found by the author on the Reef at Howick (Madman's Island), and on the vacant pages of which he wrote the book.

... this was the log of the 'Seafoam'...
Madman's Island, 1938

CHAPTER XIII

THE WELL

For much of that time they didn't share or cooperate, came to blows... Madman's Island, 1938

The author's impression of Gallipoli.

...it would be a very bloody war...
The desert column, 1932

And this morning, as Jethro was finalising his repacking on Noble, Jon was paddling slowly in circles twenty metres off the mangroves as I stood in the shallows adjusting deck lines. What Jethro and I heard was a screech that seemed so out of place that, for a moment, I imagined teenagers in a mosh-pit. Jon's reaction was probably ahead of realisation – some sort of fight or flight neural short-circuiting. Maybe, but that scream was followed by furious splashing and as we turned to look he was yelling: *It's a crocodile, a fucking crocodile. It just came up next to me, I hit it with the paddle. A fucking crocodile...*

It was probably just curious, and when Jon struck it disappeared – at least from the surface. Meanwhile I was in the mother-ship and paddling, and Jethro's repacking hit a new level. Within a minute we were in formation and heading north with another tale. Not our first experience, we've seen plenty of crocodiles in and around Cairns and along the coast. Crocodiles are part of the environment and if you want to get out there you need to accept that it's a shared space, and be sensible. Don't camp in stupid places, avoid going up remote rivers, particularly in the Wet, don't stand around in muddy shallows where fishermen dispose of fish frames, don't go into the water at night – and don't go wandering around in the mangroves. Which is, of course, exactly what we were doing the day before. In a mangrove forest set in clear water on white sand, on an island way off the coast. But crocodiles travel enormous distances; we've seen slides on islands further from the coast. And they can be almost impossible to see, even in what seems like clear water. Maybe as we set sails and paddled north we were a bit wiser ... maybe.

With Noble and its crocodile astern we pointed northwest to Barrow Point with Ninian Bay in its lee, stopping for a lunchtime break on the northern shore of Barrow Island just off the Point. Ninian Bay is about five kilometres deep and backed by sandhills with the Melville Range to the northwest and Bathurst Bay far beyond. The mangrove-lined coast west from Barrow Point gives way to beaches that stretch in a fifteen kilometre crescent to North Bay Point. Hidden from sight behind a small hill with commanding views across Ninian Bay is the site of a long abandoned homestead, Abbey Peak, a cattle lease that was granted to a returned serviceman in 1916 and transferred in 1920 to Allan Critchley Instone. Although fishermen and tourists sometimes blaze four-wheel-drive trails through the fragile ecology to the beach, the country is now deserted. But in Instone's day it wasn't. In the Bay his motor-boat, *Iona*, may have been riding at anchor alongside Japanese *bêche-de-mer* luggers, maybe even the black lugger, there to find workers or women. Captain Dan Monaghan's *Spray* might have sailed in, as it did in 1914 to drop Jack and his mate off. The mission vessel *Pearl Queen* also made regular appearances; Jack knew it from the Bloomfield, but it also came north with *Muni* from the Cape Bedford Mission. And scattered all around the bay were the traditional camping sites of the *Gambiilmugu-warra* people of Barrow Point.

Muni had it in for Dan Monaghan, the Japanese fishermen and Instone – he thought they were all responsible for the *starvation, misery and syphilization*[118] of Aboriginal *tribal remnants* between Cape Flattery and the Flinders Islands. He wasn't the only one; Sergeant Guilfoyle, the local Protector, wrote to Charles William Bleakley, who'd progressed from inspector of pearl-shell and *bêche-de-mer* fisheries on Thursday Island to become Chief Protector of Aborigines in 1914, about what he thought were suspicious movements of Instone's motor launch between Cooktown, Cairns and Thursday Island. Bleakley then got on to *Muni* suggesting that: *there is suspicion as to what use Mr Instone puts his launch to, probably opium traffic.*[119] And maybe some local use; like *Muni*, Walter Roth also blamed Asiatic aliens for venereal diseases in *tribal populations*[120] and had an idea about what the currency of exchange was:

> *Opium, obtained mainly from the Chinese, is exerting a far more deleterious influence on the aboriginals than alcohol: the usual method of indulging the craving is to mix the smoked ashes (opium charcoal) with water, and drink it.*[121]

While Jack was around Ninian Bay he may have met a woman called *Tharrwiilnda* from the country by the Mack River to the north. Two years later she had a child at *Iipwulin*, just east of Instone's homestead. The father was thought to be Maurice Hart, who had a cattle lease on

Wakooka Creek to the south and that boy, Roger Hart, was one of the last of the *Gambiilmugu-warra* people to be born at Barrow Point. That was the mob his Aboriginal father, Charlie Lefthander, belonged to, and Charlie cared for him after his mother was *abducted*. But eventually, in 1923, Charlie decided that the mixed-race child should stay far to the south at Cape Bedford. Roger told anthropologist John Haviland about it fifty years later:

> *I didn't know they were taking me to Cape Bedford you see. I heard that old fellow saying to me* 'Nhanu walaarrbi nuthinhu nagaar,' *I'm going to give you to the Beard there to the east. Well, I couldn't understand what he was meaning ... That is when they told me they were going to leave me with the white man, the* walarr *'beard'. That's what they called the missionary at Cape Bedford, although I didn't understand them at that time ... When I saw Mr.* Muuni, *I was frightened of his beard.*[122]

Eventually all of the *Gambiilmugu-warra* people were rounded up, Bleakley saw to that, sending the government cutter, the *Melbidir*, with native troopers on board, to find and destroy the camps along the coast and take that last mob to Lockhart River. They didn't stay but their options weren't good and their leaders either died or were caught and sent to Palm Island. All except one, who avoided Bleakley's net. He stayed at Barrow Point, alone, and died there during the next war – the last of his people to die on country. By that time Roger Hart was far away. He'd been sent south with the *Guugu Yimithirr*, taken from Cape Bedford along with Reverend Schwarz. As *Muni* was being led away to internment, I wonder if the old man thought about resisting, as *Gambiilmugu-warra* did twenty years before when they were consigned to his care.

Sixty years after being left at Cape Bedford Roger returned to Barrow Point and John Haviland recorded the words and stories that came back to him. One of them was about *Wurrey – Old Man Fog* – a trickster myth-hero. *Wurrey* relished deception, telling lies and elaborate stories, leaving credulous listeners duped and deprived of food – *mayi*. But while the trickster always came out well fed and on top, the unwitting victims were usually led on as much by their own flaws as by *Wurrey's* malice, be it their greed, vanity, ingratitude, disrespect or irresponsibility. Like Jack Idriess.

Two years before Roger Hart was born, Jack set off from Barrow Point after hearing from Captain Dan, who was taking the *Spray* to Thursday Island, that there was a war in Europe. He knew next to nothing about the causes or the combatants and had no illusions about the King or Empire in whose name he would fight. But like tens of thousands of young Australian men he just wanted *to get to the bloody war*. There was no way he was going to miss out, even if it meant walking to Cooktown; even if he had to ford Wakooka Creek, and the Howick River, and the Jeannie, and the Starkie and McIvor, all of them crocodile-infested. He set out with hubristic enthusiasm and ended up sleeping in a wongai tree for safety, before coming to his senses and heading back to Ninian Bay to wait for Captain Dan. That experience may have remained with him; nearly thirty years later he wrote *In crocodile land: Wandering in Northern Australia*[123] with tips, from experience with a prospecting mate, for setting up camp near waterways on Cape York.

Idriess hadn't counted on crocodiles – or *Wurrey*. But he didn't miss out; within two months of the opening salvoes on what would become the Western Front he'd made it to Townsville and enlisted, and by Christmas he was on HMAT *Persic*, a White Star liner converted to carry troops and their horses, bound for Egypt. His next sea trip was from Alexandria on the *Lutzow*, a captured German steamer that had just returned with the first waves of casualties from the Dardanelles. The 477 officers and troopers of the dismounted 5th Light Horse were on their way to Gallipoli. Only 107 of those men were part of the evacuation in December 1915.[124] Jack was right – it would be a very *bloody war*.

From Barrow Island it was another two hours across Ninian Bay and then west around the headland of North Bay Point, with a half-kilometre further to a landing in the afternoon shadows of tall trees on a rise behind the beach and the eastern face of the Melville Range. *Thuurrgha*, that was the name Roger Hart said that *Gambiilmugu-warra* called the scrub python that travelled north from *Manyammar* near Cape Bowen. *Thuurrgha* was attacked by *Gujal*, the eaglehawk, and went underground, resurfacing somewhere near Cape Melville, just to the north. He died there and was turned to stone – the Melville Range.

A kilometre along the beach the boulders of *Thuurrgha's* remains spill across the sand and into the ocean forming a point around which we clamber and swim to reach the next bay. To the north the rockwall that is the eastern face of Cape Melville continues to the horizon. That's tomorrow, this afternoon is about rubbish. This is one of the places on the coast that concentrate flotsam and jetsam; there's another just south of Cape Bedford that we called Zen-chair beach, after a sofa grounded above the high tide mark in the middle of nowhere. But here it's even denser – plastic, glass, ghost-nets, synthetic rope, fishing floats, tangled longlines, drums, chairs, thongs, life-vests, more thongs, more and more plastic, polystyrene containers, hats, sunglasses, cameras, freezers – piled above the high-tide mark in tangled mounds and scattered all along the shore. It's horrifying and fascinating. We collect stainless steel clips from commercial long-lines and have more than a dozen by the end of the afternoon. This is just what has made it to shore and remained above the sand, a miniscule fraction of the junk beneath the surface, woven through the reef and tangled around its wildlife. And it's not just rubbish left behind.

All islands have introduced species. But with a few exceptions, such as the goats on Whitsunday Island, large animals are confined to the mainland. And there are plenty here, like the feral pigs all through the Melville Range, rooting out turtle eggs from clutches buried along the beaches on Bathurst Bay, just over the hills. They're in the shadows about our campsite, and even before heading off along the beach everything edible is suspended from tree branches or sealed in one of the rigid kayaks. Not just pigs, there are wild cattle here. But while they're not interested in our supplies, by choosing a shaded place to pitch tents we're in a favourite bovine haunt – there's dried and drying dung pats everywhere. And they burn easily and evenly. Not that there's a shortage of wood, but there's a particular aesthetic to it – at least that's how it seems to me though Jethro and Jon don't appreciate it in the same way. It was on Jethro's suggestion that Jon became Wind Boy on Noble's peak and now, courtesy of Jon, it's my turn: *I've got it, it's Dung Boy.*

— *Dung Boy... Why do I have to be the one who's the excremental tag on.... How do you hold your head high with a name like Dung Boy...*

— *Jon, don't fight it, it's karma, like Pierre the Cock-sucker.*

With a line like that from Jon I already know this is leading somewhere I've probably been before, even if I've forgotten the punch line. But with the tents up, the fire set and dinner happening, I provide the segue: *What's the connection to Pierre the Cock-sucker and who the hell was he...*

— *A famous adventurer – skiing, fencing, mountain climbing, boxing, he even ran with the bulls – the lot. You're in good company. And he was upset too. He wanted to know how come they didn't call him Pierre King of the Mountain, or Punching Pierre or something like that.*

— *Jon, I have heard this one before – I pick up one piece of dung...*

— *That's it Jon, it's karma – Dung Boy – don't fight it.*

Out there, somewhere in the darkness, feral pigs are watching three humans illuminated by the soft glow of slowly combusting cow-dung. Above them a dozen dry bags hang from branches like pendulous, overripe fruit. And just visible is a line of small rectangles; prayer flags to the teabag deities. A thankless task of long-distance kayaking is monitoring supplies and, as usual, it's fallen to *Dung Boy*. The bad news is a gross underestimation of tea consumption and, as of yesterday, we're on rations – two bags per person per day – and all bags get used at least twice. Thus the teabag prayer flags – and Teabag Bay.

Lowrie Island, July 17, 2008

8 and 9 are two low, woody islets of about a mile and a quarter in diameter. Some shoal marks on the water were observed opposite these islands, but their existence was not ascertained. Both the islets are surrounded by coral reefs, of small extent.

Phillip Parker King (1827)

Six days from Teabag Bay to Lowrie with three stops. We spent two nights at Cape Melville, enough time to go boulder hopping to the seaside freshwater springs in the caves facing out to the Coral Sea, and long walks along the beaches of Bathurst Bay in the lee of the Melville Range where, just back from the shore in a small clearing in regrowth scrub, stands a memorial inscribed:

In Memory of
THE PEARLERS
Lost in the Dreadful Hurricane
on 5TH March, 1899
Alfred St John Outridge - ("Sagitta")
Interred here, aged 50
and
Harold Arthur Outridge ("Sagitta")
His nephew, aged 25
also
Edward Charles Atthow
aged 20 - ("Silvery Wave")
"When thou passest through the waters,
I will be with thee"; 43 Isiah v. 2.

---

also
E. Jefferson - "Silvery Wave"
J. Nicholson - "Silvery Wave"
R. Cameron - "Sagitta"
R.B. Murray - "Sagitta"
C.O. Fuhrman. D. Lee – Lightship
H. Karr. D. Crowley - Lightship
50 vessels wrecked or foundered
and over 300 coloured men drowned
"The blood of Jesus Christ His Son
cleanseth us from all sin"[125]

Set in concrete below is a small metal plaque recording that, a century after the storm, members of the Outridge and Atthow families visited to remember the lives lost. As they stood in that spot they would have looked across Bathurst Bay to the Flinders Islands over which the cyclone's eye travelled in the middle of the night. And that's also the direction we paddled the next day, to the Owen Channel again, with the Castle Peaks on Stanley – *Yindayin* – to starboard, over 200 metres above, and Mount Flinders on Flinders Island – *Wurriima* – to port, reaching to 300 metres. We were driven by the easterly wind and swell, amplified in the channel and bringing us to where Jon and I boarded the ACV *Botany Bay* and waited for the *Endeavour Bay* to hitch a ride north in 2003. But we didn't stop, passing around Heming Point at the western end of Stanley and along its leeward shore to Cape Flinders, near where Phillip Parker King found the wreck of the *Frederick* in 1819. As we turned to the south-east towards Castle Peaks we were paddling into the wind again, passing two mangrove-lined bays before the next headland gave way to Wongai Beach – and *Tombiembui* Rock.

Tombiembui Rock – a sedimentary monolith at the waters edge, gouged and smoothed by tempests and time, it's a natural attractor. It draws the eye and forces associations; its textured, gnarled surface seems alive. Or dead, pocked and worn by erosion that suggests decay. *Tombiembui* – we called it Dali Rock and spent two nights in a cave just five metres away, resting up for what would be a thirteen-hour day in the kayaks. On our by-day we found the rock art of the northernmost *Gambiilmugu-warra*, from long before the survivors were rounded up and taken to Lockhart River or Cape Bedford. And as we clambered towards the ridgeline we passed above fifty feet – the height they found dolphin carcasses after Mahina's fifteen-metre tidal surge – the largest in recorded history.

Climbing on and up, over and around boulders on all-fours or jumping, I was thinking of the forces on new additions to fifty-year old legs. Two metal right hips. For years Jon's worn articular cartilages had been announcing that without the collateral of youthful plasticity, the debt taken out to the Kedron Lions Football Club was falling due, and was

was paid in titanium two years ago. Jethro had no warnings, the tumour came like a thief in the night – silently and suddenly. High-tech engineering out of sight beneath two long scars, but hidden by attitude. Attitude at altitude, and from the summit we could see where the fleet was anchored when Mahina hit, and looking north, to where we were heading – with the wind to somewhere beyond the horizon.

Two sixty-kilometre days northwest from Cape Flinders to Lowrie. The first day skirting the leeward edges of Corbett, Grub and Hedge reefs to an overnight on Hannah Island. Phillip Parker King named the Claremont Isles in 1819, seven islands in all with Hannah the northernmost and right next to the shipping channel. Entirely surrounded by mangroves, it wasn't welcoming to weary kayakers too tired to do another twelve kilometres to Wilkie Island. But we knew it had a navigation tower and where there's a tower there's a landing. Not a lot of light left when we found the entrance to a twenty-five metre-long passage through the mangroves to a dark-sand beach next to the base of an abandoned light, with the new tower thirty metres beyond. Not a pretty island but maybe before Mahina it was different. A week after that cyclone the search vessel, the *White Star,* arrived at Hannah on its way to Bathurst Bay where the fleet had been at anchor. All vegetation across the Claremont Isles was gone.

There was a wreck on Hannah, but not from Mahina. In February 1921 the ten-ton schooner, the *Sea Foam*, was lost at Hannah. That was just before Jack Idriess landed with Charlie on Howick where, in the book, he found the log of the *Sea Foam* – he had a facsimile of it placed inside the cover of *Madman's Island* and told Tim Bowden fifty years later about how he was walking on the beach when he saw: *a piece of paper of all things in the world, so I lugged it up and this was the log of the "Seafoam" - the Malay's boat that had gone down, this was his log where he kept all the ship's accounts that you've got to have on your boat.*[126] Hannah to Howick – a long way and against the weather – the ship's log didn't float there. Maybe Jack got it mixed up, or the skipper of the *Sea Foam* took it with him from Hannah and left it when the rescue boat stopped in the Howicks. Maybe he didn't want it found at all, lots of maybes and nobody left to explain.

Yesterday, with clear skies and consistent winds from the south, we were pushed towards the aftermath of another cyclone. Our sails were up and, for kayaks, we were flying along the leeward drops of Magpie, Noddy and Ogilvie reefs, riding swells channelled and reflected from their turbulent edges only a few metres away. Skirting around dazzling sandbars and across shallows alive with darting rays and fish. Sometimes too shallow – one of the traps of sea kayaking along the Great Barrier Reef is presuming a clear passage where there's nothing breaking the surface. With reefs kilometres wide it's unwise to chance being stranded on a falling tide, so the kayaker needs to be alert to not only what breaks the surface but also to indicators of what's going on below – turbulence, diffraction of wave patterns and changes in colour. Even so, there was enough going right for Jethro to set up a trolling line and by the time we were off Morris Island he had a Spanish mackerel on board. Not big, but caught food, and Morris was a good place to gut and fillet it before the last push. But by late afternoon with the sun low over the mainland range it was clear that we wouldn't make it to Night Island and we shifted course to the default – Lowrie Island.

Lowrie is typical of the low-lying mangrove cays north of Princess Charlotte Bay stripped bare as Mahina made its way south. Approaching two years after Cyclone Monica passed directly overhead in 2006 gives a sense of that fury. Monica was Category 3 when it hit. It wasn't spent, and reformed as it crossed the Gulf, hitting Junction Bay west of Maningrida as a Category 5 with a tidal surge of around fifteen to twenty feet. But even as it passed over Lowrie the whole island would have been submerged.

Lowrie is now a crescent of rock coral open to the north-west, with the battered trunks of what in better times were struggling trees clustered like forlorn funeral poles on the one small patch from which topsoil and sand haven't been blown or washed away. It's only as we paddle into the lee, threading through exposed coral as far as the kayaks will go without grounding, that we appreciate the desolation. There's no beach landing and the boats need to be emptied and everything portaged to shore. In the half-hour before night closes in we've managed to get tents up without pegs – there's no point trying to hammer pegs into rock – and a fire going.

Just – on what's left of Lowrie there's not a lot of dry fuel as not much of the island escapes the high tide's reach. Which, we realize, is another problem.

Our tide table's nearest reference points are Leggatt Island two hundred kilometres south and the Torres Strait more than that to the north – both a long way from Lowrie. They give a sense of what is happening here, but as the water edges towards the tents we're tracking its progress. The kayaks are already as high on the island as it's possible to go and tethered fore and aft. We're prepared to shift camp but who wants to on a cold, wet, windy night – from one bit of rock to another. Ironically, the only bit of marine trash we found before darkness was a metal sphere about half-a-metre in diameter, with secured ports, brackets for instruments of some sort and a metre long antenna. Its markings are indecipherable but our best guess is that it's a monitoring device to track current and tidal movements. Jon's worried and reminds me of an earlier conversation about how to judge the speed of the tide's movement – we'd talked about it on Eagle Island and I repeat: *The rule of twelfths; if you know the tidal range, in the first hour it rises or falls by one twelfth, in the second hour by two twelfths, in the third by three, the fourth by three, the fifth by two and the sixth by one – a bell curve. If you were keen you could fashion an indicator, like a marked stick, and check it every half-hour or so.*

— *Do you really think that would work…*

— *No, but it would probably be reassuring doing the math.*

— *Fuck the math… and fuck the Pickabeen Five Pipe and Flute Band.*

The *Pickabeen Five Pipe and Flute Band*. Who knows what trips or which islands it was, but it's been told more than once and this time Jon's started with the punch line. *My dear old dad could never finish it without laughing*. His dear old dad is alive and kicking, not far from where Jon grew up, and probably still trying to tell the story to its end. There's a touch of *Old Man Fog – Warrey –* in Jon's jokes. The victims all have reason to be deserving – like Pierre's vanity. It's the same with the protagonist of the *Pickabeen Five Pipe and Flute Band,* but Jethro and I have both heard it before. Jon's probably miffed that we don't follow the lead that's left hanging, slowly dissipating like the fire's warmth. In the silence that follows I'm left thinking about humour – and László.

It was something I thought about a lot in the 1990s and early 2000s. Not that people who are psychotic don't laugh; mirth may be a feature of uncommunicable experiences in some psychotic states – idiosyncratic, unshared connections. But humour isn't typical of paranoia, and László was paranoid for years before clozapine. Not that he couldn't appreciate double meanings or that an expression wasn't to be taken literally. Like the *psycho the rapist* standard – László understood polysemy, didn't think that I was a rapist, and would have known that cartoon for what it was – a visual joke with multiple interpretations. But for László the implicit contradiction of healer and villain, the heart of the joke, was both a statement of fact and a code, it was a message, a realisation, an epiphany – and for him alone; whether others shared it was irrelevant. The real paradox wasn't in the joke. It was that it wasn't; for him it was a statement of categorical truth and, at the same time and despite his repeated use of the phrase, he clearly didn't believe it was true, literally, of me. At least, not until I let him down, but that was later.

But humour can also be therapeutic, even with psychotic patients. I've had agreements with some that we tell at least one joke at each session – that's about sharing, trust and the ability to tolerate degrees of ambiguity. It's a slow process and I always test the waters with humour at my own expense. With *Murri* patients it's the *silly old whitefellow* trope, there are lots of options and all with the same comeuppance, something like: *I was talking to these old ladies a while back and they were all shy and looking away and whispering. I figured that they just must think I was very important or handsome or something until one lady got up and whispered in my ear that my fly wasn't done up.* A winner in the right situation.

Not with László. Anything at my own expense simply fed into existing beliefs in unpredictable ways, like when there was a desktop calendar with Gary Larson cartoons from *The Far Side* on the table. On display was the Greystokes at marriage counselling with an ageing Tarzan blurting jungle cries as he beat his chest while Jane, who's over it, comments: *Lord of the*

Jungle? Lord of the jungle?... Ha! You couldn't make Lord of the compost pile... Oh, great. Here we go with his little chest-pounding routine. László knew exactly what it was and probably why it might have been considered a joke. I doubt that there was any concrete or idiosyncratic interpretation, but I wouldn't have known, he didn't seem to look at it. In fact it took me minutes to recognize a connection from Jack Idriess to Michael Fomenko via canoes and Howick: *You're the paddler doctor Hunter, you have to paddle your own canoe. In the sea or the river or the canal doctor Hunter, the canoe canal. In the canoe canal to* The Island. *In a double canoe with Charlie doctor Hunter...*

— *I saw the copy you'd borrowed from the library, I guessed it was you who made all the notes in the margins and text.*
— *Music doctor Hunter, notes of the melody. You need to be able to read Jack's score, to hear the music. It's the Requiem doctor Hunter. It's the Madman's Requiem, the Golgotha mass. Michael made it, Michael was there for the mass.*
— *Michael...*
— *Fomenko doctor, but not Fomenko, someone else, an alter ego, for sacrifice doctor. At Golgotha – the alter of ego...*

Michael Fomenko – Tarzan. László knew him, or knew of him, including the dugout trip to Dutch New Guinea in the 1950s, and of Michael being taken away to a different kind of *Madman's Island* down south. Michael probably didn't go to Howick but hugged the coast around Lookout Point and north past Noble to Barrow Point and Teabag Bay. But as far as László was concerned he'd been on Howick and got there by canoe. I can't imagine Michael on Howick but I can at Teabag Bay – fresh water, fish, shellfish, maybe even a wild pig to eat. He sometimes ate carrion, consuming the meat cold and putrid – the smells that followed him are legendary. And it's unlikely that he stopped on Lowrie, like further south he would have stayed close to the mainland where there was predictable water and food.

As the tide's advance slows and halts about three feet from our campsite then starts its retreat it seems appropriate to mark the reprieve from an uncomfortable night. Axel's Mace – fashioned from the sea's rejects on Two Isles, carried over thousands of kilometres between Clairview and Cape Weymouth, forgotten then found again in the Howicks – now tops a cairn of rock coral on possibly the most inhospitable island we've stayed on. But in the darkness, with the tide waning and as the wind dies and the fire's glow fades, even Lowrie starts to feel OK. Particularly when there's fresh fish to be had. Jethro's on dinner and the pots on the fire are boiling as the conversation turns back on itself – again: *Dung boy, I've got it…*

— *Jon – Wind Boy – I presume you're talking to me…*
— *Who else. I've been thinking about Jethro, he's excelled himself today. Out there, trolling along the edge of the reef. He was in the zone – Mackerel Man.*
— *Mackerel Man… He caught one fish – which wasn't all that big. How come Wind Boy and Mackerel Man and I'm stuck with Dung Boy…*
— *It may only have been one fish Jon, but remember Pierre. And it may only have been one piece of dung. Karma Jon, don't fight it.*

Wind Boy   *Mackerel Man*   *Dung Boy*

CHAPTER 9

2000-2001: epsilon

Karma. Connections; past lives, this one and others. Fate – *don't fight it*. Jon said it, often, as a space-filler or a link between jokes. He's not here on *Madman's Island* – he can't be. I wonder if he thought about karma four days ago while he was sitting on the floating jetty, watching two kayaks disappear northward; as he shouted: *DLB – don't look back. Don't look back*. We've all thought it. Back in space, back in time, behind – before the now. Maybe it actually is all about karma; look back at your peril lest you glimpse where you're going. But that's what we do; we all look back, we all want to know – even when we don't. Sometimes it must be like this, here on Howick, staring into the darkness from *The Peak*, trying to ignore the insistent light slow-strobing in the distance, drawing us like insects of the night. And their predators – *karma*.

Looking back – going back; sometimes we don't realize it until we're there. There in an imagined then; it's always an approximation, a distortion, you can never really go back, it's never as it was. Except in dreams. On the wings of dreams and at the mercy of night-winds howling along the cliffs and crevices of our unconscious, the past is changed but always the same. *Don't look back* – it doesn't apply to the sleep-world. Dreams are primed and populated by the past, a past the dreamer may or may not want to revisit. And for some rare dreamers, like László, it's not even their own past.

Finch Bay, July 9, 2000

A week out of Cairns and heading north to the Howicks and on to the Tip. Before the millennium is out – before fifty. Before it's too late. But today is a one-day break in Cooktown, the kayak outside my unit at the Seaview Motel across the road from where Idriess first stepped ashore from the *Musgrave* over ninety years ago. He would have looked north and seen Indian Head in the distance – for me that's tomorrow, then to Cape Bedford and on. But for now it's going back. Along Charlotte Street and past the West Coast Hotel where once there was an equine crime scene profile on the road. Mick told me about that. Then up Howard Street and into the hospital. Past the reception desk and the reassuringly humming Coke machine, and there on the wall to the right – just by the crossroads – a photo on the wall of doctor Mick in Akubra and khaki – totally Mick, except for the eyes that fix the viewer's gaze, it wasn't like that in person. But the smile is him, the unspoken joke shared with the Ned Kelly body armor mounted on the corrugated metal wall behind. Maybe taken at the West Coast, almost certainly after a few beers.

No hospital business for me today and soon I'm wandering through the Peninsula Caravan Park – home to more than a few of my patients including László. A short stop then a brief walk on to the Botanic Garden and past the orchid house. The Cooktown orchid, *Vappodes phalaenopsis* – Queensland's floral emblem. Through the Solander Section, dedicated to fellow travellers with Cook. Vera Scarth-Johnson was inspired by Banks and Solander and after settling in Cooktown in 1972, aged sixty, she set about recording the plant-life of the Endeavour River valley, working with the *Guugu Yimithirr* over decades. Mick knew her; they met when he was a relieving doctor around the Cape in the early 1980s. She must have liked him because she contacted him in 1988 when he was in South Africa to let him know about the medical superintendent job at Cooktown. He got it. By that time Vera was in her old age and Parkinson's had closed her art project at around 160 magnificent paintings. But this garden is also her legacy, and though she died a year ago the fruits of her activism live on. And there's one special struggling sapling – new growth – marked in commemoration of her efforts:

This tree was planted
In 1999
In loving memory of
Vera Scarth Johnson
Common Name BLACK BEAN
Guugu Yimithirr CUM-UU
Castanospermum australe

Then finally I find what I'm searching for, a ring of small granite stones surrounding a more recent planting, this one Cascading Bean, *Maniltoa lenticellata*, a memorial to someone who lived less than three months beyond Vera Scarth-Johnson but whose life was cut far shorter, and who died far away but whose heart, like hers, was here. A different kind of legacy:

IN MEMORY OF
DR. MICK MCLOUGHLIN
28th May 1955 – 9th August 1999

Dedicated to Rural Health
Respected for his cause
Motivated by his desire to serve
Innocently unique
Caring for his patients
Khaki's 'n boots
The 'down to earth Doc' friend and mentor of
Cooktown and surrounding communities.
MEDICAL SUPERINTENDENT
COOKTOWN HOSPITAL
1988-1994

Vale Mick.

Cooktown, September 27, 2000

Five weeks ago I was paddling around The Tip, discharging a flare that disappeared into a cloudless sky to mark having made it, before fifty – before it was too late. One thousand kilometres in a kayak and just one more day before it all ended in Bamaga. Then the reentry – to the other reality. Back at work it's as if I'd never left except that my thoughts are still somewhere else; with sights, sounds and coincidences in remote places. *Swallows and Amazons* and other rabbit holes – to childhood and my father. Unexpected treasures like Hannibal Island and the wonder of watching an eagle's lazy parabolic overflights, monitoring the nest and her two chicks just a few feet from where I sat at the top of a navigation tower, the coast and the other world in the far, far distance.[127]

And today I'm back at the Seaview where I broke that trip to find the memorial to Mick. Ironically there's a new monument and it's right across from the Seaview. Maybe it's a replacement for the statue at the other end of town near where the railway passed, the line that didn't make it past Laura when they realized the party was over. And like railways, statues have a use-by-date and that one passed it long ago. It's successor by the harbor strikes a different tone that resonates with the vibe of a town on the rebound as the sealed road edges closer. A stop on the *history trail*, the memorial channels Cooktown's wild, glory days for grey nomads checking out the wharf and remaining pubs, or on their way to the bowls club or RSL for the all-you-can-eat buffet and the pokies. Mick would have appreciated it, they call it *Mick the Miner*.

> *At this spot on the 24th October 1873, the vessel "Leichhardt"*
> *discharged its cargo of government officials, miners, horses and*
> *supplies for the trek to the Palmer River. This was the start of the*
> *famous "Palmer River Goldrush" and the birth of the port of Cooktown.*
> *Miners from all around the world, numbering in tens of thousands,*
> *quickly followed. The flow of people, supplies and gold through the port,*
> *established Cooktown as one of Queensland's most prosperous*
> *towns and the State's second busiest port. This statue represents a typical*

miner on his way to the goldfields in the 1870s, and was commissioned by the Cooktown and District Historical Society to mark the 125th Anniversary of the establishment of Cooktown. 31ST OCTOBER 1998

From *Mick the Miner* along Charlotte Street and past the West Coast, a walk now familiar from dozens of visits over the last decade, the landmarks and structures marking a virtual place, a ghost town – the Cooktown of a century ago. As I walk west I think about Jack Idriess and Errol Flynn wandering down this street and I imagine them meeting, yarning about gold and maybe opium smuggling, swapping stories of China steamers and strange luggers off the coast, about the people of the north – the miners, mariners and missionaries. And the misfits and madmen, there would have been plenty back then too and, like now, Cooktown probably provided asylum.[128] Asylum – protection or oppression – doctor Mick used it in both senses; he'd be smiling as he quipped that *Cooktown is Queensland's largest open asylum*, but grim-faced with darting eyes and twisted grimace when, in exasperation or resignation, he'd mutter that *Queensland Health put the lunatics in charge of the asylum.*

No more doctor Mick, but not much else has changed except that the new Multipurpose Primary Care Centre is up and running and the bush medicine garden is just a memory. But the hospital is only a base for me, most of my patients are to be found rather than expected. This morning I need to track down Jimmy from Coen, in town with his cousin Frank from Laura. Both psychotic, in and out of jail and in town to drink with countrymen after a funeral. Then a trip down Poison Creek Road to visit a young man from Holland, and his teenage partner who drifted north from Sydney to Cairns when she was fifteen. They live at the back of a property in what was once a caravan. Neither of them accept the diagnosis of mental illness – the doctors in the ward where they met and where romance bloomed didn't understand that they just needed each other. And gunja of course, and that's not hard to find around Cooktown. All of them are on Involuntary Treatment Orders – *The Act* – they know that if they don't go along with the treatment they'll end up back in hospital.

But every time they're due for their injections it's resistance and bargaining. That's the script and experience teaches that time, a cup of tea, some humour and maybe even a favour or two pay dividends in the long term. And it's the long term that matters, long enough to develop a relationship.

But even with a modicum of trust it's wise not to presume too much about relationships forged through coercion. Of course there are some psychotic patients in Cooktown who aren't compelled by The Act and who actually come to appointments on time – like László. And this morning, as usual, he's in the waiting room early: *Good morning doctor Hunter. You were in the radio last night doctor Hunter.*

— On the radio I think you mean László and I don't think I was.
— In the radio doctor Hunter. And yes, you were.

He's sitting under a wall-mounted screen that flickers mutely across the waiting room – the best view is from the receptionists' cubicle. Background television, calculated to make everyone feel at home – standard – in the Cooktown Mutipurpose Primary Care Centre and all the other waiting rooms across Cape York and the Torres Strait. That's what was in the design for a better, caring system. László will refuse the offer of meeting early even though his appointed time is an hour away – it would *upset the order of things*. But a cup of tea won't and I know how he takes it. A few minutes later as I hand it to him and casually apologise for the chipped rim, it's like it's a cue: *Chip off the old block doctor Hunter, we're all off old blocks, or out of the blocks. Racing, doctor Hunter, racing time and tide. Do you race the tide doctor Hunter, in your canoe…*

As random as the trajectory seems there are predictable stations along the way – words, phrases, set exchanges, like using canoe instead of kayak, which triggers an expected riposte: *Not a canoe a kayak, László, and only if I've screwed up the planning.* Then suddenly through that station and switching to another track: *The planning; the doctor wouldn't screw up the planning, not when it's so grand doctor. The design, the grand design. That's what you said last night. In the radio doctor Hunter, in as in sin. You should know about that doctor Hunter, psychiatrists know all about sin. Sin is what we die for doctor Hunter.*

In as in sin – nice, echoes of *in like Flynn*. Whether it's code or chaos depends on who the receiver is and making sense of it can be almost impossible second-hand. The notes of a recently-graduated nurse or junior doctor after meeting someone like László may be a seemingly endless, verbatim record, like the transcript of a police record-of-interview, as if missing any single element risks losing the key to the whole, to the internal crypto-world. By contrast, *ongoing thought disorder* – or – *psychotic rambling* may be all there is in the review notes of a hassled mental health nurse or a harried locum.

And there's no doubt that László rambles. Sometimes he's derailed by a play of words or prosodic associations and only the enthusiast can follow the trail. Other times it's lost and whatever triggered the shift across tracks is veiled or hidden entirely – he's in a tunnel. László is still psychotic, despite treatment. But he's changed; in the past, in the shunting yard of his ideas and sensations his stream of thought would sometimes spontaneously fragment, as if the carriages had all been decoupled. And at other times it might abruptly halt, as if the tracks had suddenly ended. Like the Cooktown to Laura railway – just over the river and going nowhere.

But there's progress of sorts. There are no more paranoid accusations that I'm manipulating his thought processes and controlling him through mysterious powers and mechanisms. The voices that reinforced those beliefs, talking about him and sometimes to him, have gone – or at least don't intrude unless he's under stress. Cutting out the cannabis helped. He still argues that the process is corrupt and that he's a victim of a pathological system – the nurses who administer his depot injections are *needle-dependent psychopaths* and I'm one of the *psycho-the-rapists*. And, of course, he still tells me I should *take the fifth*.

Maybe I did. When László was discharged from hospital he was placed on an Involuntary Treatment Order. He had to comply with the recommendations of his treating psychiatrist – me – or risk being returned to hospital. Each time he was interviewed by the Mental Health Review Tribunal he arrived on time, and was polite and cooperative. There was nothing to suggest he posed a danger to himself or others and drug testing confirmed what he said – he'd stopped using gunja. Since returning to Cooktown he's lived independently and the only complaints anyone knew about were from the library – minor stuff. László can look good and in obvious ways he is. But he's learned to be selective about what he reveals of his inner world. What and to whom.

Doctor Mick was one of the few people László opened up to but Mick won't be back. Although the door isn't opened for me in the same way he leaves it slightly ajar, maybe because he believes that I know some of the code; like the Bletchley Park team breaking the *Enigma* cypher I don't get it all and what I decrypt isn't usually in real time. But for the most part we talk about the day-to-day stuff – problems at the caravan park, how to stay on the same side as Mary at the library, whether he should accept Biata's invitation to visit Silkwood again... Then, in the same conversation, I'll recognize fragments that link directly to his past, such as the *ÁVO* or his father's role in the Olympics, or to Idriess, as when he mentions Shark-eye Park or Charlie – or Jack himself. And like the comments, codes and symbols in the margins and inside the covers of his borrowed library books, biblical references are scattered through his conversations and monologues.

Sometimes I think I can make out the connections to a virtual world laid out in his mind; just about anything to do with the Bible and everything that involves Jerusalem maps to Howick. Return and redemption point in the same direction – and so does sin. But there's a lot that I don't know and László won't discuss. Like how he decodes Idriess, particularly *Madman's Island*. What I know about that is from other sources. After one more complaint I went to the library and Mary showed me his annotations, and I've seen notebook pages inscribed with words and whorls – symbols and signs, comments and connectors – like medieval cartographic imaginings. I understand that László sees the text itself as a palimpsest. For him, to know the truth requires seeing deeply, beneath the surface. László believes that only he has that insight, that skill. And he does have some uncanny abilities, particularly when he's asleep. When I became aware of his dream states he realized it was something I was interested in, and for a while he seemed to relish taking me there – I thought I'd found a direct route to his other world. But not for long, the door suddenly closed and I never figured out why.

By and large I rely on the set piece of the clinical interview and as long as I don't dig too deep he can look great. But I know that if I scratch the surface his thought disorder is there and I can amplify it with particular questions or comments, like probing and irritating an open wound.[129] For the most part, I don't do that, and maybe it's the assurance of being in the safety of a predictable space and relationship, with someone who understands that there's a metalanguage and gets some of it, that allows László to share his inner world with me. He's learned from experience and he knows what not to talk about with others. But, even now, the veneer cracks if they take him there. And that's after being on antipsychotics for five years. He's had different drugs at a range of doses – always by depot injection. He refuses to take tablets even though that would mean less toxic options. *The needle*, it always ends with *the needle*, but now it's an unstated compromise that supports a fiction that's important to him – that he's being coerced.

So although I knew László was still mad when the Mental Health Review Tribunal considered his Involuntary Treatment Order for the fifth or sixth time I stepped back from the decision process – maybe I *took the fifth*. What I didn't do was push the buttons I knew would turn up the dial on his thought disorder; I didn't invoke the precautionary principle. What the Tribunal saw and judged was a stable man whose psychotic symptoms were in remission and who was cooperating with his treatment team. There was no history of violence and he seemed to be making an informed decision to take responsibility back for maintaining his well-ness. I also thought that if he became a voluntary patient and we could maintain a relationship it might create an opportunity to talk about a trial of a more appropriate medication – clozapine. In the short term the big question was whether he'd stick with treatment once the heavy hand of *The Act* was lifted. He did.

László waited until his designated appointment time and is now seated stiffly next to the desk in the consult room. There's an examination table in one corner, various bits of clinical equipment around the room and a cutaway anatomical mannequin next to a surgical wash-basin. Not an ideal mental health setting but it's a multi-purpose system, so it's what you work with. And although he doesn't look at me directly I know he takes notice of little things. But like a bowerbird he's choosy, what he registers and retains is particular. To a casual observer that bird's collection seems unstructured though they may note an odd feature, like the colour blue. The gathering process may look random – but it's not. And although there are lots of things that László knows about me from observation, conversation and gossip, some are carefully selected and stored away. For instance, he knows I trained in the United States and regularly probes to see how I'll respond to discredited theories and treatments. We're back there today: *When you were in America did you use cattle prods on your patients doctor Hunter… They say it's painless – I wonder if that's what the cattle say doctor Hunter, before they die… And sleep therapy doctor Hunter, they use that here in Australia doctor Hunter, deep sleep, the sleep of forgetfulness. Make us forget the needle-dependent psychopaths and rapists. Or do you use an orgone accumulator doctor Hunter, did they train you about how to do that in America, or how to do lobotomies… They got JFK's sister doctor Hunter. Settled her right down…*

He's informed and reads more than just Idriess. But as bright blue objects are for the bowerbird, Idriess fragments are for László – everything that relates to Jack is selected. I wouldn't recognize most of them, but I know they're being arranged and stored in some idiosyncratic but orderly way. Anything about *Madman's Island* or Jack's military service guarantees particular attention and questions. He wants to know what I know, what I think, he's not interested in convincing me of anything. The picture I've built up of how the fragments make sense for László is by inference from chance associations. Like talking about Jack at Gallipoli and the wounds he received at Lone Pine, or Trooper Idriess in Palestine, László might suddenly be off on a riff about Golgotha, the three hills, wounds and nails – *three nails doctor Hunter*. For László there is some equivalence between shrapnel and nails; his wounds and stigmata. Jack on the cross. At least that's how I read it.

Then there's Howick, though he never uses that name. It's always *The Island*; and it's *The Book*, not *Madman's Island*. I assumed it was the arresting title that had grabbed his attention and held it, as it did mine – *The Island* as metaphor for institutional oppression and coercion, or for isolation or abandonment. But I gradually realized that it's way more complex. It wasn't *Madman's Island* that led to his obsession with Idriess – he'd been reading Idriess or listening to Jack's books being read to him from childhood by the first Doris well before his psychosis began. Idriess was already important to László and *Madman's Island* had special status – it was Jack's first book, published as fiction but then revealed as fact. It can be read as tale, truth or fable, and the setting is rich with opportunities for allegorical invention – a remote island with a history of tragedy, at the whim of nature's caprice and with peculiar topography. Other than three elevations that each take on particular meanings in the story and together channel biblical landscapes, it's an impenetrable mangrove forest broken by a maze of tidal races alive with dangers.

Kayaking entered our conversations after learning from Biata that his father was a junior champion before the war and had been a coach at the Melbourne Olympics. Maybe because of his father he seems to avoid using the word kayak and always talks about my canoe. He's aware of the difference but canoe/kayak has become part of a standard exchange. He knows about Michael Fomenko and his dugout canoe voyage to New Guinea – where László was headed when I first met him in Bamaga. And he was aware that I was taking time off, going on a similar journey north, following the islands to The Tip.

Just ten weeks ago, as I was breaking that trip in Cooktown and visiting the memorial to doctor Mick, I walked through the Peninsula Caravan Park and there was László outside his donga, sitting in a camp chair in the shade of a sagging awning with a folding card-table next to him. He seemed entirely unsurprised, as if it had been scripted that I'd walk by. On the table was a small radio and I immediately recognized the ABC regional network. Separating his space from the next donga was a sheet of recycled plywood, unadorned save for a row of hooks from one of which hung a solitary pannikin. Other than the radio, the only objects on the tabletop were a writing pad and a library book that had been placed in one corner with a ballpoint pen neatly beside. The bicycle that I'd seen him riding around town and which was always outside the hospital when I arrived on those days he was scheduled to see me was leaning against the wall. Through the open door I could make out jumbled piles of clothes, dishes and boxes. Just as it was when I'd visited in the past, an internal chaos sharply marked off from a veneer of order. I didn't need psychiatric training to see the parallel to László's life.

Boundaries; containing the chaos or holding the world at bay – like his stones. Precisely marking the edge of a virtual veranda, tracking the space covered by the awning, were lines of smooth, white river stones. László had gathered them over years from the beach at Finch Bay – I'd seen him there, picking them up from where the creek empties into the sea. He was very discerning, they had to have an almost translucent quality, broken from quartz seams in some distant past and worn to perfect smoothness in their journeys to the sea. There seemed thousands of them outside his donga with spaced piles that suggested looking down on the crenelated walls of a fortress. Just a line of stones, but more. As I remained outside and László within the security of his donga-keep he spoke without getting up or making eye contact: *You came by canoe doctor Hunter. On your way to the islands. To the islands doctor Hunter...* And as scripted I corrected: *Not canoe, a kayak. But right now I'm going to see if I can find the memorial to doctor Mick, I was told it's in the botanical gardens. Do you ever go by the memorial...*

— *There's lots of memorials doctor Hunter, Mick the Miner is a good memorial doctor Hunter. That's the memorial I visit doctor Hunter, a memorial to the real times.*
— *I know about that one, I'll be leaving from near there tomorrow morning. I'll see you when I get back.*

— *There's no back from the islands doctor Hunter. It's to the islands doctor Hunter.*

He knew I'd know as soon as I found it and ten minutes later I was reading the inscription that spells out DR MICK, a plaque set in stone around which there was a mound of smooth, white, almost translucent river stones, with a few sitting precariously on the face of the plaque – maybe to keep the *golem* at bay. And the next day while I was portaging my kayak with all the gear I'd calculated was essential for another month paddling north, a dozen trips from the Seaview to the boat ramp by the wharf, I recognized László's bicycle locked to a streetlamp just a few metres away. I didn't see him over the hour it took to get it all together, but I know he was watching – as I headed to the islands.

That was just ten weeks ago and now we're back in our office relationship and I'm trying to figure out whether locating me *in the radio* is a hallucination, delusional thinking, or some kind of idea of reference, inferring me as the source of a communication that while broadcast over the radio was specifically to him or for him. And whether it's relevant, connected to a stored fragment, or simply psychotic white noise. Maybe this relates to my trip north, although I've already told him I didn't get to where Jack and Charlie set up camp on Howick. I chose not to tell him we'd camped at the island's northern tip. *It's very difficult to get to* The Island *doctor Hunter* – that's all he said. *In the radio* is still on my mind as I shift across to a different tack and check that it was local ABC he was listening to. I don't get to finish the question: *D-E-F doctor Hunter, that's deaf doctor Hunter, you're not deaf, you know I listen to the ABCDEF. But you don't need me to tell you doctor Hunter.*

All I can do is try again: *László, I'm trying to understand what this experience means to you. Last night, my voice was on the radio…* But I get no further: *In the radio and not your voice doctor Hunter.* In the radio but not my voice – not me but me. And as far as László is concerned I shouldn't need to have it all spelled out. In the end you just keep approaching from

different angles: *OK, last night while you were listening to ABC local on your radio you heard a man's voice…*
— *Not a man doctor Hunter, you should know, you were there. And you've been there doctor Hunter. You've been to the islands and you know what she said – what you said. Aren't you going to talk about treatments doctor, that's what you do, talk about the madman and drugs…*

It's not going well at all – he's never used the word *madman* before. That and *been to the islands* must relate to the trip, to the Howicks. He's agitated, with changes in voice tone and less coherence in the sequencing of his thoughts. The tremor that's usually only obvious in his right leg now involves both. Held with palms flat on his knees, his hands appear to be softly drumming. A side effect of antipsychotic drugs that he seems to accept – to wear even – as a signifier of coerced status, the stigmata of oppression.

Time to back off, to deal with the here and now, back to *the needle*. We go through our routine – reviewing his medication, the side effects, the need for compliance. One more time I raise a trial of clozapine – he already knows the potential benefits and the risks. It's usually thrown back at me as an accusation – *aren't you satisfied with robots doctor Hunter, drug dependent psychopaths filling me with neuromuscular toxins…* Who can argue with that – that's what we do, fill people with toxic chemicals. Sometimes we make things better. Sometimes we don't. *You want drooling doctor Hunter, breaking my heart … you want blood*. Not exactly *want*, but basically all true – clozapine is a drug with some pretty common side effects and a remote chance of serious toxicity – potentially fatal. It's been around for decades though not used regularly for those reasons. But it can make a difference for people whose psychotic symptoms have responded to nothing else – like László. As long as it's done carefully and monitored closely with blood tests – yes, we *want blood*.

Around it goes, one more time, his second cup of tea untouched. The session wanders over well-covered ground but occasionally the territory is unfamiliar. Maybe a hint about his refusal of clozapine – *you want to send me away, don't you doctor Hunter, away.* Correct – he'd have to go to Cairns for a few months to be stabilised. Change – not something László does well. As liminal as he is in this fringe and redneck place it's home, and he's as stable as he's been for decades. And there are connec-tions – in this world and in some other. Every now and again the voice in the radio filters into the conversation but when I pursue it – it's gone.

The space doesn't help. I prefer to talk to patients away from the clinic where the accoutrements of clinical practice don't impede communica-tion. These consultation rooms are designed for procedures, to elicit infor-mation in a one-directional flow where even the clinician's gaze isn't part of the exchange, glued to a screen or print-out of requests and laboratory results, the patient sitting immobile at the side of the desk. If I have to use that space I disrupt it; shift the furniture, use a table as a connector not a separator, and share something – *the tea ceremony*.[130] But it's still an asym-metric relationship. Despite the social pretence and freedom for each of us to ask questions, it's the doctor who probes, who gets personal. That's the script, but not all patients stick with it and it can be the patient who gets personal, triggering standard devices to get things back on track – *what interests you in my background ... I can understand that it's difficult being the one to answer all the questions ... the important task for us to work on is what's best for you, what's really going on with you right now...*

Every psychiatrist knows the feeling of a patient's comment or question that's so close it's like rubbing raw flesh. Whether it's intentional or not, it often signals real problems in the relationship – *proceed with caution.* That's less common when the patient has a psychotic illness where the questions are more like blunt force than incisive probing. And sometimes, particularly with someone like László, it's a matter of timing, of coinci-dence, a momentary eddy in the flow of thoughts that suddenly connects in new ways. As long as there's someone listening. The clinician may or may not be tuned in to all the implicit meanings but they have to be atten-tive, they have to be interested. So, maybe a dozen times we've been over the ground that goes – *why did you become a psychiatrist doctor Hunter, why did you decide to join the psychopaths...* But today, even though the stream continued uninterrupted, the torrent took me to another space, one of my own – he connected: *Where did you come from doctor Hunter… It wasn't a virgin birth doctor Hunter, I know about virgin births – not for you, not for the antichrist. Where are you from, where are your islands, doctor Hunter…*

My islands – right – where are my islands…

Cairns, November 27, 2000

When Jack Idriess passed through Cairns on the way to Cooktown in 1912 it was a knock-about, polyglot town of around thirteen thousand souls, the main port of the region and the terminus for the railway from the south, connecting to lines up the range to Chillagoe, Mareeba and Herberton. Within a couple of years – in the same month that peace was shattered in Europe – the first biplane landed just to the south at Queerah. New technologies and new cultures were being stamped on a town reclaimed from marshland. On weekends Jack might have joined the locals promenading along the Esplanade on the shores of Trinity Bay and taken in a concert by the Cairns Citizens Brass Band under Band Master Arthur Prime.[131] Strolling back into town he may have dropped in to The Popular Café on the corner of Abbott and Shields streets, or gone to see a moving picture show at The Lyric, which opened that year. The streets were still unpaved and while motor vehicles hadn't long appeared, bicycles were everywhere. Walking along Sheridan Street he would have passed over an improvised cycling and running track, illuminated by gaslight for evening events run by a Chinese bookmaker.[132] Nearly a century later and a block farther down Sheridan Street, on the corner with Upward, are the offices and studios of the ABC Far North Queensland.

Two months ago, just a few days after getting back from Cooktown, I went there. It's an unassuming, single story, brick building, and inside the front door the low-key ambience continues. The reception area was empty and the only evidence that I wasn't alone was an occasional glimpse of a young man in T-shirt and sandals shuttling between offices and studios out the back. After ten minutes a woman with a set of headphones around her neck and carrying a mug appeared in what I guessed was the corridor to the kitchen. *Front desk* – that was all she called, but soon after the young man approached and a few minutes later I was in the kitchen, explaining to them both over a cup of coffee why I was trying to find out if anything about the author, Ion Idriess, had been broadcast recently on the ABC regional network. An hour later I left with a name and a book title. Beverley Eley, author of *Ion Idriess*, had been interviewed and it had been broadcast on the regional network on September 26, the day before I saw László.

Within a couple of weeks I had a copy of the book from Gleebooks in Sydney – across and up the road from Cornstalk. Angus and Robertson published Idriess, he was their biggest selling Australian author for decades. Beverley Eley worked for them and one of her main sources for the book was Wendy, Idriess's daughter. Most of the story I know – his first years in Tenterfield, a stint at opal mining in Lightning Ridge before heading north, his war years at Gallipoli and in Palestine – and north Queensland. But there's not a lot about the north, Eley was mainly interested in the established writer where there are plenty of sources – and she has lots to say about his private life. Even so, there are things about the younger Idriess I didn't know, like the death of his mother in Broken Hill in 1908 after Jack had come down with typhoid fever: *He survived but Julia, the mother he adored, contracted typhoid while nursing him and died before his delirium had passed.*[133]

He survived... But probably not unscathed. Not long after that his wandering years began and he drifted on to Lightning Ridge. His best mate there was another opal digger, Tom Peel, who encouraged his *scribblings*. And it was with Tom that he was suspected of having killed an elderly prospector – rumors enough to leave town and head north. To Queensland, which Eley seems to gloss over with almost nothing about *Madman's Island* although she claims that after Howick his health wasn't good and he went to stay with his sister in Grafton. Not for long though, he returned north and from 1926 to 1928 was moving between Cooktown, Thursday Island and the Fly River.

But Idriess wasn't a young man any more, he was about to turn forty and according to Eley he decided that he was going to leave the north for Sydney. A big move for someone wedded to the wild, he was heading from the bush to the city to make a living as a writer at the very time that the Depression was forcing the newly unemployed from the city to the bush searching for whatever work was going. Jack went the other way. That year he received a letter from Angus and Robertson declaring the first version of *Madman's Island* a failure and suggesting he give up writing books. He didn't, and his career was about to take off with *Lasseter's last ride*, *Men of the jungle*, *Flynn of the inland* and *The desert column* all published in the next three years. From then he was on a roll and continued to mine his past experiences for the rest of his life. Including Howick, with the non-fiction version of *Madman's Island* coming out in 1938.

Jack Idriess, Beverley Eley, doctor Hunter – ghosts *in the radio*. While I was listening to the interview with Eley in the ABC studio I imagined the Sony radio on the table under the awning outside László's donga, local news and human-interest stories floating out from the keep, disappearing between the gum trees and palms of the caravan park. He might not have been listening consciously, just scanning for fragments. And then: *On the line we have Beverley Eley, the author of a recent biography of Ion Idriess, best known for his books about life in the bush.* Back 'o Cairns *is one I personally remember but he wrote a lot more about the north. Beverley, welcome to ABC North Queensland, can you tell us how…*

All coming together at once – perhaps with the force of revelation. The broadcast was the day before his appointment with me, with the doctor who knew about Shark-eye Park in New Guinea and who'd appeared at Bamaga when László had tried to get there. And who understood about Charlie and *The Island* and had tried to go there too – maybe had. To Golgotha, lair of *Ördög*. Whoever else was in the mix and whatever the connections were, the message was for László, and it was received in clear over the background static of an interview. The evidence was there, and my complicity was probably confirmed by my confusion, which he may have read as feigned to cover an attempted deception – *not in the radio, on*

… the unspoken joke shared with the Ned Kelly body armour …

… Mick the Miner.

… a hint of the tropics on the edge of the Arctic Circle …

the radio and I don't think I was. But László wasn't being fooled – *in the radio doctor Hunter, and yes, you were.*

Just like the passing mention of Shark-eye Park, which gave me the first inkling of a link to Idriess, the convoluted chain to Beverley Eley took me a few days to appreciate, and this time it took me to Jack's life story. And that wasn't the only slow fuse from the meeting with László two months ago. As I drove back to Cairns, down the coast road, through Wujal and over the range to Cape Tribulation and on to the Daintree ferry I was aware of his parting question circling somewhere in penumbral awareness – *What are your islands doctor Hunter... Where are your islands...*

Tresta, April 18, 2001

— *We're been lippenin you.*
— *Mary, I'm so sorry – but I don't know what you mean.*
— *We've been waiting for you.*

Tresta – just along the A971 at Evrabister, across the Weisdale *Voe* in the Shetland Islands. A place to learn about my islands, stories that spread around the world under sail and steam, stories that lead to mine, passing through the goldfields of Australia, and to Nova Scotia – and Jerusalem. Stories that go way back, traceable to at least 1468 when the Shetlands were given in lieu of a dowry by the financially-strapped King Christian I of Denmark, Norway and Sweden, to King James III of Scotland – an act of impignoration. Although Princess Margaret died before she made it into the arms of the Crown Prince, James kept the dowry. But he did agree to respect Norse law and language – the seeds of problems that germinated four hundred years later when the clearances across Scotland eventually came to the Shetland Islands. Udal inheritance, from those Norse ancestors, was shared, like in Ireland, and based on custom and verbal agreements. For the newcomer lairds and absentee landlords from mainland Scotland it was like *terra nullius*,[134] and with the clearances the Hunters who had lived for a century in Weisdale, and before that in Vidlin and Lunna, were forced off the land to make way for sheep. Just like Australia – fortunes built on the backs of sheep and by seeing the backs of blacks or, in this case, the coat-tails of crofters.

They say the last to leave was Johnny Hunter, rowing some of the 300 evicted crofters across the *Voe* in the 1860s. He worked for the new masters but they got rid of him too. Accused of theft and arrested, he called on the heavens for retribution and the storm on the day he was released was talked about for generations. And two old women who refused to leave their croft and were walled in by the estate men to starve them out cursed the evictors. Curses, what else could you do; the Earl of Zetland got what he wanted in the end.

Born before the evictions my great grandfather, Henry Hunter, a whaler and farmer, married Barbara Morrison and settled in Tumblin where they raised ten children. They knew the future lay elsewhere and all their sons grew to be seamen and their daughters were sailors' wives. The sea was survival and escape. Their seven sons became captains except for the first, John, who jumped ship in Australia to get to the goldfields. Maybe from Cooktown to the Palmer River, but probably Fremantle to Kalgoorlie. The seventh child was David, my grandfather, whose first two children – Beatrice and Harry – were born in Nova Scotia and the last – Ernie, my uncle and namesake – in Glasgow. On his travels David commissioned a painting in Naples, a copy of a photograph taken of his elderly mother, Barbara, outside their croft in Evrabister. In that painting Barbara is in an ankle-length black dress, with matching stockings and shoes, and a dark shawl tied beneath her chin – maybe she was in mourning for Henry. She stands at one side of a path that disappears into the distance past walled fields and scattered buildings which all look the same – small and windowless. Barbara holds a bowl in her crooked left arm and looks down at the chickens she's feeding from her extended right hand. The landscape around Evrabister is treeless now – as it was then. When David returned to pick up the painting the Neapolitan artist said that he felt it looked too empty so he'd added some trees, which stand in a copse at the right of the picture. He painted what he knew and the result was palm trees – a hint of the tropics on the edge of the Arctic circle – nice touch.

David's firstborn, Beatrice, had that painting in Rutherglen, Glasgow, and I saw it when I was visiting from boarding school in the 1960s. My father, Harry, stayed there waiting for the end, which didn't come – not there, not then. Beatrice had lived in that house for over half-a-century but even in old age mourned the loss of her childhood in Port Hastings, on Cape Breton Island, Nova Scotia, where David was stationed and where he'd married a local woman, Margaret McDonald. Beatrice wrote about that distant decade, a record of a childhood that remained vibrant in her memory seventy years later. After her death I was given that document which was unread for a decade until recently, twenty pages of close, precise handwriting that ends just after the first War as my grandparents, my father and Beatrice sailed up the Firth of Clyde. Glasgow, second city of the empire then – there was still an empire but not for long. Clydeside just off its peak – for Beatrice the old world but a new one, and definitely not Port Hastings. There's an extra page that doesn't fit in that narrative, but made sense when I then opened a book gifted to me decades earlier that had also lain unread – *Captain Kidd and his Skeleton Island: The discovery of a strange secret hidden for 266 years.*[135] Like *Madman's Island* and *Swallows and Amazons*, inside the cover is a map of an island. and also a facsimile signature attributed to Kidd dated 1699. In the top corner of the following page is another signature, much more recent but still old, my father's – *H.C. Hunter*. On Beatrice's last page:

> *Kidd's cove was a very romantic place to me. All around it was tall spruce trees and you seemed to look down on the cove. It got its name from the notorious pirate Captain Kidd. He always brought his ships into the cove when he was in that part of the world. And the story goes that on a hill overlooking the cove is where he buried his treasures. As custom with pirates they always killed one of the crew so his spirit would guard the treasures. Many and many times people would come down to Hastings to try and dig for the treasure and always there was a tragedy and never has the treasure been discovered. Many and many a time I went up the hill with Grampa and saw the big holes. I always imagined I saw a diamond sparking in the sunlight and sometimes a skull. Mama told me as long as she could remember men have tried to dig for the*

treasure but were always stopped by some unseen hand.

Unseen hands, maps – Skeleton Island, Wild Cat Island, Turtle Head Island – maps, magic.

But now I'm in Tresta, almost by accident though I sense not. A few enquiries in Glasgow on the way back to Australia after Jerusalem and within days I'm visiting relatives I didn't know I had. Met at the airport by someone I'm told is a distant Shetland cousin – Mark Hackbarth – doesn't sound very Shetland. And it's not – American. His mother, Davida, was sister to Mary whose welcome I'm decoding. For girls the sea was not a means of escape from the Shetlands but the Second World War brought opportunities. Mark's father, Robert Hackbarth, had been flying Spitfires with the American 31st Fighter Group and was shot down over Anzio in February 1944. Recuperating in Edinburgh after being liberated from *Stalag Luft* 1 by the Russians in the last month of the war he met Davida who was a Red Cross volunteer. They were married in Madison Wisconsin the year after the war and eventually Mark was born. A widow at forty when Robert died in 1967 she went back – back to the islands she'd escaped from. And with her, Mark, whose enduring American accent broadcasts an outsider status that seems to lift only in the company of his aunt, Davida's only sibling, Mary, into whose house we enter.

Tresta, April 19, 2001

We're been lippenin you. I was here yesterday, invited into a cottage set in a *daal* at the end of a winding, stone path shaded by sycamore trees that survive where there's shelter from winds that spare few trees other than the occasional rowan and crab-apple. Going back in time, with Mary Houston, my father's cousin. Entering a house and a family – my family – lost until now. Back at Tresta House again as Mary continues a commentary about memorabilia on walls and tables, artefacts from the ages of sail and steam. Her father, Adam, was Henry's tenth and last child and my father was his cadet, on the same ship in which a very young Mary and her mother accompanied Adam around the world. Mary talks of Harry affectionately, larking about as a teenager off the coast of Chile in the 1930s – before another war. Her father and two of his brothers, John and Henry, lost ships to enemy action in the First War. Then another surprise, a connection to that war and the one that followed, and to where I've just been – Jerusalem.

I flew to Scotland from Israel just a few days ago. I was teaching at Yad Vashem – the Holocaust study centre and memorial in Jerusalem. My topic was the complicity of medical professionals, particularly psychiatrists, in supporting the ideology that enabled race killing. Not only as functionaries in *Aktion T4*, the euthanasia program, or *Aktion14f13* which saw the lessons, expertise and personnel from that program support industrial murder in the east, but as the drivers in developing and refining the underlying ideology and rationale. *The permission to destroy life unworthy of life,* first published in 1920, was authored by a jurist, Karl Binding at the University of Leipzig, and Alfred Hoche, professor of psychiatry at the University of Freiburg. It was a winner when Hitler came to power and psychiatry provided willing subalterns seduced by opportunism.[136]

Far from the centres of industrial extermination that have been silent for more than half-a-century, there are lessons for Australia, a country in which there's also a history and legacy of racism in health – Aboriginal health. Forced treatments, lock hospitals, discriminatory legislation across the continent and continuing – and I'm part of it. Two conditions, leprosy and syphilis – both introduced but reconstructed as native diseases – resulted in thousands being incarcerated. With sometimes terrible consequences; a third of those suspected of having syphilis by *honorary protectors* and sent against their will to Dorre and Bernier Islands, dismal specks off the Western Australian coast near Carnarvon, died there – and they didn't even have syphilis.[137] Maybe they were the lucky ones; Idriess heard stories from Womba Billy, an ageing, heavy drinking whitefellow who'd lived with Kimberley blackfellows for most of his adulthood – he had a half-caste daughter who was taken away to Forrest River Mission around the time Gribble was there. One story was from Womba's early days in the north when he'd been a young man on the luggers off Condon Beach:

A fortnight at sea, and the master found out that venereal disease had broken out among the coloured crew.

"My God!" he exclaimed.

"Why?" Inquired the surprised boy.

"Because it means death! And we thought the fleets were clean! This will spread like wildfire. Not so much aboard, but the infected men will take it ashore, the native women will catch it, the curse will spread throughout the fleets."

"But can't you cure these men?"

"Cure venereal disease!" sneered the master. "Don't be a fool. There is no doctor within hundreds of miles, and even if there was, do you think the fleets would lay up just to take these swine to a doctor? There is only one cure for venereal disease at sea, and I don't know of any other certain cure on land."

He lined his coloured crew up against the rail, and examined them. Only one man, the cook, was infected.

"I'm going to cure you!" said the skipper evenly, staring into the man's frightened eyes. He pulled out his Bulldog and shot the man through the heart. As the man fell back into the sea, the master growled: "That is the only way to cure venereal disease at sea."

He rowed across to the companion schooner and by coincidence found the cook aboard infected also. He cured this man similarly.[138]

Maybe Womba Billy could tell Idriess that story because he didn't kill anyone, he wasn't really involved – just a bystander. Victims, perpetrators and bystanders, plenty of each – then and now. And in teaching about the bystander during the Holocaust a key resource is a poem by Martin Niemöller. Military hero with an iron cross for his services as a U-boat Captain in the First War, he became a Lutheran pastor and theologian, and ended up in Sachsenhausen and Dachau concentration camps from 1937 to 1945 for his opposition to the Nazis. He survived to protest Vietnam. I recited that poem just one week ago in Jerusalem:

*First they came for the Jews
and I did not speak out
because I was not a Jew.*

*Then they came for the Communists
and I did not speak out
because I was not a Communist.*

*Then they came for the trade unionists
and I did not speak out
because I was not a trade unionist.*

*Then they came for me
and there was no one left
to speak for me.*
                                   Martin Niemöller

The connection is among the memorabilia we sift through over the afternoon. I'm handed an obituary for Mary's father, Adam, from the *Shetland Times* of 7 April, 1959:

... *on October 21st, 1917, Capt. Hunter, in command of the s.s. Gryfevale—first "armed" merchantman to enter New York and whose cannon delighted the cartoonists there—met and engaged U151. Splitting of the gun's muzzle ended the fight but surprisingly, Gryfevale was able to increase her distance and steam out of range. Panic amongst the Chinese firemen, however, caused another crisis and the U-boat was enabled to re-open fire. Capt. Hunter, forced to run his ship ashore near Dakar, was accommodated with his crew by French lighthousemen. For the price of a bride-buying sack of sugar, their native servant retrieved from the desert the Master's close companion, Jellicoe, a smooth-haired fox terrier, who was given shore leave for the remainder of the war. Many years later reading From U-boat to Pulpit, Capt. Hunter learned that his antagonist had been the now-celebrated pastor Martin Niemöller.*

Degrees of separation across oceans and generations – me and Martin Niemöller. And bystanders; Niemöller knew about bystanders and what it took for them – what it takes for all of us – to remain complacent. Denial, rationalisation or trivialisation – whatever it takes.

Cooktown, September 12, 2001

It's a sunny, dry season morning and from the veranda of the Seaview the horizon to the north is clear – but although I've stared at it dozens of times, today it's not the same. And Charlotte Street seems wider and more deserted although it's probably always like this early in the morning. The hospital and the Multipurpose Primary Care Centre are as they were when I was last here – but not. From the moment I turned on the TV as the kettle boiled in my motel room everything is different, reality crumbling with the collapsing Twin Towers. Hypnotic images and a shocking realization somewhere along the mundane routine of showering and breakfasting that the commentators' alarm is not contrived, it's not April Fools' day, not Orson Wells, not the world I thought I had woken to.

It's everywhere, including on the TV in the waiting room of the Primary Care Centre. Muted sound, just looping images of the fall – as if you need to see it a hundred times to believe it. As if you can choose not to see it, which adds to the unreality. So public – so private. I feel like nobody in the clinic except me gets the existential crisis, an exploding matrix of actions and consequences. Maybe our media masters have immured us to disaster on any scale – it's just another spectacle. The receptionists sitting opposite only glance up occasionally as they'd usually do for their morning doses of Oprah or some other distracting nostrum. And sitting under the monitor, facing away from the screen that seems to silently scream to me of the end of days, is László. He's watching me though his gaze seems elsewhere: *Good morning doctor Hunter, it's not like you to be late.*

That's right, it's not like me to be late, even when absence is hardly noticed. Not like me to let anything upset the system's routines and rhythms. But this isn't any *thing*, it's *something* – something that feels even more incomprehensible broadcast in real time from across the world to a motel and clinic waiting room in Cooktown, far north Queensland. Unreal – repeated in comments and commentary, so banal, so true – so not true. Collapsing towers, falling bodies – crumbling empires of certainty. I'm surprised, maybe irritated by his comment and attempt to explain the unnecessary, that like everyone else I was watching what was happening in New York. Echoing my words he leads me far from the unfolding tragedy: *Watching what's happening in New York. You should be watching the watching at the caravan park doctor Hunter. ÁVO are watching there. For the Party, always watching. New York – perhaps you were dreaming doctor Hunter. Dreaming of New York. Or maybe you're dreaming of Cooktown. I might be dreaming that you're going to ask me if I want a cup of tea…*

What's happening in New York – László knows just as much as I do. Radio or TV – it's saturation coverage. But while I'm re-running the images in my mind – the last seconds of people forced to choose fall or fire – and brooding on apocalyptic implications, it's the goings-on in the Peninsula Caravan Park that's driving his paranoid projections. New York just isn't a meaningful fragment. And dreams – he used to talk about dreams a lot. Not just the old chestnut of challenging my understanding of reality when his own is questioned – *if you can't be sure when you enter or leave dream reality doctor Hunter, how can you be sure you can judge someone else's reality* – he also knows more than most about dreaming, an oneironaut of sorts.

Oneironaut – László introduced the term three years ago when I followed his lead into a dream-scape. He'd asked me if I could remember the first time we met, in Bamaga. That was easy, the memory and images were vivid and detailed: *You're creating space in a virtual field doctor Hunter. Your imagination is one of infinite space-time possibilities – it's real in your mind. And multiple realities are also possible in this shared space doctor Hunter, the space with the two cups of tea at midday on a Tuesday in Cooktown in 1998.*

Like psychoanalysis, compelling but loose enough that it's hard to tie down or refute. I wasn't interested in challenging, just going along, but that took me back to a psychiatric space: *This reality is not always as it seems doctor Hunter. You might be an imposter – and by realizing it reality is changed. Like when I was in Silkwood, the ÁVO replaced Biata's son, Dom. I don't think Biata knew but I knew. Just about everyone in Silkwood was ÁVO. And it happened at other times; even Biata when she visited the hospital in Cairns doctor Hunter, they replaced her.*

Capgra's syndrome, *l'illusion des sosies*, they picked that up when he became agitated and threatening in Cairns Base Hospital in the mid-90s. Described in the 1920s – *the illusion of doubles* – the replacement of someone known and often close by an imposter, an exact copy. It wasn't clear whether it was Capgra's or the *illusion Frégoli*. Dates from the same time and named for Leopoldo Frégoli, a *fin de siècle* performer who was so good at rapid transformations of character on stage that he was accused of having a double – he didn't. People with the syndrome believe that the bodies of various people have been taken over by the same person. For a few months László was in a hazy Capgra's/Frégoli's borderland. Whichever it was probably didn't matter, both are delusional syndromes and hard to treat. But with László it settled with antipsychotics even though the paranoia and thought disorder remained. And a few years later, when he seemed to be doing reasonably well, he took me into dreamland: *And when you dream, doctor Hunter, you're somewhere else but how do you know…*

— *Because you wake up.*
— *Don't you know when you're dreaming doctor Hunter, can't you guide your journey, that must be very confusing…*
— *I know that's possible László, it's called lucid dreaming, I don't think it's ever happened with me.*
— *A pity doctor Hunter, I thought you might be a fellow oneironaut.*

A fellow oneironaut. I didn't know what that was back then, I thought he'd made it up, one more neologism. But the ability of the sleeper to guide the dream I knew – lucid dreaming. Uncommon but not rare, the lucid dreamer is aware of self and of being in a dream, and also has access to non-dream memory, to their waking-life past. The sleeper who has self-awareness in their dream can make choices and direct the narrative. That's one of the ways it's been tested, getting lucid dreamers to signal actions while dreaming that researchers can detect in the electrical sleep record. Some people believe it's a skill that can be cultivated and there are resonances with spiritual traditions like Tibetan dream yoga. I'd heard about lucid dreaming and dream yoga around the same time as I was into TM, trying to master the flying *sidhi* when I wasn't taking chemical shortcuts. Neither worked.

An oneironaut is different and I had to do some searching. It's the ability to enter into other people's dreams – telepathic dreaming. Evoking sci-fi and Carlos Castenada, it has connections with shamanic traditions. As I began to understand I remembered a remarkable Aboriginal elder, a *Djaui* man from Sunday Island, *Ewenu*, at the entrance to King Sound, who I first met in the 1960s when I was a teenager working at Derby Hospital and he was admitted following a crash on the road along the Dampierland Peninsula. Seriously injured, his stoic, quiet acceptance of what was needed over the hours it took to get him to hospital marked him as someone special. Two decades later our paths crossed again and I realized that Aubrey Tigan was not only remarkable for his stoicism but also for particular talents and skills, gifts maybe, including healing – and dreams.

It was in the late 1980s that I met Aubrey again, at One Arm Point, *Ardyaloon*, and he told me that, years earlier, he'd lost those gifts when the grog got on top of him; I suppose they demanded clarity and focus. But he'd stopped drinking by the time we re-met and re-focused his life, and we talked about how he worked as a healer. Of course, he knew everyone in that small community and was related to most of them, so he always understood the back-story. When someone came to him with a problem they'd talk and then he'd sleep on it. He'd dream – he'd go on a journey and meet his countryman, then they'd go to where the problem was: *Those dreamings come together when we go that way*. A little later they'd meet up and talk some more: *I'd tell him what I found, tell him which way he got to go*. I tried to pin him down about whether his countryman remembered the same dream journey. He just smiled. Some years later the dreams led Aubrey in a new direction, he told Nicolas Rothwell:

The dreams came back to Aubrey Tigan in earnest some seven years ago, when he began carving his ancestral designs on Kimberley pearl shell once again. The cyclonic swirls and stepped meanders, the tight chevrons and wavelet lines he glimpsed insistently in his mind's eye: what were they but the remembered essence of his island home?

"I saw an old man, in my dreams, and he would keep coming, and telling me to carve that shell," murmurs Tigan, a reflective, reserved Aboriginal man in his mid-sixties. "It was a calling. Those dreams were coming to me, in my imagination, telling me to go and carve the pearl shell. And you have to listen to your dreams, not just leave them. If you leave a dream you know, it can do you harm and you can die."[139]

When I told László about Aubrey he didn't react; it was a distraction, not a noteworthy fragment. *Oneironaut* – his uses of the term were idiosyncratic and sometimes contradictory, at least that's how it came across. But he was in a good space when we had those discussions in 1998, coherent and engaged; I was happy to follow his lead: *Explain it to me László, as an oneironaut, what happens...*

— *What happens doctor Hunter. Nothing just happens, it is. In the dream sequence it is. In the dream sequence I can talk to László Halassy. It's very interesting talking to László Halassy doctor, you should know that.*

— *You mean you're talking to yourself...*

We'd been meeting for years but his facial expression was still hard to read. I knew that was partly due to the antipsychotic drugs but with most patients there is something you can pick up that gives insight into their internal state – their level of arousal and feeling state. But not László – just his eyes. Even though he never seemed to meet my gaze I thought I could detect a change in intensity and I sometimes commented on it. I called it a *cat moment* – a narrowing of his lids that darkened and deepened his pupils even though his gaze remained fixed straight ahead. Or so it seemed. And as soon as I said *talking to yourself* I registered a classic *cat moment* – and then an immediate reaction: *Mad people talk to themselves – you know that too.*

— *I'm confused, who's talking to László Halassy in the dream sequence…*
— *Well that depends, doesn't it, it might be Dick Welsh, or Cross-Eyed Joe. Or it could be me. Jack, doctor Hunter, Jack Idriess.*

László was describing vicarious dreaming, also uncommon but well described. In vicarious dreaming the sleeper's protagonist, the character experiencing the action in the dream, is someone other than the person who's asleep. Years ago, around the same time I was failing at becoming a lucid dreamer I tried to induce vicarious dreaming by briefing myself before falling asleep, concentrating on people I thought it would be inter-esting to inhabit, my heroes and antiheroes. That didn't work – in my dreams I was always me. But in László's dream the protagonist was Jack Idriess. It was always Jack, and over time I recognized other characters and settings from Idriess books.

As I sat listening to László in the consult room the complexity and confusions didn't stop there; in what he described of his vicarious dream-ing world his protagonist, Jack, was aware that he was in a dream nar-rative and could direct it, like lucid dreaming. And in the dream narra-tives László related, Jack as protagonist talked about László's other reality, the one that included me in Cooktown, as happening in his sleep world. Dreamed Jack might tell another character in László's dream that when he was sleeping he'd discovered what the *needle-dependent psychopaths* in Cooktown were trying to do – to László Halassy. And just as with other lucid dreamers the vicarious protagonist had access to memory of his self, except that self was Jack Idriess – a young Jack Idriess.

Although he didn't talk about it, I knew there were commonalities in the back stories of László and Jack, like Tenterfield, losing a mother and being cared for by an older woman, and going on a journey north. It raised all sorts of intriguing quasi-philosophical questions that László himself summed up one day: *I dream therefore I am, doctor Hunter.* I was cornered into a response as banal and evasive as it was true: *Interesting.* But as a psychiatrist I was also trying to imagine how someone with a fragmented, psychotic sense of self would engage with that self as a third person – in a dream. But I couldn't frame that question for him and I just went along with the dream narrative, as if I was part of it. Maybe I was.

That was 1999, nearly three years ago. From a clinical perspective he was doing reasonably well. He wasn't defensive and we talked dreams regularly through most of that year. Then it stopped – he didn't want to go there any more. Maybe he thought he'd told me too much, or that I was too curious about *The Island*. Around that time I mentioned my plan to kayak from Cairns to The Tip for the millennium year, possibly even to visit the Howicks.

Two years without any mention of dreams and today – *maybe you're dreaming of Cooktown*. As I wander to the kitchen to get two cups of tea there are a few more figures standing in the middle of the waiting room facing the television. Heads shaking – *a terrible thing* – and then they get on with the rest of the day. So do I, I don't need to see more angles, more talking heads, more updates from experts who have no idea what's going on or what's going down. Back in the consulting room László is seated as he nearly always is with his back to the wall – no slouching or leaning. The tremor and blunted facial expression are all as usual. But his eyes are different, he's looking straight at me – even if his affect is blunted his eyes are alive. That's not typical László and his speech now seems clipped, projected with what seems vexation or irritation: *They're all dreaming doctor Hunter. Locked onto realities that were hours or a millisecond ago, that just keep repeating. It's the same in the caravan park, they're all living vicariously doctor Hunter. You told me about living vicariously. Living vicariously in dreams. Do you remember that doctor Hunter…*

— I do, we haven't talked about dreams for a couple of years. I'm interested that dreams have come up again.

— *Yes, I know doctor Hunter is interested in dreams. Interested in what comes up, up from the depths, from where your canoe can't go, below the surface doctor Hunter. In your canoe you're trapped on the surface.*

Trapped on the surface… Set in a face that seems emotionally frozen, the nuances of expression flattened, his eyes seem out of place. The effect is amplified by an almost total absence of blinking – he just stares, but not a vacant gaze, it's piercing. For the first time I feel uncomfortable with László. Even when he's been floridly disorganised and paranoid I've been at ease. But today is different and I shift his cup of tea towards him – a small attempt to bridge the space between as he takes me to new territory: *We were on The Island, doctor Hunter. All four of us, usually there are just three, like the hills of Golgotha…*

— *You've never described a dream set on Howick before László.*
— *Your memory is accurate doctor Hunter. We have never visited The Island together – before now. But you know that doctor Hunter, you were there.*
— *I didn't make it to Howick on the trip, I got close but couldn't get ashore.*
— *Maybe you did and maybe you didn't – Ernest – but you were there. We were all there.*

Ernest – most of my patients call me Ernest. Some feel more comfortable with *doc* or *doctor Hunter* and that's fine. László has always referred to me as *doctor Hunter* and repeats it in almost every sentence as if to ground us both in the asymmetry of the relationship. *Ernest* – it was formed with such precision that the word seemed to be suspended between us, somewhere below the unshifting, unblinking gaze.

We were all there – he's quite clear – *all four of us.* Jack, Charlie, László and me, on *Madman's Island* in his dream, his oneironautic journey, somewhere in his lucid dream, vicarious dream world. And this is the first time that I've been included. In the past it was always just Idriess characters and Jack himself. I try again to move it forward: *Do you want to tell me what happened, I'm presuming…*

— *Presuming Ernest, not like you to presume. You're always so certain about realities, about what is and what's not. You shouldn't need to presume when you know it already Ernest.*
— *I'm not certain about many things László. There are lots of things that end up being judgments…*

— *Judgments. You see, you do know – we were making judgments, we three. It's the time of judgment.*

Only his mouth moves, his rigid torso making the fine tremor of his hands and fingers, and the coarse shaking of both legs more obvious. Everything on the peripheries is in motion but the centre is still. I'm not sure where to go – if I'm reading this correctly László believes that I know exactly what was going on in his dream. As far as he's concerned I was there and I shouldn't need to be told what I already know. My only way to move forward is to go back: *László you remember when we talked about dreams a couple of years ago and when I found out that you had dream-state skills, you'd walk me through the dream narrative in the first person, present tense…*

— *Of course I remember, Ernest, we were both there, we both remember. I know you know, and I know you have the needle-dependent psychopath script with you. It says you should return to the scene, Ernest. That we should go back together. I'm on The Island near Gihon spring, the waters flowing to the Pool of Siloam. He's walking down from Golgotha, from Calvary, it's almost as if he's floating down.*

— *What's he wearing…*

— *Nothing Ernest, absolutely nothing. I can see the wounds on his hands and feet, and the scar across his stomach, it's glowing. Even in the daylight – it glows.*

He's talking about Charlie and the hole that's sealed over is the stoma that Jack saw Charlie use to *flush out the gas* when they were together on Howick. *It glows* – maybe it's a reference to spear wounds and Christ on the cross. Howick, that's where we are now – and not. The Pool of Siloam, Golgotha or Calvary, the City of David – in his annotations and diagrams I saw in the copy of *Madman's Island* that Mary managed to claw back for the Cooktown library it all mapped to Howick. Again, another piece falls into place – in the last six months I've been to Howick – and to Jerusalem. László knows that, I told him before I left. *Maybe you did and maybe you didn't, Ernest, but you were there* – that's what he said and he's right on both counts, I was there. And I remember now his response when I told him I was going to Israel, what I didn't decode then – *take the Dung Gate doctor Hunter, Jack always enters through the Dung Gate to confuse* Ördög. Since I've been to Jerusalem I know that the Dung Gate was the southern entry into the Old City, leading directly to the Western Wall, to the Temple, to the heart of Jerusalem. It was downwind, where the refuse was taken, where one's smell wouldn't alert the Evil One. *Ördög* – he knew where I was going and whether it was *The Island* or Jerusalem, he was warning me.

Moments of insight – they're not as frequent or enlightening as clinicians like to think. But when fragments fit together other pieces light up. László stopped recounting dreams around the time he found out that I was planning to go to Howick and Jerusalem. When I stopped in Cooktown to find Mick's memorial during that trip László came to the boat-ramp as I was getting ready to leave, but he didn't show himself, he just watched. Then a few months later when I was back in Cooktown and in my clinical role he was agitated – I was *in the radio*. The night before, he'd listened to the interview with Beverley Eley on regional ABC giving the back-story of László's dream-character, not only the youthful Jack in Tenterfield and heading north, but the later life Ion Idriess, the heavy drinking establishment writer who never sorted out his personal and family life. And a major informant for Eley was Wendy, Ion Idriess's daughter – the later-life daughter of László's dream-protagonist, Jack Idriess. Maybe in some way it all threatened the back-story, Jack's memory of self in the dream.

I imagine László sitting outside his donga, suddenly hearing a voice talking about Idriess. A woman's voice; but even in this reality László knows that others can masquerade as familiar people or as many people. Maybe he thought I was communicating with him directly, telling him that I know the back-story – not just of László, but of Jack. *Doctor Hunter, psycho-the-rapist, the needle-dependent psychopath*, that's who's really interested in back-stories, who gets into people's minds. And there I was to see him in person the next day.

I thought you might be a fellow traveller, an oneironaut. When he said that I didn't take it literally. Perhaps I should have – telepathic dreaming – he could be talking about me entering into his dream from my own. That's understandable if I'm in his Cooktown reality which is Jack's dream, and now also in the dream reality on Howick. Whether it's me as a character in László's dream of *The Island*, or me as László's psychiatrist in Jack's dream it might fit – except that they wouldn't know if I had come through my own dream. This is doing my head in. But László continues, he's still in the first person, in the moment. I've got no idea where we're going but I push the narrative and László shifts to the other two dream characters on *The Island*: *There are two figures walking out of the forest, out of the darkness. The tide's falling and they are on sand that's exposed at low tide. It's you, Ernest, and László Halassy. Walking along the beach, very slowly, Ernest and László Halassy. We are standing by the spring; those who approach are smiling, they want to share the sacred waters – and to touch the cross. He doesn't seem concerned but I see the deceit, I try to get his attention but he doesn't see it. He's not aware of the deception, that* Ördög *is with us again, the antichrist is in our midst. I'm the only one who sees, who has real sight, who knows* Ördög.

— *That the creature or antichrist has arrived with László and me and is walking towards the well… Ernest Hunter – me – I'm the antichrist walking along the beach…*
— *No, Ernest, László Halassy is* Ördög; Ördög *is László Halassy. And I know the purpose and plan, it's written in* The Book.

We've been together for nearly an hour. Across the world there are fighter jets above New York and every civilian airport in the US has been shut down. John Howard is there, striding the world stage at a defining moment in history, putting Australia in the frame. In the waiting room outside, the receptionists are probably looking away from the TV screen only to register new patients, maybe someone else to see me.

In the consult room László hasn't moved and the tea is long cold. And now he's describing entering Jerusalem on foot through the Jaffa Gate as Allenby did on 11th December 1917, but it's an eidetic amalgam – *we're wearing capes of emu feathers* – I'm guessing that's a connection to the Light Horse plumage and trooper 358 of the 5th Regiment. For a moment I interrupt the narrative by stepping out of the story: *Jack never made it to Jerusalem, he only saw it in the distance.*[140] A tear across the fabric of the dream reality. As the comment seems to echo behind us I'm aware of my mistake. Even with the background rigidity of the neurotoxins he seems to stiffen, but the impression is probably more in his eyes than his body – a *cat moment* – he seems to be about to stand, to leave, but responds: *One of infinite virtual fields, Ernest, perhaps you read about it in a dream-book.* The torn threads of dream-telling are all I have to bring us back together – to take us back: *The Jaffa gate, entering the Holy City from the west...*Silence as heavy as his unwavering stare – but he takes up the thread: *Past the Tower of David Ernest. David street to the street of the chain – from Jaffa Gate to the Temple...*

Back in the story we're walking through a space that exists across time, merging nearly two thousand years from the city entered by Allenby, maybe conflated with a dream avatar of Trooper Jack Idriess of the 5th Light Horse, to the Crusader kingdom and the Jerusalem of Herod. And the Temple – before the fall. Cutting to an insignificant, uninhabited island off a deserted north Queensland shore. Collapsing time again, *The Island* of Jack and Charlie seventy years ago – and now. In László's retelling it's all now and he's shifted from reciting a dream – telling a story – to communicating with a dream being. And three of the four characters are here, in this room, only the Christ-Charlie is missing.

As a psychiatrist I try to balance an appreciation of what a patient expresses in terms of their experiences, whether psychotic or not, with an understanding of what those experiences mean as symptoms and signs of mental illness. So, while it's important not to dismiss content, I also need to avoid becoming so preoccupied with it that I'm reinforcing it or missing what it means in terms of illness. That's not always straightforward and, as I'm discovering now, almost impossible when it's being presented as a dream.

At some point you rely on experience and make a judgment – a slippery term that's already triggered biblical associations with László. But it's what a clinician does; weighs up as much information as possible to make an informed decision. It's incremental and although over the last hour a picture is slowly emerging, it's still confusing. László has never been free of symptoms, there's always been some paranoia, rambling thought disorder, and difficulty getting his act together beyond the solitary routines around which his life revolves. Not surprising for someone who has schizophrenia, but now there's a change that's subtle but significant, and hard to define. The clinical vibe – a crude measure but it's been a lifesaver in the past. And as he talks on about the Howick dream, about being on *The Island* or in the City of David as Idriess with the Christ-Charlie, László Halassy and me, I'm realizing that his Cooktown and dream worlds blur into one another, as do the identities of Jack Idriess and László Halassy. And as I struggle to understand, to find some category to fit this into, the more I'm convinced that whatever is going on, it's not good. If I could place myself in his dream, listening to Jack Idriess talking about someone he knows well – László Halassy – insisting that he's been replaced by a malign imposter, I might think that this is in the Capgra's or Fregoli's syndrome space, just as László had when he was hospitalised in the mid-90s. But it's a dream, and there's no clinical practice guideline for schizophrenia that has recommendations about how to deal with psychotic symptoms in a sleep state; just about everyone has quasi-psychotic sleep-related experiences – dreams.

The phone rings and I leave it, probably the receptionists to let me know there's another patient accommodating to exploding worlds and New Yorkers' real-time reactions – reality TV. I'm back on content, back in the dream. *The judgment is that Ördög must die.* Jack's words on *The Island* through László. Heard from the intended victim in the Cooktown Primary Care Centre. Jack is talking – there's a just discernible change in register from the voice I know as László's – he says he's seen into László's heart: *There's nothing there Ernest, just stone – a black stone.* And Charlie and I have agreed that László Halassy – *Ördög manqué* – must die. I'm listening as a clinical bystander as my character is complicit in planning a killing in someone else's dream. As much as I try I can't clarify what this means for László in Cooktown. In his mind there seems to be an equivalence – *There's no difference Ernest, you know that* – and in trying to come back to his status as a patient, to get some reassurance from László about what this means in the here and now, I'm stymied. He dismisses my attempt to suggest a connection to his mental state. He rejects the whole notion of psychosis: *We both know that's a false premise Ernest*. As far as he's concerned my suggestion that he should take some extra medications and stay a few nights in hospital in Cooktown simply confirms that it's me with the problem, and he brings it full circle: *You're dreaming Ernest, dreaming*. And as he rightly points out, he's a voluntary patient now.

Some clinical decisions balance competing principles, and today that boils down to respecting László's autonomy and trying to use the least restrictive intervention, versus a precautionary approach, which weighs up the probability of a particular outcome against its magnitude. In this case the end game could be László dead by his own hand. Even though that probability is unquantifiable I believe that, whatever its likelihood, it's trumped by the potential magnitude of harm. László is unwell and I can't be sure of his safety. As I continue to try to find a way to get his cooperation I've already decided that he has to go to the mental health unit in Cairns and that will mean making him an involuntary patient again and getting the police involved. Not nice. It comes to the pointy end – the decision. I explain my reasons and what's going to happen. He knows the drill, he's been here before: *Back to the lair of the drug-dependent psychopaths Ernest. Cattle prods and psychosurgery – can they cut out dreams with surgery now Ernest, is that what you want…*

The police arrive but they're not needed and remain in the background while the paperwork is done. As I expected, László refuses to take the tablets that are offered but climbs onto the examination bed and offers no resistance as an IV line goes in and the *neurotoxins* begin to flow. As the sedation kicks in, the tremor of his arms and legs settles – he seems completely still except for his eyes that continue to follow me and fix mine whenever I turn towards him. I go to another room, call the Cairns Base Hospital and ask for the admitting psychiatrist. It's Bruce Gynther who answers and I get straight to the point: *Bruce, Ernest in Cooktown. I have a complicated situation and I know I'm erring on the side of caution with a guy called László Halassy who I'm sending down to be admitted. He was in the Base about five years ago, I think that was before you came to Cairns.*

Tell me the story… Bruce listens quietly but I know he's as busy as I am and probably also has patients waiting. That's what happens when you're the admitting doctor. My schedule for the morning is long abandoned. A few calls and I've postponed a home visit, and in the waiting room outside, one of my patients has agreed to return in the afternoon and the other has scored another cup of tea. The image of George Bush has replaced the rolling repeats of exploding planes and collapsing towers. Americans are being reassured – *we go forward to defend freedom and all that is good and just in our world…* In the consult room on the other side of that world László is sliding towards what is probably dreamless sleep, and just as his eyes close he addresses me one last time: *You're dreaming Ernest. You should have taken the fifth. Always, take the fifth… Ernest… the fifth… doctor Hunter… the fifth…*

CHAPTER 10

2011: Elim to Restoration Island

Tell me the story… Hundreds of times that's what I've done, condensing lives to fragments of clinical code. Reducing a person to a diagnosis, comorbidities and a summary risk score. Recited to a doctor or nurse who doesn't really want to hear about another admission in the middle of a crowded shift. I know – I've been on the other end of the phone. But that's what you do; frame it to get over the line, across the threshold. Keep it simple – black and white – even when it's all grey.

And it's always grey – always – and not just with patients. Colleagues, friends, lovers; our images and understandings of fellow travellers are drawn from passing glimpses as journeys coincide or collide. Together for a moment or more – but that's all – the destinations are never the same. What we think we know about others is always a product of our own journey, a projection of ourselves. What we learn – if we're able to at all – is about ourselves. About the grey.

There was a lot of grey about László, but not for him. For him the world and the people in it – including me – were precisely defined. There was no ambiguity, that was how he saw it – that's how it was. In certain ways Idriess was similar. Ion Idriess was Jack Idriess – and not. Jack was an identity, a lived device, the chrysalis from which the author flew free. Jack was grounded, down to earth; he lives on the page in black and white. Ion Idriess was different, he wasn't of that world – he constructed it. And the result was a vibrant caricature of frontier life; stories told and retold from a decade in the bush, revisited and elaborated for another half-century. A journey where time stopped – among pioneers and prospectors, soldiers and settlers; in rainforest clearings and under heated skies in Palestine and the outback – until time caught up with him in June 1979.

The ghost in the darkness somewhere nearby is Jack, not Ion. Their early years may have been the same – Tenterfield, Lightning Ridge, the tin fields of north Queensland, the War – but not after the bush. Jack's not buried in Mona Vale, he's sitting with me now. But I can think about Jack and Ion and hold them both in my mind. That's something László couldn't do; he couldn't reconcile the older author and his ageless alter ego without collapsing the scaffolding of the dream edifice that leached into his waking life.

In that dream world all three of us were here and maybe like right now, in the early hours of the morning just before moonrise, the Coquet light would have oriented us to the unseen world. And in line behind that light, fifteen kilometres beyond the Turtle Group, there's a mainland rise, an unexceptional coastal bluff that James Cook named Point Lookout.

Lookout Point, August 15, 2011

Eleven miles beyond the cape, in a North 45 degrees West direction, is Point Lookout, forming a peaked hill at the extremity of a low sandy projection whence the land trends West by 1/2 North for twelve leagues to Cape Bowen.
Phillip Parker King (1827)

Nearly a quarter millennium ago Cook climbed to the top of this headland hoping to see a passage to the west – he didn't. Instead, there was a scattering of sandbars and reefs to the northern horizon. But in the distance to the east he saw a high island and back on board that night he decided to leave the *Endeavour* in the lee of Point Lookout and take the two-masted, settee-rigged pinnace under sail and oar to check it out. Cook didn't know that it was called *Jiigurru* but he saw shelters on the island and realized that other people visited. He had no idea that those voyages spanned thousands of years. By the time he returned to the *Endeavour* three days later it had another name, Lizard Island, and he'd found a way out.

It took us just as long to get to Lookout Point. We arrived in Cooktown with three kayaks stacked on an ageing Land Cruiser and the next morning headed north to Axel's suggested departure point. The boats' shark-like profiles were silhouetted on the roadside scrub by the rising sun, their protruding bows vibrating as we sped across the bridge over the Endeavour towards the end of the sealed road. And then on, through Hopevale in the early morning with the dew still on the ground, past Q-Build houses that would all look the same but for the boats, Toyotas and yet-to-be-cannibalised car wrecks in the yards. With the mist lifting from the hills and the community quiet, dawn is a nice time of day and outside the front doors of half-a-dozen dwellings the early risers were enjoying their first pannikins of tea and waved as we passed. An hour later we were following dual-rut tracks along a corridor cut through the mangroves to the sea, the last twenty metres wet from the tide retreating over the beach just to the west of Cape Bedford – Elim.

In Exodus, on their journey to Mount Sinai, the Israelites camped at an oasis in the Wilderness of Sin - Elim. *Guugu Yimithirr* knew this place from well before Cook, before the mariners and miners who came after, and before the missionaries who renamed it. Elim was near the first mission and a failed farm, and *Muni* set up a *bêche-de-mer* curing camp there in 1927. The mission was eventually relocated to Hope Valley. But Elim remained a camping site – it always was and still is. From that tidal beach *Guugu Yimithirr* built and launched their own seacraft, dugout canoes of mango bark trees, *Canarium australasicum*, or beech, *Gmelina macrophylla*[141] – *gundar* and *detchi* to the *Guugu Yimithirr*. Dugout canoes were made from Cape Grafton to Papua and, further north, had two outriggers. But from Princess Charlotte Bay south there was a single outrigger to starboard fixed by multiple double booms that passed through washboards lashed to the gunwales on both sides. Walter Roth, a keen observer, watched them being made and launched in mission times:

> *Here at Cape Bedford, the dug-out is generally dragged down to the water's edge by three individuals, then put into the shallow water, and punted along with two poles – one at the bows, the other at the stern – until such a time as the water is deep enough for the paddles to be made use of.*[142]

The English-born child of a Hungarian refugee, Roth arrived in Queensland in 1887, the same year as *Muni,* and a decade later he sailed into Cooktown as the newly appointed Northern Protector of Aborigines. *Muni* was waiting and with twenty-five men walked to town to tell him what was really going on. Roth listened, he was always listening – listening, observing and recording; before a decade was out he was Queensland's Chief Protector and had run a Royal Commission into abuses of Aboriginal workers in the north of Western Australia. All of which landed him on the wrong side of powerful economic interests in both states – echoes of the Gribbles. Claiming ill-health, his departing letter of 1905 was a mixture of resignation and resolve: *Though I propose leaving the State I shall ever continue to champion the cause of the natives on whose behalf I have already devoted no small amount of my life.*[143] And he did that, for nearly three decades – in British Guiana.

Roth and *Muni* didn't see eye to eye but they both spoke their minds about abuses of Aboriginal men and women by pastoralists and miners – and on the lugger fleets. Roth was responsible for bringing some regulations into the *bêche-de-mer* industry in the Torres Strait and along the coast – he understood what went on above and below decks. He knew the coast well, travelling its length on the government ketch, the *Melbidir,* and would have stopped at Elim many times. Maybe even where we launched the three kayaks, racing to beat the tide retreating across mudflats and shoals.

Three boats retracing the two vessel journey of eight years ago when Axel abandoned his kayak on Lizard Island and Jon took over from there to Cape Weymouth. For Axel a journey and a life interrupted by three years in Lotus Glen Correctional Centre. As it all unfolded through courts, prison and parole I couldn't help thinking of the five stages of grief of Elisabeth Kübler-Ross. Before we left Cooktown and on the trip to Lizard it was all denial – *they've got nothing on me, it's all bluff*. But it wasn't, and it only took a few calls from the public phone in the Yachties' Bar on Lizard for denial to be trumped by reality. Bargaining – over the next year, as he was dragged along in a legal storm-surge he held fast to a hope-preserver, a set of fictions sustained by lawyers and police who had nothing to lose. The fiction was that he could trade his way out. He couldn't, though he tried hard and money changed hands. The bargaining peaked during the first six months in prison with frenetic instructions and demands to his long suffering ex-wife for actions that would have someone unpick the fabric of the whole nasty dream. Maybe they could but they didn't and the bargaining gave way to anger. Who could blame him – a shit of a situation.

Somewhere around the end of that first year, when there was still more time to do than had been done, it all went quiet. Probably about as close to depression as Axel could allow. But by the time he'd crossed the saddle of his sentence and could see down the valley to the road out in the distance he'd figured out how the system worked; he kept his own counsel, didn't take sides, got on with work without being obsequious or standing out, didn't cause problems – a model prisoner. He'd accepted that there was no short cut and at the end of the third year he was on work release stacking shelves in the Innisfail library. Polite and a good worker, they wanted more like him and he got a farewell party on the way out.

At first glance, when he re-appeared in Cairns three years ago, it was like he hadn't been away – the clothes, the jewellery and the same artisanal intensity. But he wasn't the same; like Aubrey Tigan the dream-healer from One Arm Point who lost the healer's touch while he was drinking, Axel had lost his mojo in prison. But while Aubrey reclaimed it when he gave up the grog, it didn't return for Axel after he was released. Despite all the old gear he no longer had the confidence and carriage of the shaman. But we got back into paddling and did some trips south of Cairns – the

Barnards, the Family group – familiar territory. Axel got on with his life and took on a job at a crocodile farm – he was a natural.

Crocodiles – Axel knew a lot about predators. He lived just outside Cooktown on the north arm of the Endeavour River for a decade through the '80s and early '90s and had been down nearly every track in the region in his V8 Ford F100. Lots of stories from those days of fringe life in the bush; stories of sad characters, mad characters and bad characters. And the bad ones were really bad – or so he said. Dope deals gone wrong, jealousy out of control, people gone missing leaving only a trail of rumours. As Axel often said – *I know where the bodies are buried*. He meant it literally and my guess is that he was telling the truth. Maybe that's why he didn't give much away when the law came for him.

Axel thought Elim would be a good place to launch but we'd made a beginner's mistake. The tide tables for the area reference to Leggatt Island, just south-west of Howick and one hundred kilometres north, and Port Douglas, which is twice that to the south. The beginners' mistake, as it turned out, applied to experienced kayakers – we didn't get local intelligence. So, with twenty minutes to launch without being stranded it was all rush and no reflection getting the kayaks off the roof and gear stowed, moving them incrementally further out to keep up with the waning tide and then dragging them through ankle-deep water for fifty metres before they were floating and we could get in. And another hundred metres touching bottom before we were in deep water. Each of us parallel processing without taking in what the others were doing. Not a good way to start.

That was three days ago, and as we paddled clear of the mudflats and sandbanks, with Cape Bedford to the south-east and the beach beyond Elim merging into the fragile, stratified cliffs of Coloured Sands that stretch north-west towards Cape Flattery, I knew this trip would be different. The excitement of a journey's first day and the feeling of crossing a threshold and leaving cares behind weren't there. Even before the earth-tones of the shallows had given way to the night-shades of deep water, and with the south-easterly sea breeze hours away and the heat building, I was already calculating how long this journey would take – three weeks, maybe more.

Storms and squalls excepted, the worst conditions for long distance sea kayaking are hot, windless days. Without any swell the glass surface slowly, haphazardly undulates, merging with the sky at a horizon that disappears in sea mist and mirage. With wind and waves the vessel responds to the elements and you feel part of the movement; when it's still and silent, after an hour you feel like you're pushing through the sea and after a few more you are.

Four hours it took to Three Isles. Four hours and maybe three to four litres of water. With cloud cover and a cooling breeze astern, a sea kayaker may only need two litres or so over a six to eight hour paddling-day. Minus the clouds and breeze and with high temperatures that can quadruple. From Three Isles there was another four hours paddling into an easterly headwind to the casuarina-lined beach of Two Isles. By that time I'd been through five litres or more – and there would be another in dinner and tea. On my first trip from Cairns to The Tip I'd started out with seventy litres of water, half the storage capacity of the Feathercraft and more than I needed, but I'd figured on at least two weeks supply. I also had a filter-pump for fresh water ashore, and a solar desalinator for seawater in an emergency – I was over-prepared. Paddling with seventy kilograms of water is not such a hassle but trying to drag a kayak with that weight in addition to everything else is a nightmare and portaging not much fun either. Every trip since I've carried less water and the pump and solar desalinator are long gone. I conserve by using rapid-hydrating grains like couscous and cooking in a mix of fresh and sea water. But most important, I know where the fresh water is along this coast and only need enough for a week. Counting on averaging five to six litres a day I was set for this trip with around forty litres.

One of the problems of being an organiser is that when you take responsibility others relinquish it. But over a decade of trips with one or more mates I'd stopped checking and directing. I'd gone from being over-prepared and pushing everyone else to do the same – to *laissez faire* planning. And that worked, or seemed to until we'd set up camp on Two Isles in the late afternoon, looking toward Cape Flattery as the lights on the silica-loading wharf began to shimmer through the sunset. It was then I realized that between them Jon and Axel had only thirty litres of water and had already used up about a third of that. A bad start, and I said so bluntly. I guess I was in a bad mood and even though Axel pointed out that we could get water at Lizard, I wasn't listening.

Axel was correct, that was two days away if we'd gone as planned – Two Isles, Rocky, then Lizard. Fill up there then to Nymph, Howick, Noble, Teabag Bay and on to Cape Melville and the Flinders Group where there's a rainwater tank. That would have been tight and without any reserve. But my reaction was about me, not the situation, and I convinced myself and them that this was a monumental fuck-up and that we should head to Flattery to get containers and water and pass on Lizard. It would mean pushing into headwinds all the way and they had both already been there – that was the rationalisation. But I was also shortening the trip, even though by doing so it would be more difficult to get to Howick – again. From the in-shore route through the Turtle Group, Howick would also be into the wind, but I was thinking about the end of the trip rather than being in it.

So yesterday we paddled back to the mainland, past the silica-loading wharf at Cape Flattery and around a headland to staff accommodation blocks where we located off-duty workers and left with half a dozen plastic bottles, enough for about twenty litres in all. That gave us ninety litres by the time everything was filled. We also scored a few beers and our plans to push on went down with them. Instead, we camped in a nearby sheltered bay, climbing up a gully with stepped, fresh-water pools and onto a headland to see where we'd come from and where we were now not going, with Two Isles in the mid-distance and Lizard on the horizon.

Early this morning we launched onto a still sea heading northwest towards the Turtle Group, a thirty kilometre journey with only Decapolis Reef then Lookout Point around the mid-way. By the time we reached Lookout Point there was a south-easterly breeze, just as there was when the *Endeavour* approached in August 1770. Then, as now, it was *cloudy, hazy weather* and Cook dropped anchor just off the mainland and climbed to the highest point.

> *Excepting Cape Flattery and the point I am now upon, which I have named Point Lookout, the main land next the sea to the northward of Cape Bedford is low and chequered with white sand and green bushes &ca for 10 or 12 miles inland, beyond which is high lands. To the north of Point Lookout the shore appeared to be shoaled and flat some distance off, which was no good sign of meeting with a channel in with the land as we have hitherto done. We saw the foot steps of people upon the sand and smook and fire up in the country, and in the evening returned on board where I came to the resolution to visit one of the high islands in the offing in my boat, as they lay at least 5 leagues out to sea and seemed to be of such height that from the top of one of them I hoped to see and find a passage out to sea clear of shoals.*[144]

We must have paddled within metres of where the *Endeavour* rode at anchor while Cook took the pinnace to Lizard Island and sighted *a passage out to sea clear of shoals*. We rounded the headland into shallows with a two kilometre sandbeach merging into mangroves that disappeared into haze to the west-north-west. Scrub-covered hills back a narrow beach, sand-flats exposed by the waning tide stranding isolated mangroves that moments before had been islands of green hovering above an aquamarine mirror. By the time we'd wandered ashore and contemplated continuing to the Turtles or staying where we were the kayaks were fifty metres from the waterline.

Within two hours the beach expands from a rim of sand to a two hundred metre tidal flat furrowed by corrugations tuned to the ocean's rhythms, and cut through by a latticework of rivulets and depressions alive with sea creatures. Above the high tide mark the rhythms change and the corrugations are replaced by ridges in the beach that give way to sand-hills shaped by the wind, against which pockets of shrubs and streaks of groundcover seem to desperately cling. Clinging on to a sea of sand – two hundred million tonnes of it – slowly being eaten away by the biggest silica mine in the world, run by Mitsubishi, behind the coastal dunes at Cape

Flattery. Joseph Banks appreciated the potential when he was here but was tongue-in-cheek when he commented: *The Sand itself indeed with which the whole countrey in a manner was covered was infinitely fine and white, but till a glass house was built here that would turn to no account.*[145] Indeed, it's very fine sand, valuable sand, and in the lee of Lookout Point it adheres like talc and lifts as mist from ridges and crests as the wind shifts to the east and hooks around the headland.

There's only one built structure on this beach. The remains of a shack that seems to hover above the shifting sand, supported by eight posts with the sheet-metal walls starting about half-a-metre above the ground. The floors are long gone, as is half the roof, with the sheeting over what was an ocean-view veranda held precariously in place by jury-rigged poles. We walk through the virtual front door into a magical, sand-carpeted room, one half of which is in shade and the other open to a cloudless sky. The walls are intact and the spaces for windows frame views along the beach towards vegetated dunes immediately behind, where a wild, black pig is watching. Inside, there's no furniture except for the bed. Or the remains of a bed – the rusted head and foot of an old-fashioned metal frame suspended above the sand by fencing wire from exposed roof bearers. Whoever did it got it right.

Whoever did it... The shack is probably around five decades old, but this place has been a campsite forever. Oysters and shellfish along the rocky base of Lookout Point, fish in the creeks of nearby mangroves, and tidal pools forming a network of natural fish-traps. Of course it was a campsite, and it had a name – Roger Hart called it *marramarranganh*. It was a campsite before the missionaries and after. There were reports that troopers and native police landed from the *Spitfire* in October 1881 found articles here from the Watsons' *bêche-de-mer* station on Lizard Island. Two decades later *Muni* set up an outstation for dugong hunting – *Wawu Ngalan* – and he tried to bring in the tribes from Barrow Point – one step closer to the mission. All the adults would have had memories of the reprisals following the Lizard Island attack and probably weren't enthusiastic, but by May 1927 there were around forty people living along this beach.

By that time Roth was long gone and *Muni* had a new Chief Protector of Aborigines to deal with – John William Bleakley. With the numbers at the camp growing Bleakley appointed a local elder – Long Billy – as native policeman of the Point Lookout Station to bring some control to the camps. *Muni* was sceptical: *The appointment of Billy as "Native Policeman" for Pt. Lookout and its surroundings will prove of some value provided the present kings in that vicinity are deprived of their authority and their plates, the signs of such authority, otherwise Billy will be unable to do anything with these people.*[146]

In the end Billy wasn't going to get involved. On a moonless night King Nicholas and the Barrow Point mob left by dugout canoe with mission blankets as sails, and by daybreak they were at the Starke River and heading north. There may have been food and blankets, but *Wawu Ngalan* wasn't home for the *Gambiilmugu-warra*.

And not home for us, just another journey interrupted, a space that seems empty but is really a place of meetings and memories. As always, the campfire takes and flares over unseen, deep, storied strata. People gathered around a fire, staring into its heart, words washing over them and into the night – at this place and all along the coast – forever. But sometimes the silence is the message; unspoken, the decision has been made to head directly north. Jon knows that there is something different about this trip and that we're bypassing Howick again: *Jon, what was that name, you talked about him on the last trip when we camped nearby…*

— In 2008, yes, we did. Idriess, Ion Idriess or Jack Idriess. Howick, Madman's Island *was the book.*
— *Axel doesn't know that story.*

That's right, *Axel doesn't know that story* – I told him we were heading that way in 2003 but he had too much on his mind. And he's probably not interested now. He's preoccupied, somewhere else – like me, on the trip but not in it – but Jon takes us back anyway: *And that bloke who was your patient, what happened to him Jon… What happened…* Somewhere in the night-clad scrub the sounds of sudden movement remind us that we're not alone. Pigs probably; it's their territory though, like us, it's not their country. We all just happen to be here for now. The metal walls of the shack glow in the firelight, the support-posts lost in darkness. A shimmering screen for projecting the story of what happened to László nearly a decade ago; how he was admitted to hospital and finally started on clozapine – and improved. Although he's heard it before Jon wants the story, he always wants stories – he's interested in people. Axel isn't – or not in the same way. There are three of us around the fire but it's like he's outside the circle, sitting in cross-legged isolation. Full *siddhasana*, pretty impressive for someone close to the end of his seventh decade. I can't do it and it's not even conceivable for someone with a titanium hip; Jon's sitting on his usual seat improvised from my ten litre water container and an inflatable mattress. Even though only Jon is listening I tell them both about László's long stay in hospital, his slow improvement and how he was eventually discharged to his relatives in Silkwood, another cue for Jon: *Silkwood, I remember it from repping. There was a store there with cobwebs over the owner. He had this balsawood box filled with Woodbines, they'd been off the market for years and there were holes in the packages – weevils. I said I'd replace the lot with new stock and do up some smart shelving. But he told me the locals liked it the way it was.*

More sounds from the night momentarily halt Jon's reflections and suddenly I have a vivid memory of that empty street and what seems like an isolated and abandoned store. It seems to emerge from the fire and is gone as Jon resumes: *I guessed the only locals who'd been there in the last decade had been lost. Silkwood Jon, a weird place. Some kind of religious festival every year, I went once but didn't get cured, woke up the next day and I was still a bastard.*

It would take more than the Feast of the Three Saints to sort Jon out, but in the end he was cured of repping – he became a youth worker. And László may not have been cured but I saw him in Cairns before he went to live with Biata. He no longer had the shakes or the wooden expression and his thinking was clearer. He had plans – he was going to help Dom on the farm and maybe do some study. Literature was what appealed to him and given how much time he'd spent in libraries it seemed a good choice. When I raised Idriess he answered in a matter-of-fact way, without any suggestion of private meanings or shared interests: *Ion Idriess may be a good subject, I'm interested in first hand accounts of the north.* Not Jack – Ion – and he spoke as if the years of obsession hadn't happened. What had made him crazy and, I suppose, interesting, was gone, or so it seemed. Even the dreams, I asked about that too: *I don't know whether it's the medication I take now, doctor Hunter, but I don't dream at all.* And that was it, his care was transferred to the mental health team working out of Innisfail and our paths no longer crossed. I was sometimes copied into emails afterwards, but even that dried up and I heard nothing more – until just after the last trip past Howick.

It was Biata who called me, nearly seven years later, some time before Christmas 2008. It was a voice triggering a cascade of associations: *It's Bea here doctor, Biata Cannizzaro, Larry's aunt in Silkwood.* It had been twelve years since I had sat in her living room eating strudel as a life passed in slow motion through a series of faded monochrome images behind yellowing plastic. The scene was vivid but, other than Biata, the names were gone and I apologised for not recalling her husband's. As she answered she sounded much older than the woman I remembered: *Gino doctor – Gino. He died four years ago, it was cancer. Dom is the head of the family now, he says it was all the chemicals. Gino was always spraying doctor. He never used a mask or anything, said it would kill weeds but not him. He was a stubborn man doctor. But a good man – Gino was a good man and a hard worker.*

A good man and a hard worker – a life in a sentence or a life as a sentence, who knows... Biata was around seventy, a woman transplanted across the world by historical events from Budapest to Australia – to Silkwood. Magyar and Calabrian roots now woven deep into cane-country soil – *Dom is the head of the family now.* Dom – also a good man and a hard worker. Biata got straight to the story: *It started a year ago doctor, Larry had been doing so well, I don't know whether it was the medicine or being around family.* I could have told her that it was the medicines that allowed him to be around family – but I didn't, I let her talk on. *Gino didn't believe in medicines doctor, he thought they were dangerous.* Gino also believed that pesticides and herbicides are innocuous – he was wrong about that too.

The story wound back on itself, shifting across time and place. It always returned to László but the figure was insubstantial – in the house but never really part of the family. And there was a sense of passivity, without agency or direction; I asked about his plans to do some study: *He talked about it but it didn't seem to get going. Even on the farm Gino and Dom were always keeping him on track. He wasn't lazy doctor, but seemed lost. And he was always going to the library. Whenever he was in town he'd go to the library. On Rankin Street doctor, across from the Cathedral, it was like a second home for him.*

The Innisfail library – he might have run into Axel in the stacks – he was on work release there in 2007. I hadn't thought about that possibility before and Axel, drawn back into the conversation and story, was unsure: *Lot's of weird folk in the Innisfail library and they wanted us busy not talking with the punters, but he could have been there.* Maybe too many coincidences. But coincidences happen, and I remember one from the conversation with Biata three years ago – a voice from the radio: *It was the beginning of 2007 doctor, there was a change before Easter. He'd been listening to the radio – he always had the radio on doctor, always the ABC. I could never tell if he was listening or not, but he had it on. We don't listen to the ABC doctor, but Larry would have it on in his room or on his transistor, he took that with him everywhere.*

— What was the change…
— *He became quiet, in a strange kind of way doctor. He said he'd heard a witch on the radio. A witch, doctor, that's the word he used. And then he was talking about Jack Idriess. Dom and I figured out that it was the author who wrote stories about the Tablelands, doctor. I remembered that he used to talk about Idriess a lot when he was in hospital after he came down from Cooktown.*

A witch and Jack – not Ion, *Jack* – and something to do with the radio again. I had no idea who the witch was or what it represented. But I knew it was meaningful and guessed that the radio would be a clue; I made a mental note to visit the ABC offices again as Biata continued her story: *He's been wandering doctor. He and Dom gave a lift to that man Michael – Tarzan – when they were coming back from Cairns one time. Maybe a couple of times. Took him somewhere along the Russell River past Gordonvale. We've all seen him; we know he's not right in the head doctor – but harmless. Dom said that Larry seemed to know all about him. Then a year or so ago Larry went looking for him.*

— Went looking for him...

— *Yes, doctor, said he was going to talk to him about something. But Tarzan doesn't really talk to anyone. He just walks.*

He just walks. That's Tarzan all right, up and down the Bruce Highway. And if László was getting exercised about Jack Idriess again and trying to link up with Michael Fomenko I knew all wasn't well. Whether it was triggered by the interview with Beverley Eley years before or something else didn't really matter. With the phone on speaker and Biata's accented voice in the background, I'd opened CIMHA, the Queensland Health clinical information system and found what I wanted – Halassy, fist name Larry; other names, Laszlo. I was dual-tasking – listening and reading.

We can't watch out for him doctor, and he doesn't tell us about those tablets he takes... His case manager had changed probably four times over the years. He was a voluntary patient by the time Biata called, and the page-long entries following his discharge from hospital seven years earlier had contracted to telegraphic checklists with occasional comments about clozapine levels and blood tests. Cooperative, compliant, a model patient – until 2007. *We tried to talk to his doctor, but they told Dom that they wouldn't speak to us without Larry's permission...* From 2007 there were a few missed appointments, brief comments about leaving messages on his mobile or with his family. And he was probably less diligent with his medicine; the blood levels dipped several times but that didn't seem to be pushing buttons with his case manager. And there were occasional comments about his family at Silkwood that read like they were the problem. *I don't know what he says to them doctor, but I don't think he tells them about Michael, or about locking himself in his room...* I was sure he wouldn't mention Tarzan and they wouldn't ask. Whoever was his case manager probably knew nothing about his interior life and certainly wouldn't know if there was an oneironaut on the loose – Idriess, dreams, *Madman's Island* – buried in cyberspace.

I don't know what to do doctor, he was doing so well... And that was the problem; doing so well because he knew what the system wanted. An understanding – *don't tell us what we don't want to hear and just take your tablets.* The tablets, the hook that maintains the dance – if he misses his tablets for more than a few days they have to get him back into hospital and start the process of building the dose up slowly to avoid life-threatening complications. Because he's voluntary that's complicated and a lot of extra work. So there's an unstated agreement – *just keep taking the tablets and we won't hassle you.* And from his blood tests it looked like he hadn't stopped, which was reassuring, because if he had it would be a real mess.

Despite its dangers, when clozapine works it can seem a miracle for carers and relatives who've known nothing but madness for years. *It's like having my son back* – that kind of thing. Or: *it's like the film,* Awakenings, *when Robin Williams brings Robert De Niro back*. Robin Williams' character was based on Oliver Sacks who in the 1960s administered *l-dopa* to patients who'd been institutionalised following the pandemic of *encephalitis lethargica* in the 1920s that had left them: *frozen in deeply parkinsonian states, some stuck in catatonic postures – not unconscious but with their consciousness suspended at the point where the disease had closed in on certain parts of the brain.*[147]

Sacks' patients had been in that state for decades – *suspension of memory, perception and consciousness.*[148] When he used L-dopa in a small trial the results were startling: *At first, nearly all the patients' responses were happy ones; there was an astonishing festive "awakening" that summer as they burst into explosive life after having been almost inanimate for decades.*[149]

If that was the end of it... But it wasn't, and as miraculous as it seemed the awakenings were fragile. And that's another parallel to clozapine; sometimes there are serious complications and it has to be stopped, or the patient refuses to take any more for her or his own reasons. When that happens the psychosis can rebound and a parent or partner may have to watch as the person that's been returned to them takes their leave again. And not just drifting into that other world – the psychosis can explode.

As Biata's story wound towards its end the results of László's latest clozapine blood levels appeared on the screen. Whatever was happening in his head he still had some of the drug in his system. But something had changed; either he wasn't as diligent as he'd been before 2007 or he'd been missing doses and trying to preload before his blood tests. *Is there anything you can do doctor, Larry used to talk about you regularly, for years, about doctor Hunter – he still does…* I could feel Biata's desperation and I knew she wanted me to get involved, to take control – to sort it out. But what made the difference with László was that the relationship I had with him was more than clinical; although I always maintained a distance, there was a level at which we both knew there was something else. Beyond the standard questions and exchanges there was a connection, a relationship. That's what persisted for László; not Ernest Hunter the psychiatrist and *needle-dependent-psychopath*, but the person who listened and was interested in his story.

What was going through my mind as I listened to Biata was whether I should respond as a representative of the mental health system with its protective shell of clinical governance that would allow me to deflect responsibility to the latest iteration of his treatment team, or really get involved again. Even before closing the conversation I'd chosen the safe option – convenience. I had too much on the go; it was nearly Christmas, I was going away, it was a long time ago… I would pass the buck, pressure the players into action and cover myself with a trail of emails documenting a *good enough* response. It's what the system expected. But as I carried through with that plan I kept recalling the refrain of Martin Niemöller's poem that I'd taught in Jerusalem and recalled in a cottage in the Shetland Islands a decade ago: *and I did not speak out, because…* I wasn't there when they came for László and I didn't speak for him – just about him. And I still got to go on leave – I chose to be a bystander.

Or maybe almost a bystander; with the *witch and the radio* still pushing buttons, a few days later I was back at the ABC North Queensland office on Sheridan Street in Cairns, and within an hour was listening to Gretchen Miller interviewing Beverley Eley about her relationship with Wendy, Jack's daughter.[150] It was broadcast on Saturday February 10, 2007, nearly seven years after the first interview with Eley that László had heard as he sat outside his donga at the Peninsula Caravan Park. It was the second time I'd heard Eley and she sounded much older. In a voice that seemed rasped by years of heavy smoking, over background sounds of ice cubes bouncing at the bottom of a tumbler, Eley described: *a ladies man, a writer, a wanderer, a romantic.* A man of contradictions, not to be understood from surface appearances: *everyone regarded him as happy Jack, but I knew the other side from Wendy – he was not happy Jack.*

Gretchen Miller spliced in Tim Bowden's interview with the aged author that had been recorded three decades earlier.[151] Idriess's delivery was halting but his mind was still sharp and when Miller first heard that life-worn voice she tried to reconcile the adventurer who'd been able to sell more than three million books with the man: *who spent his last days drinking sweet sherry with milk.* The contradictions, that's what interested Eley, his life after he returned to live in Sydney in 1931. Close to St Vincent's hospital, she explained, because he thought he might have cancer. While she was working on the biography she'd spoken to someone at the hospital who with a bit of prompting dug out his file – he'd had a melanoma. But he lived for another three decades with a steady stream of books building his reputation as the chronicler of frontier fortitude just as his private life was measured in compromises; his partner of decades, Etta Gibson, shared her life with another man and had children by both. Idriess had gifts, but also some pretty significant problems relating to the world, an observer and describer rather than a participant. Eley summed it up: *I often wonder if he saw himself as part of the human race.* After the phone call from Biata I briefed László's case manager, and called back a week later to tell him about the radio and Idriess, and what I understood was happening. But I knew the details weren't being registered – not in an attentive way, not by someone who understood the back-story and cared.

...whoever did it got it right.

...they were rescued by the government cutter, the Melbidir, *heading south with Roth on board.*

...solidly in the tradition of EJ Banfield...

With the fire's last dances on the shack's floating metal walls the weight of the story has almost exhausted conversation. But in the way that meandering tales have of doubling back over unuttered thoughts this one, around the campfire at Lookout Point, brings us back to Michael Fomenko via one more of Jon's repping tales, this one about the first time he picked up Tarzan on the way back from Silkwood: *I gave him lots of rides along the highway. Took him to Aloomba once, he was staying behind a cane farm near the river, and another time I took him to Mount Sophia where he was building another dugout canoe. It wasn't going to go anywhere, but he was on the job. I stopped the car and opened the boot to put his hessian sack in the back but he tried to climb in. I guessed somebody had made that a condition of transporting him in the past.*

— And you did what...
— *I got him into the front and took him into town, dropped him off near KFC. He loved KFC. When he got out there was an outline of his torso in dust and gravel on the seat. Every time I got into the car for weeks afterwards it smelled like a campfire.*

It smelled like a campfire – like magic. We know that smell; it can transport us from a suburban garden where someone is burning off on a Sunday afternoon while we fret about the looming Monday deadlines, to the time-suspended stillness of an island hearth. Tarzan didn't dream it, he lived it along this coast – and my story ends here: *Michael probably had a campfire right where we are now. He would have stopped here when he was heading north in the dugout in the late 1950s on the way to New Guinea. No doubt about it, he was here.*

No doubt about it. Tarzan was here. And maybe László too, heading north with him in a dream-vessel.

Night Island – August 25, 2011

Night Island, its north end in latitude 13 degrees 13 minutes 8 seconds, and longitude 143 degrees 28 minutes 40 seconds, is a low woody island, two miles long, but not more than half a mile wide; it is surrounded by a coral reef, that does not extend more than a quarter of a mile from its northern end. On the south side, and within it, the space seemed to be much occupied by reefs, but they were not distinctly made out, on account of the thickness of the weather. There was also the appearance of a covered shoal, bearing North 55 degrees East from the north end of the island, distant four miles.

Phillip Parker King (1827)

Nearly two weeks from Lookout Point, bypassing Howick to Noble and on to Cape Melville, westwards from there to the continental islands of the Flinders group and then south for a few days rest at Bathurst Head before a ten-hour slog across Princess Charlotte Bay to the Cliff Islands. Then north, threading the necklace of mangrove islands and islets marking the reef's inner edge. For me it was familiar, sand cays appearing suddenly, crescent flashes along the leaden line of shallow water above the reefs from which they grow. They are its visible pulse, small cays surfacing and disappearing, their older siblings, established and vegetated on leeward fringes, expanding and contracting with the same lunar rhythms. Like Morris Island, which sits as a protected lip on a two kilometre reef, appearing like a seductive, vertical mirage – two hours before keel meets sand.

From fifteen kilometres Morris is a mast on the horizon that when first seen and map consulted can only be the navigation tower on Heath reef four kilometres west. But an hour later, as the island beneath it comes into view, its real identity is revealed; it's probably the most famous coconut palm on the Great Barrier Reef, and the reef navigator's bible – *Cruising the coral coast* – has entrenched the legend:

Morris Island also reminds us of the British Admiralty policy of the last century which was to provide many of the Great Barrier Reef islands with a means of support for ship-wrecked crew. To this end, they put goats ashore and, in the case of Morris, planted coconut palms with sisal trees close by. The latter were intended as a means of knocking down ripe nuts, the sisal producing a long stick from amidst its needle-sharp leaves. They have proliferated here while, as stated, only one adult coconut palm remains.[152]

One adult coconut palm – unapproachable through the dense tangle of razor-edged sisal that now covers the island save for a small clearing in which the grave of a long-deceased mariner continues to be festooned with visitors' discarded cans and bottles. An anonymous grave on an island named for someone nobody remembers. It could have been Eclipse Island.

At sunset on Wednesday December 6, 1871, the *Governor Blackall*, a twin steam-engined, steel-hulled brigantine which was at that time the largest ship built in New South Wales, anchored off Number 6 Island in the Claremont group. Aboard were thirty-three scientists and other *gentlemen* led by Robert Ellery, President of the Royal Society of Victoria and Government Astronomer at the Melbourne Observatory.[153] The islet they named Eclipse Island had been selected as one of two possible sites to observe the solar eclipse, the first in Australia since the advent of photography as a scientific tool. The teams from Melbourne and Sydney brought with them the most advanced technology but, with predictable academic rivalry, operated in parallel, even though from the same site.

But to Ellery what they named Eclipse and is now Morris seemed less than an island: *it was a most uninviting place – a mere sand-bank, over which an 8 ft. tide would have swept, clothed only with a few miserable bushes, and infested with myriads of rats.*[154] The journalist in the Expedition, Henry Britton, agreed about the rats: *possession of the island was hotly disputed by rats, who behaved in the most impudent manner.*[155] And nearly a century-and-a-half later Morris Island remains *hotly disputed by rats* – at least at night – and they still behave *in the most impudent manner*. With no natural predators on land and protected from raptors above by an echidnoid, sisal carapace, with darkness they claim the beach. And anything on it, running over bodies, settling on ground-sheets, sitting immobile in our headlights' glare just inches away. Rats – totally cute – but rats.

Eclipse Island was an unfortunate choice because on Tuesday 12th December, the day of the eclipse, it was raining. Disappointed, the team packed up and were ready to go by evening the next day when a schooner, the *Matilda* under Captain Watson, sailing from the Torres Straight to

Sydney with a cargo of pearl-shell, anchored nearby. They'd been at Night Island on 11 December. Henry Britton later wrote in the *Argus*:

> *the master and first officer reported having seen the eclipse very distinctly while near Night Island, in lat 13° 9' S., long. 143° 39' E., about 15 miles from No. VI. Island. They were not aware that the eclipse was going to occur, and at first took the darkness for approaching bad weather, until one of them happening to look under the mainsail, observed the phenomenon. Though wholly unprepared for the eclipse, they gave a very intelligent account of it.*[156]

Night Island – they should have been there then; we're here now, half way between Morris and Cape Direction. It's a mangrove island with a small beach on the north-west facing Bobardt Point, with Chester Peak and the Meston Range behind. Named for two men who cast long shadows over Aboriginal lives. Henry Chester brought his experiences in remote byways of the empire to north Queensland as police magistrate at Somerset, Thursday Island and Cooktown. Archibald Meston was at different times a journalist, politician and Protector of Aborigines in southern Queensland, and was responsible for a report that became the foundation for the *1897 Aboriginals and Restriction of Sale of Opium Act*.[157] And Meston knew this country. In early 1909 he spent three weeks inspecting camps set up by Hughie Giblett to cut and prepare sandalwood for the China market. There was big money to be made, but along this stretch of the coast it was only possible with the cooperation of the sandbeach people – the *Uutaalnganu* – whose country is as far as the eye can see from Night Island, southward to Friendly Point and north to Cape Direction where Giblett had his main base. There were also camps further north at the mouth of the Pascoe River on Weymouth Bay – *Kuuku Y'au* territory – and to the south at Cape Sidmouth – *Umpila* country. Meston was impressed, so much so that he wrote to the Minister for Lands for a license to cut sandalwood on the Lloyd Bay Aboriginal Reserve in partnership with Giblett. He realized that Aboriginal labour was critical, including *inland blacks* of the scrub-lands and mountains. Although Giblett had strong relationships with them Meston had reservations:

It would be useless signing on these bushmen as they will work from one day to a month and then go away at their own sweet will for a week or two, and would certainly not tolerate any restraint, as in that case they would merely clear off to some other locality or report their own inability to find any sandalwood.[158]

The Sandalwood King, that's how Giblett was known around Cooktown before he, like Jack Idriess, left for the War. But it was years earlier, soon after he arrived, that Jack heard the stories. He was sitting outside the West Coast Hotel one evening, watching what was going on in the houses and shops of Chinatown across the road. A load of sandalwood was stacked at the wharf to be loaded on the *Empress of China* and an old-timer, a cattleman from up the Cape who'd spent time at Hughie Giblett's Cape Direction camp, was describing the *Christmas beano* that Hughie ran for all comers after the last ton of sandalwood was shipped out before the Wet: *Mobs of natives were pouring in to the settlement, excited as girls at a double wedding; you'd have thought all the abos in the Peninsula were gathering for the world's great corroboree.*[159] Hughie had a *quaint sense of gunpowder humour* and lubricated the proceedings with grog and trinkets, the cattleman recalling fondly that:

Hughie thought it great fun as shrieking gins staged tugs of war over some bright-coloured garment or other until it ripped apart and they fell squalling on their backsides – sometimes into the fires. Then they'd snatch up a firestick and get into one another hammer and tongs. My heavens! There were some howling fights with skin and hair flying all over the place – if anyone new to the country had come among us sober he'd have thought the night had gone mad.[160]

Meston commented on the liberality of Giblett and the distribution of goods – *flour, tea, sugar, golden syrup, jam, rice, tinned beef, tobacco, pipes, matches, rugs, shirts, singlets, coats, trousers, hats, caps, dresses, lava lavas, accordions, mouth organs, tin whistles, mirrors, wool for dilly bags, beads, combs, scissors, knives, tomahawks, medicine, belts, etc etc* – but he probably wasn't thinking of the Christmas beano. Grog and trinkets – division and diversion. Here on *Uutaalnganu* country and right across the continent. Then and now – all that changes are the trinkets.

Giblett's innovation was to ship the sandalwood out on luggers to Thursday Island where it was transferred to China steamers. During the cutting season the lee of Night Island would have been a safe anchorage for luggers waiting to load. Just five kilometres off the coast, it's around three kilometres in length by several hundred metres, almost entirely mangroves to the south with a beach area facing west at the northern end, reached over reef drying at low tide. To the south of the landing there's a corridor of tide-cleared sand between mangroves and backing scrub. To the north a straight shelf of rock, dry at low tide, creates a causeway through an emerald tunnel alive with the sounds of the mangrove forest and rivulets running with the tide. On the exposed reef soft coral lies like an assortment of collapsed, placentoid organs, with small sharks, rays and fish racing in the tide pools between clams grown round with coral, only their vulvular lips protruding.

This is the fourth time I've been to Night. The second time, with Jon in 2003, a fishing boat was at anchor and two deckhands, Andrew from Bribie Island and Flick from Noosa, appeared in a tinny, each with a beer in hand – and more in the boat that they made no move to share. Andrew was small and wiry, his gaze all about and down but not engaging, his suntanned face framed by a beanie and a beard. He smoked continuously and seemed conscious of his irregular teeth; he had the look of someone who'd had a difficult passage. Flick was tall, with a stubble beard and precise dentition and quickly let us know he'd almost been a professional golfer – he could have been a contender. State Junior Champion on three occasions and expelled from school for truanting to play golf. To his parents' despair he gave up golf to apprentice as a chef, then left that to work on trawlers and had been at it for four years. His vision was to have his own vessel and get a block of land at Portland Roads. Fishing, that was his ticket and obsession. When we met him the boat had been anchored at Night Island for four days to wait out the full moon – time to do some recreational fishing. He told us he was making a documentary video of trawler life: *I got this great fucking groper off Chatham – just sitting there and sucking them in. And sharks. And prawns – I got shots of these enormous fucking prawns up in the Torres. Put a packet of ciggies next to them. Everyone knows how big that is. It runs for more than two hours now.*

I was lost for a response that would do justice to the enterprise and I was beginning to worry that we'd be invited out to the trawler to crowd around his laptop and take it in, although I might have been lured by the prospect of a beer. But Flick had already changed course; fishing wasn't his only interest, he also collected sea horses and dissolved them in absolute alcohol: *Chinese are into it in a big way – top money. Best sex they reckon, gives blokes the horn.* Offended or defensive, he appeared to stiffen when I asked if it worked, but returned to creative thoughtfulness when I suggested it could be good for the documentary. Flick seemed to weigh up the suggestion – a good angle versus the possibility that the long-haired, zinc-covered old bloke may be taking the mickey. I shifted the trajectory: *Check this out – watch:*

— *Fuck, what was that...*
— *Trap-jaw ant; its jaw is the fastest moving predatory appendage of any creature on earth.*
— *Fuck, I wonder if I can get it on film...*

He'd have needed a camera that did a lot more than capture dead fish. *Odontomachus* species have jaws that open to 180 degrees and are internally spring loaded, reaching speeds on closing of over 200 kilometres an hour when sensory hairs on the mandibles are activated. For flight rather than fight, the ants on Night Island seem to jump backwards but are really catapulted, flung defensively dozens of times their body length. I had Flick and Andrew imagine a football player soaring from one goal-line to the other, which led to a potentially endless inventory of fish jumping that Flick had missed getting on film. There seemed only one escape: *Can I have one of your beers...*

That was eight years ago and it all looks the same. Other than jetsam and rubbish left by the crews of trawlers and yachts sheltering in the island's lee, it's probably pretty much unchanged from when Phillip Parker

King first passed in 1819 – fine in a fix but not a great place to be stuck. And some were stuck here. At the very beginning of the last century, when Chief Protector Walter Roth was trying to regulate the pearling and fishing fleet, an Aboriginal crew commandeered the lugger *Annie*. The *Johara*, sent with native police under Sergeant James Whiteford to sort out the mutineers was wrecked after rounding them up, stranding them all on Night for weeks until they were rescued by the government cutter, the *Melbidir,* heading south with Roth on board.[161]

Someone else who spent time on Night and whose description of it in the 1860s was as it is now was John MacGillivray. The son of an English ornithologist, MacGillivray left medical school to sail for Australia in 1842 on the *Fly* under Francis Price Blackwood as apprentice to Joseph Beete Jukes.[162] MacGillivray returned to England in 1846 but left soon after as naturalist on the *Rattlesnake* under Owen Stanley in company with Thomas Huxley, not a good person to fall out with – which he did, and not just Huxley. Both journeys included surveys of this coast but he was back again in 1860 on the *Julia Percy* under Captain Banner.[163] *Captain Banner was a jovial, upstanding sea rover with a broad, keen face above a luxurious black beard* [164] – that's how Idriess described him when the *Julia Percy* sailed into Somerset in 1868 on the way north to harvest *bêche-de-mer*. Idriess relied on others' descriptions but Banner was well known as the man who on that voyage found pearl-shell off Warrior Island and changed the course of history in the Torres Strait.

But eight years earlier the *Julia Percy* with Banner and MacGillivray on board reached Night Island on August 14th. Over the following days MacGillivray visited the mainland twice looking for sandalwood and on the 18th crossed for a third time with a party exploring to the south. On the way back they found the country fired and were suddenly confronted by: *a mob of Australian natives (about 150 in number, as I afterwards ascertained), daubed and streaked with white paint, each man with his throwing stick and bundle of spears.*[165]

Overconfidence may have been what led to MacGillivray's falling out with Huxley but confidence probably helped on that day: *Being the only one of our party who knew how to deal with wild Australian natives other than by shooting them, I was allowed to manage the business as I thought proper.*[166] Experience mattered; when MacGillivray was on the *Fly* as apprentice to Jukes twenty years earlier it had anchored off Night Island with its sister survey ship, the *Bramble*. Jukes and a shore party were returning after taking magnetic observations from a hill opposite Night Island when Jukes' weapon misfired as he was attempting to prevent the fatal spearing of a crewman, Baily, from the *Bramble*.[167] Two decades on in pretty much the same place MacGillivray seems to have managed the situation well, a mixture of openness, humour and gifts; they made it back to the longboat and returned to the *Julia Percy* at Night. Eight years later he described his second encounter in detail: *as it may be of service to others on future occasions* – going on to add:

> *They were generally well made for Australians. None of those we saw exceeded five feet seven inches in height. The moustache and beard were usually very scanty; the hair of the head had not been subjected to any peculiar treatment; the artificially raised scars on the body and arms were few in number; circumcision or any analogous rite had not been practiced; but the loss of an upper front tooth was universal among the men. One man was light enough to have been a half-caste, but he shunned observation, and got out of the way when I wished to examine him closely.*[168]

The man MacGillivray saw probably didn't want to be examined closely, and he wasn't *a half-caste*, he was a Frenchman – Narcisse Pelletier – and he'd been stranded on this shore after a shipwreck off New Guinea in 1858.

Pelletier wasn't the only castaway adopted into Indigenous societies in north Queensland. In 1863 James Morrill, a survivor of the 1846 wreck of the *Peruvian* on Horseshoe reef near Cape Bowling Green, left the Aboriginal band in which he had lived for nearly two decades and returned to European society. Briefly celebrated, feted and married, he was dead within three years. And Barbara Thompson, who stayed with the *Kaurareg* on Prince of Wales Island for nearly four years after her husband's cutter, the *America*, was wrecked on Brampton Shoal. She was the only survivor and, as the story goes, they thought she was a ghost-daughter, Giom, of a local chief, Piaquai. A great story – Idriess wrote a whole book about it, *Isles of despair*, and Wongai, the escaped convict from Norfolk Island who became the *Wild white man of Badu*, was obsessed by her. Idriess has Wongai watch her on the deck of the *Rattlesnake* as the crew were hauling up the anchor and climbing along the yardarms to unfurl sails – preparing to sail away: *Something deep within him told him that the ship was taking his island queen that should have been – away from him for ever. And his island kingdom would vanish with her.*[169]

There were others, but Narcisse Pelletier's story is different, he didn't escape.[170] Pelletier was born in 1844 and shipped from Marseilles as a cabin boy in 1857 on the *Saint-Paul* bound for Sydney via Hong Kong, where some three hundred Chinese embarked for the goldfields of New South Wales. The course of the *Saint-Paul* under Captain Emmanuel Pinard was through the Louisiade Archipelago in the Solomon Sea where it hit a reef near Rossel Island in September 1858. After attempts to refloat the *Saint-Paul* failed, Pinard and ten men including Pelletier set out in a longboat heading towards the Australian coast, leaving the Chinese and a number of crew to their fate; although six crew who made it to a nearby island were rescued by the *Prince of Danemark*, only three Chinese survivors were found alive when Pinard returned in January 1859.

But before that Pinard had successfully guided the longboat to the Australian coast, covering 1200 miles to landfall near Night Island, where the nine survivors spent days looking for water and food. There are differing accounts of how Pelletier was abandoned, but whatever the truth the longboat left without him – the fifteen-year-old cabin boy was stranded. When MacGillivray sighted a native *light enough to have been a half-caste* in 1860, Pelletier was seventeen. On 11 April 1875 – fifteen years later – Captain Joseph Frazer of the *John Bell*, which was anchored in the lee of Night Island, heard from a returning shore party that there was a European man among local natives and they were sent back to bring him aboard. Narcisse Pelletier was thirty-one years old – he'd been with the *Uutaalnganu* for seventeen years.

It wasn't until Pelletier was ashore at Somerset that someone realized that the wild, European man was French, and on 13 December 1875 Narcisse Pelletier disembarked from the *Jura* in Toulon. He was home – maybe… The cover of Stephanie Anderson's collection[171] about Pelletier has a posed photo of a muscular man, bare to the waist, with striped pants visible below his crossed arms. Along his right shoulder are vertical scars at right angles to a set of parallel cicatrices crossing his chest. His hair is short and neatly combed, and he has wispy whiskers and a clear complexion. His gaze is distant, past the camera, perhaps at the studio photographer, and turned slightly to expose his right ear with a pendulous, incised lobe. Turn the book over and on the back Pelletier wears a high-collared frockcoat buttoned to its top to reveal only a hint of a scarf. Whereas the front cover has him standing face on to the camera, on the back he's sitting, his crossed legs clothed in the same striped trousers. Again, his gaze is distant and he's facing more to his left, exposing only his deformed ear as a signifier of the *sauvage*.

In France Pelletier made some money from an account of his experiences, married in 1880 and died without children at age fifty in September 1894, having lived and worked at the harbour of Saint-Nazaire. In different accounts his death was attributed to sorcery and to *neurasthénie*.[172] Maybe both; his distant, haunted gaze seems to locate him somewhere else, perhaps still with the *Uutaalnganu*, just across the water from Night Island. And save for visits they are gone now. But the land is marked still by their presence over thousands of years, the ecology changed by fire and seasonal practices that have clustered edible plants[173] – it's still *Uutaalnganu* land.

Restoration Island – August 27, 2011

Restoration Island, off the cape, is high, and of conical shape; about a mile East-South-East of it is a small rocky islet.

Phillip Parker King (1827)

Restoration Island – Resto – just a couple of hundred metres from Cape Weymouth, which Cook named when he returned to the safety of the inner passage through Providential Channel to the east. He probably mistook Resto as part of the mainland – or so thought Bligh, who came through the reef on Thursday 28th May, 1789. They landed the longboat the following day, which Bligh thought was propitious:

The day being the anniversary of the restoration of King Charles the Second, and the name not being inapplicable to our present situation (for we were restored to fresh life and strength), I named this Restoration Island; for I thought it probable that Captain Cook might not have taken notice of it.[174]

Bligh Boat Channel is around thirty kilometres south of Providential Channel, and a small island inside the reef must have seemed ideal under the circumstances. Three weeks before reaching the coast the longboat had landed on Tofua, just five days after the mutiny on the *Bounty*. Initial Tongan friendliness had morphed into hostility and as they escaped quartermaster John Norton was killed: *I saw five of the natives about the poor man they had killed, and two of them were beating him about the head with stones in their hands.*[175] That would have reinforced existing wariness; twelve years earlier he had been with Cook on his last Pacific voyage and had seen him killed on a Hawaiian shore by islanders they thought they knew well. After Tofua he wasn't going to risk any more landings than absolutely necessary. But because of Cook he had a general understanding of the northernmost coast, which Cook had charted two decades earlier – including Providential Channel. With just the memory of a map and a latitude to guide him he set a course over 3600 nautical miles of uncharted ocean to pass through the reef just thirty kilometres south – and made it to Restoration Island.[176]

Resto is a continental island that in a kayak approaching from the south looks like a mainland peak for most of the three hours it takes from Cape Direction. Three hours with filled sails, pushing through swells driving from the south-east. Little and Big Lloyd Islands slip by to the west, Cape Griffith passes and Restoration Rock appears on the horizon to the east of the island. Eventually, to the west, glimpses of white coalesce into a dividing line between sea and rainforest stretching all the way to Cape Weymouth – Chilli Beach. On the eastern flank of Weymouth facing across to Restoration Island is Casuarina Beach, Hobson camps now, *Kuuku Ya'u* country. But lots of squatters over time, particularly from the 70s to the 90s. And just before Casuarina is Wongai Point, where the man I knew as Gordon was camped in his wrecked Falcon in 1993 when the police came for him – the man I next met in Cooktown in 1994 as László.

But I steer close to Resto, along the boulders at the base of the windward cliffs, near enough to ride the swell as it builds and sweeps around the island's western face. The sail flips nervously as the wind that's propelled us for three hours is divided and tormented before it dies in the lee and we pass even ground with coconut palms and casuarinas down to a sandy shore. A scimitar spit is exposed with the water surrounding it absolutely still, but with whitecaps in the channel just fifty metres away. Respite from the wind and weather as it's been for mariners for hundreds of years and which it probably was for Robert Watson who was based here collecting *bêche-de-mer* when he was found at the end of October1881 and told that the fishing station on Lizard Island had been sacked and that his wife, Mary, their son Ferrier and two Chinese employees were missing. He headed straight back and, as he told the inquiry, spent the next month: *untiring in my search for traces of my wife and child, assisted by the police and Harbour authorities and others, among the islands and coast between Cooktown and Cape Melville.*[177] Two months later he viewed the remains of Mary, Ferrier and Ah Sam, and the belongings found with them. He never returned to the sea and died twelve years later in Cooktown hospital from lung complications of mining. He was fifty-six.

Restoration for Bligh; desolation for Watson – it all depends on circumstances but for me Resto is magic, familiar from many visits over two decades. I've landed by kayak three times before; alone the first time and then on to the Tip, the second arrival with Jon, and the third with Jon and Jethro. Each time it's special and this time it's with Jon and Axel, but there's a sense of something closing off. The journey has been about getting to rather than being in. We didn't even consider stopping at Lowrie Island to see if Axel's Mace was still there. Although it hasn't been stated we each know this will be the last trip with Axel – our headings are different.

But for now we're together and with Quasimodo to welcome us. Quasimodo is used to strange arrivals and bounds along the beach – howling. From Lockhart River via a departing teacher, his mother was a pit bull, his paternity somewhere in the seething Lockhart canine gene pool. But the result is something like a German shorthaired pointer – the only dog on Restoration Island. Maybe that's why he's of uncommonly civil disposition – his universe is this small space inhabited by a constantly changing cast of human beings arriving from across the water and leaving the same way. His world stops at the beach; he's survived crocodile attacks and cyclones and seems to know that the sea is not his element. But the island is, and the one constant in his life isn't far behind, Dave Glasheen – Resto Dave.

Resto Dave is solidly in the tradition of E.J. Banfield who, more than a century ago, popularised the romantic notion of remote, island escape, spending a quarter-century on Dunk Island off Mission Beach. Thought to be terminally ill when he arrived with his wife, Bertha, Banfield was rejuvenated by island life: *This – this was our life we were beginning to live – our very own life; not life hampered and restricted by the wills, wishes and whims of others; unencumbered by the domineering wisdom, unembarrassed by the formal courtesies of the crowd.*[178]

Resto Dave's mainstream malaise was financial but the cure was the same and he arrived on the island in the mid-1990s when John Pritchard moved across the water to Cape Weymouth where he recorded my arrival with Jon in 2003 – *trussed up like a working bullock*. At first sight, Dave fits the stereotype of beachcomber and island recluse and looks no different to my first meeting, or when he picked up journalists Mark Whittaker and Amy Willesee at Portland Roads a decade ago: *Dave comes into shore and beneath the wild white beard and hair is an even whiter set of teeth and watery blue eyes. He is in his late fifties but his body is lean and deeply tanned.*[179]

He's got the look – but he's no recluse. Fishermen, drifters, locals, celebrities, people looking for paradise and others trying to escape it – and the media – are drawn to Resto. Eccentricity is a good angle but Dave feels Whittaker and Willesee took kiss-and-tell advantage of his hospitality. And there's plenty of that, including to kayakers. Even before we're ashore and kayaks secure Dave has set up an esky filled with home-brew on the concrete slab that serves as a table in the beach bar. Thrown up with what's been blown ashore, it's a jury-rigged marvel held together by constant attention, and has survived storms and innumerable celebrations. Arriving always feels like coming home and Dave is an inextricable part of the ambience.

After a few beers and tales I return to my Feathercraft that is beginning to lift with the tide – it's time to unload and drag it up to high ground. Each time I do this it's with less enthusiasm and I think about how I first got hooked on collapsible kayaks. It was Christmas 1984 and I was in Union Square, New York, when I passed the Klepper Kayak Shop – and went in. Johann Klepper was a tailor in Rosenheim near Munich, and developed a folding model of an Inuit kayak in 1907 that went to mass production in 1910. He was in the game at the right time; a new century and an expanding middle class with soaring interest in sport and communing with nature. Women were getting in on it and kayaking democratised entry into water sports. One person who slid into a kayak in the 1920s was Franz Romer, who paddled a custom made Klepper in 1928 from Cape Saint Vincent in Spain to Saint Thomas in the American Virgin Islands. He'd made it across the Atlantic in fifty-eight days and the reports were front-page news around the world. But his journey hadn't finished and in September he set course for New York – and disappeared in a hurricane. Twenty-eight years later Hannes Lindemann, a German doctor who'd been working in Liberia and had crossed the Atlantic in a sailing dugout canoe two years earlier, left Las Palmas in a seventeen foot production Klepper Aerius double that had been reconfigured as a single. After seventy-six days and crises almost nobody would have survived he reached Saint Thomas.[180]

For almost a century Klepper kayaks have been the gold standard, but Klepper wasn't the only German company making news with folding kayaks, and when Oskar Speck paddled out of Altona near Hamburg in 1932, aged twenty-five, he was in a double kayak made by Pionier

Faltboots. Seven years and several kayaks later he landed on Saibai in the Torres Strait just three weeks after war had broken out in Europe. Although he escaped once, he spent the next six years in Victorian internment.[181] After the War he stayed on and died in New South Wales in 1995. Folding kayaks have a track record.

Klepper kayaks were introduced to the US by Dieter Stiller, but I don't remember whether it was Dieter or his son, Eric, whom I met in New York; probably Eric, because he talked about Special Service and Marine Corps operatives using Kleppers for reconnaissance and infiltration missions, even launching shoulder-held missiles from them. That's in his book, which starts with an Australian walking into the same store about seven years after me. Tony Brown was working as a male model in New York and convinced Eric that they should paddle around an island – Australia. In the end they made it from Sydney to Darwin, and Eric's book, *Keep Australia on your left*[182] was good enough to get a commendation from Paul Theroux on the front cover: *I have the highest regard for [Eric Stiller's] courage as a traveller and imagination and skill as a writer.* Theroux is no slouch as an author and knows a bit about kayaks, and what they have in common in their writing is that they tell stories about people and places.

And that's quite different to just describing a journey. Terry Bolland is a fair kayaker and made it around Australia in 1990 by kayak, foot and bicycle. In October he arrived at Chilli Beach, going on to Cape Weymouth with a passing comment on Resto: *A fishing vessel was anchored in the lee of the island, on which stood a house and a shed on a small flat section not too far from the high tide mark. Another little piece of paradise.*[183] After which the inventory of dates, places, hours exerted and hardships encountered continues. It was self-published.

But two years later Eric and Tony arrived in their Klepper, *Southern Cross*, and were met at the shoreline by Pucky and Ta'u – from the Bard and *Kuuku Ya'u* for foot respectively – like Quasimodo, displaying the hybrid vigour and friendliness typical of Lockhart camp dogs tempered by the sanctuary of Resto. On the beach with them was Resto Dave's predecessor and our Weymouth host, John Pritchard, who welcomed them into his humble quarters:

> *The bunk-style bed hadn't been washed, much less made, in a great while. Light green was the color of choice for the interior, highlighted with college-beige tapestries like you would find in a college dorm room. A detailed butterfly identification chart was positioned on the wall bordering John's bunk and was among the very first sights for him every morning. More books on birds, flora, fauna, science, and by Stephen Hawking dominated a middling-sized bookshelf. A Conan the Barbarian comic book appeared to be the current read and a B-52s tape had recently been ejected from the tape deck. Some notes on plants and weather were scribbled on his desk.*[184]

Not much about kayaking, but that's the point; reading about ocean kayaking is as interesting as watching it on TV. When Eric Stiller got back to New York and began writing he had a diary to work from, not just trip notes. And he went on to set up the Manhattan Kayak Company and a career in personal fitness and public speaking – a good storyteller.

There are lots of other kayak stories involving Resto that haven't made it to print. Like Sandy Robson, a Western Australian sea kayaker who's just set out to repeat Oskar Speck's voyage to Australia – she reckons she'll finish in five years – 2016. But in June 2007 she tried to circumnavigate Australia and got as far as Villis Point just south of Cape Direction – we passed it yesterday after leaving Night Island. As she was paddling ashore a crocodile the length of her kayak appeared astern and struck the rudder, following her in to shore and forcing a crash landing and emergency exit. She eventually retrieved the kayak, portaged it to another beach and contacted the police at Lockhart River on her satellite phone. But after she lit a fire on a nearby hill it was Resto Dave who found her and towed the damaged kayak back to Resto. The end of that trip, but she's paddled on.[185]

And then there's Freya Hoffmeister, another German but this one a multi-sport athlete. Too tall for gymnastics she took up body-building, shooting, sky diving – and kayaking. Also a businesswoman and model who placed sixth in the Miss Germany competition and then, in her forties, after circumnavigating Iceland and New Zealand, she tackled

Australia, getting around unsupported in 322 days in 2009, beating the time of the only other person to do it, New Zealander Paul Caffyn, three decades earlier. *Fre-ya Hoff-mei-ster* – Dave delivers the name syllable by clipped syllable, whether admiration or an imitation of German isn't clear: *She's going around South America the whole bloody way, it was on the radio yesterday. She's leaving Buenos Aires in a couple of days. Nearly thirty-thousand bloody kilometres. And she'll do it. What a machine – what a woman.*

Dave has been in awe since she climbed out of her kayak and onto the beach at Resto two years ago. It was Dave's Bond moment; Ursula Andress as Honey Ryder emerging from the sea – two years before Freya Hoffmeister was born. Freya knows the effect – her website is: *Freya Hoffmeister – Goddess of love to the seas*. Dave reverentially opens the red visitors book that goes back to the 1980s to show me an entry for April 15, 2009: *Freya Hoffmeister – The mermaid coming from the water. Thanks for getting me restored on the circumnavigation of Australia – love Freya*. Dave seems transported back to his Bond moment: *what a woman.*[186]

Lots of kayakers in the red book including an entry for June 1, 1992 from Eric Stiller and Tony Brown – *Southern Cross kayak expedition to the Tip*. Concise – I guess they already knew they wouldn't make it the whole way around Australia. Maybe they were starting to think about the Gulf of Carpentaria. In the end, they got across the Gulf, but not much further. And someone else who crossed the Gulf, in 2004, stopped at Resto with his paddling companion on August 17, 2001. Again, the red book has it: *Paddling from Port Douglas to PNG. Great place, thanks for the hospitality.* Ben Eastwood's companion was determined to be the first person to cross the Tasman Sea and set out on his second attempt on January 11, 2007. Andrew McAuley's kayak was found on February 10, 2007, fifty kilometres short of Milford Sound – he didn't make it.

CHAPTER 11

2013-2015: zeta

It's full-on man, it's fuckin' full-on. It's an excellent adventure, provided I make it... Older by some forty years than the light on Coquet Island that's visible in the distance, the lighthouse on Sydney's South Head was where Andrew McAuley's family and friends gathered and heard those words. They looked to the east, the direction he headed, into the swells and winds of the Tasman Sea. That's why his wife chose the location for the service and where the recording found in his kayak was played – *It's full-on man, it's fuckin' full-on. It's an excellent adventure, provided I make it...*

Tragedies – lots along this coast. People who didn't make it and others who were just lost – marooned. Like Narcisse Pelletier and Barbara Thompson, but also Jack and Charlie. And getting rescued may have very different meanings. There are those who don't want to be rescued and some who don't realize they're stranded. Plenty of those in north Queensland now and they don't attract much attention – nobody notices, nobody cares. And then there are people like László and Michael Fomenko who might argue that it's us who are marooned, stuck in physical and social spaces where the guardians are *programmed to limit degrees of freedom and to close quantum portals*. László's words, two decades ago, before I began to realize it wasn't all crazy. A lot of it was – but not all of it.

Andrew McAuley was heading into the blue because it was hard – he sought it out, he was searching for the edge. Tarzan's life was hard too, but he wasn't looking for the edge – the hardness just came with the territory. Maybe it was the same for László. And then sometimes the hardness just comes from nowhere – *shit happens*.

Le Mole sul Farfa, Mompeo, September 2, 2013

— Ernie, is that Ernie Hunter…
— Yes, who's calling…
— Ian, Ian Cole, mate – sorry to disturb you.
— Ian. Hi, what's up. An unexpected call, We're in Italy…
— I know, I'm afraid I've got bad news.
— Bad news…
— Yeah, it's Chris, he's had an accident, he's in the Base Hospital.
— Chris, you mean Jon – what happened…
— Yeah, Jon. He had a bike accident, he's broken his back.
— Where…
— Crush fracture – T12 L1.
— And the cord…
— Not looking good.

Cairns, July 23, 2014

Although most mail is electronic now I'm still not good at clearing what's left of hard copy correspondence. That only gets attention when the mailbox reaches critical. A quick scan is usually all it takes to reduce the load by half, the rest disappeared into the recycle bin. This morning it's almost all gone with the first cull, leaving just a couple of journals and a large, reusable, manila envelope, the last but one addressee being the only clue that its contents should be checked – *CMH, Innisfail*. That's where it landed before it was sent on to me and Innisfail isn't somewhere I work or where I get mail from.

Placing the journals aside I open it to find a forwarded envelope addressed to *doctor ernest hunter* in neat cursive script over a roughened oblong marking where the original address label had been stripped. Yellowing sticky tape reinforces the seal-flap on the back and below that is the archaic logo of the Queensland government. Gold, wheat, cattle, sheep, sugar cane; the pioneer quintet celebrating a myth that's alive and well, the rampant brolga a belated recognition of native populations to offset the interloping deer; bird and beast staring at each other across the signifiers of exploitation and below a symbol of appropriation, a medieval great helm – whatever it takes. Scrolled at the base – *AUDAX AT FIDELIS* – Bold but faithful. An acknowledgement, I suppose, that boldness can be entirely self-serving, without loyalty. So the conjunction is critical but leaves open what the object of faithfulness is if it's not just profit. And below that, *Mental Health Review Tribunal*.

It's a standard, official A5 envelope that could have been months or years old and the contents are rigid, it feels like there's cardboard inside with something round and loose that moves about like a marble. The moment I peel back the self-adhesive fastener it falls out and bounces off the desk to the floor – a small, white, almost translucent stone. Immediately I visualise the trailer at the Peninsula Caravan Park and the stones scattered around the memorial spelling out Dr Mick. And László walking along the beach at Finch Bay picking them up, turning each over, rejecting some and pocketing a select few.

The reaction is instant and uncomfortable, with cascading connections bypassing awareness and triggering an immediate sense of deflation, of emptiness. Then as memory and reflection catch up the emotions follow. Guilt I suppose – not for what I should have done but what I could have done. Even though it was seven years ago that I spoke with Biata and way over a decade since I last saw László in Cooktown as he was being loaded into an ambulance for the journey to Cairns – it could be yesterday. But this feeling is familiar, close to the surface, and it always triggers associations – a lover I'd let down; Jacques, the dog I grew up with whose absolute loyalty and unconditional affection was unwavering even as we left him behind; my dad, Harry, who needed the son to be father of the man as his mind disintegrated, while his only surviving child was getting on with teenage life, far from the locked ward Harry would never leave. Close to the surface but buried by selective inattention – maybe that's just what it takes to survive; insight is a liability that unmasks the bystander self.

I know that this response has something to do with unworthiness, of undeserved admiration or love. Perhaps it's a perverse twist on narcissism, hungering for admiration but uncomfortable with its expression – and the expectations that follow. Maybe discomfort is the price of insight and I suppose I should be grateful; idealisation always comes with baggage – especially for a psychiatrist. When you work with people who've been traumatised, being thought special is part of the territory, of a privileged therapeutic relationship. But plenty of psychiatrists have fallen into the trap of believing that they not only have a privileged relationship, but that it's privileged in a special kind of way – that they are special. Enough that even in the small pool in Cairns there's been sufficient flirting, fucking and infatuation to land colleagues in jail, disgrace and/or exile.

My relationship with László Halassy was special, but in a very different way. He was neither idealising nor an object of desire, and he was precise and uncompromising about physical and social boundaries. But there was something special and we both knew it. Because of that there were expectations – *special* doesn't allow for bystanders. So when he needed more than the system was likely to deliver and I did just enough to satisfy its expectations and left him to its mercy, I was complicit. On the cusp, I suppose, of being a perpetrator. While my head says that's irrational the emotion is still guilt – just like I felt as a teenager turning away from my father.

I look at the stone for maybe half-a-minute before picking it up, it has been so smoothed by time and travel it seems unnatural. As I roll it across my palm it feels lighter and looks brighter than an object broken from a subterranean seam of rock should. But it's not a random find, it's been selected for its qualities – it's special. And so are the other contents of the envelope, the first in view being the red, cloth cover of an old book, cut at the spine. I don't need to read the faded title, I have what is probably the same edition and I turn it over to see the outline of *Cape York Peninsula* with an inset map of Australia in the top right corner and a single arrow identifying *Madman's Island*. Identical to my copy except for a sticker next to the spine: *Rural Libraries Queensland*. And a fish-shaped scrawl across the bottom of the map, from coast to coast of Cape York.

The last item is blank except for a near circular character in the middle of the page and I realize I'm holding the back cover of a paperback book upside down. The scrawl on the inner cover of *Madman's Island* isn't a fish, its *alpha*, and this is *omega*. Revelations – *I am the Alpha and the Omega – the beginning and the end*. The beginning and the end; I turn the back cover over and I'm looking at a small colour photograph set against a blue background representing the sea, a picture of a gently undulating surface above, merging with a stylised graphic below. In the photo sea and sky are divided by a thin beach-line and the contours of land with two, possibly three low hills. Howick Island from the south, I've paddled by, I know it. Above the photo, a synopsis:

> *For five months late in 1920 and early in 1921, Ion Idriess and George Tritton were stranded on Howick Island, a tiny inhospitable scrap of land off the coast of the Cape York Peninsula in far-north Queensland.*
> *Idriess later became one of Australia's most popular and most published authors. His fifty-three books sold millions of copies and some of his books are still in print more than thirty years after his death. His first book,* Madman's Island, *told the story of his stranding on Howick Island with George Tritton. Idriess called George "Charlie".*
> *In* Madman's Island *Idriess claimed George (Charlie) went mad and tried to kill him but there are two sides to every story.*
> *This is the truth about Charlie.*[187]

The truth about Charlie – the truth. The Mental Health Review Tribunal envelope is on the desk, it had probably carried a letter to László letting him know he could attend a meeting of the Tribunal that would consider whether he should remain on an Involuntary Treatment Order, or not. Maybe he went; maybe he didn't – but he kept the envelope. Trying to replace the three items I find something else inside, a single sheet torn from a spiral bound notebook with László's neat handwriting: *take the fifth – live the dream.*

Silkwood, August 6, 2014

Turning right, away from Murdering Point and onto the Silkwood-Japoon Road, I remembered the first time I met Biata – eighteen years ago. I knew she wasn't going to be there now – Dom had already told me that she died in 2012. And the closer I get the more my memories are challenged. There's no rusted android by the side of the road – *Benno, by the drive, he's yellow and holding a post box.* Benno's gone, and so has the classic, cane-farm Queenslander. What sat lightly on the land as a testament to a pragmatic synthesis of function and form accommodating the demands of north Queensland's climate and resources has been upgraded and upsized into a folly of concrete and columns that dominates the land-scape like a cold-sore on the lip. The only resonance between past and present is with the then already crumbling, concrete *lipicai* stallion that seemed to be leaping to escape a pond of mediocrity. Nothing mediocre now – its Romanesque replacement standing rampant before a structure that's mesmerising in its banality. I don't know what Biata would have thought but no doubt Dom is proud.

I'm led into the fully-air-conditioned home and past Dom's wife to a room dominated by a flat-screen TV and the trappings of State-of-Origin paraphernalia. On a table to the side where I imagine business is conducted without risk of interfering with wide-screen view I recognize the now ancient-seeming album that Biata guided me through nearly two decades ago. Next to it are several cardboard boxes filled with the afterglow of lives. Biata's mainly, but also László's. Dom didn't have a lot to say when I called and from his body language this visit probably won't add much more: *We haven't seen Larry for ages doctor. Probably three years at least. He stayed with us after he left Cooktown, until he was sent back to hospital. I don't know when that was.*

It was Christmas 2008 that Biata called me because he was withdrawing, wandering and spending time with Tarzan. Five years ago, and I'd deflected responsibility to his treatment team in Innisfail. I was overseas when he was taken back to hospital, but because I'd pushed the buttons for something to happen I was copied into email traffic around discharge planning which was just starting when I got back to Cairns two months later. He was still in hospital in February 2009 and not doing well.

László had been on clozapine since I sent him to hospital in 2001 – eight years. As far as I was aware it made a difference. At least in terms of the notes I'd seen on-line, his case managers didn't report anything that might be in the Capgra's or Fregoli's syndrome space. But there was also no mention of dreams, or of Idriess or *Madman's Island*. In fact reading those notes didn't tell me much about László at all other than that he was taking his clozapine and wasn't causing trouble.

That all changed after I made the call and they went to check on him just before Christmas 2008. Maybe it was because he saw that as breaking trust, rupturing what he thought was an agreement – *I'll stick to the tablets and clinic visits if you leave me alone.* But it was unstated and asymmetrical and even though he was no longer on an Involuntary Treatment Order the power was still with the clinicians, they could still send him back to hospital – it just took a bit more paperwork. They had all the power – except to make him take his tablets. That was his trump card, his only trick; to be on clozapine he had to consent to take the tablets, and when they turned up he withdrew his consent. Or as the notes recorded, he told them to *fuck off.* Which they did, but they were back not long after with the police. They'd done the paperwork.

His trump card – his protest – landed him back with the *needle-dependent psychopaths*. Not that the psychiatrists on the ward didn't try to get him back on clozapine; they did, but I guess that as far as László was concerned he thought he'd had a deal and it had been broken. They started with reason and carrots but when they tried to convince him that he should trust them their appeals fell on ears plugged by experience. They moved to bargaining and eventually sticks. There was no choice; they knew that when he stopped the clozapine his madness wouldn't slowly declare itself, it would burst into the firmament like a comet, burning brighter than ever. And it did. The thought disorder, paranoia, Capgra's and Fregoli's in spades, desperate attempts to defend himself in a threatening environment filled with hostile persons in disguise – ending up with seclusion, ECT and, eventually, the needle.

And from the notes I knew they were using lots of it. In the years that I'd been László's psychiatrist the depot antipsychotics had never eliminated his psychosis and I'd chosen to accept residual symptoms rather than increase side effects. By and large that worked – he had some tremor and rigidity, and sometimes his face was expressionless, but he was alert, independent and got on with his life in Cooktown. From what I'd read about his last admission, after he refused to take clozapine the antipsychotics were increased – and increased – until his terrified and erratic behaviour settled and there was no more enacted madness. Or much of anything other than sedation and side effects, and nobody knew what was happening under the surface. Probably not a lot of effort went into finding out and when his challenging behaviour was flat-lining he was deemed ready for discharge – but not to Silkwood, he refused to return to his only family's home. Whether that was because of what he believed was their breach of trust, or because he still thought Biata, Dom and the others there were *Ördög*, *ÁVO*, CIA or other sinister pretenders, I don't know. So after nearly three tortured months they found him a place to live in Innisfail, a boarding room on Glady Street facing Anzac Park. The email traffic I was being copied in to stopped when the discharge planning was complete and his care was transferred back to the Innisfail team.

I hadn't checked his file since that time, March 2009, until I found the envelope forwarded from Innisfail a month ago – five years later. Within a few minutes I was reading his electronic record, tracking the home visits to his flat that started weekly, reduced after six months or so to fortnightly when his injection was due, and then monthly when they changed him to a newer antipsychotic. He was probably glad to have less to do with the *needle-dependent psychopaths* and they thought he was doing just fine. So fine, in fact, that by early 2012 the Mental Health Review Tribunal revoked the Involuntary Treatment Order and he was a voluntary patient, again. That's when the entries became sparse and spare – *did not attend … not at home …* – until eventually they stopped. The final entry – *contacted by real estate agent. Larry has not been seen for several weeks. Attended with police and a box of personal belongings retrieved and taken to relatives in Silkwood. They report no contact with Larry. Believed to have left the region. Case closed.*

Believed to have left the region… That was two years ago, but the envelope addressed to me had made its way to Community Mental Health in Innisfail some time before July 2014. He hadn't left the region, he'd been bureaucratically disappeared. And a month later I'm in Silkwood chasing his shadow across cane country. All shadows are elusive and this one particularly so – it's clear Dom feels that the less he knows about László the better. I try to keep it simple and ask about László's belongings that Dom told me on the phone had been dropped off: *Yeah, it was about the time mum passed that the nurse from the mental health came to the farm and left that box. I never got around to throwing it out, it's just been with mum's stuff. She used to worry about him. I told her he's a grown man and can look after himself. I know he was family and that he was sick in the head but, well, I guess I can say we didn't get on. I didn't like the effect he had on mum. She would always be upset after she saw him.*

She would always be upset after she saw him – I had presumed that there was no contact after he left hospital in 2009. Dom clarifies that László never came to Silkwood again but that Biata went to him: *He stayed in town in a dump by Anzac Park. Not fit for animals. Drunks and druggies. But mum would go and see him. She'd take him some cake or make some sandwiches. He'd never show he was grateful but she still went.*

She still went – went to her last remaining connection to a life a world away, no longer behind an iron curtain but shrouded anyway by distance and the passage of time. Or so I thought until Dom's qualifier: *And that all got worse when she tried to tell him about his sister.*

I'm so surprised I automatically repeat those two unexpected words – *his sister* – Dom continuing as if not registering the relationship or my reaction: *Yeah, his sister in Hungary was trying to make contact and she found mum on Facebook. There's a Magyar Facebook thing in Australia and once mum got an ipad she was on it all the time. The woman in Hungary had been trying to find out what happened to her father – Larry's father – after he defected. He had a wife and daughter back in Budapest, that's what mum said. Jewish side of that family – mum wouldn't talk about it much, said that they were heavy party members.*

Although we're talking about Béla's daughter, Biata's relative and so Dom's too, it doesn't seem to mean much to him and I have to push before Dom gives more details: *She told mum that Béla Halassy was her father. She knew he'd died in the seventies or eighties, while the communists were still in power. That got back through the refugee community – the Magyars were tight in Sydney. And somehow she knew that he'd had a child in Australia, that she had a brother. Then it was all up to Facebook.*

A half-brother in fact, but a brother nonetheless. László would be over fifty now and she would be close to sixty. A half-brother courtesy of social media – the other side of the planet and arguably on a different one. It's close to midday and Dom's wife has brought tea and biscuits, Arnott's Scotch Fingers – no home-baked Hungarian delicacies. In the background the flat-screen is alive, like a window into another reality that insistently draws Dom's gaze. He's over his Hungarian relatives and he seems to be over me too, but I bring him back to Biata's attempts to tell László about his sister. His expression suggests he wants me to know I'm imposing, that there are more important things to be getting on with, and with a pained look towards the door continues: *His sister, yeah. He didn't want to know. Mum was very upset, she said that Larry's sister was sick, maybe didn't have long to live. Mum kept going to try and find Larry. He'd avoid her, head off bush with that Tarzan freak. And then he was gone, disappeared. A couple of months later mum died. I think the stress made her heart worse, the woman in Budapest had told her she wanted to come out, to try and talk to Larry. Just after mum's gone we have a visit from the psycho team with that box. Junk, just junk.*

A visit from the psycho team … just junk… It's a standard cardboard archive box, now holding a life's jetsam, washed up in a bed-sit in Innisfail two years ago. Dom takes his eyes off the midday TV to check his watch. I've overstayed, maybe overstepped – it's time to move on. He shrugs when I ask if I can check out the box, cutting me off and closing the meeting when I try to assure him that I'll get it back, by standing up and shaking his head with an emphatic: *Don't bother.*

Cairns, August 7, 2014

As I drove north from Silkwood yesterday I was conscious of the ghost of László on the seat next to me. It was after sunset by the time I arrived home and even though I'd carried the archive box from the Cannizzaro living room to the car, when I picked it up again its lightness surprised me. Not the only surprise – or parcel; I found another in the mailbox. I knew what it was before I tore through the wrapping to expose a paperback book, the covers blue and the back the same as had arrived from László – but without the omega.

The book could wait, the box came first. It was nearly empty, the contents jumbled at the bottom like discarded refuse. And that must have been what it seemed to whoever had been sent by the Innisfail mental health team to clear out his room. What I was looking at was probably all that didn't go straight to the bin, and as far as Dom was concerned it probably should have. Maybe he didn't even open it.

I immediately recognized the book. The front cover was gone but I knew it was *Madman's Island* even before I opened it to see the running head and densely annotated text. Words underlined and circled, whole paragraphs marked with double vertical lines next to which were question or exclamation marks, and biblical references – page after page. At the bottom of the box, beneath a litter of old envelopes, some the same as the one that had been forwarded to me from Innisfail, were a few items of clothing, a metal pannikin, an assortment of old cutlery, two chipped plates and a black plastic bag, the kind you find at beaches for dog owners.

I opened it to confirm what I knew by feel; inside were half-a-dozen, almost identical, white stones.

There was only one other item, which stood out as being neither recycled nor rejected, an A4 envelope with *László* written across the front. The protective cover hadn't been removed from the self-adhesive strip; it hadn't been sealed and may never have been opened. Inside were two sheets of paper with four black and white images, computer screen shots from Facebook pages, photo-shopped to look like they were from an old album, complete with faux photo-corners and electronic cursive script at the base as if they had been labelled after the last family holiday. The oldest was of a couple standing in front of an elaborate fountain with a little girl in the foreground. The day it had been taken must have been sunny but cold; the man and woman were completely covered, with scarves at their throats and hats on, and the girl was in a belted coat and wearing a bonnet with a bow. She was the only one smiling, her small arms held high as if showing off for the camera, and while the resolution was grainy and indistinct she seemed to be holding something in each outstretched hand that looked like an egg – perhaps an Easter egg. The title below: *Húsvéthétfő 1955, Dóra, Béla, Júlia* – Béla, László's father, the year before he defected at the Melbourne Olympics.

Dóra and Júlia; I couldn't tell from that photograph or the one below who was wife and who daughter; the second picture was mother and daughter in a countryside setting, perhaps on holiday. That photo had been taken in warmer weather; both women were wearing light frocks and from the trees in the background it seemed like an autumn scene. The label confirmed the identities: *Dóra, Júlia, Balatonyörök, 1968*. The younger woman, László's sister, looked to be in her early- to mid-twenties. In that photograph she wasn't smiling – nor was her mother. A holiday scene maybe, but neither mother nor daughter looked like they were in the mood, they were gazing in different directions and seemed to be preoccupied with something in the far distance, perhaps too far to see. It would have been very hard to remain relaxed that autumn as troops and tanks from Bulgaria and Hungary were moving west to join Warsaw Pact allies in crushing the Prague Spring. It was all over quickly in 1968 but, for Hungarians, the uprising of 1956 was a recent memory, if not talked about. And probably not by either of these women whose husband and father might as well have been a casualty.

From the captions to the two images on the second sheet of paper I realized that Dóra was Béla's wife – she didn't appear – and Júlia was László's sister. In the older photograph she was with two children in front of an intricately decorated Christmas tree, and across the base: *Karácsony, 1995, Júlia, Emma, László. László* – I was startled by the name on the page. There was no way of knowing whether it was a coincidence or whether Júlia, who would have been in her mid-forties, had named her own child after a brother she had heard about but never met. And it wasn't even clear whether the two teenagers were her children. But they seemed relaxed and happy – it was years since the collapse of communism across Eastern Europe and the departure of the last Soviet troops to their bases in Russia. Maybe there was something to smile about.

From child to middle-aged adult, Júlia was identifiable across the first three images, a woman who was strongly built, with a round, handsome face. Her youthful long, dark locks were gone by Christmas 1995. Looking directly to the lens her face was framed by hair that was carefully layered and emphasised her bright eyes. She seemed like someone who would have worked with people, not things. A receptionist maybe, or a nurse, perhaps a doctor.

The last picture was of Júlia alone. Her name was not in the caption – *Barlangfürdő, Miskolc, 2011* – but it was her, though very different. While the bright eyes were the same, like the image of her as a teenager they seemed to be engaging with something far away. And she was gaunt; the woman in this photograph, who would have been around sixty, no longer had a round face. And it was impossible to tell if it was differently framed by her hairdo because she had a wrap wound tightly around her head. And her body was hidden, this Júlia was sitting in a deck chair wearing a towelling robe covering her entire body save for the calves, her feet in slippers. Behind her there was a pool or small lake and the entrance to a tunnel or cave. Perhaps she was on holiday or taking the waters at a spa, but as I examined her lined face I imagined a woman on the journey through cancer treatment. This photograph was taken around the time she was in contact with Biata. Maybe she was on another journey – to find her brother before she died.

That was last night, and after I'd replaced everything in the archive box I took up *The truth about Charlie*. The author, Rob Coutts, is a social worker from Brisbane who counsels veterans and their families, and runs the website – *idriess.com.au*. He'd understand Jack's diary entry for January 2, 1918 when he was in the Port Said Hospital after being evacuated in a delirium from a field station near Jaffa, which came under artillery fire. After nearly three years of bloodshed: *I am to be returned to Australia as unfit for further service. Thank heaven.*[188] Jack left the War but war never left him; he wrote eleven military books including six manuals in *The Australian guerrilla series* during the Second World War – *Shoot to kill, Sniping, Guerrilla tactics, Trapping the Jap, Lurking death* and *The scout*.[189] Like the shrapnel that returned to Australia buried in his flesh, he never really got war out of his system.

Coutts is an Idriess buff – I suppose I am too. He was directed to the trail of George Tritton by local historians in Cooktown who'd already made the connection and had been to Howick to see if the description in *Madman's Island* fit the topography, which it seemed to. But Rob Coutts wrote the book without getting on to the island. Then again, neither have I, at least not where it counts.

By the time I finished *The truth about Charlie* it's another day. It's not a big or challenging read and I haven't learned anything about Jack Idriess, or the story of *Madman's Island* that I wasn't already aware of. But in terms of George Tritton I was starting from scratch. He was born in Cork but raised in Devon, and set off for adventure and fortune in Queensland as a teenager with his older brothers, arriving in Townsville in 1888 on the *Quetta*, two years before its final voyage ended on the rock that would thereafter carry its name. According to Coutts, not much is known of George over the next fifteen years but he seems to have been around Innisfail just after the turn of the century and lived most of the rest of his life in Cooktown and Cape York. Except for the War.

George Tritton had a very different war to Jack Idriess. He'd enlisted in his mid-forties in June 1917 and arrived at the Western Front around Christmas, not long before the 41st Battalion of the AIF faced a final desperate German offensive in the spring of 1918.[190] Whether George saw much action wasn't clear, but from Defence Service Records Coutts discovered that he'd been in and out of hospital for the rest of the conflict and was seriously ill when the guns finally fell silent. It was in the first year of what they all thought would be a lasting peace that George underwent a laparotomy, his file recording:

Chronic constipation and trouble with bowels on and off for some years – became pretty bad last June and evacuated and returned – came over on leave and reported. Has had ileectomy, colostomy and appendicostomy done. Washes his own bowels every other day. Is getting a belt to (?stop) faeces coming through wound now.[191]

By mid-1919 George was back in Australia and arrived in Cairns on the *Bombala* in October. Within a year he was at the West Coast Hotel in Cooktown showing two other ex-soldiers, Jack Idriess and Dick Welsh, specimens of tin and wolfram that he told them he'd been given by *Old Tarquay*. Soon after, two of them sailed for Howick.

From all the sources Coutts pulled together he concluded that George wasn't crazy but that both George and Jack had problems:

Whether or not George was living with depression and whether or not Jack had PTSD both of the men stranded on Howick Island certainly had their emotional problems. Given their predicament, their similarities and also their differences made conflict inevitable.[192]

Whether or not… Jack certainly thought George had lost it and Coutts devotes a chapter to an article in the *Cairns Post* of February 1921 in which Jack is reported to have told the journalist about his time on the island and the person he'd left behind:

He is suffering very much from a wound in the stomach which he received in the war. In my opinion he is strange in his head. On two separate occa-

sions he was partially out of his mind for a week on end. Then he pulled himself together again, and became quite normal.
He has a great deal of pain in his stomach, and in my opinion this trouble has affected his head...
During the last three months I tried to persuade Tritton to leave the island whenever a boat would call in answer to my signals, but he would not hear of leaving. He said he might as well die on the island as in the Cooktown Hospital. He added that civilisation had never done anything for him, and he was sick of the rotten ways of his fellow men.[193]

Sick of the rotten ways of his fellow men – understandable given the circumstances. The isolation on Howick probably served his purposes and George didn't seem to be mad when Constable Brown checked on him a month or so later. But although George refused to leave then, he was soon back on the mainland, living for another six years around the Cape before he died, as he'd hoped he wouldn't, in Cooktown hospital. His death certificate listed: *"(1) Neuritis" then "(2) Debility" then "(3) Cardiac failure"*[194] – George was fifty-four years old. As I read the last page I got to what Rob Coutts believed was the truth about Charlie:

Over six years before George died he would have read the Cairns Post *article with its derogatory references to his mental state. He would have been angry at that time. Then Jack's book appeared in Cooktown. It must be more than likely that George read Jack's book before he died. The book would have been widely read and discussed in Cooktown for about seven months before George died. George Tritton (even when nominated as "Charlie") would have become known as the "madman" of* Madman's Island. *The melancholy conclusion of this book is that George was dying when he was wrongly branded as a madman and he took this unfair label to his death. This sad thought is the truth about Charlie.*[195]

I don't know if Rob Coutts got it right about George or Jack but as I closed the book I tried to imagine what László would have made of it. And what the message was that he intended for me. The front cover of *Madman's Island* and the back of *The truth about Charlie* inscribed *alpha* and *omega*. And between them – nothing. Maybe the truth about Idriess. Or László's own revelation: *I am the Alpha and the Omega – the beginning and the end.* And why to me, after a decade…

Cairns Base Hospital, September 16, 2014

Ernest, more than happy to talk colons – yours or not… Per os or per arse, Alan De Costa – *Professor Alan De Costa, colorectal and general surgeon –* knows more than a little about the inner workings of health staff in this part of north Queensland, including mine. I suppose I do as well, though those I've had dealings with are conscious when they give up their secrets. The person I'm talking to him about was traumatised and had some pretty significant colon problems – George Tritton – a name I'd never heard until a month ago. *Yours or not…* You can't help smiling despite the disclosure, maybe because of it. Even with an attentive cluster of white coats hovering nearby, in each of which there's someone who looks too young to drive. Students, registrars, maybe both, I'm meeting Alan on his turf, the surgical ward of Cairns Base Hospital. I had no idea whether clarifying what the abdominal surgery was that George went through would help me understand what was going on in his head. But I explained the background to Alan and he was up for the challenge, so I sent him copies of the relevant sections of both books. He smiles and touches his brow with playful deference as I approach and addresses the students: *Professor Hunter is one of our eminent psychiatrists but we don't see him much in the hospital. Nevertheless we are honoured Ernest. It's good of you to drop by.*

— *Alan, please, it's me that's honored that you would consider giving time to such a trifling request.*
— *Ah – not a trifle. A mystery Ernest, like the workings of our mortal coil – a mystery, and this one with a solution. I've taken the liberty of doing a rough drawing and have written a report of sorts but, if you'll indulge me, it may be instructive for this group who one day will be leaders in the Cairns surgical fraternity – or sorority, as the case may well be.*

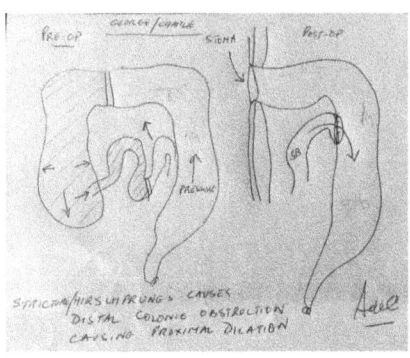

... a rough drawing...

... I invented a pair of pump-up pants.

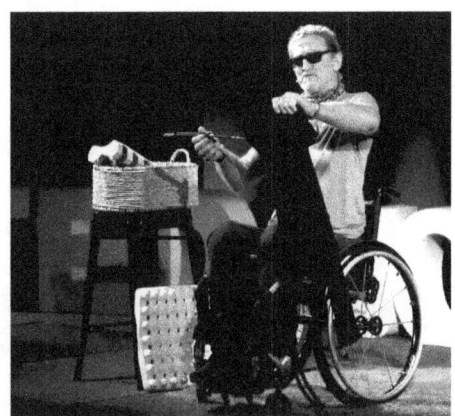

... less legs and more seeing...

...at the end of the beach where there are lots of coconut palms...

Alan is an expert at balancing a sense of humour that teeters on indiscretion with a style that seems like a parody of reserved formality. But looking at the young faces switching their gazes from Alan to me and back, I'm not sure they get it. From the dapper surgeon with the bearing and accoutrements of the profession, to *one of our eminent psychiatrists*, a bearded, long-haired and greying apparition in jeans, tee-shirt and sandals – I can imagine the cogs turning as they try to lock in on it. We probably both enjoy being able to hold an edge of uncertainty with an audience, maybe it's just humour, maybe it's control – but I'm happy to go along with it: *Professor De Costa, I'm prepared to be as dazzled as I was when I first came across your classic paper on obturator hernia – please lead on.*

I'd looked that up before I arrived, just in case, and Alan smiles as he removes a hand-drawn diagram from an envelope and places it on the counter of the nurses station, the white coats gathering around. Against the background sounds of the surgical ward Alan's voice is clear as he switches to the tight language of case presentation: *A forty-five year old single, white male was admitted to a hospital in England in 1919. Is there any importance to that date...* For fifteen minutes Alan gives a demonstration of dialogical teaching, leading this group – attentive to what is as much a mystery as a case – through what might have happened to George a century ago. He's good at it and has me hooked too. Then the youthful eyes are all back on me as Alan folds the diagram and replaces it in the envelope: *And for this intriguing vignette of surgical and local history we have Professor Hunter to thank.* With a nod and a smile he's back on task. As I head to the lift I can hear his voice in the background as the ward round moves on. I've heard the story but I'm already reading the report:

Ernest, these guys did it tough. I take it that Charlie in the novel was George. Trying to summarize the medical aspects:

George had a problem for many years before he went to war. The main symptom was constipation. Most cases (the figure given is 95%) of Hirschprung's present in early childhood. There are variations of the condition as well but this does suggest a congenital condition, eg a forme-fruste of Hirschprung's or indeed a congenital stricture of some type;

He was admitted to hospital in England with a subacute-bowel obstruction. His doctors clearly had a tricky problem on their hands. A huge proximal dilated colon and possibly terminal ileum. Oper-ating on this kind of "unprepared" bowel in the pre-antibiotic and pre-stapling era would have brought considerable technical challenges to the surgical team, and a real risk of mortality to the patient. But twixt Scylla and Charybdis…;
He had a major operation;
He subsequently seemed to survive with irrigations through a stoma of some sort;
He does not seem to have had a bag – that would have been obvious; His bowel must have been in continuity from the hole in his anterior abdominal wall to his anus;
This suggests to me that the operation was a right hemicolectomy with some ileum, "the ile-ectomy". This may have been forced on the surgeon, who may have been dealing with a very dilated caecum, ascending colon and possibly ileum. These changes would not have addressed the underlying pathology, which is in the distal ano-rectum. They would have dealt with some of the consequences of proximal bowel enlargement caused by an incomplete distal colonic obstruction and allowed him to function (see diagram);
The distal small bowel may have been joined to the ascending colon or transverse in an end-to-side manner leaving a short length of colon proximal to the anastomosis coming out through the abdominal wall. If this was long enough stool may not have come through this, but would have supplied an access channel for colonic irrigation. This is in fact a neat example of a "continent" stoma. As this opening was not very active it would have had a tendency to stricture hence the need for regular dilatation with his "scope":
A most interesting project Ernest, and good luck with it, Alan.

James Cook University, October 3, 2014

The Auditorium in the Cairns Institute is full. The first TEDx talks to be held at James Cook University have nearly finished, the topic: *Torrid talks – Why Aristotle was wrong.* Fifteen presentations through the afternoon and cameras rolling as the last speaker enters the zone – TED's trademark red circle. Ten minutes to get a message across, and the title: *Legless and all at sea.* The speaker, Chris Wighton, his wheelchair constrained by the invisible boundary of the circle. No longer *Wind Boy*, he's *Wheel Boy* now – but he's still Jon.[196]

I came unstuck about two-and-a-half years ago when I crashed a mountain bike in my line of work as a youth worker. I had a group of kids with me who were having trouble at school and we were taking them on an adventure-based resilience program to learn how to handle adversity. I didn't know that I'd have to put that stuff into place in my life sooner than I thought. The short story is that I crashed my bike and broke my back at the T12 level, so I'm paralyzed from the waist down. And the funny thing about the crash is the only thing I remember is that I heard the sound of my back break, but I had no pain. That came later, in hospital, where I spent five months. Physical stuff, but emotional as well; my brain wasn't coping with the change from being a guy who loved to run up the steps, to being someone who couldn't get out of bed on his own. For me it was a matter of identity. If I was someone who before the accident lived an active life, who was a singer songwriter, loved swimming and paddling my ocean kayak, the question was – what for me now…

Prior to my prang, friends and I had some amazing adventures along the Great Barrier Reef from Rockhampton to Lockhart River in trips that could cover distances up to five hundred kilometres. Big adventures – and I wanted to get out and do it again. So, someone had the wild idea for me to get back in my boat and try again. It was an inspiration. The plan was to paddle from Forrest Beach near Townsville out to Great Palm Island, on to Orpheus Island and in to finish at Lucinda. That's about 120 kilometres.

The first thing I had to do was to learn how to swim. My swimming ability was completely gone; when I went into the therapy pool at PA hospital I sank like a stone. We decided to find a way to keep my legs straight and I'll show a couple of ideas we came up with. This one, a fairly simple design, black for all occasions – it goes with anything – wrapped around my legs at knee level. It had plastic rods that went down my legs. We tried that – completely useless. Then I invented a pair of pump up pants. You can laugh – and they did laugh at the Tobruk pool when I was there pumping them up – I had racing tubes down the side doubled up. Again, didn't work, back to the drawing board. Eventually I went back to the basics and cut some holes in a Pull-Buoy for my knees to fit and to keep my legs straight. Once I'd achieved that goal of getting back into the water, my next challenge was getting into a boat and staying there.

When you're sitting in a sea kayak without knees to brace with, and a four-pack where a six-pack used to be, staying upright isn't easy; so we developed a seatbelt that seemed to do the trick. But if you've ever been in a sea kayak upside down out at sea, trying to find the spray deck to pull off to exit is hairy enough without trying to undo a dodgy seat belt as well. So I'm glad I found this seat which fitted nicely into my cockpit and kept me in position without the seatbelt. But I also had to learn how to fall out of the kayak and get back in again – that's part of the deal. So, Ernest, my great paddling buddy and friend, and I experimented. I learned to pull myself onto the boat – flopped over it like a beached whale – then rolled myself into the cockpit. But I ended up sitting sideways with my legs crossed. Not bad if you're riding a horse sidesaddle, but not good for paddling. So the trick was to get my legs and feet back into the cockpit on to a rubber mat that I put there so I wouldn't get pressure sores.

The next step for us was to get some paddling kilometres under our belts. We paddled for an hour, two hours, three hours, and built it up so I was fairly certain I could handle a six hour paddle. Before I knew it a year's planning came to fruition and we were heading for Palm Island – and a dream realized. You can't do it without the support of friends and family.

And the Great Barrier Reef – the gorgeous thing we've got just off our doorstep – that was my muse and inspiration to get back out there.
That's my story and I'd like to leave you with a take on a proverb: if necessity is the mother of invention then, surely, adversity could be the father – maybe a blood test. And now I'd like to play you a song that I wrote about one of our trips up north that sums up our experiences – Gone for shore.[197]

Kowanyama, November 11, 2014

Kowanyama – place of many waters. Armistice day – ninety-six years ago Jack Idriess was already back in Australia and George Tritton was on leave in England, unwell and about to be readmitted to hospital. Peace – it didn't last long. And not much peace in Kowanyama, like Lockhart River an Anglican ex-mission, but this on the west coast of Cape York. Separated by distance and a lot more, the Lockhart mob and the Kowanyama mob face off regularly in Cairns; about the only thing that brings them together is taking on the Aurukun mob.

Place of many waters and place of many troubles; when I first started visiting more than two decades ago it was the most violent community on the Cape. I remember bunkering down in the old clinic as a teenager drove around outside in a stolen car taking pot shots into the building with a rifle – his father was inside. *Rivers of grog* – that term was picked up in the press when the political winds blowing through remote Aboriginal communities shifted again. But it was pretty accurate for Kowanyama. The second highest throughput of beer in Queensland – that's what we were told. And probably the highest output of casualties – they had to upgrade the air-strip in the 1980s to keep the RFDS planes coming to keep the canteen open, so that the revenue would continue to flow into Council coffers. Just like Lockhart, Aurukun and other *ersatz* communities – since mission days, economic empowerment has been a rollicking ride. Economic empowerment – recycling Commonwealth welfare payments through *Murri* communities to the State government and the brewers – everyone's a winner. And like Hopevale and Lockhart, relocation and a new name along the way. Kowanyama was Mitchell River

Mission, relocated from Trubanaman after the First World War. The baptismal font – a giant clam shell – that's about all that remains from the original mission.

Even in mission days Kowanyama was different to the communities on the east side of the Cape. This was cattle country and Aboriginal stockmen rode high – until mechanisation and wages. The traces are still there; during rodeo time at Kowanyama, getting to the yards and arena means passing through a field full of utes and horse-floats. Wiry men walking tall in polished boots, cowboy shirts and stand-up hats. Forty-four gallon drums strung up between trees with saddles for the kids to practice on; old men with bowed legs and horned, dinner-plate-sized belt-buckles – there was real pride in that history, a time when *Kokominjena*, *Kokoberra* and *Kunjen* men could get a job on stations anywhere across the Gulf country.

Mission days are gone and the pastoral industry has been transformed by workplace efficiencies and corporate interests. The top rodeo riders have left for Normanton or Mount Isa where there are still some real cattle jobs and life is easier. Though the violence settled when alcohol was banned in Cape communities in 2004, sly-grog arrives in Kowanyama in waves and there are constant pressures to re-open the canteen. *It'll cut down on humbug and fights* – I've heard that hundreds of times, memories are short. But today is a day of memories, Remembrance Day, the armistice. And an armistice of sorts in Kowanyama; a funeral, another premature death.

An hour ago, from inside the clinic, I could hear mourning cries as relatives gathered at the morgue, then silence as women prepared the body before it was transported in the Council vehicle to a viewing. That will go on for an hour or so with more keening before the final journey to the church for Father Wayne and Deacon Val to do their duties, and then on to the cemetery to a freshly dug grave in a field of crosses above forlorn garlands of faded plastic flowers. Turned out in their best – some families in matching outfits sheltering from the midday sun under a makeshift tent, others back in the shade of trees. There will be more women wailing around the grave, and silent men with sombre expressions while children play. And cellphones everywhere.

Funerals are the most unifying events in these remote communities, moreso than births or birthdays, and weddings don't really feature any more. And a chance to make money, from the funeral directors who target communities to salesmen flogging funeral insurance – *you won't even notice, we'll do the work for you, it'll just be a small deduction...* From Centrelink; a small deduction over a lifetime, along with payments for electronics and white-goods. Concentrating welfare-dependence in remote communities has created a cash-cow for entrepreneurs and death is just one more business opportunity.

At least during funerals it's quiet, although that may change if there's grog around afterwards as the blaming and payback kicks in. There's almost always blame; if it's not another family it's *purri-purri* – black magic. Elders have already been in to smoke the health centre, where the death occurred, so that spirits are hurried away – and business can resume. Now that remote clinics are almost entirely staffed by locum workers many nurses are unfamiliar with funeral routines, standing back with reverential concern lest they cause offence. But there are plenty of others keen for spare time, rationalised as cultural sensitivity. *You don't go to a community during funeral time, it's not respectful* – self-serving bullshit from outreach employees happy to cancel a trip and stay at home. As if funerals were illness-free zones. *Out of respect...* And with the constant turnover of nursing staff it's hard to recognize faces from one visit to the next, let alone voices, but as I pass by the pharmacy a nurse's greeting triggers familiarity but not recognition: *Ernest, I heard you were here, it's Jan...*

— *Jan...*
— *Jan McLoughlin.*
— *Jan, it's been, I suppose, twenty years. And you're in Kowanyama...*

Jan McLoughlin, Mick's wife. The last time I saw her I was sitting on the veranda of their house just past the Cooktown cemetery on the road to the airport and Hopevale. Looking over what they hoped would be a mango orchard. There was a shed at the back of the property where László lived for a while. Jan was a nurse and met Mick when he started visiting Hopevale. *The waiting room was always full when Mick ran a clinic, they didn't mind waiting* – I remembered Jan talking about how much work he caused. By being a good doctor. But now the conversation is Kowanyama: *Relief work, but it's OK, not like Hopevale. I started a year or so ago. Not much reason to stay in Collinsville after Mick died. But he said they were the best years of medicine he'd had. Didn't have to deal with all the crap. Now I'm back. Fly in and fly out, I spend a bit of time in Cairns between trips. In fact you won't guess who was talking about you a while back – Larry.*

Larry – you mean László… I still have the archive box that I retrieved from Dom just a couple of months ago. And the envelope with the book covers that arrived before that. And now, in Kowanyama, someone who was as close to family for him as was possible – until she and Mick left too: *László yes, Mick and I always called him Larry. I didn't realize it was him, but he knew me. It was around Christmas. I was in the queue at Bunnings next to a bearded guy with long hair and no shirt, carrying a length of white poly-pipe and some other stuff. He turned around as if we were friends and said hello Jan – and started speaking to me like it was just yesterday that he was working at our place.*

Around Christmas, that would be somewhere near the end of 2013, maybe six months before *alpha and omega* arrived. *A bearded guy with long hair and no shirt* – the person I recalled sitting quietly in the clinic waiting room or walking along the beach at Finch Bay was always clean-shaved, hair short-cropped, and was never bare-chested: *He still had the same odd stare but he seemed more talkative. Marginally maybe, but he didn't approach people like that in Cooktown days. He told me he'd been studying boatbuilding. Somewhere near Fishery Falls. But he'd lost his teacher and he'd decided to get a boat of his own. He had it on the roof of a ute in the carpark. He showed me. Someone was giving him a lift south.*

Studying boatbuilding, near Fishery Falls, he'd lost his teacher... The *teacher* would have been Michael Fomenko and he was probably going somewhere near Aloomba or Mount Sophia. If László had been helping with boat building it was a dugout that was never going to be launched. He'd *lost his teacher* – was Tarzan gone… Over the clinic intercom the nurse on first call is being paged, I know Jan has to get back to work and so do I, but there's more I need to know about the boat. Jan obliges with another surprise: *It was like a Canadian canoe. It seemed a bit weird to me but that's when he mentioned you. He said that he knew people who'd gone up the Cape. He said his teacher had done it, and Ernest. He called you Ernest.*

Ernest – the only time László used my first name was when he was more unwell than usual. At least he'd realized that a dugout sailing canoe was a lost cause, but a Canadian canoe isn't designed for the open ocean, and it sounded like that's what László was planning. And from what he'd sent to me his destination was Howick. As we walk down the main corridor to the nurses' station and waiting tasks, Jan describes the boat she saw: *He took me to the ute; there was a guy inside who looked dodgy and wanted to get going. The canoe was red, about the length of the ute, made of plastic with wood trim around the edge. Both ends were covered in and there were two seats. He said that he was going to use the poly-pipe as an outrigger and put some kind of sail up. It didn't look seaworthy but he was full of confidence.*

Full of confidence – that's how people look when they're on a mission, even when it's doomed. Like when László was stranded in Bamaga with an octogenarian two decades ago on his way to join Shark-eye Park on the Wau. Confidence – not reassuring. With nurses and health workers hovering nearby there's time only to ask if Jan had any idea where he was heading, or when: *He said he had work to do before he left and he knew someone who would give him a lift up to the Bloomfield. And then, just as he was getting into the ute he reached into his pocket and pulled out a couple of stones. Polished white pebbles, like the ones he collected at Finch Bay, and he gave me one. Then he was gone.*

Then he was gone – but I know where.

High Island, September 23, 2015

Frankland's Islands consist of several low islets one of which is detached and of higher character than the others, which are very low, and connected by a reef. The largest island may be seen five or six leagues off; it is in latitude 17 degrees 7 minutes 45 seconds.

Phillip Parker King (1827)

— *Moby's dick Jon.*
— *You mean Moby Dick...*
— *No Jon, it's a joke – what's fifty feet long and...*
— *Jethro, he's on a riff, I knew it was a problem to break out the biscuits, no more till after we get the tents up*
— *Fuck the tents and give me another cookie. I knew I should have brought the disability sticker, what do you have to do to get service. ..*

Humour must help and it keeps coming. *Like a beached whale* – that's what started the last rave, Jon rolling from one side to the other of a tarp on a sloping beach. I felt Jethro touch my elbow as I was about to help, a simple gesture that said *let him figure it out*. And he did, finally getting into a sitting position with his back braced by a fallen tree-trunk.

A sloping beach on the windward shore of High Island – not where we'd intended when we left Bramston Beach. The plan was to paddle to a camping area facing the mainland, a *dingly-dell* of sorts out of the wind with the added bonus of a picnic table courtesy of National Parks. Jon and I had stayed there before, the last time with Axel just after he got out of prison. This time with Jethro we knew we weren't alone before we landed; there was a yacht off the beach, not a good sign. And it didn't get better; a man with a French accent standing on the beach made it very clear that we would crowd his fun-space and was totally unmoved when I mentioned that one of the paddlers in the double kayak was paralysed. There was no point trying to push any other buttons or to force the issue – a beach as far away as possible on the island sounded appealing.

Cook named the Frankland Group – Normanby, Russel, Round, Mabel and High Islands. High is about five kilometres offshore and around thirty-five from Fitzroy Island where we're going tomorrow. And High for an obvious reason, there's not much flat ground, and when we paddled to the windward shore the *other beach* appeared as a narrow band of sand between tide and hillside, boulder-strewn in the water and ashore, and clearly a bugger of a place to stay when the south-easterly was kicking. Which it wasn't, so the experiment started.

The experiment – unsupported camping offshore with a paralysed paddler. Last year we managed a distance journey with a maritime caravanserai in support. Wheelchair, commode, guitar – it was all loaded and unloaded at each stop – Forrest Beach, Palm, Orpheus and back to Lucinda. It worked and was a lot of fun, but the goal is to get back to journeying independently and this is the first time we've tried beach-camping. It wouldn't have come off without humour.

Before we set off for Palm Island in 2014 we'd figured out how to paddle comfortably and safely, but to camp without support we had to solve other problems: how Jon would get out of the kayak and up to a campsite with just two old guys to assist; enabling some kind of dignified mobility with a minimum exposure to risk; allowing him to get in and out of a tent on his own; the minor issue of catheterising and the less minor of shitting, and; what it would take to be a participant in the journey and not just a passenger. Laughing lubricated practice and in terms of mobility we'd managed to get past the ropes and pulleys and wildly-impractical tracked devices, to trials of the inflatable rollers we used to beach-drag our kayaks – which didn't work either. What did work was *rolling about like a beached whale*.

That would have been fine if we hadn't given in to the hash cookies. But even so, after a few hours Jethro and I were sufficiently together to get the tents up and two hours later, in the twilight of a setting sun we can't see because of Gallic inflexibility on the other side of the island, we three are as we have been on dozens of beaches across thousands of miles of magical coast. *Legless and all at sea* – that was the title of Jon's TED talk. But for all three of us it's less legs and more seeing that's allowed it to happen. Seeing the funny side and beyond limitations. There's always a funny side, even when it's not funny: *How many beaches…*

— *Too many Jon, or not enough. How would you know…*

— *Maybe when you run out.*

It always winds towards reflection as the fire dies, as the embers hold thoughts in suspension, patches of life-tapestries. And truth is somewhere in the warp and weft of that momentary, shared fragment. Whatever it's a piece of, it seems meaningful in the firelight, probably more profound than it possibly could be, but deeply felt all the same. A bloke-thing perhaps, but a real-thing too, revisiting other lives and past journeys: *Why don't we hear from Axel any more Jon… I remember we spent an afternoon under the picnic table on the other side of this island in a deluge a couple of years before I broke my back.*

A couple of years before I broke my back – a different life, still Wind Boy then. And a year before Jon and I paddled from Elim to Resto with Axel. I think Axel had already taken leave – he was around but not, and the shaman had departed much earlier, discarded somewhere between Cooktown and Lizard as the past caught up with him. Too much baggage in the north and we probably reminded him of it – of the fall. A fresh start, that's what he wanted and now he's gone. Another shift: *And the mad Magyar, what happened to him…*

No longer mad Jon – no longer. It's almost a year since I met Jan McLoughlin in Kowanyama. I saw her again a month ago but that will be the last time. No more remote community work for me, the service has been so degraded that I resigned in protest and the rest of the remote psychiatrists will go too. A quarter century with Queensland Health; enough time to hear a lot of stories – enough to last a lifetime. Jan had no more news for me about László but I had for her, and as I started to update her the characters and stories woven through the place László said he was heading when they'd met in Bunnings in Cairns danced in my peripheral consciousness – the Bloomfied.

There are lots of stories about the Bloomfield and Cedar Bay, which is further north and where there's no road access. I guessed that was where he would head, the same place Tarzan used to hang out in the 1970s and 1980s. Sixty years before that Jack Idriess did as well, at Ayton – *the end of the Bloomfield mailman's track. From here he turned back to Cooktown*[198] – and at the Lion's Den up the road, probably more time than scratching for tin. Jack also spent time on the banks of the Bloomfield waiting for the *Pearl Queen* to be towed up the river to Pierce's Landing with supplies. And it was just across the river, by a fern-draped pool, that Jack first caught sight of Mee-Lele, a Thursday Island-educated coloured girl. As he secretly watched her bathing he seems to have been instantly smitten: *By Jove, a man's life can hold some glorious moments! My heart thumped at my first perfect thrill.*[199] It was the beginning of a brief relationship and, whether sexual or not, as he wrote more than two decades later, it left its mark: *I have never forgotten Mee-lele, lovely little animal, warm little human soul. Her eyes would fairly dance to the smile on her lips. She would give all her heart, or else hate passionately. But she liked thrills too much; trouble was the breath of life to her.*[200]

And more trouble than Mee-lele was on the horizon; just a couple of years later he was sailing off to the War and a few years after he returned from the Middle East Jack Idriess set off with George Tritton to Howick Island. Bloomfield, Idriess and László flashed through my mind as I updated Jan – László and Idriess again. It shouldn't have mattered to me; László hadn't been my patient for more than a decade, Queensland Health had closed his case, and in another couple of months I would have been over Queensland Health. It shouldn't have mattered – but it did. On a remote island a year later the story is interrupted by the sighs of zephyr-stirred casuarinas, the breeze lifting a swarm of embers that, for a moment, draws two faces out of the darkness and a comment from Jethro: *You identify with him, with being an outsider. You think you're an outsider but you're not. You like to dip into it, that's part of what these paddling gigs are about. But we always go back. And now you think he's heading north with a kayak because he knows you've done it.*

Not a kayak, a canoe... It's almost like I'm talking to László again, a corrective that wasn't necessary, he understood the difference but it was part of our script nearly two decades ago. He knew what a kayak was and he'd seen mine as I left Cooktown in 2000, heading north. And now I had a better description of his Canadian canoe than Jan provided when we spoke in Kowanyama. It had been reconfigured with double booms supporting a sealed length of 200mm poly-pipe as an outrigger. A hole had been drilled in the front seat and a mast stepped through it that, in theory, could support a genoa-like sail tethered to a running line between the mast and the bow. There were compartments fore and aft that were sealed, with access through deck ports. That gave a small amount of dry storage and a modicum of flotation. He'd rigged a deck cover of sorts from a tarpaulin that somehow fixed to the wooden gunwale, presumably an attempt to keep it from swamping. There was no rudder and steerage must have been with sweep strokes from the stern. The whole thing sounded totally unseaworthy when Bruce described it.

Bruce Gynther knew László, he was the psychiatrist on the ward at the Base Hospital when I transferred László from Cooktown in 2001 and Bruce discharged him to stay with Biata in Silkwood. Three years later Bruce joined the remote team and has been covering the Cooktown area and the Torres Strait since. But he wasn't the first person I contacted when I decided that someone should be on the lookout, that László was heading to sea. A few calls to the clinic at Wujal Wujal on the banks of the Bloomfield tapped local intelligence.

Local intelligence, the *Murri grapevine*. Even out in the backblocks of the Daintree rainforest it doesn't take long for the word to get around about someone new, particularly when it's someone like László. *Kuku-Yalanji* people around the Bloomfield; the Lutherans arrived just a few years after they started the mission at Cape Bedford, but it was different country around the Bloomfield and the missionaries had to compete with other players – lugger crew, tin scratchers, cedar cutters and passers-through. By 1902 the missionaries had left and the *Kuku-Yalanji* stayed where they'd always been. It was a disappointment to the Lutherans, or so said the President of the Queensland Lutheran Council, Dr Otto Theile, in the 1930s: *It fills the heart with sadness when it is realised that sixteen years of effort and sacrifice remained without result. During those years not a single native was baptised.*[201]

The missionaries and the government eventually came back but the *Kuku-Yalanji* had learned from watching and waiting. They're still good at it, and reports reached me that between Christmas and Easter last year a person who could only be László was camped behind an abandoned shed off Weary Bay. He was there well before his message arrived in my mail-box in Cairns. By the time Jan McLoughlin mentioned the Bloomfield in the Kowanyama clinic, László was just another weird outsider who'd drifted into the rainforest and seemed to have taken root, no crazier than most and less disturbed or dangerous. He'd been categorised by the locals; what he had to offer and what he had to take had been determined. Without much of either he'd have been left alone and that was probably exactly what he wanted. And with nobody taking notice no one knew he'd left.

But he didn't disappear completely and around the time I was gathering intelligence he was still seen every couple of weeks at the Ayton store. I guessed he could access his pension payments there, get his supplies and be gone before any locals had time to hit him up. Sometimes someone would see his boat on the beach and they thought what I'd guessed – he was camping north of Rattlesnake Point at Cedar Bay.

The comforting campfire sounds of driftwood reducing through heat and light to ashes are the only background sounds as I approach the end. Drawn closer by the embers' contracting warm embrace, Jethro's voice seems to come from the fire: *I don't get why you would have felt you should do anything. There have been plenty of alternates hanging out at Cedar Bay, including Tarzan – would Michael Fomenko push the same buttons...*

He scores; Michael Fomenko was hounded by the authorities even when he was harming nobody. Until he got brand status that is – once he was a local character rather than an outsider he was left alone to do his thing. Placing the last log on the fire its final dance begins, motes of memories floating and flickering as the embers are stirred to life, lighting the way to more corridors, some familiar and others long forgotten, illuminating images of the past for a moment too brief to hold or interrupt the flow. Jethro's comment brings one – Bamaga in 1992 and the man I met as Gordon. He was out there but not out of it. He might have been crazy then, probably was, but if it wasn't for the old woman he called his wife he wouldn't have been on my radar. And if I hadn't been given privileged access to his thoughts and dreams over the years in Cooktown he would have been just another local character – like Michael Fomenko, who ran along the beach at Weary Bay and built his dugout canoe at Cedar Bay half a century ago.

Thoughts lifting into the night, uninterrupted by pressures to fill the silence with words, time to think through what Jethro has thrown down: *Fair point. I think it's about similarity – or resonance. I can't really speak about Tarzan because we were passing in different lanes, there was a fundamental otherness. With László there was a kind of resonance. Ideas and interests I suppose, but also a sense of aloneness that I could identify with.*

Aloneness – we're all alone, even if we don't realize it, and each of us in our own unique way. Maybe it wasn't László's aloneness that I could connect with but his lostness, and Michael Fomenko wasn't lost. I'm struggling to get to the essence of it for Jethro: *It wasn't the same with Tarzan, he was more like what Ion Idriess talked about as a jungle man, he'd rejected the world we're familiar with – and its conventions – and was doing it alone. With László I always had the sense that he had never been part of it. Maybe what the resonance was with is that part of me that feels it's never managed to fit – maybe that part of all of us. I think that's why I called Bruce Gynther.*

I think that's why I called Bruce Gynther – I think that's why but I'm not really sure. I could have done nothing – nobody was pushing alarm buttons. I could have gone and checked it out myself. That might have taken time, but was doable. But I didn't. I rationalised that Bruce was the psychiatrist covering that area – he went to Wujal Wujal regularly and knew László from the inpatient unit. Maybe that was the mistake. I didn't say that to Jan McLoughlin when I last saw her, all I knew then was that László was somewhere around Weary or Cedar. I was still working on Bruce to go one step further – to walk to Cedar Bay from Home Rule. The fire-dance has settled to its agonal glow.

Home Rule was situated under a frowning range about three miles over the south side of the river from the Rossville road.[202] Jack Idriess knew Home Rule, the tin was running out when he was there and mining is long gone, but the frowning range is just the same. Home Rule is now a rainforest lodge that goes global in an outback-sort-of-way in September each year when it hosts the Wallaby Creek Festival. Not Bruce's thing but bushwalking is, and he agreed to stay over for a weekend when he was visiting Cooktown and hike to the Bay. Jethro has been stirring the coals but stops and looks up, surprised that I would make such a big request. I can only agree: *It was. But he did it and stayed overnight. He found László's camp at the other end of the beach where there are lots of coconut palms. There was a machete there and a stack of discarded husks next to where he'd had a fire, with a pretty primitive shelter and the usual squatting stuff around. A fair amount of rubbish. Not your tropical beach idyll.*

How did he know it was your man… It's not all making sense to Jethro who knows the place but not the people. Bruce knew because he found the canoe pulled up above the high tide line. It was just as Jan had reported it, but now with an outrigger and a mast with a furled sail. Bruce described it in detail. It was mid-afternoon and he waited around for more than an hour but there was no sign of László. But he was there, Bruce felt like he was being watched – he was. Jethro's not convinced: *How do you know that Jon, and why would he hold back with someone prowling through his camp – you'd want to look after your stuff…*

— He knew that it wasn't a coincidence and that this guy was looking for him specifically. And he knew Bruce, he'd been his doctor. He would have thought that there was some kind of plot – and he'd have been right.

László was there, he was watching until Bruce left to go to a camping area of sorts at the north end of the bay. László's camp was as far south as it was possible to be from there, he didn't want anyone around. And Bruce spent the night alone and exposed as the wind built up from the south-east. From what he reported it wasn't a comfortable night and he was up early to begin the trek back. Before he left he went to check the site he'd inspected eight hours earlier. All that was left were the coconut husks and the rubbish, everything else was gone. Just a drag-line to the high tide mark. László wasn't coming back. With the darkness closing in on us I can feel them both staring at me as Jethro speaks – slowly: *You mean he took off in the dark in a canoe…*

— Yep. Maybe there's a deeper story to it. The *Kuku-Yalanji name for Cedar Bay is* Mangkalba *and there are story sites there. One of those is* Murabaymba – *the canoe story site.*

Murabaymba – *the canoe story site...* László had his canoe and there were lots of stories, but it wasn't the right place or time. He launched into a south-easterly that kept building. The coast south of Cooktown is the windiest stretch along the north Queensland coast and by the time Bruce was back in Cooktown it was howling. That continued for the next week with winds gusting at over forty knots and swells of two to thee metres. I knew what László's course and destination were – he was heading north – to Howick. In that weather there was no choice, it was north or nothing.

Maybe he sent the parcel to me as someone, like Michael Fomenko, who was a fellow traveller. I'm the only person who knows the code and is interested enough to use it. Perhaps it was just for my information, to close the chapter. But it might have been a different message, an invitation to a rendezvous and a journey. In his psychosis, in his dreams, or in some other reality he may have thought we should be back on *The Island* – together. Maybe that's what would close the chapter – or *The Book*.

After Bruce reported back I contacted the health services, the police, the Maritime Safety Authority and the airlines flying over the region. I was listened to but not much happened. For the mental health service no active patient was missing – Larry Halassy had left the region and was discharged from the service. As far as the police were concerned there was no body, no wreckage, no anxious relatives or friends, no evidence of crime or misadventure. Just me. But I could only tell them part of the story – there was no point talking about an oneironaut – and to them it didn't seem to add up. But it's only here, on the island and another journey north, that the real story is spoken. Jethro gets it: *It's like I've heard this before. I remember you talking about how you counsel families after a suicide. You said that you try to explain how we all attempt to undo events by rewinding and rescripting. You called it the* what if trap *because, when you rescript you take personal responsibility for decisions made or not. And if you do that you end up accepting responsibility for whatever happened and blame yourself.*

He's right, that's exactly what I would do as a clinician. But with Laszlo there are some pretty critical decisions that I really was responsible for; decisions to do certain things and not to do others. *Responsibility* – I had it and I didn't; he was no longer a patient of the system let alone mine, but I still chose to go to Silkwood, to plug into the *Murri* grapevine, and to convince Bruce he should go and check him out. I guess I did that because I knew the system had let László down and, in the end, so did I. Whatever the meaning of the message to me – it was for me. Perhaps he knew someone was putting out feelers around the Bloomfield, and if he did he would have realized who that was. Was there so much junk around his camp because he was waiting… Waiting – like my father in his asylum solitude, crowded by lost souls, with no future because his past had already been stripped away. All that was left was waiting, in a present that wasn't. For László it was all present, he was in the moment – the journey and the dream. But the journey was on hold – he was waiting. Waiting for *doctor Hunter*, or *Ernest* – I'll never know. *You're right Jon, you'll never know. But maybe he was just crazy.* As always, Jon is protective, even when he knows I won't believe it.

But I do know that it wasn't me who went to Cedar Bay and his camp. And I also know that he read the situation accurately – Bruce was there because I'd sent him. Perhaps he interpreted that as conspiracy, whether it was the *needle-dependent psychopaths*, *Ördög*, the *ÁVO* or some other paranoid fantasy. But I think he also read it as disappointment – I'd let him down. *Responsibility* – the bystander is also responsible – however the events were interpreted it was because of me that he set sail into a tempest. Into the night – oblivion. And on the windward shore of High Island with a gentle south-easterly stirring the last driftwood embers there's no more to say.

CHAPTER 12

2016: psi

Shit happens – and life goes on, the journeys continue. Lots of journeys – lots of loose ends. And not enough time to sort them out. In an hour or so the moon will rise and not long after that the Coquet light will flash one last time as the sun crests the opposite horizon and disappears the night. And with it, like *Rattus rattus* on Morris Island retreating through daylight hours into their sisalised fortress, the ghosts will disappear. Charles Jeffreys and Phillip Parker King, Mary Watson and Ah Sam, Jack Idriess and Charlie, Ion Idriess and George Tritton – and László and all the others who have passed this way. Maybe they'll return, summonsed by memories and memorials, testimonials and tales, brought back to life in imagination and dreams. Maybe there's time for the loose ends.

Cairns German Club, February 28, 2016

Out of thirty-four degree heat and soul-sucking humidity into an air-conditioned hall decked out like a franchised Bavarian *bierkeller* – the Cairns German Club. There are lots of new-age German backpackers in town, out on the reef and in the rainforest as they tick off the antipodean must-dos. But they're not here – this escape from tropical Queensland was set up for a post-war generation for whom northern Australia wasn't holiday but exile – and where the locals weren't necessarily welcoming. That was the cane farmers' world that Bruno Jung came to, a tough life where there was safety in numbers and newcomers kept to themselves – Punjabis, Italians, Islanders and the Germans – better to drink where nobody might mention *the War*.

Near the door a trestle table has neatly arranged rows of the book – *Michael 'Tarzan' Fomenko: the man who dared to live his own exotic dream*[203] – and there's a display just beyond of photographs and newspaper clippings. Ingram Jung adjusts a microphone and gradually the background chatter settles. He's Bruno's son and brother of Harold, whose trove of materials relating to Michael Fomenko was inherited by Ingram when Harold died of cancer in 2011. A decade ago I sat next to Harold on a plane from Sydney to Cairns. We talked about north Queensland and almost immediately the subject was Tarzan – and it stayed there. The young man I was speaking to was intense and he spoke of Tarzan as a person and as a passion – he had a mission and that was to record Michael's story.

To the obvious question – *why* – he responded that his father had a cane farm at Deeral and Michael Fomenko had lived on the bank of a creek at the back of the property when Harold was a child. Tarzan built one of his dugout canoes there. Whatever the connection between that solitary man and the child was, it was intense, and when I met him there was a sense of urgency. He seemed driven to finish a book, *the* book. He didn't say that he felt pressure to complete this task, but he did say he'd been treated for cancer of the stomach. The doctor sitting next to him listened and knew that Harold Jung was dying. So what did the Tarzan project mean for a young man with not long to live… Probably many things, from the insistent traces of childhood wonder to a consuming escape from the haunting imminence of death. And it took him to Sydney, to Michael's relatives who weren't open to more questions about their sibling who'd brought unwanted curiosity for four decades – not then anyway. But Harold wasn't stopping, and as we flew over Gordonvale and the inlet on the southern approach to Cairns he pointed to places where he'd go to intercept Michael along the Bruce Highway, his project would continue – and it did.[204]

Ingram introduces Chris Rossi, who recites his 2011 bush ballad, *Tarzan's Grip*, and retired historian Peter Ryle, who took on the task of making sense of what Harold left behind. Ryle speaks of the intolerance and injustice of systems unwilling to accommodate the likes of Michael, and the need to consign them to categories of madness. Over the background pulse of struggling air-conditioning and chatter across the bar, he reminds an attentive audience of the familiar outsider whose path all those present have crossed. The outsider – Jack could have been describing Michael Fomenko when he wrote of Womba Billy, for whom time and tide had not waited, from a different time and a continent away:

it had left him stranded, bewildered, sullenly hostile. Time and tide for him was the rapid settlement of a continent, even in his lifetime. Pushed ever farther north, it seemed another world now to those far away days when as a young Tarzan he had come in from the bush to gaze upon the beach at Condon.[205]

Peter Ryle is celebrating two lives and returns to Harold's efforts to ensure Michael's left a legacy in memory, and to the bond that had enabled him to persevere in the face of death – the relationship between Harold and Tarzan, between two men at the edge of the world. As the speeches continue I'm scanning through the copy I've just bought to the account of his trip to Dutch New Guinea in the late 1950s and it takes me back to boarding a junk-rigged boat off Turtle Head Island near the end of my first trip to The Tip in 2000, and a gift of wongai jam:

He stopped at many small islands to replenish his water supply, to search for turtle eggs and to catch fish. He also collected coconuts and what he called "Indian dates" but which were probably wongai plums, a delicacy that grows in the Torres Strait. A legend of the area states that once a person has eaten a wongai plum they will always return to the area. One of Michael's favourite foods was a jam he made by boiling a mixture of these "dates" and sugar.[206]

Sugar – Tarzan lived off the land but he loved sugar and in his later life junk food, particularly KFC – same but different, scavenging. In the background Peter Ryle's speech is winding down and he closes by noting that he's sent a copy of the book to Michael Fomenko – to an aged-care facility in Gympie. They got him in the end. But Gympie…

Melbourne, March 6, 2016

In Lego - *liberty and justice for aboriginal australians – gary foley*. Andy Warhol/Ai Weiwei at the National Gallery of Victoria, and in Lego by Ai Weiwei himself – *Dr Gary Foley*. Well, in fake Lego – *letgo* – after Lego refused a bulk order to avoid any compromise of their market in the People's Republic. Ironically the substitute is made in China – that works for Foley.

The exhibition was on the to do list for a Melbourne visit, but Foley in faux Lego was a complete surprise. But Gary always enjoys surprises when he's the surprise. And the years have brought many – professor Foley now and concerned about his legacy. But still some fire as we sit talking at the Fairfield Boathouse overlooking the Yarra. He's slowed down and walks with a cane. That is, slower compared to the last time we were in the same room, twenty-three years ago at the University of Sydney and there was no chatting then. But we can now and Gary has many stories.

After a cloudy and fresh late summer morning, the early afternoon Melbourne sky is clear, and distant voices drift through the gum-trees from kayakers below. And background noises of nature – breezes in the trees, dogs in the distance but, although I didn't notice till he pointed out, no bird sounds: *The birds, that's one of the things I like about this place. It's my favorite café haunt and usually there's tons of birds around.* He's in a space that's familiar, as is the conversational topography – the old guard, partners in protest, fellow travellers on the long ride. On the bus or off the bus – he was on it. Talk swerves to the present but we don't lose the subject – Gary – and I try to get the backstory to the Ai Weiwei show:

Buggered if I know how that happened, first thing was a phone call out of the blue from someone asking permission. I got some stick because he's been critical of Mao – letting down the Party. The Party - not many left.

Not many left who can hold an audience like Gary, his one man show in Melbourne and Sydney in 2012 was a sellout – *Foley* – no surprises there. I pick up his trailing qualifier: *Not many left, I must remember that. You're mentioned in dispatches in a book I'm working on. Struggling with maybe. It's a journey of sorts, loosely wrapped around some works by Ion Idriess…*
— *Idriess. I read just about every fucking book he wrote when I was a kid. soon as I got my library card at the Tenterfield Public Library. I used to go and read Idriess in the same room that Henry fucking Parkes delivered the Federation speech in 1889. That's where I got my interest in history from. From the bloody Tenterfield Public Library.*

Tenterfield; Foley came up when I did an internet search looking for connections between Tenterfield and Idriess – I'd forgotten. But it doesn't explain what Idriess meant to Foley and I follow the unexpected lead: *Well, he told a good story and he wrote about Aborigines, about blacks. Not just bush blacks or station blacks or drunk blacks, but about real people – like Nemarluk. I was nine, and for an Aboriginal kid that wanted to read there wasn't a lot of choice, not many writers were interested in blacks.* Foley scans the trees, maybe still looking for birds or thinking about childhood in Tenterfield more than half-a-century ago: *Arthur Upfield was one of the few others, I liked the Bony stories. Idriess and Upfield may have written fiction but it was closer to the truth than anything else around then. The Tenterfield bloody Public Library. Got me fired up on history – and the rest is history.*

Nemarluk, The red chief, Man tracks, The vanishing people, Our living stone age, Our stone age mystery … As our conversation takes other directions I imagine an Aboriginal boy drawn by the colourful dust jackets, flicking through the photographs and drawings and taking in the stories. Not just Aboriginal stories, tales of islands and Islanders too: *Drums of Mer, Coral Sea calling, Head hunters of the Coral Sea, Isles of despair…* Connections; nearly a quarter century ago I'm beginning a journey with

In Lego – liberty and justice for aboriginal australians – gary foley.

…which is what this Mary did…

… at its center, is an American bomber…
The Removal.
Roy McIvor (2015)

Idriess in Cornstalk Bookshop and dodging Foley's invective down the road at the University of Sydney. Foley – then the arch-outsider but now an establishment elder looking for a safe home to house his archives – for posterity. And it started for him in the Tenterfield Public Library, in the Idriess stack. What he doesn't know is that when Parkes was delivering what became known as the Tenterfield Oration in that space, Walter Owen Idriess was in the room – Jack's father. He talked about hearing it in *a grimy little hall before half a dozen bushies.*[207] Jack was born one month before.

Cairns, July 16, 2016

CIAF – Cairns Indigenous Art Fair. In its seventh year and now a highlight in the north Queensland cultural calendar. Feel-good for everyone – local and state politicians, Cairns cultural *cognoscenti*, small business proprietors, gallery owners and artists from around the Cape and the Islands. And thousands of *Murri* and Islander families who come for the buzz – art, music, dancing, food and connections.

The refurbished cruise-liner terminal is home to CIAF and heading towards the exhibition the view is across the inlet towards False Cape Grafton – beyond that it's Yarrabah land. For the duration this space is for all Indigenous people. Loosely grouped by community, you can walk through sections with works from Aurukun, Pormpuraaw, Kowanyama, Lockhart, the Islands and more. If you'd never been to those places this exhibition might suggest an artist's tropical idyll; Gauguin in the bush. But I have and they're not. I suppose art stands as an affirmation of capacity and integrity despite the realities.

Just beyond the terminal's industrial doors the backing music and commentary from the dance performances outside echo through the vaulted space, mixing lightly at eye level with greetings, laughter and conversation. A collage of sounds, textures and colours, a space of recognition and surprise. A place where you expect to be drawn to the big and bold, and there's plenty of that. But it's a small work of deceptively childlike figures in rust and metallic tones that locks my gaze; it's from an etching on zinc plate with the surface treated with bitumen to diffuse lines – the final dappled appearance could be mistaken at a distance for raindrops – or tears. The most striking feature, at its centre, is an American bomber, obvious from the single-star-and-bars roundel, two engines on the starboard wing, landing gear deployed. An A-20 Havoc maybe, except that had twin-engines and only one ball turret mounted on top of the fuselage behind the cockpit. That turret is there in this image but there are also ball turrets fore and aft below the fuselage. It could be a Liberator bomber although the overall shape suggests something smaller.

The markings date it; side-bars were added to the American roundel to avoid confusion with other allied war-planes after the Torch landings in north Africa in 1942. Before it crash-landed in Lae in 1942 *Little Hellion's* roundel had no bars, by the time it was flying along this coast as *The Steak and Eggs Special* it probably did, and when Rude Vucelic brought the final, streamlined incarnation – *Steak & Eggs* – to rest on Low Wooded Island in June 1944, the bars were on. The elderly artist knew about *Steak & Eggs* and maybe its ghost is in the machine on this print. But other elements date the scene precisely. Standing back, the images spiral around the aircraft, starting in the top right corner where there's a hill, two trees, and maybe a campfire and a family. As it arcs to six o'clock it passes through an American truck, the star insignia clear on the cab and with small figures crowded into the back. From there, soldiers wearing slouch hats with rifles at the ready are scattered across the landscape, the truck seeming to be headed directly to a ship that has a boarding ladder at its side, with small, stark figures at the stern and a dog at the base of the ladder. On the bow, plainly marked, is the boat's name – *Poonba*. The spiral continues past nine-o'clock into a train that snakes towards midnight – soldiers all the way. The journey ends above the war-bird in a field of crosses and a tombstone inscribed with a name – *Emily*. The scene can be dated precisely. Victor Cobus described being in the spiral from Cape Bedford Mission:

On 17 May 1942 we heard the rumble of trucks carrying the armed American soldiers who loaded us onto them without the chance to even get our things. It was frightening, we didn't know what was happening to us, children were screaming and crying, [my wife] Violet thinks she was one of them. Muni [Schwarz] was handcuffed and taken away while we were taken to the Cooktown wharf all the time under armed guard. We were loaded onto the boat called the Poonbar [sic] which took us on to Cairns, there to be herded onto a guarded train in cages like frightened animals.[208]

The *Poonbar* would have berthed almost exactly where the exhibition now stands. The *Guugu Yimithirr* were escorted under armed guard to the Cairns station where they boarded a train heading south to Baralaba and another to Dauringa, the final hours of the journey by road to overcrowded and unfinished shacks at Woorabinda. That's where the graves are. And that's where Emily is buried, the artist's sister, one of many who died in the years of exile. The print is titled in pencil at its base, *The Removal*, and Roy McIvor, who was born at Cape Bedford in 1934, was in the spiral. If the dappled effect represents tears, they are his.

Cooktown, September 13, 2016

The *Poonbar* – there's a ceramic rendition on the *Milbi* Wall – the story wall – in the park across the road from the Seaview in Cooktown. Below the vessel, with five stylized black figures staring blankly at the viewer from the foredeck, an inscription:

> *The people were put on board*
> *the steamship the Poonbar and*
> *transferred South to a community*
> *near Rockhampton. They fought*
> *with the government to*
> *return to their homeland.*
> *Some did return in 1950.*

The Seaview; fifteen years and one day ago I woke up in this hotel to rolling clips on breakfast TV of the Twin Towers collapsing. Indelible memory traces: *where were you on September 11, 2001...* As lower Manhattan was blanketed in dust when the second tower collapsed it was midnight in Cooktown. By the time I turned on the TV at the Seaview it was another day – but one like no other. *Bent time* – László used to talk about it, the *spacetime continuum*. September 12, 2001 will always be the day before – and a blur, except that I remember organizing for László to be taken to hospital in Cairns. All that's left that's clear from that day are the Twin Towers and László.

Today I did that same drive, along Charlotte Street and past where the West Coast Hotel stood for more than one-hundred-and-thirty years before it was blown away by Cyclone Ita in 2014. And I didn't turn to the hospital but went straight on to Hopevale. I haven't worked as a clinician at Hopevale for over a decade and gave up working for Queensland Health a year ago. I don't know whether I gave up on Queensland Health or it gave up on me. Anyway, now it's a different gig – but familiar faces.

Hopevale is pretty much as I remember it, nestled gently in a soft valley landscape embraced by the north and right arms of the Endeavour River. As you drive in you're transported on the mission's history; McIvor road that becomes Thiele street, past the old people's hostel and the Lutheran church to cross Muni Street and turn into Flierl Street. Just out of sight are other traces of Cape Bedford Mission – Kotzur, Kernich, Wenke, Keller, Prenzier – and from Flierl Street you can take a left onto Elim Road and go all the way to the beach – Elim, the oasis in the wilderness of sin. But I turn right into Muni Street, past the council offices and store to a small duplex on a corner.

Beyond the gate there's a narrow passage to the door across a veranda stacked with the gear of lives on country and the sea – camping, hunting, fishing, boating – modern devices for ancient practices, now the stuff of weekends and holidays. An elderly woman appears when I knock at the half-opened door, an expression of faint suspicion giving way as I explain why I'm there, and as recognition filters through the mists of time: *You used to stay at the old people's hostel, with your wife.* She's right, a quarter century ago it was the only place for visitors in Hopevale, and Thelma ran it.

Inside is as cluttered as outside but with photos, pictures, magazines, books – memorabilia. At a table burdened with the bric-a-brac of reflective retirement an old man is sitting with his lunch in the only cleared area.

… *My mate Dick…*

… *you never know when you'll find a golem…*

… *and do up the chalkboard.*

Roy McIvor has a distant smile, his movements slow and with a faint tremor as he resumes eating. Although his voice is halting, when I tell him I bought his picture his eyes light up: *As soon as I walked into the exhibition at CIAF I saw* The Removal. *In fact what I saw was the bomber.* He puts down his fork, his speech clearer but still in short phrases: *The Liberator...* I mention that when I first saw it I wondered if it was the plane that went down on Low Wooded Island. Suddenly Roy is with me on the island I've paddled by four times: *That plane on Low Woody. I haven't been there for years. The boys say the propeller looks new. Just like it crashed yesterday.*

Thelma and Roy are in the moment – it's lunch, it's right now. Even though I'm only in Hopevale to help with a project, I'm caught up in schedules – in a different time zone – there are people waiting outside, another meeting to get to. Too quickly I explain how I interpreted the spiral around the Liberator, from some sort of domestic scene at the top right corner, through the arrival of troops, to the ship that in his picture has the final *r* missing, *Poonba*, the misspelling perhaps symbolising something, but maybe just time and old age. And finally to the train and on to the graves. Roy's smile doesn't change – it was a long time ago, a lifetime. And I'm rushing, fitting time and relationships into pre-determined containers, preoccupied – about stuff – in a time-trap of my own making. Thelma cuts through to point out what makes *The Removal* really special: *It's the last art work he'll do. And you haven't heard where the story starts, what's going on in the top corner.*

Thelma hands me a book on the cover of which *wandarr* and *ngurraarr* – white cockatoo, black cockatoo – share the same tree-branch. It's Roy's story, his artwork. She opens it and points to a paragraph mid-page:

It was 17 May 1942, my sister Emily's birthday. That day we walked up with Mum and Dad to Spring Hill to get a couple of fowls. Dad killed them and they were cooking in the boiler with some pumpkins and other vegetables from the garden. We were sitting around on logs, about to be served with this big stew, when we heard people coming through the scrub. When Dad saw they were wearing uniforms, he knew they must be soldiers or policemen. They came up to the camp, stood there and asked what we were doing. Dad explained that it was his daughter's birthday and that we were about to have a birthday celebration meal.

To our surprise, they responded by saying, 'No. Leave that. Leave everything here.' So we never ate that wonderful stew. 'Come on, get up,' they said. 'It's time to move. Leave everything.' We had no choice. There was clothing and bedding nearby, but they refused to let us take it. 'Leave everything.' they said.[209]

A few pages on are the details of his sister's death in 1943 at thirteen years of age. Forty years later Roy returned to Woorabinda: *Emily's was the only cross left standing. The others had rotted away.*[210]

Two hours and a meeting later, on the way back to Cooktown, I stop among other ghosts in Cooktown cemetery, the history of a region in stone, including those on the fringe. One such was the Reverend Francis Tripp from England via New Zealand where he'd apparently been *considered an eccentric*, which may have been why he ended up being sent to Cooktown in 1874, where he died ten days after landing. Just a few metres away is a wooden cross with a rusted metal heart at its centre, crowned with the remains of plastic flowers and below it:

In commemoration
Of the NORMANBY WOMAN
Who was buried in the vicinity of this ground in 1886.
No one knows where she came from… or who she was
she took that secret with her
She was a European woman brought up by the Normanby
Aboriginal tribe (60km S.W. of Cooktown)
She was captured by the European authorities and brought
To 'civilisation' in which she could not survive.

Not far away is an elaborate headstone over the grave of Reverend Albert Maclaren, who was on the *Albatross* when it was joined by the *Merrie England* after the sinking of the *Quetta* in 1890 to rescue survivors stranded on Adolphus Island, and who read the service of the Church of England over the site of the wreck as Pilot Keatinge stood by. All clustered in the Protestant sector. In another area the Catholics were laid to rest and there's a small Jewish section and a Chinese Memorial located at a distance. That's where the remains of Ah Sam were buried on Sunday 29th January 1882 in a ceremony that followed Mary Watson's funeral. And I find her grave back with the Protestants – born in Cornwall and resting forever in Cooktown. More plastic flowers, on a cross with a faded representation of the lamentation of Christ – Mary cradling her dead son – which is what this Mary did:

In Memory of
Mrs Watson
HEROINE OF THE
LIZARD ISLAND TRAGEDY OF 1881
And her infant son Ferrier

Robert Watson is also buried in the cemetery, separated from his wife by work then tragedy. There are no flowers on his grave and the separation continues – he's with the Catholics. Then, after half an hour of searching, a small metal plate set in granite catches the afternoon sun, a name familiar from reading Idriess:

RICHARD ALBERT WELSH
PE 2033
52BN
Died 1933
Aged 39 YEARS

Dick Welsh – *My mate Dick* – the best friend Idriess ever had. He and Jack were together along the Bloomfield, on Lizard Island – and in the bar of the West Coast when the tale began. And just ten metres away a small tree shields a grave I've passed half-a-dozen times without noticing. The headstone is relatively new and beneath an insignia that was a hangover from the new nation's first military adventurism in the Second Boer War, a crown surmounting the motto *Australian Imperial Force*, is inscribed:

5130 PRIVATE
GEORGE TRITTON
26th A.S.C.
6th MARCH 1928

George Tritton – Charlie – within sight of Dick Welsh. The marker stands on a cement base in a bed of leaf litter and rough, gravel pebbles through which are scattered a small number of smooth, white stones. I select half-a-dozen and place them on the top of the headstone – you never know where you'll find a *golem*. And the grave is only a kilometre from where George, Jack and Dick met and where it all started in September 1920, just a few days before Jack and George headed to Howick:

> *Dick and I had met Charlie for the first time when recently we returned to Cooktown from a long prospecting trip in the Bloomfield-Daintree mountains. Charlie had installed himself as "honary" barman in the West Coast Hotel. To Dick and me, he threw over the bar counter several small black stones.*[211]

It's just a two-minute drive from the Cemetery, along Charlotte Street, to the West Coast. The bar on which George Tritton's *small black stones* fell in front of Jack Idriess and Dick Welsh is gone, all that's left of the old hotel is the façade of the veranda at one side. What did survive cyclone Ita was the drive-through bottle shop – product of a different era – and now there's a temporary bar. Between them, where the main hotel stood, is an empty lot fronted by a two-metre high metal-link fence and a bolted gate. On the other side a grey Great Dane sprawls lazily in the shade of the bottle shop at the feet of a man who is probably only marginally bigger, sitting Buddha-like scrutinising papers. After a few yells the dog is in action along the perimeter line, ears back and hackles up. Part of the security system in a town where break-and-enter is a minor-league sport and a bottle shop fair game. I imagine the frenzy after the cyclone when locals heard the pub had been taken out. Two decades ago one of the Seaswift barges supplying Lockhart River dropped a pallet of beer over-board during transfer off Quintell Beach. No big deal for Seaswift, just an insurance claim. But that's 1,440 cans, and within half an hour the word was out and just about every car in Lockhart was mobilised to get the boys down to the landing for search and recovery operations. Possibly similar scenes after Ita went through the West Coast.

The man is much slower to respond but eventually comes to the gate. He announces he's the manager and was here when Ita hit; the West Coast was one of only a couple of buildings taken out by the cyclone – but he's philosophical: *Ita, April 11, 2014. I won't forget that day. But we'll rebuild. We've just opened the temporary bar. Your interest is...*

I explain that I'm writing a book that involves the West Coast, a story that goes back to events a century ago, but it doesn't seem to spark interest: *Lots of stories about the West Coast.* He reaches out to stroke the Great Dane that's on its hind legs, front paws on the fence and its head – more equine than canine – at eye level. I'm not sure which one I'm talking to, but I explain that I'm returning next week to paddle my kayak north, part of the tale, and I'd hoped to stay at the West Coast but realize that isn't going to happen. His answer has the finality of a dismissal: *That isn't going to happen.* Despite no hint of interest or encouragement, master and hound remain behind the fence, so I press on. Neither of them can figure out what my angle is – everyone has an angle when it comes to grog. It's not clear if he's restraining or encouraging the dog but eventually he seems to understand that I'm coming to Cooktown with friends, something to do with a book, and that there's an offer to put on some music at the West Coast for free next Thursday night. And the bloke who plays guitar is in a wheelchair. I'm left with the Dane that's still on patrol on the other side of the fence and not getting friendlier while the manager walks off. A minute later he reappears through the bottle shop, the look of suspicion replaced with a smile and his arm outstretched: *Dave, Dave Gay. We don't have much left but we've just opened a beer garden behind the bar, we can put something on there. Thursday night's a bit iffy – pension day. Might be a goer though, they like their music round here. Send me something that I can put out on Facebook.*

We're in business, and as he starts to write out his email address – dgay1@... – I have to ask how often people look at it and make some comment about dyslexic Aussies. He responds without looking up: *every time mate, every time.*

CHAPTER 13

2016: Cooktown to Howick Island

omega

Who is the tranquil gentleman who won't salute the State
Or serve Nebuchadnezzar or proletariat
But thinks that every son of man has quite enough to do
To paddle down the stream of life his personal canoe.
      Dooleyprudence. James Joyce, Zurich, 1917[212]

To paddle down the stream of life – nice. Sunrise from *The Peak*. Jethro's tunnel-tent is rocking and swaying in our camp below, a pupa tensed and tormented, its butterfly-being about to rupture through into the air – into the world. I've seen it dozens of times – I know it – his morning ritual of deflating his mattress and stuffing his sleeping bag into a dry-bag before he emerges into the day – free of the fabric chrysalis that collapses into a pool of colour on the ground. If Jon were with us there would be banter from tent to tent. Forestalling the routines of breaking camp and prepar-ing to resume the journey – *down the stream of life*.

Cooktown, September 23, 2016

The entrance of this river, in latitude 15 degrees 27 minutes 4 seconds, and longitude 145 degrees 10 minutes 49 seconds, forms a very good port for small vessels; and, in a case of distress, might be useful for large ships, as it proved to our celebrated navigator Captain Cook, who, it is well known, repaired his ship there after having laid twenty-three hours upon a coral reef.

Phillip Parker King (1827)

Cape Bedford in view in the distance across an ominously flat sea. An early morning departure from the floating jetty across from the Seaview. Leaving again from where Jack Idriess first stepped ashore. Jethro to starboard as our kayaks glide past fishing and dive boats being readied for the day. From somewhere behind us Jon's shouts hang in the still air – *DLB, remember DLB, don't look back*. That's what I told him as we paddled away from Lizard Island thirteen years ago – *don't look back*. It's better not to see the following swells coming at you, just focus ahead. Don't look back, Jon on the jetty looking with us into the distance, with us but not with us – *Wheel Boy*.

Cooktown, the second time I've been here in a fortnight. This time we arrived in a convoy two days ago and on the road, over the backing diesel sound-track, snatches of voices – of coincidences – seemed to come together as melody. For moments only, listen too hard and it was gone, but it was there – pieces falling into place.

Two months ago I was sitting on the back deck of Jon's house drinking Peroni and talking to James Vyver who was producing a radio program about Michael Fomenko for the ABC. Jon had called the station when he heard James interviewed on local radio and told him he had a painting of Tarzan on his wall, the classic image of Michael bare-chested and carrying the hessian sack. For good measure he added that he'd kayaked along the coast Michael had passed half-a-century earlier and that he had a mate, me, who knew that coast better than anyone. A week later we were being recorded and two days before we left for Cooktown the program was broadcast on Radio National. As we drove through dense rainforest on the range road above Port Douglas our podcasted voices were in the soundtrack. But more interesting was an old woman, Inessa, Michael's sister.

Inessa related the story of the family's journey before the Second World War, through Siberia, China and Japan to Australia, and others told of their contacts with Michael over the decades since. All of that was familiar, but towards the end the narrator revealed that in 2013 the eighty-six year old had set out to walk from north Queensland to Sydney. No explanation, he just did it. But he became unwell on the way and was admitted to hospital – that's how he ended up in Gympie. And that's where Inessa finally made contact through her daughter, Lucia, who went to see him at the Cooinda Aged Care Centre. Lucia reported back immediately to Inessa who told James Vyver:

She said, I saw him and it's really Michael. And he's got a lovely room facing the park. His legs have given out and he's in a wheelchair, he does exercises every day and they're looking after him very well. She said as soon as he realized who I was, when I was in his room, she said he clammed up and he wouldn't talk to me.[213]

Dom Cannizzarro's voice filters into parallel consciousness – *the woman in Budapest had told her she wanted to come out, to try and talk to Larry.* Biata was struggling to connect László with his dying sister who he'd never met, but just like Tarzan he didn't want to know. The past in the present; the present in the past. I'm part of a radio broadcast that answers questions I didn't know I had. Tarzan ended up in Gympie because he'd set off on another journey – but he didn't make it, he was stranded by eighty-six year old legs. Pieces falling into place – a sister's efforts to reach out and reconnect with a younger brother lost for half-a-century – Inessa and Michael. And Júlia and László. And Júlia /Juliette – the sister László never met; the mother Idress lost. And something else clicked as I imagined Michael Fomenko staring out at the world from *a lovely room facing the park* – why László had disappeared from Innisfail. No doubt there was madness in his reasoning, but he left because he'd lost his companion – Tarzan. And I've figured that out just days before setting out for *Madman's Island* – in pursuit of Ion, Jack, Charlie, George – and László.

In Cooktown we took over a wing of the Seaview, two kayaks on the grass in front of the units, rooms filled with dry-bags and gear. An afternoon consult with Dave Gay in the beer garden of the West Coast about Jon's appearance: *It'll happen, we should get a few, the fishing mob is in, I'll do up a sign for the front.* The bar was completely empty except for Greg, who'd been working hard on the trawlers for decades and drinking harder and longer. Chest-sized white beard marked by a chain-smoker's yellowed flair, with every other table empty he planted himself at ours, shaking hands with a firmness that seemed to compensate for unsteadiness. While we discussed plans for the concert he floated in and out with *non-sequiturs* delivered with the assurance of the perpetually drunk.

Half-an-hour later we were at the cemetery as I reprised the findings from the week before – Mary Watson, the Normanby Woman, Dick Welsh – and George. And then to the hospital to see the photo of Dr Mick. Paul Mathews, erstwhile battler against the forces of cultural and environmental bastardry in north Queensland, who came with us to Cooktown for the ride and the concert, seemed reflective: *Classic Mick, he was probably taking the piss.* I was surprised he knew Mick: *Yeah, I was at school with Mick at St Joseph's College on Gregory Terrace. Like that photo, he always seemed to be laughing at some unspoken joke. You never really got to know what the joke was but you knew it was about the absurdity of the world. He was always trying to hide the fact that he was sniggering – that he was the one that got the existential joke. It didn't really matter if nobody else did.* Paul continues without looking away from Mick's likeness, their gazes meeting in a moment of fond reflection: *He lived at Holloways before he went to work up the Cape. At the Jade Hut on the beach, just enough space for a bed and a hammock. But that's all Mick needed. And a beer fridge. Just the essentials. If there'd been a door it would've always been open – but there wasn't. He was a bloke with a big heart.*

A bloke with a big heart. That heart eventually gave out in Collinsville. A big heart in a larger than life man and we'll never know what the joke was. And from the hospital we moved on to the Botanic Gardens, past the Black Bean dedicated to Vera Scarth-Johnson and to Mick's Cascading Bean. With some imagination a few scattered white stones in the vicinity of the plaque could have passed as having been placed intentionally. Maybe too much imagination. But what was a sapling when I passed by in 2000 has reached the canopy – Mick would smile.

And Mick would have smiled at the evening gig in the rump West Coast Hotel – he would have been in his element in the motley mob that showed up for some songs and, courtesy of Dave Gay, free prawns. He'd have had a beer and maybe would have ended up taking Greg back to wherever he was camping just to make sure he got there. And Greg was there, a cigarette in one hand and a can in the other, calling out requests and swaying with Jon's music. Just over a century ago Jack Idriess walked into the West Coast and met *Paddy and kindly Mrs Devaney, and their lively crowd of growing daughters*. It was his base camp in Cooktown, and a decade and a war later he was back, with Dick Welsh when the *honary barman*, George Tritton, threw *several small black stones* that he'd been given by *Tarquay the Malay* on the bar. Soon after that Jack and George were on their way to Howick Island. And that's where Jethro and I are heading now.

Lizard Island, September 26, 2016

Lizard Island, about three miles long, is remarkable for its peaked summit. The latitude of which is 14 degrees 40 minutes 20 seconds, and longitude 145 degrees 23 minutes: on its south side is an extensive reef encompassing three islets, of which two are high and rocky: the best anchorage is on its western side under the summit; with the high northernmost of the Direction Islands in sight over the low land, bearing about South-East by compass: the depth is six and seven fathoms sandy bottom.

Phillip Parker King (1827)

... Michael bare-chested and carrying the hessian sack...
Michael. Greg Dwyer (2009)

... only two of the three hills at the eastern end of Howick were visible...
Madman's Island, 1938

... the three granite mounts that for Laszlo was Golgotha.

A decade after the longboat had returned to the *Endeavour* at anchor off the island, a member of the shore party that had climbed Cooks Look remembered:

Gliding over the multi-coloured coral bommies, I watched tiny pink-and-blue shell fragments pulsing on the sand with the movement of the waves. Goggle-eyed parrot fish flicked out of reach between clumps of emerald seaweed.[214]

That was in August 2001, one year after my first kayak trip from Cairns to The Tip, and Iain McCalman was taking part in a re-enactment of Cook's transit through the reef on a replica of the *Endeavour*. He'd climbed to the Look with a scientist from the research station on the island who'd spoken to him bluntly about the status of the reef: *she and her scientific colleagues at Lizard Island believed the entire Reef system to be under threat of extinction.*[215]

Fifteen years later the reef around Lizard Island is still there – but it's dead.[216] Scraping over the reef between South Island and Lizard Head on a falling tide and into the Blue Lagoon, what the scientists predicted for the Reef as a whole and have demonstrated now at Lizard is clear from a kayak – it's dead. And although less precise but more compelling, personal experience of kayaking something like ten-thousand kilometres along this coast over nearly two decades reinforces the sense of agonal decline of the system as a whole. Since my first voyage to The Tip even the life on the surface has changed; on that trip I saw more than a dozen dugong floating lazily above the sea grass beds of the inner reef. Those were the last dugong I've seen, and whether because of pollution or predators – they've gone. That's not the case for crocodiles.

In 1974 Queensland became the last jurisdiction in the nation to ban the hunting of saltwater crocodiles – *Crocodylus porosus*. The dramatic post-war decline halted and forty years later the juveniles of that time, survivors of a selective culling that harvested profitable larger reptiles, are now mature, big and numerous. And to kayakers – close-up, exposed and vulnerable – that's obvious from sightings and slides on mainland beaches and islands as far out as you care to go. They're unseen fellow travellers, unperturbed by our passage and moving with the freedom and impunity of apex predators protected, for the moment, by a fragile legislative safety net. Too fragile for the dugong whose grazing areas are contracting and for whom protections are porous with persistent pollution and provisions for traditional hunting – which goes on in untraditional ways.[217] The moment belongs to the apex predators, crocodiles for the time being and – for the reef as a whole more dangerous through disregard than intent – humans.

The Blue Lagoon; according to lizardislandinfo.com the: *well-developed fringing reef encircles a 10 metre deep Blue Lagoon with fantastic snorkelling over pristine coral.* In the past maybe, but not now, not when Jethro and I coast across under sail, pushed along by the south-easterly hooking around Lizard Head. We pass Palfrey Island to the east, Mangrove Beach to the west leading to Research Point with Casuarina Beach stretching north to South Bay Point, beyond which is the resort. Before we get there, as we approach Loomis Beach fronting the research station, there are two women standing in the shallows – one waves and we paddle over. Researchers; when I ask about their topic the first to speak does so with enthusiasm that resonates with memories of my own early career: *Aboriginal marine resource use on the reef through the Holocene, the last ten-thousand years or so. What that means in practice is studying shell middens, mainly trochus –* Tectus niloticus *and other species. There are middens here that date back thousands of years. At Mangrove Beach and all around the lagoon. And there was seasonal or permanent occupation on Lizard, Cook saw the structures when he was here.*

Cook did: *The inhabitants of the Main visit this Island at some seasons of the year for we saw the ruins of several of their huts and heaps of shells &ca.*[218] As she continues to share her passion her colleague tempers her enthusiasm – *findings yet to be confirmed.* Maneuvering our kayaks into the vestigial wind as we talk, I'm reminded of a chance meeting and conversation near Lockhart River a year ago, and a passing comment about Lapita pottery fragments on Lizard Island. I was so surprised I googled it and found a report of research from a decade earlier documenting evidence of a maritime economy from Melanesia stretching far down the coast of

Cape York – and far back in time. Lots of ghosts on Lizard and they go back a long way. Millions of years in the making, sustaining human voyagers and societies for millennia, a couple of centuries of that by Europeans – the Great Barrier Reef – in maybe five or six decades the largest living structure visible from space will have become the largest dead one. The ground beyond Loomis Beach looks ideal as a campsite and I make the mistake of asking. Probably predictably, a polite refusal: *We couldn't OK that, but there's the National Parks campground past the resort. A bit Spartan though, they just burned off. But come back for drinks at sunset.*

Drinks at sunset – sounds nice but unlikely, it's a long walk. And the campground is familiar from 2003, with Axel and when he left, with Jon. Jethro and I set sails, harnessing the last breaths of the south-easterly as it slides around the island, slowly coasting Casuarina beach to North Head Point where we turn north-east along a windless lee shore with the buildings appearing on the ridge line and then the beach. Not far away – apex predators in resort-wear.

Madman's Island, September 30, 2016

Howick's Group consists of ten or eleven islands, of which No 1, remarkable for a hillock at its south-east end, is in latitude 14 degrees 32 minutes 40 seconds, and longitude 144 degrees 55 minutes 20 seconds; it is nearly three miles long; the rest are all less than half a mile in extent, excepting the westernmost, Number 6, which is nearly a mile and a half in diameter.

Phillip Parker King (1827)

We spent the night before last on Coquet Island where Jethro and I stayed with Jon in 2008 after a day of big following winds as we paddled and sailed from the Turtle Group. This time, over fifty kilometres from Lizard heading west-north-west, pushed along by an easterly that didn't falter all day. Howick's high ground was on the horizon for three hours, the light on Coquet visible for two hours and the beach from an hour out. Destination Coquet because we know it but, more importantly, because the only way to land where Jack and George went ashore from the *Spray* is at high tide and that's in the morning – if we'd tried at the end of the day the reef would have been completely exposed. Yesterday, high tide was at 08:20 and with an hour paddle from Coquet we were there for it.

Approaching from the south only two of the three hills at the eastern end of Howick were visible, the three granite mounts that for László was Golgotha. The highest is the easternmost, bare on its windward side with boulders at its base and a wisp of scrub climbing the leeward ridge. That's what Jack called *The Peak*. Half the size and hidden from view behind is *The Hill*. To the west along the southern shore is *The Mound*, pale granite boulders forming the windward ridgeline, seeming to cascade down to meet the sea on its leeward face. In the morning light the border between sea and sky resolved as we approached, becoming a rifle-green line stretching far to the west. At high tide mangrove foliage floats darkly on the sea – an illusion of substance that here extends more than three kilometres to where Jon and I camped, miserably, thirteen years ago, an unmarked grave behind us and Watson Island silhouetted on the horizon by the setting sun.

Howick is not a high island but it is continental; the surrounding reef has grown by accretion around a submerged hilltop. It doesn't have as precise a boundary as the outer reefs but is just as dangerous. According to Idriess, George heard about the tin on Howick from Tarquay who'd been marooned there when the *Sea Foam* was lost. A mistake by Idriess that Rob Coutts makes much of; *Sea Foam* was wrecked on Hannah Island. But the survivors of other shipwrecks did end up on Howick; from a lugger, the *Jessie* in 1889, and in 1897 a naval vessel, the *Ringdove*, rescued passengers and crew from the *Myrtle* after the schooner bound for Cooktown from Port Moresby grounded on the outer reef.[219]

Even in kayaks that only draw inches, getting ashore is tricky; it would have been a lot harder for desperate survivors after nearly fifty miles in an open boat. Dan Monaghan's ketch, the *Spray*, couldn't get closer than the edge of the reef so Jack and George would have ferried their provisions and mining gear to the shallows and portaged from there. But they made it, probably to the same small stretch of sand and rock at the base of *The Peak* where we uncurled from our cockpits and stepped ashore. I'd finally landed where it counted on *Madman's Island*, and in the same month as Jack and George ninety-six years earlier.

Over two decades kayaking the reef and coast I've been on dozens of islands. Every experience is unique; not only is each island different to all the others, but despite the obvious familiarity on return, there's always change. Sometimes it's dramatic; cyclones wash away beaches and strip vegetation, like Dunk Island after Cyclone Larry and Lowrie after Monica. But most changes are incremental and constant – sand-spits move, fires destroy ground-cover, tracks are overgrown, sand cays appear and disappear. And then there's the flotsam and jetsam – nothing stays the same. So, every island and each visit brings something new, memorable – remarkable. Which makes Howick all the more surprising – it's totally unremarkable.

Nearly a day on the island has been enough time to climb the three hills, to feel the tidal pulse through the mangrove forest and to search for signs of the past. And signs there are, but not of Jack, George – or László. Signs though, of many others; along the beaches and in the mangroves are woven the ghost-nets and detritus of passing fishing boats and yachts, tankers and barges. Blown away or thrown away by the careless or carefree, on all these islands the transit contrails of passers-by accumulate as our indelible footprints.

Footprints; Mary Watson and Ah Sam saw footprints in the sand on this beach and returned to the sea. And it was the sea that claimed them though they died of thirst a horizon away. But our footprints now don't wash away; they're there for generations and, at the micro-scale that matters – forever. And the prints of fellow travellers; *Rattus rattus* is here – maybe distant relatives of those at the other end of Howick that ate Jon's mouthpiece in 2003. Separated by a mangrove forest that's impenetrable to humans – a three kilometres tangled matrix of roots and branches intersected by crocodile-infested tidal races. But rats have possession of the whole island, travelling with impunity above the rips and reptiles on a canopy-level highway.

Searching along the edge of the mangrove forest behind what was probably the camp area that Jack and George set up and George took as his territory during their standoff, I can't locate the site of the well that sustained them until it was inundated by a king tide, which brought them together as survival trumped differences. I walked along what is now solid ground between *The Mound* and *The Peak* but which in the 1920s was submerged at low tide when Jack snuck through the mangroves to get water or to take advantage of George's absence to raid the camp. I clambered over the boulders that form *The Mound*, imagining where Jack hid out and where he secreted his meagre supplies when George *went west*. I could see how Jack felt vulnerable with George in possession of the only firearm and in command of the heights on *The Peak*.

Jack and George were both vulnerable, like all the men who returned from the War. Even on Howick, about as far from Gallipoli and the Western Front as it was humanly possible to be, they carried it with them. Buried in their flesh and etched into their souls, the War was the backstory of a generation of outsiders who'd survived the trenches but who recoiled at the traffic and tribulations of the new society they'd returned to. The bush; a geographic solution to an existential problem. At the end of the day I climbed *The Peak*, from where I could just see the mainland, the same coast along which Jack tried to walk back to Cooktown lest he miss out on the War. He didn't get to Cooktown but he didn't miss out on the War. And after it was all over he came back to the bush, and although he returned to the city and died there, he carried the bush within for the rest of his life.

A day of exploring and almost every feature is familiar, recalling passages from Idriess or the biblical associations that were layered over them in László's psychosis and dreams. But for all that it's an island – just another island. Different but the same. The magic of islands isn't inscribed in the topography, it's in the stories – all along this coast, everywhere – the traces of journeys. Sunset on *The Peak*, looking east with Lizard Island proud on the horizon. In the direction of Nymph Island a sail shines in the late afternoon light, probably tacking into the lee of Lizard for the night. A sail on the horizon; from this spot Jack kept watch for Captain Dan returning with the *Spray*. And he and George may have crouched here camouflaged by tussock grass watching a black lugger moving slowly offshore, searching for the container of opium that had washed ashore the day before. A *rakish black lugger* – maybe the same one that Cross-Eyed Joe followed in the *Nancy Bell* to Howick from Lizard where Jack and Dick Welsh had been left. Perhaps the black lugger Errol Flynn saw in Townsville as the *Sirocco* sailed north towards tragedy in the Gulf of Papua. Or it could have been a lugger heading to Elim to exchange alcohol and opium scrapings for workers or women. And one particular woman; just below is where the tank drifted to rest carrying Mary, Ferrier and Ah Sam before its last, short passage.

In the shipping lane beyond Coquet a freighter heads south, its steaming lights drifting on the horizon. Just after the Second World War the *Cape York* passed in the same channel, with Harry Hunter on his last sea voyage as captain. As bearings were taken on the Coquet light he may have been on the bridge with the Torres Strait Pilot, successor to Eldred Pottinger Keatinge who with Captain Alfred Sanders headed north sixty years earlier on the final voyage of the *Quetta*.

To the west the cone of Noble Island is silhouetted against a distant profile of low hills edged by the setting sun. A play of light and waves, a speck on the sea, a dot on the horizon that might have been Formasini rowing furiously back to Noble from the mainland, racing a dugout canoe manned by *Guugu Yimithirr* who didn't know Formasini's mate was dead or why the white men had come to *Wurrguulnyjin*, or what they wanted to rip from its heart. Lizard and Noble; unmistakable profiles for navigators over two centuries of exploration, commerce and recreation, but known as *Jiigurru* and *Wurrguulnyjin* to at least some of the mariners who passed this way in the millennia before that. They came in dugouts and sailing canoes, ancient technologies with modern imitators. A distant object in failing light could have been a hollowed log with a primitive outrigger, with Michael Fomenko, surviving on coconuts and carrion, drifting to a destination of the mind.

And in his mind or in his dream, László came to *Madman's Island*. He was a lucid dreamer and maybe he chose not to wake up, not to vanish us all. Vicarious dreaming; he's all of us in the story. So the dream or the story goes on. And although George Tritton left Howick and is buried in Cooktown cemetery, Charlie didn't. And while Michael Fomenko may be in a wheelchair looking out his window at a park in Gympie, Tarzan is on the side of the Bruce Highway, bare chested with a hessian sack across his shoulder heading north. And he's off a deserted shore in his dugout canoe under a clear, starlit sky.[220] Into the night. And László is with them both, and with me too.

In the dying light the dim line of hills to the south and west is fading into the moonless night, the coastline I've followed five times – always heading north – in the end *I took the fifth*. With the wind falling the last whitecaps are gone, leaving only the cadence of distant forces in a gentle swell that pulses slowly over the reef, lunar powers driving the tide that's now moving with speed. We're on the cusp of a new moon and as the western horizon disappears the island is transformed by the twilight into a space of magic and memories, with only the flashes from the navigation light on Coquet intruding from the other world. Looking down from *The Peak* the tide is creeping across the silvered streak of sand and rock coral between reef and high ground. It takes me back to the Kimberley, to being enchanted by my first viewing of the *stairway to the moon* on the tide-flats of Roebuck Bay. Below me the starlight picks out the boundary between worlds – land and sea; life and dream. And with the sure but fragile presence of a dream, shells, rocks and coral pucker the surface of the shallows and from this distance it seems transformed into a pathway, each stone glistening against the night sky. I can imagine holding one, turning it over, feeling it. Marble-smooth and weightless, its surface seems to absorb the light of the stars with a spectral afterglow with each distant flash of the Coquet light. Not just white – *translucent*.

I know a place in the sea,
Nobody's been there but me,
It's just a spot on a map that I've got – to get there
You'll need a wind from the south,

You'll need a vessel that's true,
You'll need a foul-weather friend
To tell you your name.
And I'll be gone, I'll be gone, I'll be gone
Tomorrow for sure.

I know this place in the sea,
Where time's an illusion,
Night follows day in a spectacular kind of way – to get there
You'll need a wind from the south,
You'll need a vessel that's true,
You'll need a foul-weather friend
To tell you your name.
And I'll be gone, I'll be gone, I'll be gone…
It's in my head, but I need it under my feet
It's in my head, but I need it…

Gone for shore
Chris Wighton, Restoration Island, August 2011[221]

…sunset on The Peak…
Madman's Island, 1938

NOTES

1. Page 23, in: Lawrence, T. E. (1962 (1926)). <u>Seven pillars of wisdom.</u> Harmondsworth, Penguin Books.
2. Page 359, in: Rice, E. (1991). <u>Captain Sir Richard Francis Burton.</u> New York, Harper Perennial.
3. Page 186, in: Ransome, A. (1985 (1930)). <u>Swallows and Amazons.</u> New Hampshire, Jaffrey.
4. Page 35, in: Idriess, I. L. (1938). <u>Madman's Island.</u> Sydney, Angus & Robertson.
5. The quote is an adaptation of the last entry in the record that Mary Beatrice Phillips Watson maintained after she, her infant son Ferrier and the wounded Chinese house-servant, Ah Sam, left Lizard Island on Sunday October 2, 1881, which was probably written on October 10 or 11: *Still all alive. Ferrier much better this morning. Self feeling very weak. I think it will rain today, clouds very heavy, Wind not quite so high. No rain. Morning fine weather. Ah Sam gone away to die – have not seen him since 9. Ferrier more cheerful. Self not feeing at [all] well. Have not seen any boat of any description (No water. Nearly dead with thirst.)* Page 12, in: Stephan, J. (2013). Mrs Mary Watson: "The heroine of Lizard Island". Cooktown, Cooktown Historical Society.
6. Page 196, in: Idriess, I. L. (1938). <u>Madman's Island.</u> Sydney, Angus & Robertson.
7. Page 1, in: Stow, R. (1958). <u>To the islands.</u> London, Macdonald.
8. In: Bottoms, T. (2015). <u>Cairns: City of the South Pacific - A history 1770-1995.</u> Cairns, Bunu Bunu Press.
9. Ernest Gribble died in Yarrabah in 1957. The following year Randolph Stow followed Patrick White as the second recipient of the Miles Franklin Literary Award for *To the islands*. Traces of the Gribbles are not hard to find and Gribble Streets in Yarrabah and Palm Island acknowledge father and son respectively. In 1964, seven years after Ernest's death, boys from Palm Island supervised by Fred Krause – pastor, teacher and scoutmaster – cleared a small patch of land next to a shed on the leeward shore of Esk Island, six kilometres east of Palm Island, that was briefly the Gribble outdoor chapel (Keiran Michael, personal communication). Unlike the street, those traces are long gone.
10. See: Hough, R. (1995). <u>Captain James Cook: A biography.</u> London, Hodder and Stoughton.
11. All sailing directions are those of Phillip Parker King, based on three transits of the reef (1818-19, 1820 and 1821-22): King, P. P. (1827). <u>Narrative of a survey of the intertropical and western coasts of Australia performed between the years</u>

1818 and 1822. Volume II. London, John Murray. King was native born, on Norfolk Island in 1791, and sailed to England with his father (Philip Gidley King, later Governor of New South Wales) at age five, returning in 1817 to complete the work of Flinders – who was a friend of the family. Lachlan Macquarie was instructed by the Admiralty to provide a vessel and King was initially attracted to the *Lady Nelson*, a retractable-keeled, innovative vessel ideal for in-shore surveying, but settled on the *Mermaid*, an 8 ton, copper-bottomed teak cutter constructed in Calcutta, in which King undertook three major voyages, returning to Sydney in 1820 where the *Mermaid* was replaced with the much larger brig, *Bathurst*. By the time he arrived in England in 1822 he had circumnavigated the continent of Australia three times – he was just thirty years old. He died as Rear Admiral King in Grantham, New South Wales in 1856. Reconfigured as a schooner, in 1823, the *Mermaid* was the first ocean-going vessel to enter the Brisbane River, and in 1829 was abandoned after running on to Flora Reef south-east of Fitzroy Island. See: Hordern, M. (1997). King of the Australian coast: The work of Phillip Parker King in the *Mermaid* and *Bathurst 1817-1822*. Melbourne, Melbourne University Press. For more on the exploration of the north Queensland coast see: Macknight, C. C., Ed. (1969). The farthest coast: A selection of writings relating to the history of the northern coast of Australia. Melbourne, Melbourne University Press. Also: Gill, J. C. H. (1988). The missing coast: Queensland takes shape. Brisbane, Queensland Museum. And: Hands, H. and S. Hands (2009). The cussed and the cursed: The coral, the craft, the captains, in North Queensland waters. Ingham, Susan & Howard Hands.

12. Page 234, in: Richards, J. (2008). The secret war: A true history of Queensland's Native Police. Brisbane, University of Queensland Press.
13. Page 15, in: Stephan, J. (2013). Mrs Mary Watson: "The heroine of Lizard Island". Cooktown, Cooktown Historical Society.
14. In: King, P. P. (1827). Narrative of a survey of the intertropical and western coasts of Australia performed between the years 1818 and 1822. Volume II. London, John Murray.
15. As master of the *Providence* with *Assistant* in support, Bligh was also responsible for charting a path through the Torres Straits from Darnley Island (now Erub) in the east to a gap in the reefs known since as Bligh's Farewell in the west. That was in 1792, three years after the longboat journey north along the Cape following the *Bounty* mutiny. With Bligh on the *Providence* was midshipman Matthew Flinders.
16. The purported *Hobart Town Gazette* article is now regularly cited but some remarkable sleuthing by Tasmanian librarian Edmund Morris Miller and colleagues clarified the deception, see: Miller, E. M. (1958). A paper read before a General Meeting of the Tasmanian Historical Research Association on 8 August, 1958. Part 1: An unrecorded Hobart Town Gazette, May 11 1816, and its extraordinary Aftermath, a Derwent Insurrection, 1817, and a London Reprint., State Library of New South Wales. **(Catalogued under Morris, EM)**. Miller also investigated Jeffreys' plagiarism of the then unpublished work of George Williams Evans, releasing the first account of the geography of Tasmania in 1820, two years before Evans' account reached press. See: Miller, E. M. (1959). "An unrecorded

Hobart Town Gazette: A paper read before a General Meeting of the Tasmanian Historical Research Association on 8 August, 1958. Part II: First two Books on Tasmanian Geography by Jeffreys (1820) and Evans (1822); with Comments on Jeffreys' plagiarism of Evans' work and Wentworth's contribution." Tasmanian Historical Research Association 7(4): 59-65. Jeffreys transited the inner route twice, the second time (again, against orders) on the return journey to England in 1817 during which Thomas Hassall, a passenger, recorded the *Kangaroo* grounding briefly in the maze of islands somewhere north of Princess Charlotte Bay. See: Hassall, T. (1817). Journal, January - September 1817. Includes a brief account of his life, written in Jan. 1817, together with an account of the Sydney to Batavia section of a voyage from Sydney to England in Brig *Kangaroo*, 9 April-8 Sept 1817, State Library of New South Wales. **ML MSS 4364/Box 1/Item 3 (Oxley papers)**. For general accounts of Jeffreys see: Tiley, R. (2006). The Mermaid tree: How a tiny unknown ship opened Australia's north and west to development, dreams and disappointment. Sydney, ABC Books. And also: Gill, J. C. H. (1988). The missing coast: Queensland takes shape. Brisbane, Queensland Museum.

17. Page 153, in: Idriess, I. L. (1959). The tin scratchers. Sydney, Angus & Robertson.

18. Having seen armed *Indians* on the mainland after heading north from Restoration Island, Bligh chose to land on Sunday Island because its height afforded a view of the main. He recorded: *One person in particular went so far as to tell me, with a MUTINOUS LOOK, that he was as good a man as myself. It was not possible for me to judge where this might have an end, if not stopped in time; therefore, to prevent such disputes in future, I determined either to preserve my command or die in the attempt; and, seizing a cutlass, I ordered him to take hold of another and defend himself; on which he called out that I was going to kill him, and immediately made concessions. I did not allow this to interfere further with the harmony of the boat's crew, and everything became quiet.* Page 100, in: Jack, R. L. (1921). Northernmost Australia: Three centuries of exploration, discovery and adventure in and around the Cape York Peninsula, Queensland. Volume 1. London, Skimpkin, Marshall, Hamilton, Kent.

19. Arguably the most important anthropological expedition ever undertaken in Australia, the 1898 *Cambridge Expedition to the Torres Straits* was in the area from April to October, mainly based on Mer and Mabuiag. Led by Alfred Cort Haddon, it included a linguist, Sidney Ray, and Anthony Wilkin, who maintained the photo-record of the expedition. However, there were four psychologically-oriented doctors - William McDougall, Charles Myers, Charles Seligman and W.H.R. Rivers. They would also have understood Idriess's expressions of psychological distress in his account of his Gallipoli and Palestine experiences in *The desert column*. During the First World War all four were involved with developing approaches to addressing the needs of traumatised soldiers and Charles Myers coined the term *shell shock* in 1915 in the British Medical Journal – which he came to regret. Rivers served at Maghull War Hospital near Liverpool and then Craiglockhart outside Edinburgh where his patients included one of the most important poets of the First World War – Siegfried Sassoon. Wilfred Owen was

also there before returning to the front and being killed just as the war was ending, and Robert Graves was a friend of Rivers. Sassoon wrote positively of Rivers in *Siegfried's journey*, and all of them were drawn on extensively by Pat Barker for her Booker Prize-Winning *Regeneration trilogy*, Rivers explicitly. Wandering in a storage area under the Green Hill Fort on Thursday Island in 1993, completed just five years before the Cambridge Expedition to protect against feared Russian incursions, I found an old hospital visitors book. Immediately above an entry by the Bishop of North Queensland who commented *very much pleased at all that I have seen* are six entries for April 24, 1898 – all the members of the Cambridge Expedition team with *WHR Rivers, Cambridge England* in precise handwriting. The reports of the Expedition were released between 1901 and 1935 and Idriess drew on the extensive material on Mer. For information about the expedition see: Herle, A. and S. Rouse, Eds. (1998). Cambridge and the Torres Strait: Centenary essays on the 1898 Anthropological Expedition. Cambridge, Cambridge University Press. For information about the team members and their influence on psychology and anthropology see: Shephard, B. (2014). Headhunters: The search for a science of the mind, London.

20. Idriess, I. L. (1950). The drums of Mer. Sydney, Angus & Robertson.
21. Idriess, I. L. (1950). The wild white man of Badu. Sydney, Angus & Robertson.
22. Idriess, I. L. (1957). Coral Sea calling. Sydney, Angus & Robertson.
23. Paul's opinions have been popularized by retired British submariner, Gavin Menzies, in: Menzies, G. (2002). 1421: The year China discovered the world. London, Bantam.
24. See: Idriess, I. L. (1993 (1932)). The desert column. Ion Idriess's greatest stories of miners and soldiers. I. L. Idriess. Sydney, Cornstalk Publishing: 355-614. The foreword to *The desert column* was written by Lieutenant General Sir Harry Chauvel, who commented of the accuracy of descriptions of the campaigns that: *Idriess was, I think, above the average in this respect though I must say that the Australian Light Horseman was generally very quick in summing up a situation for himself.* After the armistice, Idriess's commander-in-chief, Field Marshall Edmund Allenby wrote in terms that could apply to Idriess that: *The Australian light horseman combines with a splendid physique a restless activity of mind. This mental quality renders him somewhat impatient of rigid and formal discipline, but it confers upon him the gift of adaptability, and this is the secret of much of his success mounted or on foot.* Page 791, in: Gullett, H. S. (1984 (1923)). The official history of Australia in the war of 1914-1918. Volume VII: The A.I.F. in Sinai and Palestine. Brisbane, University of Queensland Press.
25. Page 144, in: McLaren, J. (1990 (1926)). My crowded solitude. Melbourne, Sun Macmillan.
26. See: Sharp, N. (1992). Footprints along the Cape York sandbeaches. Canberra, Aboriginal Studies Press.
27. Page 181, in: ibid.
28. In his retirement Phillip Parker King, who knew the coast of Cape York as well as anyone, provided coastal instructions for Kennedy's expedition. See: Hordern, M. (1997). King of the Australian coast: The work of Phillip Parker King in the *Mermaid* and *Bathurst 1817-1822*. Melbourne, Melbourne University Press.

29. Page 421, in: Parkin, R. (2003 (second edition)). H.M. Bark Endeavour: her place in Australian history: with an account of her construction, crew and equipment and a narrative of her voyage on the east coast of New Holland in the year 1770. Melbourne, Miegunyah.
30. Page 106, in: Idriess, I. L. (1957). Coral Sea calling. Sydney, Angus & Robertson.
31. Page 75, in: Carron, W. (1996 (1849)). Narrative of an expedition, undertaken under the direction of the late Mr Assistant Surveyor E.B. Kennedy, for the exploration of the country lying between Rockingham Bay and Cape York. William Carron's narrative of Kennedy's Cape York expedition (fascimile edition). L. Hiddins. Bundaberg, Corkwood Press: 1-79.
32. Ransome, A. (1985 (1930)). Swallows and Amazons. New Hampshire, Jaffrey.
33. Ransome's counsel, J.H. Campbell, had sections of *De Profundis* read out in court with Lord Alfred Douglas on the stand. The jury ultimately determined that Ransome's text – which did not refer to Lord Alfred (Bosie) by name – contained elements that were libelous – but true. See: Brogan, H. (1984). The life of Arthur Ransome. London, Jonathan Cape.
34. See: Chambers, R. (2009). The last Englishman: The double life of Arthur Ransome. London, Faber and Faber.
35. Page 186, in: Ransome, A. (1985 (1930)). Swallows and Amazons. New Hampshire, Jaffrey.
36. Written at the beginning of the Second World War, *The great trek* is a romanticised and deproblematised account of the Jardines' overland expedition by Idriess for a youthful readership, reprised nearly two decades later in *Coral Sea calling*.
37. Page 69, in: Byerley, F. J. (1994 (1867)). Narrative of the overland expedition of the Messrs. Jardine, from Rockhampton to Cape York Northern Queensland. Brisbane, J.W. Buxton (fascimile edition, Corkwood Press).
38. Page 35, in: Mullins, S. (1995). Torres Strait: A history of colonial occupation and culture contact 1864-1897. Rockhampton, Central Queensland University Press.
39. Page 255, in: Moore, D. R. (1979). Islanders and Aborigines at Cape York: An ethnographic reconstruction based on the 1884-1850 'Rattlesnake' journals of O.W. Brierly and information he obtained from Barbara Thompson. Canberra, Australian Institute of Aboriginal Studies.
40. Not a lot of sympathy, either, from Ion Idriess, who described the attack by *the Yardaigains and Gomokudin* at Vallock Point north of Somerset, but is silent on the retribution. In: Idriess, I. L. (1957). Coral Sea calling. Sydney, Angus & Robertson.
41. Page 56, in: Prideaux, P. (1988). Somerset Cape York Peninsula 1864-1877: From spear to pearl-shell. Corinda, Boolarong.
42. Eborac is said to derive from the Latin, *Eboracum*, the Roman name for York.
43. Page 177, in: Slocum, J. (1999 (1900)). Sailing alone around the world. New York, Penguin.
44. Chapter VII, in: Synge, F. M. (1908). Albert Maclaren, pioneer missionary in New Guinea: A memoir. Westmister, Society for the Propagation of the Gospel in Foreign Parts (http://anglicanhistory.org/aus/png/maclaren1908/).

45. In a letter to George Robertson of Angus and Robertson in July 1926 as they were about to sail from Brisbane, Idriess voiced concerns: *Another point which I objected to was the boat. I firmly believe in horses.* Seeming to have forgotten his time on Howick he noted that: *Only two of us are going, the idea is that two men would agree and stick together, whereas anything might happen with more in the party, and any unpleasantness would foredoom such an expedition to failure at the outset.* Angus and Robertson at that time were preparing the second version of *Madman's Island* and, ironically, he commented: *By the way, we will be passing Madman's Island. If the weather permitted I would land and get photos if you should want any. I haven't seen 'Madman's Island' creating a furore in literary circles yet, so suppose it is not out yet. Rather conceited on my part, is it not?* In: Idriess, I. L. (1926). Letter to George Robertson, 12th July, 1926. Angus & Robertson Archives at MLMSS 314/40, Cairns Historical Society. **D20183**. Soon after, he wrote to Fred Shenstone, at that time another partner in Angus and Robertson, saying that *should weather allow* and should he be able to get photos of Howick, he would post them from Thursday Island. In: Idriess, I. L. (1926). Letter to Fred S Shenstone, 24th July, 1926. Angus & Robertson Archives at MLMSS 314/40, Cairns Historical Society. **D20183**. They didn't get to land on Howick.
46. Page 1, in: Idriess, I. L. (1959). The tin scratchers. Sydney, Angus & Robertson.
47. Page 7, in: ibid.
48. Page v, in: Idriess, I. L. (1957). Coral sea calling. Sydney, Angus & Robertson.
49. By the time Idriess returned from Palestine James Dick was dead, and in the books Jack wrote years later he's James Dickie – confused with another prospector, John Dickie. See: Dick, A. J. (2003). Peninsula pioneer: James Dick (1849-1916), visionary of Far North Queensland, a biography. Brisbane, Self-published. James Dick was also a writer and he wrote a pamphlet describing the two expeditions of Robert Logan Jack in 1879-80 – *A Geological and Prospecting Expedition Which Filled Many Blank Spaces on the Map* – which was published in the Port Douglas Record in 1913 and sent to Jack with a fancied map of the region that had numerous errors, enough to stimulate Robert Logan Jack to write his own history and description of the region – *Northernmost Australia* (1921). See: Jack, F. (2008). Putting Queensland on the map: The life of Robert Logan Jack, geologist and explorer. Sydney, University of New South Wales Press.
50. Page 161, in: Flynn, E. (1937). Beam ends. New York, Dell.
51. See: Shay, J. and B. Shay (nd). The rail to nowhere: The story of the Cooktown to Laura Railway (Based on "The Cooktown Railway" by J.W. Knowles). Cooktown, Cooktown Historical Society. Also see: Shay, J., Ed. (2009). Cooktown through the years. Cooktown, Cooktown & District Historical Society.
52. Page 21, in: Idriess, I. L. (1959). The tin scratchers. Sydney, Angus & Robertson.
53. Page vii, Idriess, I. L. (1967). One wet season. Sydney, Angus & Robertson.
54. Gribble, J. B. (1987 (1905)). Dark deeds in a sunny land or Blacks and Whites in North-West Australia. Perth, University of Western Australia Press.
55. Not Cook's only Cape Flattery named for dashed hopes. In March 1778, during his last voyage in the Pacific, he fancied that he had glimpses of the opening to a safe harbor along the fog-shrouded Pacific coast of the Americas. Disabused as he

drew closer he turned away, naming a low-lying point of land Cape Flattery. He missed the Strait of Juan de Fuca, now the boundary between the United States and Canada and the entry to Puget Sound.

56. See: Musumeci, M. D. (2014). Aircraft crashes of northern Queensland Australia 1942-1945. Cairns, Michael Musumeci.
57. These are consistent with *Koko-Yimidir* vocabulary compiled by Walter Roth with the assistance of Reverends Schwarz and Poland from Cape Bedford Mission. See: Roth, W. E., G. H. Schwarz and W. Poland (1901(April)). Stucture of the Koko-Yimidir language. North Queensland Ethnography: Bulletin No. 2. Brisbane, Government Printer. Roth (along with later linguists) pointed out the accuracy of the word list that Cook compiled while careening the *Endeavour* on the banks of the eponymous river. In subsequent publications that are cited later in this book, the meanings have been reversed. In different texts both *Muni* and *Muuni* appear.
58. For an account of the bicultural reconstruction of this encounter and its consequences see: McKenna, M. (2016). From the edge: Australia's lost histories. Melbourne, Miegunuyah Press.
59. Page 76, in: Price, A. G., Ed. (1969). The explorations of Captain James Cook in the Pacific as told by selections of his own journals 1768-1779. Melbourne, Angus & Robertson.
60. Page 75, in: Brunton, P., Ed. (1998). The Endeavour journal of Joseph Banks: the Australian journey. Sydney, Angus & Robertson.
61. Page 76, in: ibid.
62. Page 10, in: Stephan, J. (2013). Mrs Mary Watson: "The heroine of Lizard Island". Cooktown, Cooktown Historical Society.
63. Page 166, in: Flynn, E. (1937). Beam ends. New York, Dell.
64. Page 3, in: Idriess, I. L. (1948). The opium smugglers: a true sory of our northern seas. Sydney, Angus & Robertson.
65. Page 122, in: Flynn, E. (1937). Beam ends. New York, Dell.
66. Page 197, in: Idriess, I. L. (1948). The opium smugglers: a true sory of our northern seas. Sydney, Angus & Robertson.
67. Page 4, in: Anonymous (1928). Opium found. Cairns Post. **Monday, February 20:** 4.
68. From early in that race Moitessier was ahead on time, but instead of heading north after passing Cape Horn to collect the prize and accolades, he kept going east – following the roaring forties until he turned north to Tahiti and legend. Robin Knox-Johnstone won the race, but more interesting was Donald Crowhurst – a would-be electronics guru whose plywood trimaran, *Teignmouth Electron,* had blown records early in the race and, as other competitors retired, was in the lead. Francis Chichester, who knew enough about sailing to be suspicious, was. The trimaran was eventually found by the Royal Mail Vessel *Picardy* –without Crowhurst aboard. Over time the deception and his journey to madness became apparent. He'd maintained a false log, circled off the coast of South America feigning radio difficulties to explain the limited communication, and became increasingly desperate and deranged as he realized that he would not only win but would be exposed. Jumped overboard was the consensus – and the boat sailed on.

69. Page 174, in: Slocum, J. (1999 (1900)). <u>Sailing alone around the world</u>. New York, Penguin.
70. ABC Radio National, PM, Monday 5 June, 2000.
71. Page 18, in: Idriess, I. L. (1959). <u>The tin scratchers</u>. Sydney, Angus & Robertson.
72. Page v, in: ibid.
73. Theroux, P. (1992). <u>The happy isles of Oceania: Paddling the Pacific</u>. London, Penguin.
74. Page 86, in: ibid.
75. Located inland from Quintell Beach, Lockhart River Aboriginal Community is some ten kilometres from the eponymous river which was named by geologist Robert Logan Jack in his 1879-80 surveying expedition up the Cape after his Edinburgh friend, Hugh Lockhart (and also his son, born in 1878 and also a geologist, Robert Lockhart Jack). The river, no more than a creek, runs northward parallel to the coast emptying into the base of Lloyd Bay through a lattice of creeks that had been explored by Captain John Moresby in the *Basilisk* in 1873 who recorded that they: *explored one salt-water creek after another, but each was a failure, and led only to entanglement in the swamp, where clouds of mosquitoes resented our invasion of their holds. There was no river.* Page 551, in: Jack, R. L. (1921). <u>Northernmost Australia: Three centuries of exploration, discovery and adventure in and around the Cape York Peninsula, Queensland. Volume 2.</u> London, Skimpkin, Marshall, Hamilton, Kent.
76. There's more than coincidental connection between magic and medicine, but it should work the other way. The magic is creating a fleshed out story of a real person compared to just 'tricks': *Contrary to popular belief, magic is not about concealing things but about building a shared narrative that makes sense for audience and performer. The magic is in the telling, constructing a compelling world through story. Without the story you're left with just tricks. Medicine too is about creating a shared narrative that works for patient and clinician, accounting for each person's problem in the context of their life.* Page 148, in: Kneebone, R. L. (2017). "The art of magic: Performing magic, performing medicine." <u>Lancet</u> 389(19): 148-149.
77. Page 1, in: Idriess, I. L. (1947). <u>Gold-dust and ashes: The romatic story of the New Guinea goldfields</u>. Sydney, Angus & Robertson.
78. Page 13, in: Flynn, E. (1937). <u>Beam ends</u>. New York, Dell.
79. Idriess, I. L. (1962). <u>My mate Dick</u>. Sydney, Angus & Robertson.
80. Page 133, in: Meston, A. (1895). Geographic history of Queensland. Brisbane, Edmund Gregory, Government Printer.
81. Page 11, in: Stephan, J. (2013). Mrs Mary Watson: "The heroine of Lizard Island". Cooktown, Cooktown Historical Society.
82. Page 15, in: ibid.
83. Page 16, in: ibid.
84. Australian Quarantine and Inspection Service.
85. Page 220, in: McHugh, E. (2003). <u>Shipwrecks: Australia's greatest maritime disasters</u>. Melbourne, Penguin.
86. Page 108, in Layton, R. (1992). <u>Aboriginal rock art: a new synthesis</u>. Cambridge, Cambridge University Press.
87. Page 29, in: Whittingham, H. E. (1958). The Bathurst Bay hurricane and associated storm surge. Brisbane, Divisional Office, Bureau of Meteorology.

88. In: Idriess, I. L. (1938). Madman's Island. Sydney, Angus & Robertson.
89. Page 52, in: Idriess, I. L. (1959). The tin scratchers. Sydney, Angus & Robertson.
90. Page 58, in: Bayliss, S. (2015). Stories from heart and soul. Self-published, All-read-E. Since writing it's emerged that it was not Tarzan, but George Cooper, who lived on Grassy Hill from the late-1960s to 1977 (Marge Scully & Jenny Habermann, personal communication, 2019).
91. Page 125, in: Idriess, I. L. (1979 (1958)). Back 'o Cairns. Sydney, A & Robertson.
92. Page 10, in: Idriess, I. L. (1934). Men of the jungle. Sydney, Angus & Robertson.
93. Pages 34, in: Ryle, P. (2016). Michael 'Tarzan' Fomenko: the man who dared to live his own exotic dream. Brisbane, Rams Skull Press. Peer Ryle writes that this quote is based on a telephone conversation in 2005 between Harold Jung and Mary Caldwell, who met Michael on Horne Island in late 1958 when she was sailing around the world with her husband, John Caldwell, whose 1949 book, *Desperate voyage* documented his attempt to sail across the Pacific to Australia to join Mary, which ended in a hurricane near Fiji. Nearly sixty years later, with Matthew Douglas, she published *Mary's voyage*, the story of Mary, John and their children sailing from the United States to Australia and then from Sydney to the Leeward Isles of the Caribbean where they built a resort. Michael Fomenko is not mentioned in that book. Mary does, however, give advice as sound for kayakers as sailors; in relation to *giant walls of water rearing up behind,* her approach was to *never look back.* Page 109, in: Caldwell, M. and M. M. Douglas (2008). Mary's voyage: The adventures of John and Mary Caldwell - a sequel to *Desperate voyage*. New York, Sheridan House.
94. Page 768, in: Anonymous (1878). The Wreck of the Riser, Cutter, and Massacre of the Crew. The Queenslander. **Saturday 14 September:** 768.
95. Fanning, W. (1949). Magyar refugees seek life free of Red fear. The Stars and Stripes. **Saturday, January 8:** 2.
96. For a comprehensive account see: Sebestyen, V. (2006). Twelve days: Revolution 1956 - How the Hungarians tried to topple their Soviet masters. London, Pheonix.
97. While three countries – the Netherlands, Spain and Switzerland – boycotted the Games, allegedly because of the Russian occupation (others boycotted as a result of the Suez invasion), Hungary's team competed. The majority of those who subsequently defected went to the United States but several of those eventually returned to Hungary. The prestige of athletes in Hungary, as in the Soviet Union, was enormous. Before the uprising Mátyás Rákosi visited training venues to assure athletes of his personal backing. By and large, regardless of athletes' support for the uprising, those who returned after the Games continued their careers. Desző Gyarmati, captain of the water polo team that beat Russia 4:0 in the *blood in the water* semifinal and then won gold, went on to win bronze and gold in the Rome and Tokyo Olympics, to coach the national team into the 1980s and became a Member of Parliament in the first democratic government. See: Blutstein, H. (2017). Cold War Games: Espionage, spies and secret operations at the 1956 Olympics. Richmond, Echo.
98. See: ibid.
99. This may have been Jozsef Kardos, who just months after the Olympics changed his name back to Lájos Polgar and a year later took Australian citizenship. Five decades on his past caught up but he died before legal proceedings could be commenced.

100. Page 8, in: Idriess, I. L. (1959). The tin scratchers. Sydney, Angus & Robertson.
101. Page 7, in: Idriess, I. L. (1993(1956)). The Silver City. Ion Idriess's greatest stories of miners and soldiers. I. L. Idriess. Sydney, Cornstalk Publishing: 1-192.
102. Page 173, in: McKenzie, M. (1847). "Observations on making the passage to the eastwards through the Torres Strait, and the monsoons in the Timour sea." The Nautical Magazine and Naval Chronicle (April): 113-117 and 172-178.
103. Page 176, in: ibid.
104. In: King, P. P. (1827). Narrative of a survey of the intertropical and western coasts of Australia performed between the years 1818 and 1822. Volume I. London, John Murray.
105. Page 35, in: Idriess, I. L. (1938). Madman's Island. Sydney, Angus & Robertson.
106. Page 226, in: Idriess, I. L. (1934). The yellow joss. Sydney, Angus & Robertson.
107. Page 232, in: ibid.
108. Page, 234, in: ibid.
109. Page 236, in: ibid. Idriess was as interested in the tales people told as the characters who told them. Like the story he heard from Formasini on the Bloomfield about his adventures on Noble after his mate died. But that had an attribution – Formasini – and what happened to Harris and Reynolds doesn't. And Jack made it clear that not all the stories in *The yellow joss* were based on fact, so *Account rendered* was probably one of the *two exceptions,* and it's no surprise that the S.S. *Tait* and Captain Tersh don't appear in any registers of wrecks off the Queensland coast. It may even be a story that was set in another place that, for effect, he located on an island he knew well – Howick – an island that was already associated with madness.
110. Page 63, in: Idriess, I. L. (1970s). Unedited transcript of Ion Idreiss in interview with broadcaster Tim Bowden, in the early 1970s. T. Bowden. Sydney http://www.abc.net.au/rn/legacy/programs/radioeye/documents/idriess.pdf, accessed May 9, 2016.
111. Page 1, in: ibid.
112. Charnel house certainly, but there had been a radical improvement in British military medicine since the catastrophes of the Boer Wars just over a decade earlier. Doctors in the Royal Army Medical Corps, often with limited civilian experience, were thrust into roles where, as noted by Sir Geoffrey Keynes who served close to the front, they were challenged to work in conditions in which they were often forced to take technical short cuts; young doctors, who themselves came under fire, suddenly confronted with: *thousands of operations of all types from minor injuries and fractures to abdominal, thoracic, cranial and even cardiac emergencies.* Page 256, in: Whitehead, I. R. (1999). Doctors in the Great War. Barnsley, Leo Cooper.
113. Page 2, in: Idriess, I. L. (1970s). Unedited transcript of Ion Idriess in interview with broadcaster Tim Bowden, in the early 1970s. T. Bowden. Sydney http://www.abc.net.au/rn/legacy/programs/radioeye/documents/idriess.pdf, accessed May 9, 2016.
114. Page 28, in: Idriess, I. L. (1938). Madman's Island. Sydney, Angus & Robertson.
115. Page 29, in: ibid.
116. Page 34, in ibid.

117. Page 1, in: Idriess, I. L. (1970s). Unedited transcript of Ion Idreiss in interview with broadcaster Tim Bowden, in the early 1970s. T. Bowden. Sydney http://www.abc.net.au/rn/legacy/programs/radioeye/documents/idriess.pdf, accessed May 9, 2016.
118. Page 39, in: Haviland, J. B. and R. Hart (1998). Old man Fog and the last Aborigines of Barrow Point. Bathurst, Crawford House.
119. Page 103, in: ibid.
120. See: Hunter, E. (1998). ""…in spirochetes than in suffering men…": Widening the context of Indigenous sexual health." Venereology 11(3): 11-19.
121. Page 31, in: Roth, W. E. (1984 (1901)). North Queensland Ethnography: Bulletin No. 3. Food: Its search, capture, and preparation. The Queensland Aborigines: Volume II , W.E. Roth (Fascimile Edition). K. F. MacIntyre. Perth, Hesperian Press: 1-34.
122. Page 89, in: Haviland, J. B. and R. Hart (1998). Old man Fog and the last Aborigines of Barrow Point. Bathurst, Crawford House.
123. See: Idriess, I. L. (1946). In crocodile land: Wandering in Northern Australia. Sydney, Angus and Robertson.
124. See: Hamilton, J. (2008). Gallipoli sniper: The life of Billy Sing. Sydney, Pan Macmillan.
125. In the Quetta Memorial Church on Thursday Island, set among reminders of that earlier maritime disaster, is a marble plaque, much older but very similar:

      AMDG
  AND IN MEMORY OF THOSE WHO PERISHED
  DURING THE HURRICANE OFF CAPE MELVILLE
      5th MARCH 1899.

ALFRED St JOHN OUTRIDGE	)
HAROLD ARTHUR OUTRIDGE	) *SAGGITA*
ROBERT BROWN MURRAY	)
ROVERT CAMERON	)
EDWARD JEFFERSON	)
CHARLES ATTHOW JOHN	) *SILVERY WAVE*
HENRY NICHOLAS	)

235 COLOURED MEN
73 VESSELS WRECKED OR FOUNDERED.

  "When Thou passest through the waters I will
  be with Thee". ISIAH LX111-2.

126. Page 3, in: Idriess, I. L. (1970s). Unedited transcript of Ion Idreiss in interview with broadcaster Tim Bowden, in the early 1970s. T. Bowden. Sydney http://www.abc.net.au/rn/legacy/programs/radioeye/documents/idriess.pdf, accessed May 9, 2016.
127. Hunter, E. (2000). "On the gift of dreams and sitting with eagles." Australasian Psychiatry 8(4): 318-322.
128. Though they wouldn't have known it, Flynn and Idriess had a shared, place-based connection to madness. For Idriess it was Charlie and the months they spent

together on Howick; for Flynn it was Laloki outside Port Moresby where he ran a tobacco plantation in 1931 and 1932 after the *Sirocco* sank in the Gulf of Papua. In 1962 a small group of inmates made the ten kilometre journey from the Bomana prison to new buildings on a flood-prone site next to the Laloki river, ever since then the only asylum in Papua New Guinea. By that time Flynn was dead but Idriess was still telling stories.

129. Probing an open wound was exactly what was done to some lunatics in the early days of madness management in Australia – *seton therapy* – a running sore kept discharging by regularly irritating a skein of fibre or thread tunneled between skin and muscle, placed by the nape of the neck for best effect. Like many treatments then and since – not without complications. See: White, S. and W. Kealy-Bateman (2017). "Primary evidence of seton therapy at Tarban Creek, New South Wales, 1839." Australasian Psychiatry **25**(3): 293-296.

130. Hunter, E. (2008). "The Aboriginal tea ceremony: its relevance to psychiatric practice." Australasian Psychiatry **16**(2): 130-132.

131. Listen to: https://www.youtube.com/watch?v=nLwYSu-GEdw.

132. George Comino, in: Bottoms, T. (2015). Cairns: City of the South Pacific - A history 1770-1995. Cairns, Bunu Bunu Press.

133. Page 7, in: Eley, B. (1995). Ion Idriess. Sydney, HarperCollins.

134. Or *nulle terre sans seigneur* – no land without a lord – the feudal territorial divisions brought to England by the Normans leading to centuries of tension across the border with Scotland – see: Rosen, W. (2015). The third horseman: A story of weather, war, and the famine history forgot. New York, Penguin. Ironically, much later it was mainland Scottish lairds displacing Shetland crofters.

135. Wilkins, H. T. (1935). Captain Kidd and his Skeleton Island: The discovery of a strange secret hidden for 266 years. London, Cassell.

136. See: Hunter, E. (1993). "The snake on the caduceus: Dimensions of medical and psychiatric responsibility in the Third Reich." Australian and New Zealand Journal of Psychiatry **27**(1): 149-156.

137. See: Hunter, E. (1998). ""…in spirochetes than in suffering men…": Widening the context of Indigenous sexual health." Venereology **11**(3): 11-19.

138. Page 42, in: Idriess, I. L. (1967). One wet season. Sydney, Angus & Robertson.

139. Page 182, in: Rothwell, N. (2007). Another country. Melbourne, Black Inc. Aubrey was an elder of the *Mayala* people whose traditional lands encompass the intertidal zone of the Buccaneer Archipelago and is internationally recognized for his pearl-shell artistry – *riji*. He had a presence that impressed me deeply as a teenage student working in Derby Hospital, and as a research psychiatrist nearly a quarter century later – I have no doubt that presence was a critical element in his healing. Until this writing I had forgotten that I had acknowledged Aubrey in the preface to my book *Aboriginal health and history*. Aubrey died in 2014 aged sixty-nine.

140. He wrote in his diary: *Eventide. All is very quiet. The Turkish guns have ceased firing. From the hills we can see Jaffa and Jerusalem. Old Jerusalem.* The 5th Light Horse headed west towards Jaffa and soon after he was incapacitated by malaria and hospitalized, only to suffer shrapnel wounds when the field hospital came under fire, leading to his evacuation and the beginning of a three month journey

back to Australia. See: Idriess, I. L. (1917). Diary of Ion Llewellyn Idriess, 1917-1918. Australian War Memorial, RCDIG0000454 (https://www.awm.gov.au/collection/C1358584).

141. Walter Roth identified beech as *Gmelina macrophylla,* which should be *Gmelina fasciculiflora.*
142. Page 14, in: Roth, W. E. (1984 [1910]). North Queensland Ethnography: Transport and trade. The Queensland Aborigines, Volume III, W.E. Roth (Fascimile Edition). K. F. MacIntyre. Perth, Hesperian Press: 1-19.
143. In: Roth, W. E. (1906). Letter from Dr Walter Roth to the Under Secretary, Home Secretary's Office, resigning as Queensland Protector of Aboriginals due to ill-health. Brisbane, Queensland Government Archives: http://www.archives.qld.gov.au/Researchers/Exhibitions/Top150/076-100/Pages/096.aspx.
144. Page 404, in: Parkin, R. (2003 (second edition)). H.M. Bark Endeavour: her place in Australian history: with an account of her construction, crew and equipment and a narrative of her voyage on the east coast of New Holland in the year 1770. Melbourne, Miegunyah.
145. Page 75, in: Brunton, P., Ed. (1998). The Endeavour journal of Joseph Banks: the Australian journey. Sydney, Angus & Robertson.
146. Page 115, in: Haviland, J. B. and R. Hart (1998). Old man Fog and the last Aborigines of Barrow Point. Bathurst, Crawford House.
147. Page 169, in: Sacks, O. (2015). On the move: a life. London, Picador.
148. Page 174, in: ibid.
149. Page 173, in: ibid.
150. Miller, G. (Saturday 10 February, 2007). Jack. Radio Eye, ABC Radio National (www.abc.net.au/radionational/programs/radioeye/jack/3388842).
151. Idriess, I. L. (1970s). Unedited transcript of Ion Idreiss in interview with broadcaster Tim Bowden, in the early 1970s. T. Bowden. Sydney http://www.abc.net.au/rn/legacy/programs/radioeye/documents/idriess.pdf, accessed May 9, 2016.
152. Page 294, in: Lucas, A. (1996). Cruising the coral coast, 7th edition. Avalon, Halbrooks Publishing. Lucas was a graphic artist working for a Sydney advertising agency while he built his first cruising yacht, *Rendezvous,* in his Hunter's Hill back yard in the late 1950s. Over the next three years he sailed up and down the Queensland coast and wrote *Cruising the coral coast* aboard-ship in Southport, publishing it in Sydney when he couldn't get Queensland interest. See: Lucas, A. (1978). Barrier Reef rendezvous. Hong Kong, Horowitz.
153. Lomb, N. (2016). "Australian solar eclipse expeditions: the voyage to Cape York in 1871." Journal of Astronomical History and Heritage **19**(1): 79-95.
154. Page 85, in: ibid.
155. Page 6, in: Special Correspondent (1872). The Australian Eclipse Expedition: III. The Argus. Melbourne, **Monday, January 1:** 6.
156. Ibid.
157. The full title of the 1897 Act is: *An Act to make Provision for the Better Protection and Care of the Aboriginal and Half-Caste Inhabitants of the Colony, and to make more Effectual Provision for Restricting the Sale and Distribution of Opium.*
158. See: Meston, A. (1909). Letter from Archibald Meston to Hon. D.F. Denham, Minister for Lands, Queensland, re sandalwood cutting licence at Lloyd Bay, Queensland Archives HOM/J45.

159. Page 27, in: Idriess, I. L. (1959). The tin scratchers. Sydney, Angus & Robertson.
160. Page 29, in: ibid.
161. Page 108, in: Richards, J. (2008). The secret war: A true history of Queensland's Native Police. Brisbane, University of Queensland Press. Richards confuses the geography of this region and identifies this site as Knight Island near Cape Flattery, noting that Walter Roth in the *Melbidir* picked up prisoners and police and transported them to Cooktown. However, in his 1901 report Roth notes: *The "Melbidir" has also been utilised in rescuing a police party in the neighbourhood of Night Island.* Page 19, in: Roth, W. E. (1902). Annual Report of the Northern Protector of Aboriginals for 1901. Brisbane, Office of the Northern Protector (Cooktown). Richards may also have the names of the ships mistaken as there is no record of the loss of a ship named *Johara*, but a schooner, *Annie*, was lost two decades earlier. That *Annie* stopped regularly at Lizard Island under Captain Menzies and was one of the last boats bringing supplies to Mary and Robert Watson. Mary recorded in her diary for 11 August, 1881 – seven weeks before the tragedy – that another schooner: *"Kilt" arrived here making for Cooktown with schooner "Annie"'s crew. Capt. Menzies drowned, schooner lost, crew all saved.* Page 9, in: Stephan, J. (2013). Mrs Mary Watson: "The heroine of Lizard Island". Cooktown, Cooktown Historical Society. Whatever the name of the vessel it was not the only one commandeered by Aboriginal crew – in 1902 a Japanese lugger was taken over, and a 'flying detachment' of four Native Police under a junior European constable was dispatched by James Whiteford resulting in four Aboriginal suspects being shot near the Ducie Rivers. An inquiry was subsequently held at Moreton Telegraph Station under Walter Roth and the Police Commissioner W.E. Parry-Okeden. Despite publicity and controversy there were no significant repercussions for the accused but local ill-feeling about Roth's role contributed to pressures for his resignation, which followed three years later. See: Richards, J. (1999). Moreton Telegraph Station: 1902 - the Native Police on Cape York Peninsula. Paper presented at the History of Crime, Policing and Punishment Conference convened at the Australian Institute of Criminology in conjunction with Charles Sturt University, 9-10 December.
162. Over the following two decades as geologist, biologist and ethnographer, Jukes went on to become a founder of reef science. McCalman, I. (2013). The reef: A passionate history. Melbourne, Penguin.
163. Powell, F. (2010). "Review: Pelletier: the forgotten castaway of Cape York, by Stephanie Anderson." Aboriginal History **34**.
164. Page 177. In: Idriess, I. L. (1957). Coral Sea calling. Sydney, Angus & Robertson.
165. Page 4, in: MacGillivray, J. (1862). Wanderings in tropical Australia. No. II: First nothern cruise. The Sydney Morning Herald. Sydney. **Friday, January 10:** 4-5.
166. Page 4, in: ibid.
167. In: McCalman, I. (2013). The reef: A passionate history. Melbourne, Penguin.
168. Page 5, in: MacGillivray, J. (1862). Wanderings in tropical Australia. No. II: First nothern cruise. The Sydney Morning Herald. Sydney. **Friday, January 10:** 4-5.
169. Page 222, in: Idriess, I. L. (1950). The wild white man of Badu. Sydney, Angus & Robertson.
170. The story is largely based on the English translation of Constant Merland's French account published in 1876, which appears as *Seventeen years with the*

savages. The adventures of Narcisse Pelletier, in: Anderson, S. (2009). Pelletier: The forgotten castaway of Cape York. Melbourne, Melbourne Books.
171. Ibid.
172. Ibid.
173. The alteration of coastal environments by hearth-based cultures taking advantage of seasonal resources is well described, and termed "domiculture". See: Hynes, R. and A. Chase (1982). "Plants, sites and domiculture: Aboriginal influence upon plant communities in Cape York Peninsula." Archaeology in Oceania **17**(1): 38-50. Traditional practices supporting the growth and preparation of grasses, grains and tubers are described in detail by Bruce Pascoe's work, representing pre-colonial agricultural practices that were not acknowledged in support of the denial of prior occupation. See: Pascoe, B. (2014). Dark emu black seeds: agriculture or accident? Broome, Magabala Books.
174. Page 205, in: Bligh, W. (1962 (1792)). A voyage to the South Sea, undertaken by command of His Majesty, for the purpose of conveying the bread-fruit tree to the West Indies, in His Majesty's ship *Bounty,* commanded by Lieutenant William Bligh. Including an account of the mutiny on board the said ship and the subsequent voyage of part of the crew, in the ship's boat, from Tofoa, one of the Friendly Islands, to Timor, a Dutch settlement in the East Indies. New York, Signet.
175. Page 149, in: ibid.
176. With a sextant, a quadrant and an improvised log-line, but no chronometer, Bligh could estimate latitude but not longitude and was reliant on dead reckoning to determine their progress to the great reef he knew lay to the west. See: Mundle, R. (2017). Bligh: master mariner. Sydney, Hachette.
177. Page 16, in: Stephan, J. (2013). Mrs Mary Watson: "The heroine of Lizard Island". Cooktown, Cooktown Historical Society.
178. Page 15, in: Banfield, E. J. (2001). Confessions of a beachcomber. Kingston, Dixie-Price.
179. Page 15, in: Whittaker, M. and A. Willesee (2001). The road to Mount Buggery: A journey through the curiously named places of Australia. Sydney, Macmillan.
180. For these and many other stories of extraordinary voyages in small craft see: Longyard, W. H. (2003). A speck on the sea: Epic voyages in the most improbable vessels. New York, McGraw Hill.
181. At Tatura Camp in Victoria he met Fritz Weber, who ended up living in Mission Beach south of Cairns. Years after the war Oskar gave Fritz the navigation lamp, compass and sextant that he had used on the journey. The compass and navigation lamp were donated to the National Maritime Museum but the sextant was sold by mistake in a garage sale around 2000. See: Woodward, L. (2004). Hero's sextant search. The Cairns Post: Weekend Post. **Saturday, February 7**.
182. Stiller, E. (2000). Keep Australia on your left. Melbourne, Bantam.
183. Page 154, in: Bolland, T. (1998). The long way home: A 24,000 kilometre walk, cycle & kayak around Australia. Bassendean, Terry Bolland.
184. Page 302, in: Stiller, E. (2000). Keep Australia on your left. Melbourne, Bantam.
185. On November 2, 2016, Sandy Robson landed on Saibai after a five year journey from Germany, following in the paddle-strokes of Oskar Speck.

186. In June 2011 I left Auckland on a forty-foot yacht, *Caper*, bound for the Atlantic via South America. For reasons that related to chaotic changes in the Queensland health sector, I returned from Tahiti and Jethro replaced me, joining *Caper* in 2012 in Puerto Montt, Chile. Not long afterwards, *Caper* was overtaken by Freya Hoffmeister heading south to Cape Horn.
187. Back cover: Coutts, R. (2013). The truth about Charlie: the "madman" stranded on Howick Island with Ion Idriess. Brisbane, Boolarong Press.
188. Page 614, in: Idriess, I. L. (1993 (1932)). The desert column. Ion Idriess's greatest stories of miners and soldiers. I. L. Idriess. Sydney, Cornstalk Publishing: 355-614. The materials for *The desert column* were the diaries Idriess maintained throughout the war and include observing the taking of Beersheba by the 4th Light Horse. Not long after, on the night before the Third Battle of Gaza (the first two being Allied debacles), he closed the seventh diary, this one written on *The British Troops' Writing Pad* with the following: *Well I am going to leave this old diary in my kit bag, and hope very much that I see it again. If I am killed in the great battle that will take place should Gaza be forced and this diary fall into the hands of any damned military authorities, will you just forward the dairy to my father. Address: W. Owen Idriess, Court House, Grafton, N.S.W. Australia. And Damn the World.* In: Idriess, I. L. (1917). Diary of Ion Llewellyn Idriess, 1917. Australian War Memorial, RCDIG0000453 (https://www.awm.gov.au/collection/C1357946).
189. See: Feain, P. and E. Aroney (2016). Ion Idriess: An annotated and illustrated bibliography. Sydney, Cornstalk Bookshop. Idriess was also probably the first author to write about a dog at war. *Horrie the wog-dog* is based on the diary of J.B. Moody with the 6th Division of the AIF in the Middle East and Greece in the early years of World War II. A cherished mascot, his soldier-keepers attempted to smuggle him back to Australia with them prior to re-deployment to New Guinea. Although the text ends on a happy note, the book's 'epitaph' is otherwise: *Well, Horrie, little fellow, your reward was death. You who deserved a nation's plaudits, sleep in peace. Among Australia's war heroes, we shall remember you. Under Quarantine Regulations, Horrie was destroyed on 12 March, 1945.* Page 209, in: Idriess, I. L. (2017 (1945)). Horrie the wog-dog: The original tail. Sydney, ETT Imprint.
190. Australian War Memorial records show that George Tritton, Service Number 5130 was in the 31st Infantry Battalion, embarking on HMAT *Hororata* from Sydney on June 14 1917 and returned to Australia on 19 April, 1919.
191. Page 172, in: Coutts, R. (2013). The truth about Charlie: the "madman" stranded on Howick Island with Ion Idriess. Brisbane, Boolarong Press.
192. Page 22, in: ibid.
193. Page 238, in: ibid.
194. Page 222, in: ibid.
195. Page 242, in: ibid.
196. The TEDx presentation is on: https://www.youtube.com/watch?v=EAnyJJdU-9Ak&list=PL5juWrUp_f0D1h9JR3qTLyFlksjBUvT7B&index=9 (or Google: Chris Wighton TED)
197. *gone for shore* is the title of Tim Trehearn's book on kayaking the coast of northern Queensland and has an introduction by Chris Wighton. See: Trehearn, T. (2015). gone for shore: a sea-kayaking guide to northern Queensland. Cairns, Tim

Trehearn.
198. Page 174, in: Idriess, I. L. (1959). The tin scratchers. Sydney, Angus & Robertson.
199. Page 71, in: Idriess, I. L. (1934). Men of the jungle. Sydney, Angus & Robertson.
200. Page 71, in: ibid.
201. Page 237, in: Anderson, C. (1988). A case study in failure: Kuku-Yalanji and the Lutherans at Bloomfield River, 1887-1902. Aboriginal Australians and Christian Missions: Ethnographic and historical studies. T. Swan and D. B. Rose. Adelaide, Australian Association for the Study of Religion: 321-225.
202. Page 127, in: Idriess, I. L. (1959). The tin scratchers. Sydney, Angus & Robertson.
203. Ryle, P. (2016). Michael 'Tarzan' Fomenko: the man who dared to live his own exotic dream. Brisbane, Rams Skull Press.
204. The Cairns Historical Society has a permanent display dedicated to the cane cutters of Far North Queensland, featuring the life of Bruno Jung who arrived from Germany at age twenty in 1954. He was a 'gun' cutter able to clear between twelve and twenty-five tonnes per day and went on to give demonstrations into his late life, well after machines had taken over. Entering the refurbished museum a mandala of cane knives is the main feature visible from the Shields Street, a small sign recording: *Harold Jung Cane Knife Collection: The Cairns Museum's cane knife installations feature the collection of Harold Jung of Deeral. Harold grew up on his father's cane farm and was an avid collector of working tools, including cane knives. In addition to collecting the knives, Harold also noted the names of the men who used them and the area they cut for. After Harold's untimely death, his brother Ingram and father Bruno donated Harold's collection to the Cairns Museum.*
205. Page 39, in: Idriess, I. L. (1967). One wet season. Sydney, Angus & Robertson.
206. Page 37, in: Ryle, P. (2016). Michael 'Tarzan' Fomenko: the man who dared to live his own exotic dream. Brisbane, Rams Skull Press.
207. Page 19, in: Eley, B. (1995). Ion Idriess. Sydney, HarperCollins.
208. Page 58, in: Close, K. L. (2009). Invisible labourers: Cape Bedford (Hopevale) Mission and the 'paradox' of Aboriginal labour in the Second World War. Master of Arts, University of Melbourne.
209. Page 74, in: McIvor, R. (2010). Cockatoo: My life in Cape York. Broome, Magabala Books.
210. Page 80, in: ibid.
211. Page 2, in: Idriess, I. L. (1938). Madman's Island. Sydney, Angus & Robertson.
212. Page 425, in: Ellmann, R. (1982). James Joyce (revised edition). New York, Oxford University Press.
213. Vyver, J. (2016, Tuesday 20 September). On the trail of Queensland's 'Tarzan'. Earshot. K. Melville, ABC Radio National: http://www.abc.net.au/radionational/programs/earshot/finding-australias-tarzan/7852260.
214. Page 9, in: McCalman, I. (2013). The reef: A passionate history. Melbourne, Penguin.
215. Page 9, in: ibid.
216. If not dead then, at best, *in extremis*, as Anna Krein, reviewing the most recent threat – coal – has observed: "The reef isn't dead. But it can't breathe". Page 116, In: Krien, A. (2017). The long goodbye: Coal, coral and Australia's climate dead-

lock. Quarterly Essay. Melbourne. **66:** 1-116.
217. Unless one can be dismissed as an uninformed, radical environmentalist, speaking out about the traditional hunting of endangered species predictably pushes buttons, sometimes influential. The first but not last person on the phone after I did so in the Weekend Australian in 2012 was Noel Pearson. See: Hunter, E. (2012). Tradition not always the highest value, but justice is. The Weekend Australian, Inquirer. **March 17-18:** 19.
218. Page 404, in: Parkin, R. (2003 (second edition)). H.M. Bark Endeavour: her place in Australian history: with an account of her construction, crew and equipment and a narrative of her voyage on the east coast of New Holland in the year 1770. Melbourne, Miegunyah.
219. In: Anonymous (1897). Wreck of the Schoner Myrtle. Passengers and crew rescued. The Queenslander. Saturday 17 April: 829.
220. In early 2018 Michael Fomenko returned north, with the front page, banner headline of the *Cairns Weekend Post* for May 19-20 announcing: *TARZAN RETURNS: Far Northern icon swings back to where his legend began.* The story continued inside, taking up almost all of page 5, under the header – *Highway icon is home: Long-held wish comes true as 88 year old Michael Fomenko returns to Babinda.* The front page headlines of the *Cairns Post* for Wednesday August 22, 2018 read *LONG WALK OF A LEGEND: The Far North's iconic Tarzan, Michael Fomenko, has died, aged 88, after spending his last months living at Babinda.* He had died five days earlier and in the following double page article headlined *FINAL JOURNEY OF FREE SPIRIT* recollections were accompanied by recommendations for a statue of Michael somewhere along the Bruce Highway. He probably would have walked past without noticing or caring. *Vale Tarzan.*
221. Jon sings *Gone for shore* at the end of his 2013 TED talk – at: https://www.youtube.com/watch?v=EAnyJJdU9Ak&list=PL5juWrUp_f0D1h9JR3qTLyFlks-jBUvT7B&index=9

Geoff, Chris & Ernest – aka – Jethro, Jon & Jon...*Three old blokes covered in zinc...* Gloucester Island, 2004

Acknowledgements

For the quarter-century that I've been privileged to explore and enjoy the remarkable but fragile world that is the coast of Cape York my most constant companion has been Trish Fagan, my wife, who moved with me from Sydney to Cairns in 1992 and who was with me on my first kayak trip from Cairns to Cooktown in 2000. Without her support this book would never have survived its protracted gestation. The story is based on journeys, many shared with Chris Wighton and Geoff Miller, whose companionship and good humour in fine weather and foul was constant. Our paths crossed those of many others who have, knowingly or not, contributed to *Vicarious dreaming* and, in particular, I note John Pritchard and Dave Glasheen. I am obliged to many others including Mick McLoughlin, Jan McLoughlin, Alan De Costa, Ulf DeGaunt, Harold Jung, Helga Biro, Mark Hackbarth, Suzanne Bayliss, Bruce Gynther and Gary Foley. Others, who without being aware of it provided guidance, include my psychiatric colleagues of Peer Review Group 665 to whom I presented a case of a patient with psychosis complicated by complex dream states. Among the institutions I have consulted I acknowledge the Cairns Historical Society, the Cooktown and District Historical Society, the Mitchell Library and the Shetland Museum and Archives.

I have used the life and works of Ion Idriess to tell this story and I thank Tom Thompson, whose knowledge of and investment in Idriess is unparalleled, for his encouragement and for copyright permission. Idriess was a man of his time, but also ahead of it. He was one of the first successful authors to write about Aboriginal resistance heroes in the collision of cultures that resulted in their dispossession. While *Vicarious dreaming* is not about Indigenous Australians they are constantly, and purposefully, on the stage. Theirs is the backstory of all this, and for the opportunity to work with the residents of the communities of Cape York and the Torres Strait for over two decades – I am profoundly grateful. That opportunity would not have arisen had I not been inspired by my brother, Randy Spargo, who in Derby in 1967 opened my eyes to the wonders of remote Aboriginal Australia and to the importance of relationships in making healing meaningful.

Finally, through writing this book I have discovered that my passion for the sea and the boats – small and large – in which voyages are made, I owe to a man I hardly knew but whose traces were rediscovered off the deserted shores of north Queensland, a coast that he passed just after the Second World War as he neared the end of his final journey, as captain of the *Cape York* – Harry Hunter, my father.

www.ingramcontent.com/pod-product-compliance
Lightning Source LLC
Chambersburg PA
CBHW031308150426
43191CB00005B/122